THE LAST
VOYAGEUR

THE LAST VOYAGEUR

Amos Burg and the Rivers of the West

Vince Welch

THE MOUNTAINEERS BOOKS

THE MOUNTAINEERS BOOKS
is the nonprofit publishing arm of The Mountaineers,
an organization founded in 1906 and dedicated to the exploration,
preservation, and enjoyment of outdoor and wilderness areas.

1001 SW Klickitat Way, Suite 201, Seattle, WA 98134

© 2012 by Vince Welch

Distributed in the United Kingdom by Cordee, www.cordee.co.uk

Manufactured in the United States of America

Copy Editor: Amy Smith Bell
Cover, book design, and layout: Emily Ford, The Mountaineers Books

Cover photograph: Oregon Historical Society
Frontispiece: John Barnett/4 Eyes Design based upon a map that appeared in *The Explorers Journal*, Volume 60, March 1982

Background image for page 16 by Splendor and Demise, www.flickr.com/photos/thom ashebert/

Library of Congress Cataloging-in-Publication Data

Welch, Vince.
  The last voyageur : Amos Burg and the rivers of the West / by Vince Welch.
    p. cm.
  Includes bibliographical references and index.
  ISBN 978-1-59485-701-0 (pbk)
  1. Burg, Amos. 2. Boatmen—West (U.S.)—Biography. 3. Boats and boating—West (U.S.) 4. Canoes and canoeing—West (U.S.) 5. White-water canoeing—West (U.S.) 6. West (U.S.)—Description and travel. I. Title.
  GV782.42.B87W45 2012
  797.1092—dc23
  [B]
                          2012022244

ISBN (paperback): 978-1-59485-701-0
ISBN (ebook): 978-1-59485-702-7

SUSTAINABLE FORESTRY INITIATIVE
Certified Chain of Custody
Promoting Sustainable Forestry
www.sfiprogram.org
SFI-01268

SFI label applies to the text stock

For Helen,
midwife to mothers
and wordsmiths

———

Photo Credits

The author and publisher have made every effort to identify the source and identifying numbers for the photographs included in *The Last Voyageur*. Photos are listed by page number (in bold face) with the source and/or copyright holder identified, if known.

28: Oregon Historical Society, Lot 765, No. 87065; **35**: Oregon Historical Society; **39**: Oregon Historical Society; **47**: Courtesy Cort Conley; **57**: Oregon Historical Society, Lot 765, No. 87232; **62**: Oregon Historical Society, Lot 765, No. 87202; **73**: Oregon Historical Society, No. CN014964; **85**: *Oregonian* file photo, 12/1/1928; **91**: Oregon Historical Society; **103**: Oregon Historical Society, No. 87048; **108**: Oregon Historical Society, No. 2134; **119**: Courtesy Nancy Long; **123**: Alaska State Library, Amos Burg Collection, Box 4, Folder 65, No. 380; **126**: Alaska State Library, Amos Burg Collection, Box 13, Folder 220, No. 1502; **143**: Courtesy Pepper Family; **147**: Northwest Maritime Historical Museum, Port Townsend, WA, Photo © Myron Gauger; **148**: Courtesy Pepper family; **152**: Courtesy Pepper family; **159**: Courtesy Pepper family; **169**: Courtesy Nancy Long; **174**: Oregon Historical Society, Lot 450, Box 11, Folder 6; **188**: Courtesy Cort Conlin; **197**: Oregon Historical Society, Lot 450, Box 12, Folder 1, No. 87033; **202**: Courtesy Nancy Long; **207**: Oregon Historical Society, No. 765-18; **220**: Oregon Historical Society, Lot 450, Box 12, Folder 1; **226**: Oregon Historical Society, No. 87208; **246**: University of Alaska, Anchorage, Archives and Special Collections, Consortium Library. Glenn Bowersox Collection, Photographs and Papers, 1931–2005, No. hmc-0731-86; **249**: Alaska State Library, Donald Burrus Photograph Collection, ca. 1917–1975, No. P-466-92-043; **260**: Alaska State Library, Box 12, Folder 209, No. 1351; **287**: Courtesy Randy Pepper; **290**: Courtesy Randy Pepper; **293**: Oregon Historical Society; **300**: Oregon Historical Society No. 87047.

CONTENTS

Preface 9
Acknowledgments 13

PART I. VOYAGES OF THE IMAGINATION (1920–1929)
Chapter 1. Great River of the West: The Columbia 18
Chapter 2. The Mad Snake 46
Chapter 3. Down the Yukon River 72
Chapter 4. Deh Cho: Canada's Mackenzie River 98

PART II. BEYOND THE HORIZON (1930–1949)
Chapter 5. Rising Star, Exotic Climes 118
Chapter 6. Land of Fire: The Tierra del Fuego and
              Patagonia Archipelagos 136
Chapter 7. Yank in a Canoe 166
Chapter 8. Burg's Experiment: The Green and Colorado Rivers 180
Chapter 9. Boatman, Filmmaker, Spy: The Middle Fork and
              Main Salmon Rivers 218

PART III. COMING ASHORE (1950–1986)
Chapter 10. Return Voyages: The Bering Sea and the Yukon River . . . 244
Chapter 11. The Same River Twice: The Mackenzie Revisited 257
Chapter 12. A Voyageur's Lament 276

Appendices
1. Chronology 303
2. Amos Burg's Boats 307
3. A Brief History of Western Dams 308
4. Sources 311
5. Selected Bibliography 313

Index 317

What is this thing in me that enables me to leave comforts and a wide variety of entertainments and feel a strange satisfaction wandering down a cheerless and indifferent river, enduring hardships and eating very little and exposed to all sorts of weather. I feel as though I am doing the thing that I have always longed to do and that I can continue to do it forever and like it more all the time. Yes, tonight even as I sit shivering and listening to the patter of the rain, I see myself in many places all over the world wandering like a gull on the winds working with the ideals of Truth and Beauty as part of my vision to bring these things back with me for other people to see.

—AMOS BURG,
YUKON RIVER,
JULY 1928

PREFACE

The Columbia River had fired Amos Burg's romantic imagination since he was a boy. Floating in a wooden boat one sunny afternoon in the middle of the mile-wide river near his home in Portland, Oregon, he had gazed upriver to the east. Distant, snow-covered Mount Hood, symmetrical and postcard perfect, rose above the river bathed in a blue mist. The stirring image was a call to adventure that Burg would remember throughout his life. Somewhere beyond the Cascades, the dreamy youngster imagined, lay the source of the Columbia River. But where? And how far away?

Within a decade Burg would be the first to make a continuous run in his canoe of the 1,200-mile river from Columbia Lake in British Columbia's Rocky Mountains to the Pacific Ocean. He would also become the last individual to voyage all the celebrated Western rivers, source to mouth, in a small craft before dams and reservoirs would make such voyages difficult, if not impossible. Between 1920 and 1940 he paddled, rowed, sailed, and occasionally motored—the Columbia, Snake, Green, Colorado, and Yukon as well as the Yellowstone, Missouri, Mississippi, and Canada's Mackenzie.

Most of these trips lasted months. Once, he traveled in winter with an injury that placed him on crutches. He lost canoes in rapids, made blunders, and suffered inept companions, loneliness, and illness. He also experienced natural beauty and a freedom of movement that profoundly affected his view of the world and his place in it. He came to think of himself as a "voyageur," following in the historical wake of men like David Thompson, Alexander Mackenzie, Simon Fraser, Meriwether Lewis and William Clark, as well as the French-Canadian rivermen who once ranged the North American continent's waterways.

As an ex–river guide who had traveled some of these same rivers, I could not help but be impressed, even envious. Burg first came to my attention in the 1970s, when I worked for Martin Litton's Grand Canyon Dories. My fellow river runners, both men and women, and I called ourselves "boatmen." Our allegiance lay as much with our graceful wooden boats as the Colorado River. (Anyone who has ever rowed a wooden dory would forgive this sin of pride.) Each of us carried a water-stained, dog-eared copy of Buzz Belknap's *Colorado River Guide* in which a postage stamp–sized photograph of Burg and his inflatable raft appeared with this caption: "First inflatable boat to traverse the canyon, run by Amos Burg in 1938." Burg, along with fellow Oregonian Buzz Holmstrom, had run the 1,200-mile length of the Green and Colorado Rivers. *Conquering the Colorado*, Burg's 1939 short film of the voyage, became a hit across the country. Despite this impressive achievement, however, I was more interested in Holmstrom at the time. He had made the same journey a year earlier alone, rowing a wooden boat he had built himself. It was a first. Burg's story seemed destined to be an abbreviated one.

My focus on Holmstrom shifted to Burg in 2006, when I stumbled across my Burg notes and realized I had not given him a fair reading. Where Holmstrom had been a down-to-earth workingman from coastal Oregon, Burg was an idealistic romantic from Portland. While Holmstrom's 1937 Grand Canyon voyage had been a defining moment in his life, Burg, despite being the first to navigate an inflatable raft on the Colorado, seemed ready to move onto his next exhilarating adventure. Burg harbored ambitions of becoming an adventure writer and photographer; Holmstrom had only wanted to escape the tedium of manual labor. At times Burg's purple river prose sounded pretentious next to Holmstrom's homespun narratives.

Although I preferred Holmstrom's style, I set out to gain a better understanding of Burg. I contacted author, boatman, and river historian Cort Conley, who had grown close to Burg in the final years of his life and carried on a regular correspondence. When I first mentioned my interest in writing about his friend, Conley was guarded. He suggested a handful of articles to read but offered little more. I suspect it was his way of protecting Burg and his reputation as well as testing my resolve for such a lengthy project. After a year of phone calls and emails, however, Conley relented, generously offering me his collection of letters and audio tapes and allowing me to tape his own reminiscences of Burg. Conley also pointed me in the direction of the Oregon Historical Society in Portland and the Alaska State Library in Juneau. Burg, it became clear, threw nothing away. I spent another year wading through these vast reservoirs of materials.

Among many surprises, I learned that Burg's life had roughly paralleled the start of dam-building in the West and its five-decade arc of nonstop

activity beginning in the early 1930s. I assumed that the river-loving romantic would have had serious reservations about dams. His feelings, however,
were anything but clear cut. So began my own voyage into the sometimes
contradictory life of Amos Burg. Often I drove east from Portland on US 84
through the Columbia Gorge to see what Burg had seen, to stretch my imagination. Few drivers are aware that the road parallels the little-used Historic
Columbia River Highway, completed in 1922. This first scenic roadway in
the United States had been designed to take full advantage of the area's natural beauty. It was a road Burg traveled often.

Driving on US 84, I found it increasingly difficult to ignore the fact
that the dominant natural feature of the Gorge—the Columbia River—was
missing. Four dams—Bonneville, The Dalles, John Day, and McNary—link a
daisy chain of reservoirs stretching roughly 150 miles up to and beyond the
confluence with the Snake River. So much for the so-called Great River
of the West. The slack water of the reservoirs made it easy to forget that the
Columbia River, born in the Canadian Rockies, once roared over Celilo
Falls, fed Native American tribes, frustrated Portland businessmen, and ter-
rified early voyageurs, pioneers, and steamboat captains as it flowed west. Yet
I could also imagine Burg rowing downriver in his canoe, bound for the
Pacific Ocean, grinning while he sang a voyageur's chantey to fight off the
winter cold. It made me want to sing along too.

In an age where we can Google satellite images of a river and make a virtual river trip even before setting out on water, Burg's river voyages continue
to amaze. His trips remind us of the age-old, sometimes forgotten, maxims
of adventure: If you get into trouble, you have to get yourself out of trouble.
Worthy companions are a gift. Often the journey outward leads inward. Personal honor with a dash of modesty trumps celebrity.

When Burg returned to Hells Canyon on the Snake River in 1978,
he was surprised by the changes that had occurred on the river he had run
five decades earlier. His gentle disposition tempered whatever disapproval he
felt about those changes (permit systems, loss of beaches, crowds of rafters,
diminishing fish migration). He understood we could not go back to "better times," that we must forge ahead, ask much of ourselves, and do better
in terms of the environment. Modern river trips, he believed, continued to
offer much to the human spirit—an opportunity for relaxation, laughter, and

genuine companionship, and on occasion, joy, solace, wonder, and reverence in a harried world.

Burg would have been embarrassed to find himself hoisted on a pedestal. Nevertheless, he serves as a marker on the river of time, a witness to change who wore his heart on his sleeve when it came to rivers. He traveled the western waterways in pursuit of beauty, adventure, and excitement as well as companionship. His explorations were as much of the landscape as the human heart. He delighted in bringing newcomers along with him. Although he was not political by nature, long before there was an environmental movement, he told a reporter that how we treat our rivers tells us something about who we are as a people.

So much of Burg's life revolved around rivers that I have organized this book by the chronology of his numerous voyages and adventures. Like tributaries, his backstories feed into the main channel where appropriate, contributing to the narrative flow, sound, and color. *The Last Voyageur* touches upon Burg's family and friends, childhood, adolescence, schooling, and his work as an able-bodied seaman. It explores his career as a writer, photographer, filmmaker, and lecturer, as well as, of course, his travels around the world and his life in Alaska. Some digressions run like small side creeks, offering glimpses at various stages of his life; others are full-bodied rivers, important narratives in and of themselves, which deepen our understanding of the man.

I have also included stories from my own river-running days throughout the narrative as evidence that although much has changed since Burg's early adventures, much remains the same. It is my hope that these "eddies" provide context for Burg's unique voyages. A series of appendices includes a standard chronology, a list of Burg's boats, a brief history of western dams, information on sources, and a selected bibliography. Together, these appendices provide a vehicle for readers to orient themselves as they travel with Burg down the great rivers of the West.

Amos Burg, I am certain, would welcome a fellow voyager.

ACKNOWLEDGMENTS

Although rowing a wooden dory through Grand Canyon without a flip or a wreck is a notable accomplishment, no boatman can fail to acknowledge the vital role his or her fellow river guides play in the 277-mile voyage. Without their advice, experience, and encouragement, it is difficult, even for a veteran oarsman, to pilot a boat down the Colorado River without getting into some kind of trouble, often self-inflicted, sooner or later. Any river voyage is a communal effort, and so it was with the writing of this book. Over the five years it took to complete *The Last Voyageur*, I was fortunate to be traveling in generous, knowledgeable company.

To my fellow boatmen, river historians, and river lovers who aided in my research, offered counsel, corrected my historical errors, and read portions of the manuscript, I am indebted. I thank Jim Norton, Tim Cooper, Bego Gearhart, Roy Hill, Jerry "Snake" Hughes, Don Lago, Steve Young, Rudi Petschek, Richard Quartaroli, Brad Dimock, Ellie Johnson (my Utah research assistant), and June Hall (Juneau researcher). Special thanks to Rod Nash and Earl Perry, who graciously braved an early, very rough draft, and Pete Donovan, who offered invaluable suggestions at a time when I had rowed myself into an eddy and could not find a way out. And lastly, to Cort Conley, steadfast fellow guide whose quiet encouragement smoothed the waters that I might follow in my subject's wake.

Without the cooperation of Amos Burg's friends and relatives, his story might not have been told in the rich detail it deserves. My gratitude to the folks in Juneau, Alaska, for sharing their memories and hospitality with a stranger: Nancy and Ed Ferrell (Burg's stepdaughter and son-in-law, both now deceased), Charles and Ellen Campbell, Nancy Long and Butch Garber, and the members of Endeavour Breakfast Club—Mark Kissel, Fritz Funk, and R. T. "Skip" Wallen. In Washington, I was privileged to be accepted into another circle of Burg's many friends: Bruce and Virginia Garmen, Pastor Don Brown and his wife, Glenda, and their two adult children, Vickie and Phillip and the Pepper brothers—Scott, Dan, and Randy—and Randy's wife, Judy. Each had fond memories and specific insights into Burg's character. Others who knew him and shared their stories included Jim Boyce, Loel Shuler, and Lou Flannery, an ex-librarian at the Oregon Historical Society in Portland. Members of Fred "Spokane" Hill's family—Marie Brown and Elizabeth Hill Robinson—made invaluable contributions to my understanding of their father and his friendship with Burg.

Two major institutions, one at the Alaska State Library in Juneau and the other at the Oregon Historical Society, house extensive Burg collections. At both locations I was greeted with enthusiasm and a genuine interest in Burg, a boost when my energy for the project flagged. My appreciation goes to Alaksa State Library's curator James Simard, director Gladi Culp, and their staff in Juneau as well as the crew of archivists, volunteers, and department heads at the Oregon Historical Society—Kim Buergel, MaryAnn Campbell, Michelle Kribs, Megan Freidel, Scott Rook, and Geoff Wexler, Library Director.

Individuals at many other institutions were helpful throughout my research. Many thanks to Tiah Edmunson-Morton at the Oregon State University Library; Bruce Tabb and Sue Eveland at the University of Oregon; Roger Furman at the Idaho Power Company; Sandy Televik at the Ilwaco Museum (Washington); Jeffrey Smith at the Columbia River Museum in Astoria; Ryan Haley and Jeff Stolzer at the Explorers Club in New York; the crew at Mad River Expeditions in Jackson Hole, Wyoming; Polly Armstrong at the University Archives at Stanford University; the National Archives Regional Facility in Seattle; shipwrights Ed Louchard and Steve Chapin and the Wooden Boat Foundation in Port Townsend, Washington; the Pottawatomie County Genealogical Society (Iowa); Portland Public Schools and Judy Jindrich and Gwen Newborg at Grieg Lodge Library at Norse Hall in North Portland; and Bill Wilkerson at the Qayanek Preservation Center in Kwigillinok, Alaska. To any individuals or organizations I have neglected to mention here, my apologies.

My gratitude to Kate Rogers, editor in chief at Mountaineers Books, who first saw promise in the Burg story and had the good sense to pair me with Phyllis Hatfield, a freelance editor. Phyllis, with serious intent and wicked humor, guided me through her editorial process, all the while encouraging me to argue with, even swear at, her over the phone if I didn't like the manuscript changes she suggested. Burg's story is the better for her effort. Special thanks also to Mary Metz and Amy Smith Bell who came on board to help complete the editorial voyage.

And to Helen, my wife and companion on many different voyages and a gifted navigator in her own right, where to next?

BURG'S BOTTLE FOUND ON BEACH IN ILWACO

MESSAGE SENT OUT BY CANOEIST IS FOUND

Long Trip Down Columbia River Made in 90 Days— Note Will Be Returned to Sender in Portland

A brown bottle that had been floating down the Columbia River for the past four months was picked up on the Ilwaco beach Wednesday afternoon by Lark Whealdon. The bottle contained a message from Amos Burg, Jr., the Portland lad who made the trip from the source of the Columbia to its mouth, arriving in Ilwaco on that trip on January 3rd. It had been placed in Lake Columbia, the source of the river, on the day he started his memorable trip.

The message was indistinct as water had leaked into the bottle and had destroyed a part of the text. As near as possible it has been deciphered as follows: *October—I am so cold can just barely write this. To the one who finds this: I am just starting from Lake Columbia and it is very cold. If you find this bottle please send it to Amos Burg, Portland Oregon. This is my canoe 17-feet long. I am going to the Pacific Ocean.*

Then following some writing that could not be read, but a picture of his canoe was roughly sketched in one corner. There was also a notation about $1.00 that was indistinct but it is thought that he was offering that amount of money to anyone who would return the paper to him.

Mr. Whealdon will forward the paper to his Portland address.

From The Oregonian, *January 29, 1925*

PART I

VOYAGES OF THE IMAGINATION

(1920–1929)

Chapter 1

GREAT RIVER OF THE WEST: THE COLUMBIA

Twenty-two-year-old Amos Burg was in turmoil. By September 1924 his plans to voyage the length of the 1,200-mile Columbia River, two years in the making, were in disarray. A knee injury he had suffered the previous spring while working as an able seaman had forced him to hobble around Portland on crutches, indefinitely postponing his June departure date. He had delayed querying the editors at *National Geographic* magazine about a proposed article. When he finally did receive a response from the notoriously picky editors, it was not the firm commitment he had hoped for. He had to ask his father, Amos Burg Sr., for money. At times the younger Burg felt pangs of guilt when he compared himself to his hard-working father who owned and operated a commercial laundry. He scolded himself for his inability to follow the conventional path his older brothers and friends had taken. Failure clung to Amos Burg Jr. like morning fog on the Willamette River. A diarist since the age of fifteen, he wrote: "I can see now that had I worked at school I would have gotten my credits by March at the O.I.T. [Oregon Institute of Technology], finished navigation school, and voyaged down the Columbia and entered the University with full honors, but now I lack all these things and my Columbia River trip I shall never touch at all." The thought of postponing the voyage any longer was unbearable.

In his late teens Burg had set himself an ambitious, even audacious goal: to run the great rivers of the American West from source to mouth. He went so far as to make a list in his diary: the Columbia, Snake, Missouri, Mississippi, Yukon, Green, and Colorado as well as Canada's Mackenzie. The list of rivers would grow to include numerous smaller and less well-known rivers. At the time there were few, if any, dams on these rivers. Two years earlier, in 1922, Burg had taken his first step toward reaching his goal: completing a five-month, 3,800-mile transit of the Yellowstone, Missouri, and Mississippi Rivers in his canoe, *Song o' the Winds*. His younger brother Johnnie and able seaman Harry Fogleberry had accompanied him, but after a month each had departed, leaving Burg to finish the remainder of the trip—more than 2,500 miles—alone. The success of this first lengthy river voyage had whet his appetite.

One of the numerous books Burg read and reread as a youth was William Lyman's *Columbia River* (published in 1909), which offered a broad overview of the human history of the Columbia laced with, in Lyman's words, "a lively sense of the romance, the heroism, and the adventure which belong to the great stream." Given Burg's boyhood passion for the river voyageurs and his developing romanticism for that life, it is worth quoting here.

> The boatmen were French-Canadians, a hardy, mercurial, lighthearted race, half French, with the natural grace and politeness of their race, and having the pleasant patois which has made them the theme of much popular present-day literature. They were half Indian, either in tastes and manners or in blood, with the atmosphere of forests and streams clinging to every word and gesture. They were perhaps the best boatmen in the world. Upon those matchless lakes into which the Columbia and its tributaries expand at intervals the fur-laden boats would glide at ease, while the wild songs of the *coureurs odes bois* [runners of the forest] would echo from shore to shore in lazy sibilations, apparently betokening no thought of serious or earnest business. But once the rapids were reached, the gay and rollicking knight of the paddle became all attention. With keen eyes fixed on every swirl or rock, he guided the light craft with a ready skill which would be inconceivable to one less daring and experienced. The brigades

would run almost all the rapids from Death Rapids to the sea, making portages at Kettle Falls, Tumwater or Celilo Falls, and the Cascades.

Burg knew that the Native American tribes of the lower Columbia River and the Pacific Coast archipelago to the north had been superior boat build-ers, paddlers, and navigators. For a spell, the flat-boat men of the Ohio and Mississippi Rivers captured his attention. When they were replaced in the public's imagination by the river pilots of the sternwheelers (whose own careers were tapering off at the turn of the nineteenth century as transporta-tion on the river gave way to the railroad), Burg sought out the Columbia River captains for advice as much as for the pleasure of listening to their tales. In his youthful romantic imagination, they were all heroic figures. He was determined to become a member of the "fraternity of river men," past and present.

For Burg, rivers embodied aesthetic and intellectual values that could not be measured in conventional terms. They carried innate worth beyond their usefulness to irrigate crops, transport freight, float logs to the mill, or feed and water populations. They served as visual symbols and historical reminders of the westering movement of the United States that had defined the national character. They inspired poetry, story, and song that nurtured the soul. They offered recreation, pleasant idleness, and brief sanctuary from a hard day's work. These were hardly universal notions in the 1920s. River travel also provided a few adventurous young men like Burg the chance to experience the spiritual element to be found through intense encounters with nature. He viewed his voyages, in part, as personal explorations, an opportunity for reflection and self-improvement. Unlike some of his contemporaries, Burg found harmony with nature preferable to the rhetoric of conquest. In his diary he wrote: "My eyes seek the beauties of nature and my brain is fed by dreams of purple-fringed mountains and great rivers confined in sunshiny valleys. I see God in everything and my life should be full and sweet if only I make the outdoors my lover and weave its soul into my life and into my work. The longer I am with nature the more my heart is thrilled by its won-ders and the more peaceful and serene all things become."

Despite his doubts and setbacks regarding the Columbia River voyage, and with no firm date for departure, Burg pressed forward. His research was extensive, his planning meticulous. He kept pages of detailed lists—equipment, river miles, camps, meals, rapids, history, costs, contacts—which he revised regularly. He intended to use his river diary not only to record his observations and responses to nature, but as a source of raw material for his proposed magazine articles. To this end, he contacted Basil Hamilton, a historian for the Canadian Pacific Railroad. Hamilton, a Columbia River enthusiast, agreed to share his knowledge of the history of exploration on the upper Columbia. In return, he asked to accompany Burg on the first leg of his voyage from Lake Columbia to Golden, a lumber and tourist town, 150 miles downstream. Burg agreed.

Hamilton had met and advised both Lewis Freeman and M. J. Lorraine, two men who had made the lengthy voyage down the Columbia River (Freeman in August 1920 and Lorraine in May 1921). Each claimed to be the first to complete the transit in a small boat. Lorraine, a civil engineer, had traveled alone in one vessel; Freeman, a popular author, routinely hired guides and boats as necessary. Each had written well-received memoirs of their voyages. Burg had scoured both Freeman's *Down the Columbia* (published 1921) and Lorraine's *The Columbia Unveiled* (1924) for information. Together the two books complemented one another, offering a broad and compelling view of the Columbia River and the people who worked and lived along its shores. Both works unveiled the river for the first time as fact and romance to a new audience.

Burg's "outfit" was modest, second-hand, and inexpensive. Although he anticipated cold weather, he intended to travel as light as possible. He brought a bulky eiderdown sleeping bag, a large piece of canvas, an electric lantern, a marine repair kit, a .30-30 rifle, and ammunition. His clothing was mostly wool: long underwear, leather wool-lined gloves and stocking cap, a heavy shirt and sweater, extra socks, rubber-lined pants, and an overcoat. Food included beans, canned fruit, raisins, spuds, hard candy, coffee, jerky, and sea-biscuits—a staple Burg had grown accustomed to while at sea. He would supplement his meals by fishing and hunting, although he was hardly a skilled marksman or fisherman. He arranged to have his mother, Annie Burg, send jars of homemade jam and cookies to predetermined locations along the river. He would routinely rely on the hospitality of strangers.

Any article for *National Geographic* required photographs, lots of them. Burg had dry bags constructed out of "hospital rubber" to protect his most valuable piece of equipment beside his canoe—his camera equipment. He made no mention of makes, models, or the number of cameras he brought with him. He stored his photographic film in sealed fruit jars. He failed to bring a lifejacket—a troubling omission. Whether this was a deliberate decision remains unknown. He also brought strands of flesh- and pink-colored pearls he had purchased in the Orient while working as an able seaman to sell in the larger towns along the river if he ran short of cash.

He would pilot *Song o' the Winds*, his seventeen-foot canvas- and wood-framed canoe, built by the Old Town Canoe Company. The whimsical name of the boat was inspired by a line from one of Burg's favorite childhood poems, "The Wind" from Robert Louis Stevenson's *A Child's Book of Garden Verses*: "O wind, a-blowing all day long / O wind, that sings so loud a song." The canoe was a sturdy craft rigged for rowing as well as paddling. The company catalogs offered a variety of craft, ranging from fifteen to nineteen feet with prices starting at thirty dollars and running as high as seventy-five dollars. The ribs of the canoes were typically constructed of white cedar, a soft wood both flexible and tough, and western red cedar was used for planking to which an overlay of heavy cotton duck canvas was attached. Native spruce and ash were used for rails, stems, and thwarts. The hardwoods Honduras mahogany and cherry provided material for gunnels. The canoes came in a variety of colors and exterior hull designs. The company also offered to custom-fit any model with extras, such as a keel, outside stems, outer decking, and rowing set-ups. The terms of purchase: cash with order or a satisfactory reference. Special-order work required advance payment. The Old Town Canoe Company had a reputation for excellence.

Burg had not sought out a companion for the voyage. Except for the Big Bend reach of the Columbia in Canada (where he would hire a guide for the 180-mile run), he intended to make the journey from the mountains to the Pacific Ocean alone. (With the addition of Hamilton and a hired guide, however, Burg's claim of having made the first complete solo transit of the Columbia would be subject to debate.) After much procrastination, he shipped his canoe and outfit to Cranbrook, British Columbia, the point of entry between Canada and the United States, on October 15. Two days later, he limped aboard the train on crutches at Union Station in downtown Portland. A chill laced the autumn air. His family had gathered to see him off, and Burg assured his mother he would be home by Thanksgiving.

He had chosen an inopportune time to make a lengthy voyage on an unfamiliar river. In the higher elevations of the Canadian Rockies, winter temperatures had arrived early that year and dropped precipitously. He could expect inclement weather, snowfall, and temperatures well below freezing. Although Burg had previous river experience on the Yellowstone-Missouri-Mississippi Rivers it did little to qualify him for a run on an icy, high mountain river with winter approaching. He would have to line or portage his canoe at numerous rapids. Wading on crutches through bitterly cold water over slippery rocks posed a serious handicap. An outside observer might have concluded that his decision was impetuous.

On October 19, Burg passed through customs at Cranbrook. The temperature remained above freezing. The dry air and brilliant sunshine was invigorating, and locals predicted another month of clear weather. Burg hobbled around town making last-minute purchases. That evening, he began the writing task he had set for himself—two thousand words a day, which would serve as source material for a magazine article. If *National Geographic* wouldn't purchase it, some other magazine surely would. On October 22 he boarded the Kootenay Central Railroad for Lake Columbia, the starting point of his voyage. His companion, Basil Hamilton, was waiting for him when he arrived the next afternoon. A light snow fell as the two men, with the help of the railroad conductor and brakeman, unloaded Burg's outfit from the baggage car and lugged it to a shallow canal leading to Columbia Lake. Canal Flats, a low strip of land roughly a mile wide, separated Columbia Lake, headwaters of the Columbia, from the already formidable Kootenay River. The two rivers, adjacent to one another but traveling in opposite directions, delighted and confounded Burg.

Burg's voyage to the Pacific Ocean began with little fanfare. Hamilton sat in the stern while Burg, in his hip waders, towed *Song o' the Winds* to

Columbia Lake. The snow flurries continued. After a few miles of rowing they reached Lake Windermere. It was midnight before they arrived at Hamilton's bungalow on the eastern shore, where they were greeted by his wife. She prepared a warm meal and a comfortable place to sleep for Burg, who was cold and tired but generally upbeat. The voyage had begun.

The next morning Burg and Hamilton departed for Golden, 150 miles downstream. Snow showers temporarily gave way to dazzling blue skies. At Athalmer, a small town at the end of Lake Windermere, the hundred-foot-wide Columbia took on the shape of a river, albeit a slow-moving one, winding back and forth across the valley. Willow, alder, and cottonwood lined the banks; lagoons paralleled the river course. Along the way the two men stopped at isolated cabins, where Hamilton introduced Burg to numerous World War I veterans. They had come, Hamilton said, to forget the Great War. The weather held, and Burg took dozens of photographs. Hamilton was a mine of information, especially concerning the British fur man, surveyor, and astronomer David Thompson. He and his party had been the first to traverse lengthy portions of the river. He had attempted to establish trading posts for the Hudson's Bay Company and later the Northwest Fur Company. In the summer of 1811, after years of starts and stops along the Columbia, Thompson finally reached the Pacific Ocean.

Six days later, Burg and Hamilton reached Golden, below the mouth of the Kicking Horse River. Hamilton returned home to Lake Windermere aboard the train. Burg sought out veteran riverman Peter Bergenham, whom Hamilton considered to be one of the more reliable river guides in the area. Burg was disappointed to learn that his first choice had left town to set trap lines for the season. Burg's presence in Golden had not gone unnoticed, nor had his intention to run the entire length of the Columbia. His audacious plan drew sardonic comments from the locals, who could not resist an opportunity to tease a greenhorn. Only a fool would challenge the Big Bend in winter, they chortled. Burg shrugged if off—he was not unfamiliar with the exaggerated tales of doom folks who lived along rivers loved to tell. Their stories were not without currency, however. Drownings and near-drownings on the upper Columbia, even among seasoned rivermen, were regular occurrences.

Early the next morning, K. C. Knudsen, a large, self-assured Dane, appeared at Burg's riverside camp. Like everyone else in Golden, he had heard that Burg was looking for an experienced guide. He claimed to know the Big Bend reach better than anyone in the area; it was a boast all local rivermen made without hesitation. Knudsen said the 235-mile voyage to Revelstoke would take nine days, ten at most. Burg cut to the chase: how much would it cost? Ten dollars a day, plus grub, spouted Knudsen. One hundred dollars was a substantial sum, but Burg accepted—he could not afford to delay.

Knudsen failed to mention his wreck in the rapids of Donald Canyon three years earlier. There he had lost not only his canoe but all his provisions, gear, traps, and a rifle. He had been fortunate to make shore alive. In *The Columbia Unveiled*, Lorraine had written of such river mishaps: "My knowledge of swift rivers and their rapids convinces me that practically all the accidents which occur are due either to inexperience, ignorance, incompetence, or recklessness." Lorraine had met Knudsen, who readily admitted to carelessness. It is unclear whether Burg realized that Knudsen was the trapper mentioned in Lorraine's early chapters.

The deal secured, Knudsen inspected *Song o' the Winds* and expressed dissatisfaction. Burg's canoe, he insisted, was far too small for a river the size of the Columbia. He would prefer to pilot his Petersboro—a larger, more stable canoe. The favorite craft of local guides ran to twenty feet with a four-foot beam, and weighed 250 pounds. It carried a high bow and stern. Burg held his ground. To use a different boat, he argued, would break the continuity of his trip. How could he claim to be the first to run the length of the Columbia in a canoe if he began the trip in another man's boat? *Song o' the Winds* was at least as stable as the Petersboro and certainly more maneuverable. The trapper ultimately relented. Burg went into town to purchase provisions; Knudsen returned home to assemble his gear.

Snow was falling when the two voyagers launched the morning of October 31. Burg sat midship at the rowing station while Knudsen sat in the stern working the steering paddle. Neither man wore a lifejacket. The roar of the Kicking Horse River, cascading into the Columbia from the right bank, did little to calm Burg's anxiousness. He had surrendered his boat to a stranger. The shoreline raced by; gravel bars and rocky islands appeared; the braided river offered numerous channels. Which way to go?

It was a far cry from Burg's halcyon boyhood days on the Columbia near Portland. Born December 3, 1901, in the Woodlawn Hospital in the rural, unincorporated area east of the Willamette River and downtown Portland, Amos Burg arrived in a household bustling with noise and activity. His thirty-six-year-old mother had already given birth to one child every two years over the past decade: two boys and three girls. Amos, the third son, was distant in age from his older brothers, Charles and George, by ten years or more. By the time he reached ten or eleven, they would have been living away from home. Closer in age to him were his older sisters, Vera and Mabel, who doted over their new baby brother throughout his childhood and later shepherded him through the neighborhood as a child. Eventually both sisters became confidantes and allies. Two years after Amos's birth, Annabelle was born, followed by John two years later. Burg grew up surrounded by his sisters.

By all accounts, the Burg household was a happy one. There was a never-ending cycle of family outings, seasonal chores, celebrations, and neighborhood play. Birthdays and holidays were celebrated with much fanfare. Sunday dinners were the norm; afterward the family gathered around the piano, where Mrs. Burg played their favorite tunes. The family attended a local Christian church, where Amos received bible instruction and learned to play the cornet. The children roamed freely through a patchwork of yards, orchards, nearby fields, and the Columbia Slough. In summer there were berry patches to raid, and in spring a variety of wildflowers to pick. Electricity had not yet reached the east side of the Willamette, horse and buggies were a familiar sight, and the dirt roads turned into muddy bogs in winter. Eventually the area would become known as the Woodlawn neighborhood of northeast Portland.

Burg was a preoccupied boy, indifferent to schoolwork, a mediocre student at best. It was not for want of intelligence or curiosity. He had both in abundance but preferred reading stories about sea voyages and shipwrecks, trading the classroom for the library at every opportunity. He devoured Kipling, Defoe, and Robert Louis Stevenson. He liked geography and studied maps relentlessly. He found his way to accounts of the early French voyageurs, Lewis and Clark, and his favorite, Captain Cook. He followed the race to the South Pole in 1911, rooting for the Norwegian Roald Amundsen. He routinely disappeared into the Columbia Slough, spending entire days on the backwaters with a circle of friends, and when they were not available, by himself. Taking the measure of his son, Burg Sr. often wondered what would become of the dreamy boy.

Burg Jr. began his voyaging apprenticeship on the quiet backwaters of the Columbia Slough, a short bicycle ride (a bit longer walk) from his home. Located in the floodplain of the Columbia River east of the city, the nineteen-mile slough stretched from Blue and Fairview Lakes near the Sandy River in the north to the confluence of the Willamette and Columbia Rivers. The northern portion of the slough was a maze of lakes, islands, wetlands, and narrow waterways fed by Pacific Ocean tides and seasonal flooding. The area teemed with fish and fowl as well as plant- and wildlife. In 1903 Frederick Law Olmsted, the nationally recognized landscape designer, and his adopted son, John, were invited to Portland by the city council to envision a plan for a system of city parks. In their final study they identified the Columbia Slough as an aesthetic natural resource, claiming it one of Portland's "remaining great landscape features."

Shy and rail-thin as a boy, Burg spent entire days exploring the slough. He favored the warmer seasons but often took to the water on clear, cold winter days. His vessels included crude wooden rafts and battered canoes. When he could not scavenge a craft, he built or borrowed one. Of one canoe he wrote: "It was so unstable I had to part my hair in the middle just to keep from tipping over." Burg and his friends floated, fished, swam naked in the warm lake waters, camped on the islands, sang songs, and spun wild tales around the campfire. They hatched schemes and plotted ambushes in mock encounters among pirates, Indians, and river bandits. The young boy liked to paddle, but when he discovered that the local boathouse rented small wooden rowboats, he was eager to try one out.

As a teenager, he pushed beyond the familiar boundaries of the slough to make three- and four-day journeys up and down the Columbia, often traveling alone. To reach The Dalles, sixty miles upriver, he booked passage on one of the sternwheelers that left Portland each morning, and then floated down the river, stopping where he pleased to camp. For the roughly hundred-mile run from Portland to Astoria on the Oregon coast, he simply launched his canoe near the recently completed Interstate Bridge that linked Portland to Vancouver, Washington.

As an adolescent, Burg dreamed of becoming a writer and going to sea like his hero, Jack London.

After Burg graduated from grammar school, he appeared reluctant to attend high school. He confided in his sister Vera that he was restless and wanted "to go to sea," specifically to Australia and the South Pacific islands. She thought him foolish and typical of all boys his age but kept her own counsel, handing her brother off to his mother, who pointed her son to his father. In 1917 Burg Sr. helped young Amos find a job aboard the coastal passenger steamers that made weekly round trips between Portland, San Francisco, and Los Angeles.

By fall, however, Burg had returned to Portland and enrolled in high school, where his academic efforts were halfhearted. He was often tardy and more than once skipped school to go to a movie or to boat in the slough. Upon discovering author Jack London, Amos decided he would become a writer as well as "a man of action." He began to keep a diary, the first evidence of a sustained writing effort.

After one semester Burg quit high school, in January 1918, to ship out to Australia. His mother and sisters helped the young voyager prepare for the journey, making sure he had the necessary clothing and insisting that he write them regularly. The family's confidence in him seemed to give Burg the courage he needed to make another leap beyond the world of his imagination. Over the next four years he worked as an able seaman, often in rough, if not dangerous, circumstances. He never returned to high school but eventually enrolled in the Oregon Institute of Technology in Portland to complete his secondary education. In 1923 he finally received a diploma.

The guide Knudsen showed little hesitation when choosing a route. *Song o' the Winds* skipped down the deeper channels, rarely touching bottom. The Dane might be worth every penny after all. Twenty-five miles later, they passed under the steel bridge that carried the Canadian Pacific Railway across the Columbia. The river narrowed to three hundred feet, creating sharp waves and whirlpools. It was here that Knudsen had lost his own boat and outfit to the river three years earlier. They passed through the rapids without incident. At the head of Redgrave Canyon, Knudsen ordered Burg to pull for shore to scout the narrow, three-quarter-mile rapid. From their rocky perch they watched the river race by.

In *The Columbia Unveiled,* Lorraine had rated rapids in three blunt categories of difficulty: minor, medium, great. The rapids at Redgrave Canyon he estimated to be "great—a maelstrom." Knudsen casually mentioned that they would run the cataract as a kind of test. He steered *Song o' the Winds* into the storm. Immediately a series of breakers crashed over the gunnels, filling the canoe with icy water and soaking both men. The canoe floundered, then nearly swamped. Burg managed to keep it from capsizing by using the flat blade of his oars in outrigger-fashion. Knudsen dug the paddle in. Together they made for shore. When they discovered they had only lost a sack of potatoes and twelve loaves of bread they had purchased in Golden, both men were relieved.

After running Kitchen Rapids, they landed at Beavermouth, where they were greeted by Peter Bergenham, whom Burg had initially wanted to hire. The dilapidated hamlet—a rundown grocery store, a makeshift post office, the charred skeleton of a once-thriving lumber mill, and a handful of derelict cabins—was gloomy and discouraging. The operating railroad side track, station, and engine house added little to the forlorn scene. Like Knudsen, Bergenham considered the upper Columbia his private domain. City slickers and greenhorns were welcome, as long as they kept their place in the pecking order. After scrutinizing *Song o' the Winds,* Bergenham growled: "I'd sooner be in hell with my back broke than ride that thing through Big Bend."

By the next afternoon Burg and Knudsen were camped above Surprise Rapids, a major obstacle. The width of the river had doubled in size. The rapid itself fell one hundred feet over a distance of three miles. The steepest drop—21 vertical feet over a run of 750 feet—occurred at the head of the whitewater. Below lay a furious maze of monstrous confusion—gaping black holes, whirlpools, shoals, and rocky channels—that stretched farther than the eye could see. The thunderous drone of fast water overwhelmed normal conversation.

Turning over or wrecking the canoe could mean losing everything—gear and camera equipment—bringing an end to the trip. Nevertheless, Burg saw exciting photographic opportunities and delayed departing to wait for the right lighting, much to Knudsen's dissatisfaction.

In their published works on voyages down the Columbia, both Freeman and Lorraine had commented on a proposal by the Canadian Pacific Railroad to dam the lower end of Surprise Rapids. Lorraine, the civil engineer, dryly stated the expected amount of hydroelectric power and its uses in one short paragraph. Freeman, however, was zealous in his praise of the dam promoters. The travel writer who had run the rivers of the world and written of their beauty and romance wrote: "The Columbia, in a hundred miles of the Big Bend, offered the opportunity for developing more hydro-electric energy than all the west of Canada could use in the next twenty years." Neither writer mentioned how the loss of free-flowing rivers would impact voyages like their own.

Knudsen and Burg spent the better part of the next day lining *Song o' the Winds* down the right shore of the first, steepest pitch of Surprise Rapids. Icy water, freezing temperatures, snow flurries, and snow-covered boulders made for a laborious task. Burg, on his crutches, was of little help. At one point the men allowed the canoe to drift too far out into the current, forcing both of them to scramble aboard the boat or else be stranded on shore. It was a near miss. Late that night they arrived at Knudsen's tiny one-room cabin along the river.

The next morning Burg was eager to run lengthy Kinbasket Rapids, but Knudsen dallied. He started to bake a loaf of bread, using the last of the gray-looking flour from a rusty bin. By one o'clock they were paddling downstream. Steep walls along the river closed in on the voyagers; the weather cleared but remained cold. Kinbasket Rapids, although not the most technically difficult fast water on the river, was a lengthy, continuous stretch of whitewater. A minor mishap could turn into a catastrophe. Burg stuck with the oars; Knudsen steered from the stern. When *Song o' the Winds* washed up on a rock and stalled, Burg used his crutch to push them off. Although they had numerous near misses, they managed to avoid trouble.

With night falling, they pitched camp on a steep, snow-covered bank. Snow flurries gave way to a full-blown winter storm. Burg added layers of newspaper beneath his woolen long johns to fend off the bone-numbing chill. The voyagers huddled around their campfire, drying their clothes as best they could and cooking their supper. Despite the miserable conditions, Knudsen remained indifferent, Burg stoic. He slept in his eiderdown sleeping bag covered with a canvas tarp inside his canoe—all of which was tied to a tree. When they woke in the morning, they were covered with snow.

Burg insisted on stopping at Boat Encampment, the location where David Thompson had wintered over in 1810. Here the Canoe and Wood Rivers tumble out of the northern Rockies to join the Columbia, which makes a sweeping U-turn and heads south—the Big Bend. Knudsen surrendered to Burg's wish. He made it clear, however, that his interests lay in earning a living, not visiting historical landmarks. With the river's turn to the south, the Rocky Mountains gradually disappeared from view, replaced by the Gold Range on river right. The Selkirk Mountains now appeared river left. Not that the two voyagers could tell. The snow fell so blanket thick at times that both shorelines disappeared. They lost their bearings. Harsh upstream winds sliced the river surface into dull gray flashing waves. Ice built up on the gunnels as well as the inside of *Song o' the Winds.* Gravel beds, the result of abandoned placer mining, jutted out from the shoreline, adding another potential hazard.

Using Lorraine's guide, Burg kept track of the rapids in his diary—Potlatch, Gordon, Soda Creek, Twelve-Mile, Death (Les Dalles de Morts), Priest, Eighteen-Mile, Petite Dallas, and Steamboat. Lorraine had estimated the breakers in Death Rapids to be fifteen feet high and nearly impassable. Lining the cataract (along the right shore) was arguably as dangerous. A hundred yards below lay Priest Rapids, which also had to be lined. After lining Death Rapids, the pair wasted little time crossing the brief section of fast water. Once again, Burg was rendered marginal by his knee injury. Time and again he slipped on the icy boulders. Knudsen charged forward into the frigid waist-deep water. *Song o' the Winds* took a beating.

On November 7 the two voyagers landed in Revelstoke in a snowstorm. Their canoe was coated in ice. Burg's diary contained a wealth of facts and observations; he had also taken dozens of photographs. The trapper and the greenhorn had averaged roughly twenty or so miles a day, a brisk pace given the winter conditions. Burg took a room at the Hotel Royal, then made for the post office, where a letter from his sister Mabel (with money he had requested more than two weeks ago) awaited him. In a reply to her, he grumbled that he had paid Knudsen too much. A year later, however, he wrote in his diary:

> The voyage around the Big Bend with Knudsen was an education. He was indispensable as I was on a crutch and had trouble on the snow-covered bank. The information he imparted made the whole region of that great wilderness come alive. His manner was rough and abrasive. He was as foolish in trying to emphasize the extent and profundity of his wilderness knowledge as I was in trying to protect my poor abused ego. Knudsen was proud of his river running skills but I found this arrogance of knowledge typical of the Big Bend trappers. They were similar to the mountain men I'd read about—the best trappers, the best marksman, the supreme hunter, the trapper of the most furs, the bravest—everything superlative with a pitying contempt for the cheechako [Chinook jargon for "newcomer" or "greenhorn" in Alaska and northern Canada] like myself . . . but I had already been five years in ships' fo-castles voyaging the seas of the world and similar Cape Horn egotists had taught me that such talents should be duly recognized and appreciated if one is to function with them in jagged harmony. No money wasted there—just solid gold in dealing with these priceless individuals.

The distance from Revelstoke to the international border was 180 miles, the majority of the reach being the flat water of Upper and Lower Arrow Lakes. Burg estimated he could make the run in less than a week. Upon launching, however, he immediately encountered icy headwinds that would plague him relentlessly. The half-mile-wide Columbia entered a broad valley. The mountain ranges retreated; lagoons shadowed the main channel. He rowed a sluggish current, and monotony set in. Gloomy, pewter-colored skies weighed down, and it took him the better part of two days to cover the twenty-nine-mile run to Upper Arrow Lake. Another snowstorm descended. Cold winds tore across the lake, churning up leaden-colored waves that filled the canoe, soaking Burg. His feet ached from constant exposure to the icy water. Oars, canvas tarp, gunnels, and Burg himself were coated with ice. An endless round of rowing, stopping, and scraping ensued. Despite constant effort, he gradually lost the battle. Every night he was exhausted.

A quarter-mile from shore one evening, the canoe swamped. Burg pitched himself over the side into the dark water. Fortunately his feet touched bottom. As he began towing the floundering craft, his water-proof bag holding his sleeping bag drifted off—a potentially fatal loss. Burg dropped the painter and shuffled through the icy water to retrieve the precious sleeping bag. By the time he set foot on the beach, he was shivering violently. He emptied his gear and managed, not without some difficulty, to start a fire. Changing his trousers, Burg warmed himself, ate quickly, and then climbed into his sleeping bag. Nestled in his canoe, he watched a full moon rise, washing the snowbound landscape in the strange pearl-like light. The temperature dropped to ten degrees. The immense silence sharpened the nocturnal murmurs of the wilderness—wind, snowfall, and lake water. Just as he began to relax, Burg realized that one of his gloves was missing. He could not row for long with a bare hand. He stumbled out of his bag and searched the beach. He spotted the glove lying on the cobbles in the moonlight. Another close call.

Burg spent the next three days crossing the lake. It was a miserable and lonely slog that tested his resolve. When he reached The Narrows, an eighteen-mile reach between Upper and Lower Arrow Lakes, he found protection from the winds but little current. Although the storm passed, the temperature remained bone-chilling. Gloomy weather persisted. The voyager experienced feelings of deep isolation and withering self-recrimination. He recounted all his past failures. He feared disappointing his father, and he questioned his will, even his desire, to continue. Promising to reach home by Thanksgiving had been a foolish gesture.

Burg had gained valuable perspective on his previous river trips, however. He knew these moody episodes were transient and thus he endured. He firmed his resolve by maintaining a steady rhythm as he rowed. Usually quite shy, he raised his voice in song, like his much-admired voyageurs who had sung their way through hardship and miserable conditions. Wind-whipped whitecaps littered Lower Arrow Lake. He hugged the lee shoreline; it was slow going but he was out of reach of the icy winds. He camped early, allowing himself enough time to prepare his meal. As the temperature plunged, he retreated to his sleeping bag and wrote in his diary until he fell asleep. He awoke each morning blanketed in ice.

In Castlegar—a railway depot with a hotel, store, and a handful of rough houses—Burg stopped to restock and mail letters. The international border lay forty miles away. After days of flat water and icy headwinds, he felt the pull of the current as he rowed *Song o' the Winds* downriver. By the end of the day, he reached the mining town of Trail. The towering stacks of the Consolidated Mining and Smelting Company of Canada billowed smoke into the dismal sky. Two days later, he spotted the Pend d'Oreille River, the second-largest tributary of the Columbia, surging into the river from the right shore. Crossing into the United States, he let out a cheer. At Northport, Washington, he felt a rush of patriotism as he set foot on American soil for the first time in a month. The Pacific Ocean lay 750 miles downriver.

Burg quizzed locals about formidable Little Dalles Rapids. One man assured him that not so long ago, he had watched a bateau with six lumbermen capsize in a whirlpool at the head of Little Dalles. The boat was eventually recovered downriver, but the bodies of the men were never found. As Burg rowed, the dull rumble of the cataract drifted up canyon. It was a sound that would give any river traveler pause. Still undecided, he pulled ashore to scout. He later wrote in a letter: "The temperature was at freezing and it would be a risky run, but I thought I could make it so I jumped in and took off." The opportunity to avoid a lengthy portage may have been too hard to resist.

As the canoe approached the rapid, Burg realized the route was anything but clear. The river bent to the right, funneling into a channel no more than two hundred feet wide. He had been warned about the ancient reef that spanned the river. Now the current carried him toward the obstacle. On either side, basalt outcroppings jutted out, forcing the water into swift-moving channels. The combination of reef and rock simultaneously split and constricted the current. Water crashed and swirled, boiled up as waves, appeared and disappeared

Burg rowing Song o' the Winds *on Columbia River in 1924*

at random. Time had run out. Whether out of design or an error in judgment, he took the right channel. The river thunder rose up, echoing off the hundred-foot limestone wall on the right. He wrote: "Canoe went in grandly gripped by huge swirls. Starboard side dipped under gripped by whole force of river. Round and round I spun. I dropped the oars and my hand gripped the gunnels. Now the entire canoe was not only swirling but icy water was pouring over both gunnels. Pictured myself struggling in the icy maelstrom. Suddenly it eased further down the canyon and I thanked God for deliverance wet and cold as I was." The experience shook him more than he cared to admit.

At Marcus, Washington, he pulled ashore. He had another problem: he was broke and could not afford to hire a drayman to portage *Song o' the Winds* around Kettle Falls Rapid. The local newspaper editor directed Burg to the town hall, where a bake sale was in progress. He might be able to sell some of his pearl necklaces there. The editor was right. Burg sold enough necklaces to pay for the portage and then some. The woman in charge of the bake sale fumed. The charming stranger had stolen her potential buyers right under her nose. Burg wisely offered to purchase the remaining baked and canned goods. He then enlisted a group of boys to carry the treats down to the river for an impromptu picnic around a blazing fire. The next morning, a horse-drawn dray shuttled him around Kettle Falls.

A few miles below the mouth of the Spokane River, the Columbia River jogs west, forming the southern border of the Colville Indian reservation. On Thanksgiving Day, the day Burg had promised his mother he would be home, he stopped at the Shingler homestead, three miles above the future location of the Grand Coulee Dam. Mrs. Shingler set another plate at the table; Burg joined the family for holiday celebrations, entertaining them with accounts of his river journey. He wrote to his parents the next day from Lincoln, Washington, apologizing for missing Thanksgiving and requesting a list of supplies and gear to be delivered to Pasco, Washington: one six-foot canoe paddle, two cans of marine glue, twelve rolls of #118 film (Eastman with twelve exposures), one box of .30-30 shells, a hunting license, a brown wool stocking cap, two pairs leather wool-lined gloves, a pair of rubber-lined pants, and a heavy shirt. He told his family: "I stopped at Sam Seaton's ferry, where Sam was running his ferry and dreaming of the money he would receive for his ranch. It was directly on the site of Grand Coulee Dam. He was planning his strategy and viewing the future with anxiety. He was David dealing with the government Goliath."

Near the town of Patero, Washington, Burg laid over for two days aboard the steamer *Bridgeport*. He celebrated his twenty-third birthday on December 3 with a Captain McDermott, who insisted the young man have dinner with him. Burg caught up on his river diary and referred to the notes he had taken from Lorraine's *The Columbia Unveiled*. He had copied entire passages for both navigation purposes as well as inspiration. Lorraine had quoted Reverend Samuel Parker, who had navigated Cascades Rapids in 1836, about the thrill of running rivers: "The sensations excited in descending the Cascades are of that peculiar character which are best understood by experience. The sensation of fear is no sooner awakened than it subsides before the power and magnificence of the rolling surges, the circling vortices, and the roaring breakers. Let those whose energies, either of body or mind, need arousing, try the navigation of the Columbia in high water and their powers will be invigorated for almost any future enterprise."

At the head of Box Canyon, Burg stood in *Song o' the Winds* at the head of the rapid to take a final photograph. It was a careless moment. The canoe struck a reef and he was catapulted into the icy river. He clung to his canoe for a half-mile before crawling ashore. Shivering uncontrollably, he built a fire. The canoe survived the mishap with a few minor scrapes; Burg's camera, however, had been seriously damaged. In later newspaper accounts, he brushed off the severity of the mishap, holding fast to the persona of the unflappable riverman. In his diary, though, he admitted to being frightened.

Twelve miles below Wenatchee, Washington, he ran Rock Island Rapids without incident. "I had one of my finest days," he wrote. "The day was sunny and the views breathtaking as I viewed the dramatic basalt cliff bordering the river on the right and the sweeping plains of the Horse Heaven country." For weeks on the river, he had endured the cold without complaint. Sitting in the canoe for long periods, however, had left his feet numb and cramped. His injured knee now ached continually. Hoping to staunch the chronic pain, he took to shore every few miles to hobble back and forth along the beach. He ran into trouble at Priest Rapids, where seven distinct drops occurred over an eleven-mile stretch of the river. On the sixth pitch, *Song o' the Winds* ran aground on a reef. He stepped into the water to free the craft but lost one of his oars in the effort. He had no choice but to drift helplessly through the rapid.

On the afternoon of December 16, Burg reached the confluence of the Columbia and Snake Rivers. The Snake, the river he had once referred to as an "enemy," was a welcome sight. The weather further deteriorated, forcing him to remain at the confluence camp for three days. What he could not know was that a severe storm had recently pushed down from Canada into western Montana, roared across Idaho and the plateau country of eastern Washington, and was funneling down the Columbia Gorge toward Portland. Over the next three weeks the cold snap would bring river traffic to a halt, freezing portions of the Columbia to within a few miles of the Pacific Ocean. Sternwheelers found themselves trapped at their moorings. In Portland, children ice-skated while adults drove their automobiles across the Willamette River. The winter of 1924–25 would be remembered as one of the worst on record.

To stave off the cold, Burg wrapped himself in newspapers beneath his outer garments. He attempted to take photographs, but his camera froze up repeatedly. He took short walks. Bundled in his canoe in the evenings, he cooked his supper as best he could with gloved hands. Firewood was scarce. He waited for gaps in the overcast sky in hopes of viewing the stars, an experience he found uplifting given the cheerless conditions. When it became apparent that the harsh weather was not retreating, Burg could wait no longer. He launched on a steel-colored river packed with floe ice and white-capped waves. A collision with ice would be deadly. Overhead the drab ominous sky weighed down upon the lone voyager. Along the shoreline the river had frozen over, white piles of ice building on one another, catching and trapping other chunks of ice floe. Eddies, once his slow-water sanctuaries where he might escape the fierce headwinds, had disappeared. Finding a landing, usually a simple maneuver, was a problem. He was constantly forced to the middle of the river into the teeth of an unforgiving wind. It was a dangerous distance from shore should he capsize.

Burg faced a by now familiar dilemma: sharp waves splashed over the gunnels, river water accumulated in the bottom of the canoe and froze, adding more weight to the canoe, which in turn rode lower in the water, allowing even more water over the gunnels. His attempts to chip away the ice were fruitless. The weather was as strange as any he had encountered while at sea. Rain followed hail, interrupted by snow flurries blown diagonal by gale-force winds. At Arlington, Oregon, Burg was forced to pull ashore. The canvas-and-wood hull of the canoe was leaking badly. He dragged the boat up the beach, unloaded his gear, and turned her over. Somehow he managed to build a small fire underneath the canoe to thaw it out, heat the tar pitch into a thick jell, and coat the bottom of the canoe. It was a difficult task in the best of circumstances. "By making my teeth chatter," he joked, "it helped to chew gum without voluntarily moving my jaws."

Three separate reefs, a half-mile apart, stretched across the river at Umatilla Rapids. At high water the reefs disappeared and the route was straightforward. Low water revealed narrow chutes in each reef through which the river raced. In a canoe these passages were difficult to locate in fair weather, and an exhausted Burg misread his position. Too late to correct, he found himself stranded on a rocky outcropping. Icy river water roared into two fresh gaps in the hull of his craft. He wrangled the sinking canoe off the rocks. He struggled to shore to make repairs.

For the next two days Burg navigated minor rapids—Devil's Run, Canoe Encampment, Owyhee, Blalock, Four O'Clock, Rock Creek, Squally Hook, Indian, and below the mouth of the John Day River, John Day—and endured increasingly poor weather. He had not seen any boats on the river for weeks. At Celilo Falls he encountered an unworldly scene. The rapids were frozen over. Ice floes had piled up on one another, and the roar of the famous rapid—normally heard upstream for a mile—was muted. The outcroppings where Native people still fished with their gaffes and nets were encased in snow; ice dams had formed in the chutes and channels between the islands. The river groaned and creaked. Burg dare not venture below the Big Island in search of a passage for fear of being stranded. The Celilo Canal, which he had used to skirt the rapid on previous shorter voyages, was frozen over and impassable.

Lawrence Harvey, a railroad engineer, was surprised to see a solitary figure waving at him on the empty road above the Columbia in such desolate weather. He stopped his truck and picked up the young man, who asked if he had room for his canoe. Harvey was astonished when Burg gave him an account of his voyage on the Columbia. He offered to drive the voyager to Cascade Locks, forty miles downriver, but Burg refused. When they reached The Dalles, the temperature was twelve degrees. Burg spent the night on the floor of the local newspaper office.

The next day his progress was agonizingly slow, but by evening he had reached Cascade Locks, his energy sapped. As he suspected, the freezing temperatures had made the lock inoperable. He had no choice but to portage *Song o' the Winds*. The next morning he set off and immediately capsized in the lower Cascade Rapids. He drifted more than a mile in the frigid river before reaching shore. Unable to warm himself sufficiently, he returned to the river in the hopes that rowing would halt the shivering. At Bridal Veil Falls, a few miles below Cascade Locks, he beached the canoe. He was in bad shape. He boarded a local train for Portland. When he arrived home unexpectedly days before Christmas, his family was confused but excited. Newsmen from the Portland dailies arrived on the doorstep. Was the voyage over? Had

Burg returned to photograph Celilo Falls numerous times throughout his career.

Burg given up? If not, when was he going to finish his journey? Burg told them he would wait until the weather turned to continue downriver.

The week after Christmas, Burg resumed his voyage down the Columbia. The cold snap had ended, but the weather continued to be harsh. Ice floes crowded the river. Freezing rain and high winds slowed his progress. He stopped in Vancouver, Washington, across the Columbia River from Portland, where he contacted Jesse Sill, a photographer for the *Oregon Journal* and a freelance newsreel cameraman for Pathé News. Sill was one of a handful of early pioneer filmmakers in Oregon. He had been one of the first to film Portland's Rose Parade (1912) and the Pendleton Round-Up (1914) in eastern Oregon. Sill had shot footage of the construction of the Columbia River Highway as well as the opening of the Interstate Bridge between Washington and Oregon. He had also taken the first aerial photographs of Mount Hood.

Sill, who harbored movie-making aspirations, was always on the lookout for dramatic footage of current events for the weekly newsreel in local theaters. When Burg proposed that Sill meet him in Astoria and film him crossing the Columbia River Bar, Sill agreed immediately. Burg also contacted Bill Hudson, another Pathé News cameraman, in Seattle. Family, well-wishers, and newsmen saw the local hero off in Vancouver. From the outset he experienced trouble on the lower Columbia. At Saint Helens, Oregon, thirty miles downriver from Portland, floating ice trapped him along shore, nearly crushing his boat. Near Cathlamet, Washington, and again at Deer Island, the scene repeated itself. He calculated his progress at about two miles an hour, at best. It would take days, if not weeks, to reach Astoria. Burg began to second-guess his decision to depart his hometown so quickly.

Previously he had avoided the parade of passing ships bound for the Pacific for fear of capsizing in their wake. When he realized how effortlessly they cut through the floe ice and acted as a wind barrier, he slipped into the wake of one ship after another for the next three days. After nearly a week on the river, he arrived in Astoria, Oregon, on January 2. The next morning he made the twelve-mile crossing to Ilwaco, Washington. A crowd had gathered to welcome him. That evening the Chamber of Commerce hosted a banquet in his honor. Burg waited three days for the weather to clear and conditions on the bar to improve. The delay may have had another cause: although Jesse Sill had arrived, Hudson, the Pathé News cameraman, had yet to appear.

At noon on January 7, Captain Alfred Rimer, commander of the Fort Canby Coast Guard Station, towed *Song o' the Winds* out of the harbor, past Sand Island, and into the Columbia. Now Rimer piloted a new Class "E" lifeboat, powered by a four-cylinder Red Wing gasoline engine. In 1913, Rimer, among others, had received the Gold Lifesaving medal from the Coast Guard for his attempt to rescue crew members from the *Rosecrans*, a 2,970-ton oil steamer that had become stranded on Peacock Spit at the mouth of the Columbia. Ship and cargo were eventually destroyed, and thirty-three crew members perished.

It was typical January weather on the Oregon coast. Temperatures had dipped to thirty-nine degrees that morning and would only reach a high of forty-five degrees. Wind gusts out of the southwest peaked at fifty miles per hour. Nearly a half-inch of rain fell throughout the day. Rimer felt it was his duty to accompany Burg in case of a mishap. (Burg had once apprenticed as a fifteen-year-old cabin boy on the coastal steamer *Rose City* under Rimer's command.) Burg was certainly counting on the captain's judgment when assessing the chances for a safe crossing.

Accompanying Rimer and Burg were a number of prominent Ilwaco and Astoria businessmen as well as newspapermen from the *Oregon Journal*. They traveled aboard the McGowan cannery boat, *Leonore III*. Hudson had arrived at the last moment and lashed his motion-picture camera to the boat's stern deck. The mood was celebratory. The men aboard the two boats felt certain they were witnessing a historic event. Burg, for his part, did not want to disappoint. Rimer gave the signal to one of his crewman to cast off the line towing *Song o' the Winds*. The tide was on the ebb. For a few hours, river and ocean flowed west in the same direction. Burg began to row.

Absent a river delta to dissipate its force, the Columbia current raced at four to seven knots through the relatively narrow coastal gap to saltwater. When the prevailing westerly winds, aided by an ebb tide and ocean swells, rose to meet the river's swift current, steep waves (ten to twenty feet) broke irregularly on the shallow bars and shoals. Without a river pilot, small ships often lost their way and ran aground; fishing boats and pleasure craft were routinely overturned. Every year, lives were lost. Lewis Freeman had not even considered crossing the bar; M. J. Lorraine thought it unnecessary. Both pioneers had ended their voyages in Astoria, ten miles upriver from the mouth of the Columbia.

Rimer had advised Burg to follow in his wake along North Jetty, staying as close as possible to the Coast Guard vessel as safety permitted. This proved impossible—the swells made rowing difficult, and Burg soon fell behind. The cameras continued to roll. He temporarily lost sight of Rimer and the *Lorraine III,* and the canoe began to take on water. At one point the Coast Guard vessel lost power and drifted off course. The situation worsened when conditions on the bar deteriorated. One reporter described the scene as follows: "Shooting the rapids on the upper Columbia was child's play compared to crossing the Columbia Bar. The breakers were especially high and an ebb tide and a heavy wind combined to provide more thrills than he had anticipated when he started. The light craft was tossed to the crest of one breaker and then would plunge down 10 to 15 feet before rising on the crest of the next. While he did not get seasick, he admitted that he experienced all of the symptoms."

Around 3:00 in the afternoon, amid high winds and rough seas, Burg reached the end of the 2.5-mile-long North Jetty. His voyage from the mountains to the sea, from freshwater to saltwater, was complete. He had traveled in the wake of his heroes—the French Canadian voyageurs, David Thompson, Lewis and Clark—and stood the test. He had answered his boyhood query about the source of the Columbia. He could rightfully claim the first recorded source-to-mouth canoe voyage on the Columbia. The drama, however, was not over. *Song o' the Winds,* buffeted by the wind and the waves, capsized. Rimer's crew sprung to action. Burg was pulled from the surf; the canoe took longer to retrieve. Although aghast, the newspapermen were thrilled by this turn of events. Burg, cold and shivering, was greatly relieved. In Ilwaco and Astoria, local fisherman cheered him. He had nothing to be ashamed of—no one had ever attempted to take a canoe across the bar in such conditions.

Back in Portland, Burg received a hero's welcome. He gave more interviews, and his modest, self-effacing manner invited praise. Invitations to attend lunch and dinner banquets poured in. He joked that in Portland anyone could become a hero with a bit of effort. At one dinner in his honor,

Burg presented Captain Rimer with two five-foot cedar paddles to commemorate the occasion. He inscribed one with the following:

> To Capt. Fred Rimer, Ft. Canby Coast Guard Station, Ft. Canby, Wash-
> ington for rescuing canoe "*Song o' the Winds*" from Surf, Jan. 7, 1925
> 3:00 PM Columbia River Bar. The First Canoe from Columbia Lake
> to the Pacific Ocean, a distance of 1268 miles in 73 days, negotiating
> 107 rapids from an altitude of 2654 ft. to sea level,
> Signed Amos Burg

"Fame," Burg later wrote, "is the shortest of all professions."

In January 1925, Burg enrolled in Oregon Agriculture College (today's Oregon
State University) in Corvallis, seventy miles south of Portland. He had only just
completed his Columbia River voyage weeks before. Over the next four years
a familiar pattern emerged as he attempted to earn a degree as well as to learn
the skills necessary to become an adventure-travel writer and photographer.
Conventional education, however, proved difficult for the seasonal student with
wanderlust. During his first term at college, he enrolled in journalism, photography, typing, and creative writing classes. His grades were dismal. Spring
term was no better, and by April he had dropped all his classes, receiving a W
("withdrawal") with no explanation. By July he was on the Snake River. Burg
never returned to Oregon Agriculture College. Fifteen months passed before
he enrolled in the journalism program at the University of Oregon in Eugene.

There his attendance was sporadic, dictated by the rivers he ran or the
need to go to sea to earn money. His grades were mediocre at best. Nevertheless, he drew the attention of the deans of the journalism and philosophy
graduate schools who found the older student a talented, interesting conver-
sationalist. They regularly invited him to dinner and social events. A popular, somewhat mysterious figure on campus, Burg attracted female attention.
Familiar with his reputation as an adventurer, one woman told him that "he
was likely to be here today and gone tomorrow." Of his relationship with
another woman, Burg wrote: "To me it [a relationship with a woman] means
the unfolding of myself and that I experience and feel the things that make
me grow." Yet the river continued to call him.

Burg wrote a column for *The Emerald,* the school newspaper, and became an associate editor for a brief time. He continued to be mentored by the filmmaker Jesse Sill, who invited him along on assignments throughout Oregon. He also began to successfully market silks, pearls, and Oriental rugs to teachers and students alike. One spring he even managed to run the fast water of Oregon's McKenzie River with three other students. He never received a degree, however, instead claiming that like any good romantic, he strived for knowledge alone.

Eight decades before Burg landed in The Dalles that wintery afternoon, James and Nancy (Dickerson) Welch faced a similar situation. My great-great-grandparents were hardly romantic voyageurs, however. The Welches, along with their three young sons, had departed Saint Joseph, Missouri, in the spring of 1844 on the Oregon Trail. They traveled in a party of eighteen wagons (one of four such parties in a collective group that called itself the Independent Colony wagon train) and hoped to reach Oregon City, the jumping-off point for the Willamette Valley, before the snow flew. Sometime in late October the wagon train arrived at The Dalles. Despite the record amounts of rain and flooding that had delayed their passage westward, the wagon train had made good time. The long, difficult journey was about to become even more arduous. (Construction of the 150-mile Barlow Road around the eastern slope of Mount Hood would not begin for another year.) So great was the danger and difficulty of navigating the Columbia River, later pioneers preferred the Barlow Road route to Oregon City despite outrageous toll fees, extraordinary hardships, and the very real chance of being caught in a winter storm in the mountains so close to their final destination.

James and Nancy had no choice but to take the river route, thus becoming the first river runners in the family. The term "river runners," of course, is downright misleading. They were hardly engaged in a recreational activity, but it is hard to resist the idea of the river and a historical thread connecting Burg, my ancestors, and me. The first obstacle the Welches and the other pioneers faced was finding a means of river transportation large enough to carry them and their possessions. They had three options: rent a bateaux (a French term for a flat-bottomed river boat with a sharply pointed bow and stern that was first used in eastern and central North America) from the Hudson's Bay Company for roughly eighty dollars; purchase a log raft from an enterprising white person or Native American; and lastly, build a log raft themselves.

No record remains of which option twenty-eight-year-old James Welch chose or whether he hired a guide or a boatman to navigate the river. Given family lore, it would not surprise me if he built a log raft himself or teamed up with another family to get the job done. With winter fast approaching, they could not afford to wait very long at The Dalles. Historical records and an old photograph suggest that James was entrepreneurial in spirit and certainly not a man to be trifled with. Yet Nancy, with three young sons in tow, may well have insisted he hire a bateaux, providing one was available. Often the pioneers were forced to wait days, if not weeks, for bateaux to return upriver from Fort Vancouver.

As Burg discovered later, traveling the Columbia River during the winter was a hazardous undertaking. It was an icy cold, turbulent, wind-blown, and unforgiving river. Experienced pilots were few, and even those with knowledge of the river could not guarantee safe passage. Few, if any, of the pioneers had seen, much less navigated, a river the size of the Columbia. Children and adults were routinely washed overboard, as were possessions; high winds overturned sizable wooden rafts; impassable rapids (especially Cascade Rapids) made for tortuous portages lasting days. It is likely that of the four parties (involving a total of 323 people), some individuals suffered a mishap.

The Welch family survived the voyage, landing first at Fort Vancouver on the Columbia and then making their way up the Willamette River, where they reached Oregon City on November 10. Two years later, in April 1846, my great-great-grandfather loaded family and possessions on either an open scow or a bateaux and floated a hundred or so miles down the lower Columbia to Fort George (later renamed Astoria) at the mouth of the Columbia. James and Nancy Welch were the first white family to make a home at the then British trading post. They sunk roots, enlarged their family, became pillars of the community and in time part of the history of Astoria and the westward expansion of the United States.

Chapter 2

THE MAD SNAKE

Within five months of his successful transit of the Columbia River in 1924–25, Burg set off on another marathon voyage—this time on the Snake River. It was a swift turnaround given the hardships he had recently endured. Although roughly equal in length to the Columbia, the Snake's numerous rapids surpassed those on the Columbia in size and ferocity. The headwaters of the Snake rise near the source of the Yellowstone River in the Rocky Mountains of northwestern Wyoming, flowing south through Jackson Valley before bending west through Alpine Canyon, the "Grand Canyon" of the Snake. Near present-day Hoback, Wyoming, Wilson Price Hunt, the leader of the Astor Expedition of 1811, faced with the first of many gorges that looked impassable, called the Snake the "mad river." Exiting the mountains the river swings south-southwest in an arc across the arid Snake River plain, dipping into and out of isolated, steep-walled gorges with significant rapids. Upon reaching the Idaho-Oregon border, the river curves north and makes a beeline through rugged Hells Canyon, eventually passing the cities of Lewiston, Idaho, and Clarkston, Washington, before making a final wiggle west to the confluence with the Columbia River.

No one, as far as Amos Burg knew, had ever run the entire length of the river in a canoe. In May 1920 he and Fred "Spokane" Hill, whom he had met aboard the SS *Waikiki* during a round-the-world voyage the winter of 1919–20, had launched *Song o' the Winds* from Lewiston to run the 140-mile lower Snake. Confident, carefree, and inexperienced, the pair capsized more than once, lost a portion of their outfit, and nearly sank the canoe at a rapid just above the confluence with the Columbia. They continued down the Columbia to the Pacific Ocean, covering a distance of 450 miles in twenty-two days. It was the first of numerous voyages Hill and Burg would make together.

In an effort to promote the voyage down the Snake River, Burg forged several promising business relationships. The Union Pacific Railroad agreed to help with the cost of shipping in exchange for photographs. Jesse Sill, photographer for the *Oregon Journal,* lent Burg his Debrie motion-picture camera and agreed to pay to develop the film in exchange for film rights. Fred Kiser of Kiser Brothers Scenic Photographers in Portland offered the use of camera equipment to take photographs for one of Kiser's scenic booklets. Recognized as one of the finest photographers on the Pacific Coast, Kiser had been the official photographer for the 1905 Lewis and Clark Exposition in Portland. His list of accomplishments also included illustration work for

Burg and Harry Fogleberry en route to the Snake River, 1925

the *National Geographic,* and in 1906 he had come up with the well-known slogan "See America First" for the Northern Pacific Railroad.

Burg's own aspirations to earn a living remained unfulfilled. No word had come from the editors at *National Geographic.* It is likely that in the brief period between trips, he had little time to write the piece or found what he had written wanting and did not submit it. Nevertheless he was determined to place an article on his upcoming voyage with one of the popular national magazines of the time—*Sunset, Saturday Evening Post,* or *Field and Stream.* A seasoned voyager now, he left little to chance. He had become a competent paddler and oarsman, but he knew his limitations. Ever thorough in his research and the logistics of travel, equipment, and supplies, he secured United States Geological Society (USGS) river maps for the voyage.

Chronic lack of money continued to plague him. He had yet to repay the loan his father had given him for the Columbia River voyage when he once again sought financial support. The elder Burg agreed to another loan. Before embarking on the Snake, he wrote to his father: "It is not funny to have to depend on you in crisis that I should and could have overcome myself. You have struggled and conquered against great odds and I wish to do the same.... I'm certainly sorry that I have to ask you for so much Dad, but I'm sure that I can make this up to you." He was twenty-four years old at the time.

On the morning of July 7, 1925, Burg and thirty-one-year-old Harry Fogleberry, an able seaman Burg had met aboard the SS *West Kadar* in 1922, launched *Song o' the Winds* from the shores of Jackson Lake. Burg's earlier experience with Fogleberry on the Yellowstone and Missouri Rivers in 1922 had proved less than ideal, however. Fogleberry had been restless from the start, always in a hurry, and short-tempered. After a month he had abandoned the voyage altogether in Council Bluffs, Iowa. At the time Burg had been glad to see his former shipmate go. In light of this, Burg's choice of companion for his latest river voyage is puzzling. He claimed that when Fogleberry heard about the trip, he pestered Burg relentlessly. After much indecision, Burg had given in. "I just couldn't think of anyone else that would go," he wrote. "I'd just take a chance and see."

The mountain air was warm on launch day, buzzing with the sound of insects. In the distance the ragged, snow-covered Teton Mountains pierced the blue western sky. The two voyagers paddled across the dark-green waters until they reached low-lying Jackson Lake dam, which they portaged around. A small crowd of curious locals and vacationers gathered. Learning of Burg's ambitious voyage, they crowed that his chances of success were nil. No one had ever attempted to paddle the length of the Snake. That evening Burg and Fogleberry pitched camp near Moran Lodge, a well-known vacation spot in Jackson Valley. The spectacular setting was a far cry from the freezing temperatures and snowbound riverbank camps Burg had endured on the upper Columbia River months earlier. Despite the warm weather and intoxicating scenery, he suffered prevoyage feelings of dread mixed with excitement.

Around 9:00 AM the next day, the two voyagers departed. USGS flow records reveal that they launched on 5,160 cubic feet per second (CFS). Over the next eight days the water would fall to a low of 2,890 CFS on July 15, as the dam operators held back water to meet the irrigation needs of the local ranchers. Fogleberry manned the steering paddle in the stern; Burg sat forward on the camera box with his paddle. It was an unusual arrangement, given Fogleberry's lack of experience on fast water. Both men wore cork life vests. Measured by the International Scale of River Difficulty (Class I to Class VI), the rapids of the upper Snake included Class I (moving water with a few riffles and small waves; few or no obstructions); Class II (easy rapids with waves up to three feet, and wide, clear channels that are obvious without scouting; some maneuvering is required); and Class III (rapids with high, irregular waves often capable of swamping an open canoe; narrow passages that require complex maneuvering; may require scouting from shore). This whitewater taxonomy includes a caveat: if the water temperature is below fifty degrees and an extended river trip is in a wilderness area, the river should be considered one class more difficult than normal.

Burg was overjoyed to be on the river. Even Fogleberry could not suppress a broad smile. The Snake was running fast and cold, the sun shining, the air temperature a pleasant eighty-five degrees. *Song o' the Winds* raced past stands of willow, aspen, and cottonwood. Along shore, geese and ducks herded their broods to safety. Numerous gravel bars split the current, carving channels both deep and shallow. The escalation of levee-building by ranchers to stop seasonal flooding of their pasture land had not yet begun in earnest.

The first day of their journey, Burg and Fogleberry covered thirty-five miles in roughly eight hours, a swift pace. They camped early at Menner's Ferry. (Two years later, the first bridge across the Snake in Jackson Valley would be completed and the ferry would close.) It was an auspicious start. Wanting to investigate rumors of a massive landslide near Kelly, a few miles north of Jackson Hole, Burg hitchhiked into town to take photographs. There he encountered an otherworldly scene: the riverbed had been laid bare. Two weeks earlier, an enormous landslide had blocked the Gros Ventre River from reaching the Snake. Burg hiked to the earthen dam only to be surprised once again: the newly formed lake stretched for miles.

By the time he returned to camp, Fogleberry had started a campfire and supper was cooking. Sleeping bags had been laid out. Laundry hung on a section of buck-and-pole fence to dry. In a burst of affection, Burg decided he had misjudged his shipmate. "I like to watch Harry walk down a trail," he wrote, "this short, rugged, brown-skinned Norwegian seaman, broad shouldered, his hat cocked to one side, his movements in rhythm to a sailorly roll. . . . I think that Harry is an admirable character." As he had done on the previous trip, Burg banned alcohol. "Why this oaken-hearted sailor who had sailed the seven seas had respected the wishes of a twenty-four-year-old kid to not take a drink," Burg wrote, "I'll never know."

The next morning they headed downstream. Spirits were high, the current swift. They gabbed as they paddled. Fogleberry pointed out the birdlife along shore—geese, ducks, and bald eagles. Burg was pleased to see his shipmate engaged. Rounding a bend in the river, the canoe was suddenly swept close to the right shore. Neither Burg nor Fogleberry had been paying attention. They found themselves plummeting into the trough of a crashing wave and were fortunate to come out right side up. *Song o' the Winds* swamped and became difficult to paddle. Out-of-control, they washed downriver and collided with a sweeper (an overhanging tree) with what Burg later described as "the momentum of a freight car." The canoe turned over, pitching both men into the fast water.

Burg came up underneath the craft gasping for air. Fogleberry was nowhere to be seen. The overturned canoe dragged Burg downriver until the boat was wrenched from his grip. He struggled to shore. "A great roaring in my ears," he later wrote about the experience. "The canoe passed swiftly down the river around the bend. Harry came tearing down the bank and hardly able to walk in our soggy clothes we started in pursuit. One load off my mind. Harry had not drowned. Now I thought of the expedition, of the box containing the cameras, charts, and logs which were now lashed in the canoe in the mad current." The two men tramped along the rocky, brush-filled bank. They found the boat lodged on a gravel bar on the other side of the river. Burg was forlorn, certain that the camera equipment and film were destroyed, if not washed downstream. The voyage was over before it had begun. What would he tell Jesse Sill and Mr. Kiser, not to mention his father?

Fogleberry pushed a small log into the current and worked his way across the river. He clambered ashore and turned the canoe over, frantically searching for the equipment box and waterproof camera bags. When he held up the camera box, Burg broke into a wide smile. His shipmate had saved the day. Fogleberry shuttled the damaged canoe back across the river. Together they assessed the damage. The boat had taken a serious but not fatal beating. They fetched the remains of the splintered decking and lashed the canoe back together with rope. Fogleberry fashioned new paddles out of driftwood while Burg spread the camera equipment in the sun to dry. The photographic film had been destroyed; his diaries were soaked. They had lost gear and most of their supplies. It was a humbling experience.

They had little choice but to tighten their life vests, promise to be more cautious, and continue downriver. Fogleberry had suffered a minor injury to one of his arms yet remained at the steering paddle. He struggled to keep the canoe away from the banks. By the time Burg took over, the river had braided into a series of shallow channels cluttered with gravel bars and snags. That evening they camped downstream from the Wilson Bridge. Both voyagers were exhausted, hungry, and feeling down on their luck. Burg's old ear injury, received in a scuffle with another seaman years ago, flared up. If not attended to, the pain would be unbearable over the weeks ahead. He caught a ride into Jackson Hole, where he restocked supplies and sought out a doctor. When the voyagers woke in the morning, the river had dropped a foot. Burg's earache had subsided to a tolerable level.

Thirteen miles downstream, near Flat Creek, the broad floodplain of the Jackson Valley tapers abruptly. The river bends east, then south, and the terrain on both sides of the river steepens. The Snake River sheds its braided S-turn channels for a single, fast-water corridor. When Burg and Fogleberry reached the confluence of the Hoback and Snake, they found themselves in trouble. The two rivers collided with surprising force, forming oversize whirlpools that captured the canoe, pulled it down, spun it around, and sent it hurling toward a rocky overhang. More by luck than skill, they managed to avoid another wreck. They landed on the banks of Slim "Bacon Rind" Hossman's ranch. Burg offered the rancher their help with haying if Hossman would portage a portion of Burg's outfit by horseback through Alpine Canyon. A deal was struck.

Three days of labor, however, left Fogleberry restless. He snapped at Burg, claiming they needed to be heading downriver immediately. Burg attempted to appease his companion, but when the short-tempered Fogleberry lit into Hossman, Burg was aghast and embarrassed. "Since leaving Portland," he later wrote, "Harry's temper had made me miserable until I felt at times that life was unendurable. He deadened the charm of the valley, of Slim's talk, and all that was beautiful and interesting in life thru his infernal temper." The damage had been done.

On July 18, Burg and Fogleberry set off downriver, while Hossman hiked along the trail leading his pack horse loaded with gear. USGS records show water releases at Jackson Dam had increased to 7,230 cubic feet per second. Flows from the Hoback River and side creeks would have added significantly to the volume of water. The canyon narrowed. To the right, the Snake River range rises; on the left, the Wyoming Range. At Bailey Creek Rapids they stopped to scout. It was the beginning of a long afternoon of difficult decisions under trying conditions. In certain locations sloping hillsides and steep rocky cliffs made lining difficult, portaging nearly impossible. Burg's caution, plus the inevitable delays involved with lining, further annoyed Fogleberry. Burg swamped in the upper portion of the rapids and was forced ashore. He decided to line the boat down the lower section of the rapid. Fogleberry, temporarily stranded on the other side of the river, fumed.

Below Bailey Creek the current picked up speed. Constricted by the narrowing canyon walls, the river makes a series of sharp S-turns, the fast water rushing over steep limestone ledges, which creates unpredictable boils and hydraulics. Outside of the Milner reach, Alpine Canyon has the largest concentration of rapids mile for mile on the Snake. (Today the rapids, ranging from Class II to Class V depending on water levels, carry whimsical appellations: West Table Creek, Fence, Three-Oar-Deal, Blind Canyon, Big Kahuna, Lunch Counter, Rope, Champagne, and Cottonwood.)

Disaster struck halfway through the gorge near the mouth of Wolf Creek (likely today's Three-Oar-Deal Rapid). One modern guide book describes the rapid in these terms: "At high flows (12,000 CFS) the hole at Three-Oar-Deal is possibly the most dangerous on the river. As the river turns to the right, the main current flows over a sandstone ledge protruding from the left, creating a huge and potentially deadly reversal. This unassuming ledge has been the scene of a few horror stories and drowning incidents." Burg was taking no chances. Running on relatively high water, he chose to line *Song o' the Winds* around the rapid. Always difficult work, lining requires patience, cooperation, communication. By now, Fogleberry was short on all three. Increasingly irate, he began to lecture his younger shipmate. Abruptly, he grabbed the line out of Burg's hands and as he paid out the line, he allowed the canoe to drift into the current. The typically even-tempered Burg had never been angrier. He later described the incident:

> The canoe caught in the terrific current put unholdable strain on the bowline. I was holding the stern line and pulled it tight. There the canoe was stretching 17 feet across an 80-foot broadside, and pulling both of us into the river. The line would not hold much. My line was out completely and I followed to the end of the brink leaving go and then came back to give Harry a hand. The canoe capsized. The line tightened dragging Harry across rocks for ten feet. In his gameness he laid down with tattered clothes and bleeding hands. The current now gripped beneath the canoe and its force was terrific. It dragged both of us toward the river. We called to Slim for assistance. He grabbed hold of the rope. It ceased to slip through our hands. The rope tightened and began to stretch. The canoe failed to swing to shore. Instead it seemed intent on playing tag with the bluff. The line broke and the canoe passed from view around the bend.

The men stumbled along the rocky trail in pursuit of the canoe, but it was too late. The half-submerged vessel was gone. The voyage appeared to be over. Fogleberry stomped off alone downriver on the trail to the village of Alpine. Burg and Hossman trailed behind him, scouring the shoreline in search of the lost canoe.

At Red Creek, three miles above where the Snake River breaks out of its mountain passage, they found *Song o' the Winds*. The canoe was stuck fast, submerged between two boulders. The bow had been demolished; the gunnels broken in numerous places; the gashes in the hull irreparable. The paddles were long gone. With Hossman's help, Burg managed to salvage a portion of the gear. They manhandled the canoe from between the boulders and pushed it down the river. The boat floated a short distance and sank. The voyage really was over.

Sometime later, Burg and Hossman found Fogleberry waiting at the Snake River Bridge, near the village of Alpine. His face revealed both shame and anxiousness. His wallet, which contained cash, citizenship papers, and his merchant marine certificate, had been stowed with his gear in the canoe. It was a significant loss for a man who made his living at sea. But Burg in fact had Fogleberry's wallet in his own pocket. He had briefly considered holding onto it—small retribution for his companion's erratic behavior—but was not one to hold a grudge. "I thot [*sic*] it a huge joke," Burg later wrote. "Then I remembered the morning below the mouth of the Gros Ventre that Harry swam the treacherous river to salvage the outfit. I saw him as my comrade still, a man to stand by and I handed him the wallet to gladden his heart as the jammed canoe had gladdened mine."

The next day Hossman returned to his ranch. Fogleberry and Burg caught a long, dusty ride from a passing truck into Twin Falls, where they boarded a train for Portland. Fogleberry immediately made for Seattle to ship out on the next available transport. Despite the loss of *Song o' the Winds*, Burg was already making plans to return to the Snake River as soon as possible. It was the last time the two seamen voyaged together.

A month later, Burg arrived in Idaho Falls to resume his voyage. His outfit included a new canoe, purchased from the Chestnut Canoe Company of Canada. He had *Song o' the Winds* painted on the bow, *Kiser Studio* on the stern. Burg, who had used oars (as well as paddles) on his Columbia River voyage the year before, realized that the stubborn Fogleberry had not been entirely to blame for the mishap on the upper Snake. Steering with a paddle from the stern of a seventeen-foot canoe on a relentlessly swift, shallow, and braided river was more than an exercise in strength or endurance. It required a deft touch, the ability to read the river quickly, and to adapt to near-constant changes— skills that Fogleberry clearly lacked. Why Burg had allowed his inexperienced shipmate to pilot the *Song o' the Winds* remains a mystery.

Burg had oarlocks installed on the new Chestnut craft. A canoe's shape and length do not allow for abrupt changes on fast water, but he hoped to gain the advantage of making better time on flat water by rowing instead of paddling. He met with the usual skepticism about the voyage. Upon learning that he was bound for the Pacific Ocean through Hells Canyon, one naïve shopkeeper asked with great urgency if Burg was aware that the Snake River "tunneled underground" at certain locations. Burg bit his lip and smiled. The gloomy comments agitated him more than usual. "It seemed as though I too had been injected with fear of the Snake which seemed to prevail in the great valley," he wrote. "Like the early voyageurs, everyone pointed it out as the 'accursed, mad river.'"

Charlie Harderlie, a local rancher, agreed to transport Burg to Alpine, Idaho, for ten dollars. Burg wanted to resume his voyage where he left off weeks before. On the drive out, however, Harderlie suggested that he visit his ranch near Thayne, Wyoming, and begin his journey on the nearby Salt River. On August 25, after a three-day visit, Burg set off down the Salt. The small, rocky river flows north through picturesque Star Valley between the Salt River Range in Wyoming and the Caribou Range of Idaho. Several peaks reach eleven thousand feet or more. Dreary weather accompanied Burg as he picked his way through the numerous channels while encountering strands of barbed-wire fence stretched across the river. At dusk he camped on a gravel bar at the confluence of the Salt and Snake Rivers. The cloudy sky opened up; thunder and lightning followed the rain. Throughout the night Burg was deluged. He woke at 5:00 AM the next morning cold and groggy, to continuing rain. Idaho Falls lay roughly a hundred miles downstream, a seemingly insurmountable distance on a miserable morning.

Burg was traveling through Grand (Teton) Valley, a spectacular setting. A break in the weather allowed him to begin taking photographs. With the addition of Greys and Salt Rivers, the flow of the Snake River increased. The Class I and Class II rapids he encountered were few and gave him little problem. The Chestnut canoe handled well. What he did encounter was an increasing number of small, low-lying diversion dams that funneled river water into nearby fields and holding ponds to irrigate crops. Built by individual dry land farmers and ranchers, co-ops, and water districts, these diversion dams stretched across the main channel as well as the minor channels created by midriver islands. Materials ranged from river boulders, timber, and wire mesh to concrete, weir-type barriers. They were essential to the survival of the farms and ranches along the Snake. All were dependent, however, on the natural flow of the river; summer droughts rendered the diversion dams all but useless. Burg found himself dragging or lining the canoe over and around these human-made obstacles numerous times. It was exhausting work. Between the river and the rain, he was constantly wet.

In Swan Valley he found refuge at the Nelson ranch. Like many other farmers and ranchers in the area, the Nelsons had suffered much hardship because of drought, but to stint on hospitality was unthinkable. After supper, the weary voyager bedded down in a small cabin, where a fire dried his outfit and clothes. The next morning Burg offered Mrs. Nelson a string of pearls, which she graciously accepted. He also stopped to visit the Diamond K Ranch, whose owner, Bill Lage, had extended an invitation to visit three months earlier when they had crossed paths outside of Jackson Hole. When Burg inquired about conditions on the Snake, the rancher told him that two young boys had drowned in Dry Canyon recently and people were "cussing the treacherous Snake worse than ever." Dry land farmers and ranchers harbored few romantic notions about the river.

Foul weather alternated with brief spots of sunshine and blue skies. Near Heise, Idaho, Burg rowed out of the high mountains and into the foothills, marking the end of the Rocky Mountains and the beginning of the Snake River plain. After five days, he reached Idaho Falls and put up in a hotel. He spent two days restocking, mailing his film back to Portland, and writing letters. The local paper wanted an interview, and Burg was happy to oblige. He also bumped into Charlie Harderlie again, who introduced him to an attractive young woman and her mother. The young woman was keen to go down

Burg and a young woman seated in Song o' the Winds *near Idaho Falls, Idaho*

the river with the handsome stranger, but her mother joked nervously that she was not ready to lose her favorite daughter.

When it came time to portage his canoe and gear around the Porter Dam in the middle of town, Burg, short on money, decided to do it himself. While photographing the dam, he described the structure as "a monster with high concrete walls on either side and must have been 20 feet high. The dam itself was wood braced on the downside by huge right-angled blocks." As the river poured through the gates, he sat atop the wooden structure and opened a box of fudge the friendly young woman had given him earlier. A note read: "I hope that the river gods will be kind to you, Amos Burg." Burg placed wooden logs he called "rollers" beneath the canoe and pushed and pulled the craft up the steep rocky bank beside the dam and down the other side. Three hours later, *Song o' the Winds* bobbed along shore, the task complete.

On September 4, Burg departed Idaho Falls under sunny skies. He hoped to reach Twin Falls, 140 miles downriver, in five days. Below the Shelley Bridge, he encountered a series of rock-filled rapids, all manageable. By afternoon clouds rolled in, bringing rain. He continued rowing in the downpour; gusts of wind tore at the surface, sending spray into his face and slowing his progress. The canyon walls echoed the distant thunder and lightning. He was cold and, not for the last time, lonely. "Good water," he wrote in his diary the next day. Although cloudy, the temperature reached eighty degrees. With fair weather, he relaxed. The numerous islands in the braided river provided habitat for an astounding variety of birds and waterfowl. He kept track of his sightings—pelicans, magpies, hawks, gulls, cranes, and doves—in a small notebook tucked in his shirt pocket.

The difficulties of river travel receded, at least temporarily. Of the harmonious relationship between the river and his canoe, Burg wrote: "I know the limitations of my boat and I always underestimate its ability rather than overestimate it. In that way the Snake River and I have an understanding and a truce that will not be broken." He stopped in the town of Blackfoot and bought groceries from a store by the Blackfoot Bridge. He encountered another human-made obstacle at American Falls. Construction of the concrete gravity dam, part of the larger federally funded Minidoka Irrigation Project, had begun the previous spring. The once thunderous falls had now been reduced to a few meager trickles. He hired a truck to portage his outfit around the construction site, then camped on an island in the river below.

A few miles downriver, Burg found himself rounding bends, searching for routes through rock-cluttered channels and over shallow basalt reefs. The gorge walls rose, narrowing the skyline whose absence created a foreboding claustrophobic sensation. Boulders the size of automobiles split the river in channels. He held his breath and chose one, grimacing as *Song o' the Winds* bounced along the shallows, surprised when the bottom of the canoe was not torn apart. When he became confused about his direction near the confluence with the Raft River, Burg's confidence momentarily failed him. To counter his anxiety, he broke out in song. Romantic to his core, Burg wrote that he was "a lonely photographer and explorer following in the treacherous wake of men wasting their strength and fortunes with only faint return." When he reached the flat water of Lake Walcott, he pulled steadily on the oars, bucking a strong southerly headwind and unruly waves. It took a day and a half of steady rowing to reach Minidoka Dam.

Another long day of flat-water rowing and singing brought the voyager to the Milner Dam on September 10. The operator of pump station #2 was waiting for Burg. He had read about the "lone voyager" in the *Idaho Statesman* and was determined to give him the welcome he deserved. He cooked

Burg supper and later played his guitar. The next morning Burg boarded the train to Twin Falls, arranging to have his canoe shipped by train to Buhl, fifty miles downriver. He left no explanation for skirting the next reach of the river. Portages, poor weather, low water, bouts of loneliness and illness together had taken a toll on the river traveler. His schedule was in tatters. He did not like to admit it, but the detour felt a little like cheating. After picking up his mail, he had the local ferryman row him to the 212-foot Shoshone Falls to take photographs. Later, he hitched a ride to Buhl, where he picked up his outfit at the station and hired a truck to transport it down to the Snake River Bridge.

On September 13, Burg rowed a half-mile down the Snake River to its confluence with the Malad River and pitched camp in the narrow gorge. A sense of isolation overtook him as the river flashed by and the vertical walls rose sharply. Earlier voyageurs had at least had one another's company. Although Burg had skirted a dangerous section of the Snake, he was not done lining and portaging. (Modern-day river runners rate the five-mile Wiley run Class II to Class IV depending on water levels.) The Snake River remained rock-bound, meandering through a daunting, steep-walled gorge. The rapids at this time of year posed no serious navigation problems. Burg, however, was on his own should trouble strike.

The immediate environment seemed to dictate his ever-changing moods. "The Snake River ahead seems dangerous and makes me reluctant to go," he wrote. "Canyons, rapids, and falls impede my way to the Pacific and the loneliness in running the rapids only adds to the uncertainty that accompanies dangerous adventure. No one to talk to, only the winds, and they pass by too busy in singing among the trees for a poor voyageur mortal." Upon reaching the placid waters at the head of the Hagerman Valley, Burg's mood improved. The current ambled, the canyon walls retreated, and the skyline widened into a sea of pale blue. Hot springs dotted the shore. Farmhouses nestled on bluffs high above the river.

That evening he reached Thousand Springs, where the Snake River aquifer cascades from gaps and cracks in the porous basalt cliffs. He spent the evening marveling at the natural phenomenon and later that night, the stars overhead. He rose at dawn, climbed the bluff above the springs "to hail the rising sun." Of the river he wrote:

They say the Snake River is treacherous because they get wet. I figure rivers have their natures and one must know and train oneself
to master them. If they have any stretches that can't be mastered, a
voyageur knows at a glance that he must portage. People think that
river navigation is a game of chance, that the boat is at the mercy of
the current and if the gods are kind and luck is in the bow all is well.
I think that it is a science in estimating depths, currents, distance. I
have gotten so that I can tell the approximate depth and the position
of every rock in a swift channel. And for safety I always underestimate
my craft's ability.

A day later at Lower Salmon Falls, he hired a local farmer to portage his outfit around the upper and lower falls. The portage continued another twenty
miles downriver to the town of King Hill. His explanation for yet another
extended detour was forthright. "So tired was I of running rapids alone," he
wrote, "that I wanted to be around them even at the risk [of] making my
Snake River voyage incomplete." Although reluctant to dawdle, he stopped
at the Three Island Crossing near Glenn's Ferry, another historical location
on the Oregon Trail, to help a farmer with his haying in exchange for a meal
and a bed. Downstream he entered the thirty-five-mile reach of the Snake
(what is today known as the Birds of Prey Natural Area). The Class I and II
rapids eventually gave way to lengthy stretches of flat water. The "mad" river
had turned friendly for the time being.

On September 19 he portaged around Swan Falls Dam. Over the next
five days he passed the mouths of the Owhyee, Boise, Malheur, and Payette
Rivers and stopped in Weiser, the last sizable town on the river before Hells
Canyon. Short on money, he took a job packing apples at a local plant. He
immediately contacted Leigh Lint, who invited him to dinner at his parent's
house. A year younger than Burg, Lint had made trips on the nearby Snake
while still in high school and later worked for four months in Hells Canyon
for the United States Geological Society. Lint's reputation as a skilled, trust-
worthy boatman earned him a place on the 1923 USGS survey expedition
through Grand Canyon led by Colonel Birdseye.

After dinner, Burg laid his river maps on the kitchen table and questioned Lint extensively about Hells Canyon. Lint shared photographs of

the Snake and the boats he had piloted. Although he suggested caution at certain rapids, he assured Burg that "the roughness of the Snake was greatly exaggerated." People had gotten into trouble because of carelessness, poor judgment, and the use of overloaded boats. When Burg broached the idea of hiring a well-known guide by the name of John Mullins, Lint's father chimed in that Mullins was trouble. Why Burg did not ask Lint to accompany him remains a mystery. The same age and hungry for adventure, they would have made excellent river companions. Lint was certainly capable and experienced. It is likely that Lint was already employed or had lined up work on another river.

On October 6, Burg set off downriver. He had picked up an inexperienced companion: Ralph Shumaker, who had worked with Burg at a packing plant. According to Burg, Shumaker was "a good-natured fellow with long sideburns and high-heeled cowboy boots who harbored aspirations of going to Hollywood to become the next Tom Mix." He had assured Burg that he was a "crackerjack" at the oars. Burg's possible motives for bringing Shumaker along were mixed—help, company, perhaps doing a favor for the cowboy who was trying to reach Portland on the cheap.

The USGS gauge at Weiser read 11,900 cubic feet per second, medium-to-low water by today's standards. Burg manned the oars. They ran Whiskey, Gypsum, Bayhorse, and Shoofly Rapids without incident. That evening they camped at the Vaughn ranch on Wildhorse Creek. The next day they passed by the mouth of the Powder River, lined Eagle Island Rapid, and ran famous Oxbow Bend. The weather was clear and mild; the scenery splendid. Burg was exuberant, and he crowed about the "wonderful pictures that charm the eye at every bend." His excitement, however, was tempered by the suspicion that Shumaker was not all he claimed to be. It was clear to Burg that his new partner had never rowed before. Worse, he was a poor cook. By the time they reached Homestead, Oregon, Burg had decided to let Shumaker go. He felt foolish for bringing the cowboy along but responsible for his welfare.

The next morning, Burg had a change of heart. Below Homestead, however, he pulled ashore and reversed course yet again. He informed Shumaker the voyage was over. Shumaker did not argue. They lined *Song o' the Winds* back upstream to Homestead. Burg paid Shumaker five dollars for his time,

Burg hired John Mullins, a local miner and moonshiner, to guide him through Hells Canyon.

then gave him his parent's address in Portland. He wrote to alert his parents that Shumaker was coming through Portland on his way to Los Angeles. Could they help the fledgling cowboy movie star out, perhaps let him sleep on their couch for a night or two?

In Homestead, a once-bustling mining town, Burg went looking for John Mullins. For three decades the fifty-year-old hard rock miner had run pack trains for motion-picture companies and railroad surveyors through the backcountry. Burg thought Mullins might be his man. Few doubted Mullins's familiarity with Hells Canyon. Several townspeople, however, cautioned Burg about employing him as a guide. There was talk of mental instability. Two months earlier, Mullins and his wife had been on the verge of hanging a man who they believed had stolen their horse. When Burg approached Mullins about guiding him through Hells Canyon, Mullins appeared unfazed by the undertaking. Never mind that he had never paddled a canoe. He agreed to guide Burg as far as Pittsburgh Bar, at the lower end of Hells Canyon. Pay was ten dollars a day plus grub and return stage fare to Homestead.

Burg was anxious to start downriver before the weather turned. Mullins balked, informing him that he had other business to attend to and disappeared. He headed into the backcountry to check his moonshine stills. (In 1916, Idaho had adopted a statewide ban on alcohol. Four years later the state became the tenth to approve national prohibition.) Burg bided his time. He slept on the floor of the local pool hall. He had his hair cut at the local barbershop. He sold a couple of strands of pearls to local women. He explored the area around Homestead, visiting the Iron Dyke Mine. He wrote one final letter to his parents in which he outlined the deal he had made with Mullins and his readiness to tackle the project: "I have written this long letter to show you that I am trying hard to do my best, especially on this voyage. It will certainly be my last until I am well equipped to earn my way upon them. The end of the voyage will tell the tale, whether or not I am capable of going on or not. Since leaving I have been more resolute than upon my previous voyages. I think I will have a good set of pictures and my diary is up to date.... When I get home I will set to work to recuperate my lost fortunes by paying off what I owe."

A week later Mullins returned. On October 20, Burg packed the last of his gear into his canoe. Mullins informed his companion that he intended to run—not line—Kerns Rapids, a sizable piece of fast water. If *Song o' the Winds* could not manage Kerns, said Mullins, "she couldn't run anything." Burg bit his tongue. (At the time, the water gauge at Oxbow, Oregon, showed flows of 16,000 to 18,000 cubic feet per second through Hells Canyon. The major rapids downriver would have been Class IV and V.)

The sun was over the ridge when they pushed off shore from Brockman's Ranch. A handful of townspeople waved goodbye. Mullins was perched in the stern with the steering oar; Burg sat midship. Mullins immediately steered into the heart of the quarter-mile-long rapid. It was a wild ride. When the canoe emerged right side up after running the standing tail waves, Burg was thrilled. He had felt certain they would overturn. Mullins, sitting in a pool of water and bursting with overconfidence, laughed out loud. The two men now faced a series of rapids larger and more turbulent than anything Burg had previously encountered.

Long before they saw Kinney Creek Rapid, Burg and Mullins heard its thunder roar. They landed at the head of the rapid and scouted. The noise was deafening but intoxicating. The size and turbulence of the rapid took Burg's breath away. Formed by Lynch Creek (on the Oregon side of the river) and Kinney Creek (directly opposite), it looked impassable, at least in a canoe, to both men. They ate lunch, then decided to line the boat along the rocky shore. In the 1950s and 1960s boatmen piloting thirty-two-foot pontoon rafts, twenty-four-foot aluminum boats with motors, sixteen-foot cataract boats, and ten-man paddle rafts made straightforward but hair-raising runs down the main tongue of Kinney Creek Rapid. Compared to the other great Hells Canyon rapids, Kinney Creek was considered runnable.

Less than a mile downstream, Squaw Creek Rapids (Class V), larger and more furious than Kinney Creek, waited. Mullins and Burg had little choice but to line *Song o' the Winds.* When the canoe dropped over yet another steep pitch and veered out into the current, Burg clenched his teeth. He shuddered at the thought of what might have happened if he had brought Ralph Shumaker along. Mullins and Burg worked the boat back to shore and, after hours of hard labor, made camp on a narrow sandbar at the foot of the rapid. They picked apples in the abandoned orchard up Squaw Creek.

They were in no hurry to break camp the next morning as they ate breakfast around the campfire and waited for the sun to creep over the ridge. Mullins boasted that for every mile of Hells Canyon, one man had perished in the river. Many had been prospectors searching for claims, and most of them could not swim and had little experience piloting a small boat. Mullins revealed that he himself had once capsized and become entangled in the bowline of his boat. He had barely made it to shore. When he discovered that his dog was missing, he presumed the animal had drowned, but he found the pet beneath the overturned boat. Burg had grown to like Mullins. "He still had a smile on his face no matter how blue he was feeling and my heart went out to him," he later wrote. "He hasn't traveled such a smooth road in his day and the end of the trail was getting rougher. After falling off a cliff and losing his hearing from the flu, John has never relinquished his faith in men or life."

With the sun up and the temperature climbing, the two men headed downstream to scout Buck Creek Rapids. "Big, Bad Buck" (Class VI) was an astonishing display of the river's raw power. Braced by the addition of Buck Creek (on the Idaho side), the river tumbled over a basalt ledge that spanned the river from bank to bank. The steep rocky slopes and the towering walls on either side of the river made lining difficult. Later, pre-dam river runners would consider Buck Creek Rapids the most awe-inspiring display of water power on the Snake. In his diary Burg described what happened as he and Mullins lined the canoe along the right shore: "With great misgivings in my heart, John pushed the canoe into the current for the descent of Buck Creek. The current catching it wrong necessitated another try and we sent it down bow first. I let out too much line instead of pulling the bow close to the rocks. The line sizzled through my hands. The canoe was gone."

For the third time Burg had lost a canoe during a voyage. Given their isolated location, it was a serious mishap. Although his outfit was safe on shore, the equipment was more than two men could carry in a single journey back to Homestead. They took off downstream, Burg scrambling over the bluff above the river while Mullins picked his way along the rocky shore. Both routes were slowgoing. Burg, expecting the worse, was surprised to find the overturned canoe snagged on a rock above the second pitch of Buck Creek Rapids, rocking back and forth in the surge. The tension on the line was so great it looked like it might snap at any moment. He stripped down and plunged into the river, untangled the line, and towed the boat back to shore. *Song o' the Winds* was undamaged, and miraculously the oars had remained with the boat. By the time Mullins caught up, Burg had the canoe loaded and ready to go. Mullins was irritated, grumbling that they would not line the canoe down any more rapids.

At Thirty-Two Point (Sawpit) Rapids, however, they had little choice but to line. The boat again got away from the two men and was swept downstream, crashing into a boulder and shattering the stern. Yet another setback. They retrieved the boat, and Burg made temporary repairs. By dusk, they were still on the river. "The deep canyon appeared wild and strange in the twilight," Burg wrote. "We could see nothing before us, hearing the hissing waters below us, dodging great boulders with foam. Far down in the darkness, I heard the roar of Steamboat Rapids." After running Pine Flat Rapids, they landed above Steamboat Creek and spent the night in a rat-infested cabin.

On the third day of the voyage through Hells Canyon, Burg woke tired and anxious. He had slept fitfully, the train roar of Steamboat Rapids (Class V) ringing in his ears throughout the night. One look at the head of the cataract confirmed his fears. After nearly four months and hundreds of river miles, his nerves were frayed. He needed a reprieve, no matter how brief. Burg parlayed with Mullins, suggesting they lay over for a day. Mullins agreed and spent the day fishing for trout up Steamboat Creek while Burg repaired the boat and caught up on his river diaries.

The next morning Burg's anxiousness was countered by Mullins's apparent indifference to the dangerous rapid. Burg wrote:

> We made an early morning departure, fighting hard on the first bend to keep from being swept under an overhanging precipice. Directly below giant combers bursting over a submerged reef seemed rushing up to meet us. To me they looked like a lace-covered casket rolling over and over. Old John sat on the back seat grinning indifferently, plying the steering oar. We cut across the river for the left bank, already battling in the mountainous combers that carried us toward the reef. My left hand, still numb from exposure at Buck Creek, suddenly cramped under the exertion. I could not pull another stroke. John gave a warning cry as we struck the reef. We crouched low as a great wave smothered the canoe. I began to swim desperately, thinking that I was struggling in the maelstrom. Suddenly my head popped out of the water.

With great effort, they reached shore, the boat in tow. At Deep Creek (three-tenths of a mile below today's Hells Canyon Dam), they lined the canoe along the rocky shore successfully. At Copper Ledge Falls, however, they nearly capsized again. Burg's river diary got soaked. Less than a mile downstream they stopped at Studhorse Creek Rapids, which they also lined. Mullins nonchalantly pointed out the gravesite of a surveyor who had drowned twelve years earlier, when the boat he and his two companions were traveling in was dashed against an overhanging cliff and overturned. The survey company had offered a hundred dollars to anyone who would hike in and bring the body out. No one stepped forward. Burg spent part of the afternoon laying the ink-stained pages of his river diary on the rocks to dry. He made no mention of Wild Sheep or Granite Rapids, the last two formidable cataracts on the river. Either could have easily overturned their craft.

After nearly a week on the river, Mullins had grown increasingly impatient. In an ominous voice he insisted that they would run every rapid, regardless of the danger. Burg bargained that it suited him all right, but that he greatly feared the loss of his camera equipment. Mullins countered that they had passed the worst of the rapids. Burg's previous glowing, overoptimistic assessment of the man had changed. "Woe to the person who betrayed him," he later wrote of Mullins. "I was sure he would shoot a man down if he thought he deserved it—and he said so."

They headed downstream, running Bernard Creek, No-Name, and Waterspout Rapids, plus a dozen or so smaller rapids, without incident. Blue skies and easy water lightened the hard rock miner's mood. By the time they reached Bills Creek, Mullins boasted of having piloted the first canoe through Hells Canyon. He claimed he knew every rock in the river. Burg allowed that "he ought to since he'd hit them all." After running Sluice Creek and Rush Creek Rapids, they stopped at Johnson Bar, three miles downriver. Mullins decided to go home at this point—he had mines and moonshine to attend to. He lassoed a tired range horse and departed.

With more than five hundred miles to go before he reached the Pacific Ocean, Burg was on his own. He rose early the next day and started rowing. He passed by the mouth of the Imnaha and a few miles later the Lower Salmon River. By evening, he reached Christmas Creek, thirty miles downstream. Two days later, he came ashore at Lewiston, Idaho, where he restocked, wrote letters, and prepared for the last leg of his journey. Beyond Lewiston, he found himself on the familiar water of the lower Snake River. After the intimidating rapids and the claustrophobic cliffs of mile-deep Hells Canyon, the cataracts appeared benign. He reached the confluence of the Snake and Columbia without incident, becoming the first person to continuously run the entire length of the Snake River, source to mouth, in a small craft.

In early November, his voyage on the Snake completed, Burg set off from the confluence of the Snake and Columbia Rivers bound for the Pacific Ocean. Downriver, cameramen from Fox Movietone and International Newsreel were waiting for him at the town of Cascade Locks. Local and regional newspapers had been tracking his journey for weeks. Now the cameramen wanted to film Burg in action. They suggested he make a short run on the lower sections of Cascades Rapids. He was reluctant—the river was icy cold, the pitches steep and rocky, the shoreline eddies turbulent.

The newsmen didn't need to remind him that any publicity would bolster interest in his voyages, firm his reputation, and attract possible financial support. They suggested that Burg would not actually have to "shoot the rapids." If he could paddle close to shore, with the roaring falls in the background, they would shoot the film at such an angle that the audience could not tell the difference. Although the stunt would be staged, it remained risky business. When the cameramen promised to have a local man situated on shore to grab the bowline of *Song o' the Winds* when it passed by, Burg relented.

A large crowd had gathered along the rocky shore. Burg made the run successfully. The young man standing on the rocks grabbed the bowline of the canoe as it passed by and hauled Burg to shore. The newsmen claimed they had missed the shot due to a camera malfunction, and they wanted him to make another run. Two different accounts of the second run illuminate a significant aspect of Burg's character—namely, his consistent adherence to the adventurer's code. In an interview after the shoot, Burg said:

> So I had to do it again. The second time I think he [the newsman] must have bribed the kid, because he made no effort to grab my boat. I lunged forward to get to shore and the canoe took off. Well, the only thing I could do was go over the rapids. Everything was going

fine. It was probably the first canoe that ever went over after that poor Indian maiden that was said to have drowned after her husband shoved her canoe in the rapids because he wanted to get rid of her. There was a big rock ahead, and a couple of hundred people on shore. I thought I would just cut close to the rock and give them a thrill, because I would disappear from view for a few moments, and that is exactly what I did. I didn't realize that behind a big rock like that there was a big eddy. The water forms a big hole. Well, I dropped into that hole and I disappeared alright. I disappeared for about 400 feet. It was very cold. When I fell into the river, the cameramen were cold and they had their picture, so they went somewhere to warm themselves up, while I was struggling downriver. They were a heartless bunch. Then, when they found out that I had gotten ashore (two miles downstream) they came down and made a picture of me, my hair all wet, wet clothes and everything.

The reporter for the *Oregon Statesman* told a different story, however:

Amos Burg, Portland canoeist who had been making a trip by his frail vessel from Jackson Lake to Astoria via the Snake and Columbia rivers, came near death here late this afternoon when a rope tied to his boat to let it down the rapids was cut by the rocks. The canoe was about in the middle of the rapids when the rope was severed and (the canoe) immediately capsized. When it rose to the surface, Burg was hanging on, and he held his grip for about three miles down the river, with his head bobbing beneath the water at intervals. When he neared a small rock island he lost his hold on the boat, which was lost in the swift water. Burg, however, reached the island, from where he was rescued by Francis Shellenberger and Arthur Reinoble, who went out after him in a rowboat. Due to the icy water and his exposure in the rain, Burg's jaws were locked when he was rescued, but he rallied under care here.

How to explain the gap between Burg's account and that of the newspaper man? Burg was modest by temperament, a gentleman by inclination, and a romantic in spirit who revered the early river voyageurs. One never complains about hardship, draws undue attention to one's exploits, or dwells on the seriousness of a dangerous or near fatal encounter. Indeed, one sings or makes light of these incidents. Burg had adhered to the adventurer's code.

After a brief layover in Portland, he continued down the Columbia River, reaching Astoria the first week in December. Although he owed his father money and needed to find a job as soon as possible, he had completed another lengthy voyage in pursuit of his goal of running all the major rivers of the West. For the time being, he was satisfied with himself.

Decades passed before the early pioneers of commercial river running attempted to run the various reaches of the Snake with paying passengers. In 1939 Buzz Holmstrom guided Edith Clegg, a Vancouver, B.C., socialite and widow, upriver through Hells Canyon. Clegg had hired Holmstrom to guide her on an unusual voyage—a west-to-east transcontinental journey by river and lake. Clyde Smith launched the first commercial trip through the Snake River Canyon in 1940. Blaine Stubblefield began running motorized trips in thirty-three-foot war-surplus bridge pontoons in the early 1950s. Georgie White, who had swam a portion of lower Grand Canyon in a life vest with fellow river rat Harry Aleson in 1945 and nearly drowned, made several trips with passengers who became known as her "Royal River Rats." In 1962, Don and Ted Hatch ran a twenty-seven-foot pontoon and a ten-person raft down the river with members of the Appalachian Mountain Club. By 1968, Becker-Cooke Expeditions offered float trips to a growing population of river enthusiasts.

Fishermen had long known the pleasures of floating the Jackson Valley reach of the Snake River in small inflatables. In 1956 the Grand Teton Lodge Company began offering float trips on war-surplus rafts. The eight- by twenty-seven-foot-long rafts were rigged with sweep oars manned by a single boatman. By the early 1960s river guides Dick Barker and Frank Ewing had started their own company, Barker-Ewing Scenic Floats. Throughout the late 1960s and early 1970s, river running as an adventure experience grew slowly but steadily in popularity. Small river companies (often owned and operated by longtime river guides) proliferated, opening up previously unrunnable sections of the Snake and other rivers in Idaho and throughout the West.

By the mid-1980s commercial river running had become increasingly popular, so much so that corporations began to purchase Ma-and-Pa river companies. Insurance companies began to dictate which activities might be more or less dangerous. The quality and range of river gear and equipment improved. River companies began to be run as businesses. Policies dictating river routines as well as codes of conduct for boatmen were developed. Slick brochures advertising "professional river guides," promised customers a safe and fun voyage. River guides began to receive benefits: fair compensation, health and disability insurance, and a share in company profits. As river trips became more standardized, they also began to be tailored to satisfy the changing tastes of an upscale market. At the start of the twenty-first century, river running had been transformed and absorbed into the tourist industry.

River adventures like Burg's, although stripped of most of the risk, still offered the modern-day river traveler opportunities for fun, natural beauty, peace of mind, relaxation, camaraderie, and a fair amount of excitement. The pleasure of floating down a river on a sunny day in spectacular settings has proved a durable experience.

Chapter 3

DOWN THE YUKON RIVER

In January 1925, Jesse Sill, the Portland-based Pathé newsreel cameraman and filmmaker, had filmed Amos Burg crossing the Columbia Bar. When Burg expressed a desire to learn how to make "moving pictures," Sill took the novice under his wing, inviting him on assignments and teaching him the fundamentals. The following summer, he had lent Burg camera equipment for his Snake River transit, agreeing to process the film free of charge in exchange for film rights. Mutual interests developed into a friendship that lasted half a century.

Sill approached Burg with an idea for another film in the winter of 1927. Newspapers around the country had run stories and photographs of the annual caribou migration across the Yukon Flats area in the interior of Alaska. The startling images recalled the bison herds of the Great Plains, a memory still within reach of a portion of the population at the time. Sill, who had long harbored aspirations to make an epic Western based on the Oregon Trail, wanted Burg to film the migration. He was betting that motion-picture images of the natural spectacle would trump mere photographs. To sweeten the deal, he agreed to lend Burg equipment, pay for film, and develop and print the negatives in his Portland lab in exchange for film rights. Burg would receive a cut of the revenue and gain much-needed motion-picture camera experience. Their collaboration was one of the first of its kind in the Northwest.

While Sills was the acknowledged mainspring of the project, Burg saw another opportunity. He suggested that he also film another kind of journey—

a voyage the length of the Yukon
River, from Bennett Lake in Canada to the Bering Sea on the west
coast of Alaska—a distance of 1,980
miles. It was an ambitious proposal.
Sill, who liked to make his films fast,
scratched his head. Why not? Burg
suggested that the journey begin in
Juneau, where they would paddle up
the Inside Passage to Skagway and
take the train over the White Pass to
Bennett Lake. This was historic Gold
Rush territory. Sill came back with
a counterproposal: extend the Yukon
River voyage north along the Alaskan
coast to the village of Cape Prince
of Wales to film the annual reindeer
roundup as well. Burg would travel by
schooner through the Gulf of Alaska

*In the 1920s Jesse Sill, cameraman and
filmmaker, took Burg under his wing and
taught him how to operate a motion picture
camera in the outdoors.*

and the Bering Sea, making stops at various islands—King, Diomedes, Saint
Lawrence, and Nunivak—to shoot the footage. The journey would take four,
perhaps five, months. Burg accepted the challenge.

He began a diary, labeling the first page "Expedition Log #4, Amos Burg
Explorations—Correspondent-Importer-Cinematographer—World Wide."
It was a bold call to arms. He included two aphorisms: "You must always
remember the story hasn't been written until you write it. It hasn't been
done until I do it," followed by "They carried an amazingly small amount
of mechanical gear—but they did have with them an unlimited supply of
courage, enterprise, and artistic sensibility. The film they produced . . . gave
evidence of all three qualities." He was giving himself a self-prescribed dose
of encouragement and advice.

On his Snake River voyage Burg had replaced his Old Town canoe with
an eighteen-foot Chestnut. The craft had performed admirably. After miles of
river travel and rough treatment, it remained in remarkable condition. Spruce
ribs and the wood-and-canvas shell made for a lightweight craft that handled

easily but could also suffer a glancing blow. The bow was decked over to protect gear and a passenger from the spray. Beneath the bow deck, Burg now fitted iron racks to hold the valuable camera equipment. The middle thwart, where a rower sat, could be removed if necessary. The canoe was already equipped with oarlocks for rowing and a portable, lightweight step mast for sailing. Splashboards along the gunnels raised the freeboard.

Burg contacted Fred "Spokane" Hill, with whom he had traversed the 140-mile lower Snake in May 1920. Five years older, a World War I veteran, and an experienced deep-water sailor who rarely backed away from a fight, Hill was a reliable and capable companion with a hardy sense of humor. "Spoke is a swell fellow who never gets sore when you tease him about the little moustache he is trying to grow," Burg wrote of his friend. "He is jolly and kind." Hill had also voyaged with Burg during the summer of 1926, when they navigated Alaska and British Columbia's rugged Inside Passage. The 950-mile voyage from Skagway to Vancouver, B.C., had taken two months. At the end of the trip, seemingly on the spur of the moment, the two decided to repeat Burg's 1924–25 Columbia River transit. In August they arrived by train at Lake Columbia and started rowing *Song o' the Winds* downriver, bound for the Pacific Ocean. Despite their differences in age and experience, they had much in common—a can-do attitude, a love of adventure, a Scandinavian heritage, and immigrant parents who had arrived in the Northwest at roughly the same time.

Burg planned to finance the trip on a shoestring. He estimated that they could feed themselves on thirteen cents a day, eating beans, bacon, and sea biscuits, supplementing their diets by fishing and hunting. To cover transportation costs, he cut deals with the Alaska Steamship Company and the White Pass Railroad. Keen to attract the burgeoning tourist trade, steamship and railroad companies sought to promote the natural wonders of the area their lines passed through. In exchange for passage and shipping, Burg agreed to shoot promotional photographs. He also had read *Along Alaska's Great River,* Frederick Schwatka's dramatic, best-selling account of his 1883 journey down the Yukon River on a sixteen- by forty-two-foot log raft. During the Gold Rush of 1898–99, thousands of stampeders had carried the book they considered a bible with them. Burg contacted the editors of the *National Geographic* about writing a piece; his proposal was greeted with cautious enthusiasm but eventually accepted.

On the morning of June 16, 1928, Burg paced back and forth in front of the trucking office on the Seattle waterfront. His jaw ached and he was spitting blood. He had recently had three teeth pulled. His frustration, however, had nothing to do with dentists. Never again, he vowed, would he ship anything by truck. *Song o' the Winds* had failed to arrive from Portland and the SS *Yukon,* bound for Juneau, was due to depart within hours. When the office doors of the trucking company opened, Burg charged in. The short-tempered clerk ignored the impatient voyager and told him to wait outside. Burg encountered another unforeseen obstacle. The captain of the *Yukon* refused his claim for free round-trip passage, insisting that his instructions from the home office were that Burg and Hill were to receive only return passage. Adventurer and captain went round and round. Burg fumed, swallowed hard, and finally paid the forty-six-dollar fare for two. In the meantime, the canoe had arrived.

The coastal schooner transported hundreds of black, Mexican, and Philippine laborers, all headed north to work in the canneries along the Inside Passage. They jostled for space on the decks and passageways. Hill and Burg hustled their outfit aboard the ship. Hill headed directly for the forecastle to secure two decent bunks. In search of his canoe, Burg went below deck, where his worst suspicions were confirmed. He found the boat under a mountain of luggage and mailbags. Three ribs had been cracked, one broken in two. In the rush to weigh anchor, the stevedores had manhandled the canoe. Burg, a veteran seaman, guessed they were hung over from the night before. He moved the canoe out of harm's way. He would have to make repairs in Juneau. An hour behind schedule, the SS *Yukon* departed Seattle. The weather was unusually sunny, a good omen.

The three-day journey north along the Inside Passage was uneventful. The weather remained mild, the inland sea unseasonably calm. Not so mealtime. Despite regular seatings each day, the cafeteria was bedlam. Noisy lines stretched out the door into the passageways. The tables were filthy, the food beyond redemption. Hill witnessed a knife fight between one of the deck boys and a Filipino cannery worker. Three days later the SS *Yukon* landed in Juneau. Burg and Hill made last-minute purchases—screws, tacks, a mirror, needles, thread, a jug, and film for one of Burg's view cameras. Grub included fruit, raisins, butter, salt and pepper, candy, spuds, and coffee. They split a chicken sandwich and pastry for lunch. Total expenses: $7.40. Hill met a "candy girl" in one of the shops. When she heard they were voyaging down the Yukon River, she asked to go along. Perhaps another time, he told her.

That afternoon the two sailors launched *Song o' the Winds* in the Gastineau Channel, bound for Taku Inlet, southeast of Juneau. Burg wanted to take photographs before heading for Skagway. They stopped at an abandoned Indian camp for the night. Hill put out fishing lines; Burg set up the tent. The dreaded mosquitoes appeared. Over the next three days the weather held. Wind rose in the afternoon, turning the waterway into a shimmering silver sea of white-capped waves, only to retreat by evening. After hiking up to Annex Lake, Burg struck photographic pay dirt. He photographed ice floes and waterfalls, and he filmed panoramas of the area. Back on Taku Inlet, the birdlife put on a display. Ravens cawed to one another; flocks of arctic terns soared and dived as if of a single mind. Dozens of eagles perched silently on tall snags or floated listlessly overhead. On the gravel beaches they clashed with one another for the remains of decaying salmon when they were not driving off the raucous gulls. The mix of sea and forest breezes carried a familiar, exhilarating scent.

Burg made lengthy observations and descriptions in his diary. Of Hill he wrote: "Spoke will do anything to make a picture. Honestly, I do not think I could have a better partner. He has understanding and is not a hog. Most of all, he can watch out for himself. We do not sit down and gossip but just mosey along and we each look out for ourselves but both look after the equipment. We do not bicker or quarrel and we both seem to fit in everywhere." During their return to Juneau, Burg and Hill encountered a series of squalls. The passage was wet and bumpy, the rowing arduous. Once in town they took a room at the Scandinavian Hotel. Burg caught a ride out to the Mendenhall Glacier to take photographs.

The next day they departed north on the Lynn Canal for Skagway eighty miles away. The sky was overcast, the seas choppy. Swarms of gnats descended. Whoever manned the oars had to avoid swallowing and breathing the microscopic creatures while the other man retreated beneath the canvas tarp. They reached Coughlin Island, where John Petoch and his wife raised blue foxes. Burg and Hill spent two days filming and visiting. Mrs. Petoch proved an invaluable escort, guiding Burg around the island, narrating the human and natural history of the area while pointing out possible photo opportunities.

"Not many women, even one younger," noted Burg, "would be willing to work as hard as she does, at that kind of work."

At Yankee Cove they met Harvey Moore and his wife. Moore thought Alaska a "hell of a place that he would die in as he had not (enough) money to get out." Burg took photos of the couple working in their garden; Mrs. Moore would not allow Burg to photograph her face. He described the enigmatic woman as follows: "In her soiled overalls with bobbed hair and a sun-brown complexion working the garden, nimble as a deer . . . and ready for any hardship. . . . She was a puzzle to Spoke and I with her command of language and knowledge of the world. Mr. Moore was on fine terms with his wife." Burg's observations on male-female relationships cemented his belief that wilderness life made for cooperation and marital harmony, while city life pulled people apart with its busy distractions.

Days later, near Haines, Burg experienced what he recognized as a psychological letdown. "Awoke at 6 AM," he wrote, "it was with a great feeling of emptiness and aloneness as though this life that I was leading was barren of everything." Normally these episodes, the traveler's bane, came and went. He had also been feeling unwell and may have been suffering a fever when he wrote this. At camp that afternoon he took a nap, then rallied himself by keeping busy. He erected the tent, put the gear inside, washed his face, wrote in his diary, and sang a chantey. Hill appeared with a pail of wild strawberries. Burg lit a fire and Hill boiled tea from the brackish tidewater. Mosquitoes appeared briefly, but an evening breeze kept them at bay. Dinner was rice and raisins; dessert, cupfuls of Hill's strawberries. The next morning overcast skies signaled a change in the weather. They spent the afternoon bucking choppy seas and headwinds. By evening, black clouds crowded the skyline; fog descended into the canal, settling on the water's surface. They lost sight of the shoreline and were forced to drift helplessly until the fog lifted. They reached the Chilkoot Army Barracks, twelve miles up Chilkoot Inlet, in the dark.

On the evening of July 6 they arrived in Skagway. An Empress steamboat hugged the pier. The once-rollicking, lawless, jumping-off point for gold seekers was now a tourist depot. Burg and Hill rode the White Pass and Yukon Railway train over White Pass into Canada the next morning. Blue skies and sunshine on the snowcapped peaks combined with steep grades and cliff-hanging turns left visitors speechless or giddy with chatter. Burg joked to Hill that he felt like a "cheechako," an Alaskan term for "tenderfoot" or greenhorn.

By the time they reached the lakeside town of Bennett, both men were anxious to escape the crowds. Rundown cabins, abandoned buildings, rusty mining equipment and railroad cars—Bennett had seen better days. The wooden church was the only building not listing to port or starboard. The wooden sidewalk outside the lunch counter was packed with hungry travelers, hoping to purchase a meal before continuing by train to Whitehorse. Burg's reaction to the tourist trade he would encounter along the Yukon River ranged from nonjudgmental observations to mild disapproval: "Bennett now a feeding station kept alive by dollar meals."

In the Native language Gwich'in, Yukon means Great River. It is the longest river in Alaska, the third longest in North America. The debate over the source of the Yukon and the correct measuring stick—length, volume, geographical location, highest elevation—continues to this day. In any event, somewhere in the high glacier country of southeast Alaska's Coastal Range, fifteen or so miles inland from the tidal water of Lynn Canal, the headwaters of the Yukon begin, pools to riffles to numerous creeks until the nascent river reaches the southern lakes region that straddles British Columbia and the Yukon Territory. The main glacier-fed lakes (Linderman, Atlin, Bennett, Tagish, and Marsh) are relatively narrow bodies of water, flanked by snow-covered mountain ranges and low-lying forested hills, connected by equally narrow but considerably shorter arms of water. Swamps and lowlands border the lakes. A handful of islands dot the waterways. Most agree that the Yukon proper starts at the northern end of Marsh Lake, south of the town of Whitehorse, 120 miles downriver from Bennett. From Whitehorse the Great River twists and bends northwest for a thousand miles across the Yukon Flats before reaching Fort Yukon. There the river turns southwest for another nine hundred miles. At Mountain Village the main Yukon frays into numerous channels, sprawling across the delta before reaching Norton Sound.

Late on the afternoon of July 8, Burg and Hill launched *Song o' the Winds* into the ruffled green waters of twenty-six-mile long Lake Bennett. White clouds scudded across a blue sky past towering snowcapped mountain peaks. The sapphire-colored glaciers of the Bennett Range to the west of the lake stood in a stark yet complementary contrast to the red rock mountains on the east side. A following wind nudged the canoe along as Burg pulled on the oars; the first whitecaps danced on the crest of rising waves. Hill rigged the sail. Soon the canoe was leaping across the lake. Spray dashed over the bow, soaking both men. Burg had estimated the boat carried seven hundred pounds—two men, outfit, camera equipment, and provisions. The men found themselves laughing: "Only 2114 miles to St. Michael (Bering Sea)," wrote Burg.

Sixteen miles downlake, they pitched camp on a sandy pocket of beach. Hill cooked a meal of beans and bacon. The next morning they woke to fair winds and reached the village of Carcross in two hours. Upon their departure a bank of gray clouds rolled in, bringing sheets of rain. They alternated one-hour stints at the oars with good-natured complaints. Progress was slow and at the head of Windy Arm steep, rising, slate-colored waves forced them ashore. They hunkered down to wait out the storm. To pass the time, Burg read and reread an old copy of *National Geographic,* looking for ways to improve his own writing. He broke down the construction of the articles, analyzing the sentences and the narrative line. Determined to learn the *National Geographic* style, he mimicked the sentences in his diary.

The next day they attempted to head downlake, but foul weather pushed them back to shore after two miles. When blue skies and a freshening breeze from the south returned, Burg realized they would have to pay close attention to the ever-changing weather. To be caught too far from shore in a severe storm could spell disaster. The boat skipped like a smooth stone across the sparkling waters of Tagish Lake, passing by prosperous-looking cabins, then the ruins of abandoned Fort Tagish, until reaching shallow, warm Marsh Lake. To the east, swatches of forest were decorated by colorful patches of wildflowers, especially crimson fireweed. At Dixon's Trading Post, Burg purchased hard tack, potatoes, and salt. They were swarmed by mosquitoes. By evening, the winds had died down. They had covered nearly forty-five miles. Burg relaxed. "Spoke and I look for trees [submerged stumps], want to drift and sleep and dream, a good idea where the nights are only two hours long but slow," he wrote. "With the sunset flaming the clouds and casting light to sparkle on the rippling swells of Marsh Lake we pitch camp."

On the afternoon of July 15, as Hill rowed to the head of Miles Canyon, the speed of the Yukon River picked up. They had sailed across Marsh Lake that morning with a following wind and made good time. Their confidence was running high. Now the river, compressed between the walls of the narrow canyon, behaved erratically—boiling pools, sharp eddy lines, crosscurrents—tossing the canoe about like a toy boat. Good fortune trumped the voyager's raw skill. When they reached the head of Whitehorse Rapids, they stopped to scout, chastened by their experience in Miles Canyon.

They walked along the basalt cliffs above Whitehorse Rapids. "Here the whole river is funneled through a narrow rock channel, forming a mass of wild breakers succeeded by treacherous boils," Burg wrote of the sight. "Walls act like sounding boards, perpendicular columns of basalt." The wooden portage trams on either side of the river, though abandoned and falling apart, suggested that his concern was well-founded. At least two hundred men, most of them thoroughly inexperienced, had lost their lives at Whitehorse Rapids during the 1898 rush to treasure.

Burg spent an entire day filming and taking photos of the area. The quality of the northern light surprised him. He shot from multiple viewpoints—atop the bluff, from the wooden bridge downstream, along the riverbank. He kept detailed notes of the photographs: location, names, camera settings, weather conditions. After finishing his shots, he walked into Whitehorse to shoot promotional photographs of the White Pass Railroad station and Alaskan poet Robert Service's cabin as per his agreement with the railroad company. At some point he and Hill decided to hire a truck to shuttle *Song o' the Winds* and their outfit around Whitehorse and Squaw Rapids.

The voyagers spent two more days in Whitehorse preparing for the 460-mile run to Dawson. Hill purchased nineteen dollars worth of provisions: fruit, bread, butter, bacon, ham, beans, flour, prunes, salt, baking powder, pilot biscuits, soap, sugar, and new mosquito netting. Burg secured a passage permit from the Royal Mounted Police. He performed routine maintenance on the canoe at the Whitehorse boatyard, the local graveyard for Yukon River paddle wheelers, where seventy-six-year-old Mr. Taub, the acknowledged grand old man of the Yukon, held court. The ex–riverboat pilot was glad to have an audience to listen to his yarns about the Yukon River.

Burg and Hill departed Whitehorse under sunny skies. The speed of the current surprised both men as *Song o' the Winds* raced downstream, the scenery flashing by and the mosquitoes, once a constant nuisance, now a memory. The river offered few eddies; if the canoe capsized, they faced a serious swim in icy water. The unfamiliar sound of cutbanks—the river gnawing away at the banks until large chunks of soil and brush crashed into the racing water—startled them. By midafternoon they entered upper Lake Laberge, a welcome relief. Southerly winds and a following sea favored the voyagers. Hill raised the sail.

Coal-colored clouds crowded the ragged horizon by early afternoon the next day. Hill and Burg passed Richthofen Island. The wind rose steadily, and before they knew it, the once serene lake was a sea of whitecaps. With the wind came the rain. Waves broke over the bow of the canoe. But for the splash boards and the canvas cover Burg had rigged, *Song o' the Winds* would have swamped. Hill, like all deep-water sailors, distrusted shorelines of any kind. He argued for remaining in the middle of the lake and riding the squall out. Burg knew that wasn't a wise course, and the voyagers made a run for the nearest point of land. As they neared a rock-bound cove, the canoe ran aground on a shallow bar and nearly tipped over. They spent a wet night in a leaky, wind-blown tent.

The storm pinned them down for another day. When Hill grew restless, he practiced carrying ever-larger loads of equipment up and down the beach in the event they would have to hike out. In his diary Burg suffered a bout of self-criticism. He had overreached in terms of the territory he wanted to cover in the time allowed. Had it been necessary to paddle from Juneau to Skagway? Probably not. It forced the pace of the voyage, something he wanted to avoid. "By coming to the Yukon so late," he wrote, "we have to hurry to make the mouth in time to escape the ice." His enthusiasm and ambition, not for the first time, had ambushed his common sense.

On the second night of their retreat, the poor weather lifted. They decided to make a dash through the Thirty-Mile reach that ran from the lower end of Lake Laberge to the confluence with the Teslin River at Hootalinqua. In the gauze-like light of the Alaskan summer night, they broke camp and rowed for the mouth of the infamous canyon. The swift, narrow channel and the near perpendicular sand and gravel bluffs two hundred- to three hundred feet high, marked by the odd-looking rock formations called hoodoos, suggested a mysterious landscape. Although this was one of the more dangerous stretches of the Yukon, some considered it one of the most beautiful. Subarctic forests of aspen, birch, and poplar mixed with stands of pine and spruce topped the corridor. The bluffs were marked by nondescript gravesites. By dawn Burg and Hill were floating below the confluence of the Teslin and Yukon. The size of the Yukon had doubled.

Burg was aware of the legendary hospitality practiced along the Yukon toward land and river travelers. At times, however, he and Hill shied from the informal reciprocity. Already low on provisions, they camped in locations along the river that discouraged landings despite being the beneficiaries of that hospitality themselves. At the village of Little Salmon, Burg met an Anglican minister who had arrived a decade earlier from England to devote his life to the welfare of the Native people living along the Yukon. He invited Burg to accompany him on his medical rounds through the village—a trading post, a church, and handful of log cabins. On a bench above the village, the dirty-white tents of the Native people, likely of the Tagish tribe, poked through the brush. "Spirit houses," structures the size of a child's playhouse where the deceased's ashes and personal effects were placed, dotted the oversize graveyard, clear evidence of the toll the 1918 flu pandemic had taken on the people. The dismal condition of the Yukon River tribe made a lasting impact on Burg. In his travel diary he wrote:

> Most sick and forlorn tribe with an assortment of unkempt unwashed shy children—smudgy fire in front of tents with racks of drying meat above the reach of the gaunt and shaggy dogs—medical rations consisted mostly of aspirin and Lysol—tuberculosis scored 100%—Rev. told me the only thing that saved them was their sense of humor—all live in same tents regardless of afflictions which spreads disease rapidly—tubercular glands common—two old squaws in tent making moccasins shake heads and say no sick—Rev. looked at one old hag and shakes head as being beyond repair—young Indian and wife very much concerned over baby—Rev. tells them very fine looking baby, looks the same as you . . . gloomy countenance lit up for minute—girls among Indians in particular have hopeless look.

Two years later, in his *National Geographic* article published in July 1930, Burg expressed the same thoughts publicly:

> It was a dismal camp. Its wreckage of a race, like a tattered page from the gold saga, revealed primitive man crushed almost to extermination by civilization. With the bold, reckless whites who swarmed into this wilderness came also a certain riffraff catering to the savage's weakness for rum and debauching his women. Conscientious workers of Government and missions could do little against such odds to save these Indians from degeneracy. Now they are a scattered and forlorn race, merely existing from day to day in the slush along the white man's frontier. Their colorful native costumes, observed by Frederick Schwatka on his rafting voyage down the Yukon in 1883, have given place to the cheap, dingy clothes and calicos of the white trader. The bright, intelligent faces that eagerly welcomed the white man have become sullen maps of wasting disease.

At the village of Carmacks a Royal Mounted Police officer offered the voyagers a firm warning. Three days earlier he had swamped in Five Fingers Rapids, twenty miles downriver, and nearly drowned. The officer's open canoe, heavily loaded, had been swept away and still had not been recovered. Swarms of swallows, their nests burrowed in the wind-carved hoodoos above the river, signaled the voyager's arrival at the head of Five Fingers Rapid. The rocky outcrops and islands splayed the cataract into five distinct channels. It was a dramatic, even intimidating scene. It was also a photographic opportunity Burg could not pass up. After setting up his camera equipment on shore, he instructed Hill to paddle down the nearest shoreline channel. No sooner had he positioned himself than he spotted his partner in the canoe below the rapid. Hill had run the chute on the far side of the river, out of camera view.

At Rink Rapids, the last cataract of any significance on the Yukon, they hugged the right bank in the canoe. Half submerged on the rocky shoal in the middle of the river lay the wreckage of the steamboat *Dawson*. The current slowed to three knots as the Yukon flowed through a widening valley with low banks. Numerous islands split the river into slender channels. As they rowed downstream, Native camps appeared along shore, the smoke of their campfires and the smell of roasting caribou spicing the air. Burg and Hill pitched camp on a small island in the middle of the river. Two weeks earlier, several thousand caribou had crossed the river in the vicinity. If they were to film the migration, this would be the right location. At the time the Forty Mile herd was estimated to number a half million. Their range extended from Whitehorse in the Yukon Territory six hundred miles north to the White Mountains in Alaska. A decade later the huge migrations had nearly ceased. By the early 1940s the herd had dwindled to ten thousand animals. Biologists at the time cited numerous possible causes: deterioration of range quality because of fire and overgrazing as well as excessive hunting.

Burg and Hill's initial encounter with a caribou herd occurred the next day. In his diary Burg wrote:

> The next morning our caribou saga began. While cooking breakfast a band of several hundred caribou split in a "V" and passed on either side of our camp so close we could hear their clicking hooves. They waded into the Yukon and easily breasted the swift current on their easterly crossing. We followed them to the bank, swinging our cameras into action to record the dramatic scene. They made an impressive sight with their huge antlers silhouetted against the sky as they stood on the opposite shore gazing at us. All day long we encountered scattered bands swimming the Yukon . . . we often rowed into the midst of the large swimming bands, taking a chance of being swamped in an area of antlers for that one elusive dramatic shot.

That afternoon Alfred Fortier came poling upstream to the Coffee Creek Trading Post with his three dogs. Fortier, who had lived up Nisling River for three decades, claimed loudly to Burg that he was getting the hell out of Alaska. According to Burg's diary, Fortier was on his way to sell his guns, furs, boat, and dogs to "that crook, Jim Derry." For the next half-hour the small, wiry man with the drooping white moustache talked nonstop. Burg, realizing that Fortier was a rich source of Yukon River lore, decided to camp with the disgruntled trapper for the night.

Fortier did not disappoint. He was sick of greenhorns, present company excluded, and his rheumatism was getting worse. He bragged that he kept the local Native people and their dogs away from his trapping line by telling them that the wolf bait he had planted was poisoned. Coffee Jack, who had once threatened to shoot Fortier and then tell the Mounted Police that he had mistaken Fortier for a moose, was a scoundrel. And so it went, far into the night. The next morning Fortier picked up where he left off. As Hill rowed away from camp, the sourdough shouted to them one last time about an adventure he had once had with the Dawson police, who objected to his bootlegging.

On August 1, Hill spotted the bald patch (left by a landslide) on the mountainside above Dawson City. They camped on a beach near town, the sound of the confluence of the Yukon and Klondike Rivers in their ears. Hill shopped for .30-30 shells, garlic, and tobacco. Burg wandered the area, photographing fish wheels, dilapidated paddle wheelers, aban-

On their 1928 voyage on the Yukon River, Burg and Fred "Spokane" Hill filmed the caribou migration.

doned cabins, and an electric gold dredge the size of a cathedral. He visited the Moosehead Indian village, where he found the Han Indians friendly, productive, and in good health—a stark contrast to his experience at Little Salmon. The village itself had none of the earmarks of poverty or indifference. Racks of fish dried in the sun, children ran about, a small armada of boats hugged the shoreline. The women appeared content, as they performed their daily chores. After asking permission, Burg took photographs of some members of the tribe; others, wanting payment, refused to have their picture taken.

They dallied for a day, but already Burg fretted prematurely about the Yukon "freeze up" that could begin anywhere from the first to the third week in October. Once the river froze over, boat traffic halted. Another month or so passed before sled traffic was possible but perilous. Beneath the ice, the Yukon ran swift and unforgiving. To fall through a crevice or weak spot in the frozen river was a guarantee of severe frostbite at best. Flat and relentless in its forward motion, the Yukon bristled with whatever cargo—tree stumps, carcasses, *Song o' the Winds*—it carried on its coffee-colored back. Bulky, misshapen black clouds scudded across the blue sky. Brief squalls followed the voyagers, interrupting the fragile sunshine. A rainbow appeared.

At times Burg, like many other river travelers on the Yukon, experienced a vague anxiety. He was not the first to remark on the feelings of isolation and loneliness the river evoked. The scale of the landscape itself seemed to defy conventional measurements of distance and size. Rain, gray skies, endless forests, devil's club, mosquitoes, impenetrable bush, mountain ranges as far as the eye could see, and a silent, indifferent river—all seemed to conspire against individual efforts. Here was a land with a dark waterway coursing through its heart that did not bend easily to settlement, a place that did not tolerate human error or foolishness without serious consequences. Signs of failure littered the river corridor—abandoned woodcutter's cabins, overgrown gardens, derelict boats and fish wheels. Disease, poverty, and alcoholism stalked the Native as well as the white population. Come fall, the river froze over and darkness descended. A winter living along the Yukon tested a man's endurance.

On August 6 the two voyagers reached the village of Forty-Mile, site of Canadian customs. After a cursory glance at their papers, the customs official loaded *Song o' the Winds* with a generous helping of lettuce and peas from his garden, then waved the men good luck. Crossing into the United States days later, they stopped in Eagle, Alaska, on the west bank of the Yukon, 1,400 miles from the Bering Sea. The Han Indian village there had once been a thriving hub for the area's miners, rivermen, traders, trappers, and missionaries. Burg began another round of detailed notes on the habits, lifestyles, and customs of these local Native Americans. It is unclear whether he was able to differentiate between the various tribes or simply failed to write down the names. He listed population, number of students, school absences, births, and illnesses.

In his diary he wrote about their cabins as well as the role of Native women, social affairs, church habits, dances, musical ability, table manners, work habits, the law, use of tobacco, marriage rites, schools, parent-child relationships, the socialistic nature of their community, their adaptability to change, the impact of whites on Native culture, and the nature of white's (and perhaps his own) perception of Indian behavior. "Hard to see how they exist at times," he wrote. "As seen out of his native environment, the Indian appears stolid, stupid, unresponsive and sometimes arrogant. . . . At home, distinctly individual . . . Cannot lump their character anymore than white man . . . Find most of them cordial, responsive and affectionate. Also sensitive and proud. If not for the interference of unscrupulous whites, [they] would be free from suspicion and easily managed."

At Charley Creek, seventy-five miles downstream, Yukon mail carrier Ed "Adolph" Biederman greeted Burg and Hill with enthusiasm. Along the river corridor, stories of Biederman's exploits were well known. Three years earlier, while driving a team of huskies with five hundred pounds of mail over the frozen Yukon River between Eagle and Circle City, he had attempted to cross a frozen stream in below-zero-degree temperatures. The ice collapsed and Biederman had fallen in. Instead of stopping to build a fire and warm his feet, he continued to the nearest roadhouse—a mistake he later admitted. At Fort Yukon a doctor amputated the forepart of both of Biederman's feet.

On August 11, Hill and Burg reached Circle City, the first sizable town on the northeastern edge of the Yukon Flats. The town, with a population of seventy-four (fifty-seven Natives; seventeen Whites), was rundown and discouraging. The next day the ore barge *Yukon* docked at the wharf. The voyagers hitched a ride to Fort Yukon, eighty-five miles downriver. The run from Circle City to Fort Yukon had befuddled even the most experienced riverboat captains. Shifting sandbars combined with the vagaries of the local weather had caused numerous sternwheelers to run aground. Some had been trapped for days. A week before Burg and Hill's arrival, a respected river pilot had committed suicide. Local hearsay suggested that the navigational error the pilot had made during foul weather (which caused extensive damage to the sternwheeler) was the cause.

Located at the confluence of the Porcupine and Yukon Rivers, Fort Yukon was a strategic and historic location. The confluence of the Porcupine and Yukon Rivers had earlier been an important trading center for the Gwich'in Indians as well as the Hudson Bay Company, the British trading company. Now tourists, arriving by sternwheeler, crowded the wooden sidewalks. The local population, roughly three hundred people, was financially dependent on the summer crowds whose presence they tolerated. Burg echoed the chagrin of residents: "On their annual two-week vacation all with cameras snapping pictures of everything, imagining they were being philanthropists and being mainly rude while being inquisitive around the natives. Two school teachers will walk up and laugh knowingly and condescendingly as though they understood how it was to be an Indian—Probably the Indian liked it for they always come down at steamer time and sat around. But they mimic the tourists after they are gone."

Burg certainly realized that the purpose of his photographs for the railroad and steamship companies was to promote tourism. If he felt ambivalent about his duel role as adventurer and commercial photographer, he failed to mention it. He had found a way to finance his voyages. The tourist visitors, on the other hand, were none too pleased with the conditions in the hotels, shops, and restaurants in Fort Yukon.

Three days later, Burg and Hill set off downriver. They made stops at Victors Island and later that afternoon at Purgatory. William Yanert—trapper, poet, reader of books, soldier of fortune, expert wood carver, and river curmudgeon—asked Burg to carry a pair of snowshoes downriver to his brother Herman in Stevens Village. In return, Yanert shared his colorful, hand-drawn map of the lower Yukon River corridor, which proved to be an invaluable guide and work of art. The voyagers reached Tanana on the afternoon of August 21. Downstream lay a panoramic view of the barren Yukon Flats washed in gray mist. The widening Yukon River, its banks blurred by fog and distance, suggested proximity to saltwater. The Bering Sea, however, was eight hundred miles away. The sun came out and stayed, allowing Burg and Hill to dry out their gear and clothes. Once on the river, they raised sail to catch a following wind, unusual for the Yukon. A stop at a Native camp was rewarded with a gift of dried grayling. After carefully examining *Song o' the Winds,* the Native fisherman grunted his approval. In Ruby, Burg found another threadbare riverfront town with muddy streets, broken sidewalks, and boarded-up storefronts. Stores and cabins faced inland, away from the river, an unusual arrangement.

The voyagers spent time with the Gurtlers, a mixed-blood family. Burg took photos of the two children and Mrs. Gurtler at her numerous tasks while Hill helped Mr. Gurtler with a wooden boat he was building. Over the course of the day, Burg found Mrs. Gurtler to be typical of the resilient women he had encountered on the Yukon. A keen observer of human nature, including her own family, she worried about her youngest son, who ventured fearlessly out on the river in any available craft. Her oldest son, she thought, had been ruined by attending the Chemewa Indian School in Oregon. Upon returning home, he had beaten his father for mistreating her. Mrs. Gurtler remarked that her oldest daughter, Alice, was *different*. She did not care to skin beaver and cut salmon like the other village girls. Burg took a liking to Alice, whom he thought was "like the girls I had known." He also felt sorry for her because she was, as he put it, "an outcast from both races." The troubling complexity of Alice's situation gave him pause. "This evening thru a part of the clouds," he wrote in his diary, "I looked up at a star and realized how vast the universe with its immense spaces and how insignificant I was with my bickering and striving for attainment and never thinking to give—the sum of all virtues is human sympathy."

When the steamboat *Alice*, bound for Holy Cross 385 miles downstream, docked at Ruby, Burg and Hill decided to hop aboard. It was not the first time Burg had taken a "shortcut." Given his notions about continuous voyages and his criticism of Lewis Freeman's style of voyaging on the Columbia, however, the decision begs for an explanation. Burg offered none in his diary. One rationale for the change, perhaps, was his fear of being trapped by the Yukon "freeze." Such a reality would have forced him to abort the final leg of his voyage along the west coast of Alaska to the Bering Sea. Whatever the case, Captain Adams agreed to free passage and meals for both men in exchange for help unloading freight at the downriver villages.

Four days later, Burg and Hill arrived at Holy Cross. They helped the crew unload the last of the cargo onto the beach. At the trading post, Hill purchased bread, potatoes, chocolate, crackers, and cigars; Burg bought candy, soap, and a shaving brush. The Jesuit fathers at the Holy Cross mission provisioned the voyagers with fresh loaves of bread and baskets of vegetables. When they set off downstream, Burg calculated they were a mere 290 miles from the Bering Sea. He mentioned seeing his first *qayaqs* (kayaks) on the river and was greatly impressed by their construction as well as the way the local Yupik men handled the craft.

As he rowed, Burg brooded over an incident that had occurred at their campsite the night before. Awakened by a noise outside the tent, he had gotten up to investigate. It is unclear whether he failed to recognize the animal he encountered: stray dog or wolf? Both could pose dangers. He shot the animal and immediately suffered feelings of remorse. At sea he had witnessed numerous acts of casual callousness by seamen toward shipboard animals and sea life. On the Yukon dogs were routinely mistreated. Burg's diary responses to the mistreatment of animals had ranged from acceptance of unpleasant cultural norms to disgust. His explanation for his own behavior offered little: "I don't know yet why I shot him—can understand now how some people might do a thing in a fit of anger without meaning it—there was a yelp and I looked outside to find him dead in his tracks."

The run to Russian Mission, about fifty-six miles downriver, turned into an ordeal. At Nualto the Yukon River bends south and the river corridor lays directly in the path of storms born on the Bering Sea. Rain fell continually, at times pelting the river so hard that a smoky fog rose off the surface. Icy, upstream winds flushed white-capped waves over the gunnels and into *Song o' the Winds.* Hill and Burg sang sea chanteys during these challenging times. They routinely tucked into the lee of islands or fingers of land to rest. A trip that normally took one long day lasted three. They finally arrived at Russian Mission, wet and exhausted, and camped below town on the beach. The storms continued, pinning them in their leaky canvas tent. The river was transformed into a roiling sea. The size of the wind-driven breakers dismayed Burg. Not even the local Natives took to the water in their qayaqs. On shore the wind howled, driving anything not tied down skittering along the beach. A local man offered the two voyagers the use of an abandoned cabin.

Burg had always been an enthusiast of small river craft. Weather-bound, he took the opportunity to make a closer examination of the Yupik qayaqs that were unique to the region. The word "kayak" in Yupik meant "man's boat" or "hunter's boat." The single-cockpit boats, used primarily for hunting, were constructed of stitched seal skins stretched over a wooden frame made from collected driftwood. The boats were designed and built by men with the help of their wives, who stitched together the treated seal skin using intricate knots made of caribou sinew. While the qayaqs of the various villages along the lower Yukon had many similarities in terms of size and shape, no two craft

Burg purchased two kayaks at Russian Mission on his voyage down the Yukon River and had them shipped back to Portland.

were identical. Each boat was built with an individual in mind, and thought of as an extension of the user's body. The dimensions were dictated by use, general water conditions, and measurements taken from the user's body size. The boats were light in weight, quick on the water, easy to handle, and flexible in terms of repair. Burg, keenly aware of the craftsmanship, soon found himself coveting the handmade "skin boats." Before departing Russian Mission, he exchanged a rifle and money (a portion of which he borrowed from one of the local priests) to purchase two qayaqs that he had shipped back to Portland.

Although Burg was irked when he learned that the local Russian religious order expected the Natives to pay weekly tribute in fur, fish, or currency, he and Hill attended services one afternoon. Midway through the ceremony, the headman burst into the drafty building shouting "Kayak! Kayak!" The entire assembly dashed out the door to the beach. They were astonished to see *Song o' the Winds* upside down riding the crest of wind-blown waves downriver. Had the canoe been torn from its anchor on the beach, or had Burg or Hill failed to secure it? Everyone scrambled along shore in a futile pursuit. The canoe drifted around the bend and out of sight. Fortunately Burg's camera equipment and gear had been stored in the drafty cabin. Burg hired Matthew, the only Native at Russian Mission who owned an operating outboard motor, to ferry them downstream to Marshall. Provided the wind quieted and he did not die that night, Matthew teased, they would leave tomorrow. Another gale blew in; the departure was delayed.

Four days after *Song o' the Winds* disappeared, the trio departed Russian Mission. The sky was steel-gray; rain fell intermittently. Matthew's wooden boat leaked continually. Burg wondered how the three men, gear, and supplies would fit. Matthew, dressed in trousers and a thin long-sleeved shirt, appeared indifferent to the damp cold. Burg envied the guide's nonchalance but insisted that he wear his hunting jacket. Burg resigned himself to the loss of his canoe. He recalled the day on the Snake River when he and Harry Fogleberry had watched as an earlier version of *Song o' the Winds* washed away, only to be wrecked in a rock-strewn rapid and sunk. Burg's hopes were renewed when Matthew suggested that the canoe was likely to be in a large eddy a few miles downriver.

As Matthew predicted, they found the boat in the eddy floating upside down in a sea of driftwood. The bow and stern had been crushed. The splashboards were in pieces and the inside decking torn away. The oarlocks had been stripped, and a number of the ribs were cracked. A single life preserver had washed ashore. Making extensive repairs was out of the question. Burg offered the canoe to Matthew, who thought the better boat builders in his village would have little problem bringing it back to life. If Burg was upset about the loss, he did not show it. Voyaging downriver in miserable conditions, they stopped at one village after another to deliver mail and shuttle supplies but especially to socialize. No sooner had the trio finished visiting one set of relatives and friends, than Matthew was angling toward shore for another round of river neighborliness. He hoped the locals in Marshall would throw a dance to honor his arrival. Decades later Burg wrote of the Natives of the lower Yukon and Russian Mission:

> The people were honest with a sense of delicacy in human relationships. They never provoked a quarrel, and seemed to take without question whatever was offered them for their labor and produce. They showed no jealousy nor did they put great store in possessions. This was probably due to their absolute faith in Providence and its ability to always

provide them with daily necessities. . . . From our observations of these villages, we surmised that the so-called primitive village culture—evolved through centuries to fit available resources and limitations of the environment—has an extremely delicate mechanism. Uninformed, over-night wonder planners, gifted with more enthusiasm, than savvy, have usually botched cultures they did not understand. Many eventually became entirely unworkable, resulting in people suffering and in many cases destroyed.

In Marshall, Burg attempted to hire another small boat for the run to Saint Michael on the coast. No luck: the red-eyed storekeeper growled that the two voyagers might catch a lift aboard the paddle wheeler *Ensee* that was due any day. In the meantime Burg hiked up to the summit of Pilcher Mountain to photograph the tundra with the Yukon River braiding, then disappearing, into the mist. When the *Ensee* arrived, the captain accepted Burg and Hill's offer of labor for a lift to Saint Michael. Near Andreafski, 120 miles from the Bering Sea, Burg felt the tidal pull for the first time. The shoreline was jam-packed with immense slabs and chucks of ice and driftwood. The *Ensee* worked its way down the Apoon tributary of the Yukon delta. Describing the area, Burg wrote:"No current, mud channels and banks in place covered with ice and beyond with the scrawny northern growth of willow, alder and hemlock and the rest tundra moss. Very desolate country, low, soggy and mud."

Early on the morning of September 28, the *Ensee* rounded Point Romanof into the Bering Sea. Burg stood on deck, watching the scene unfold. The Alaskan coastline was blanketed in paste-like fog. As they neared the harbor of Saint Michael, he scribbled more notes: immense gray skies, piles of bleached driftwood on the rocky beach; along the waterfront abandoned piers and their decaying pilings looked like strange vertical snags that had been hand-planted; on a bluff above the harbor a semicircle of derelict, weathered buildings. Burg and Hill's four-month, 2,300-mile river journey had come to a quiet, gloomy finish.

Although his Yukon River voyage had come to an end, Burg's work had not. He had before him the task of finding passage for himself and Hill to Nome,

Alaska. There they would board the schooner *Boxer* and voyage north to film the roundup and slaughter of thousands of reindeer. They rented one of the drafty, one-room cabins overlooking the harbor, pleased to have a roof over their heads. Over the next two days Burg reviewed his notes, gave his camera equipment much-needed attention, and plotted out the logistics of the last leg of their journey.

On October 2, Burg and Hill, along with five other passengers, boarded the schooner *Good Hope*, bound for Nome via Shaktoolik. The fare was ten dollars per passenger. The two voyagers thought they had seen their share of run-down boats; *Good Hope* proved otherwise. The bilge pump lay in parts on the deck. Lines were frayed and pieced together; the schooner had not seen a lick of paint in years. Many of the windows were broken out, allowing the chill wind into the cabin. Captain Ivanoff started the ancient diesel engine by heating the frozen head with a blowtorch. The intense heat caused the already blackened roof of the engine room to ignite and catch fire. The lone Eskimo crewmember, standing by with a bucket of water, doused the flames.

It was a bumpy, wind-swept passage across the Norton Sound. The engine routinely cut out, leaving the schooner to wallow. Burg huddled on a wobbly bench trying to cope with his seasickness; Hill, immune to the sea voyager's scourge, stifled his laughter. For breakfast they were served cold cereal. When they asked Ivanoff about lunch, he asked if they had eaten all the grape nuts. *Good Hope*'s food shortage was temporarily resolved when they landed at Shaktoolik and learned the Natives had recently killed a sixteen-foot white beluga whale. The next morning, thankfully, *Good Hope* reached Nome. Burg voiced disappointment at how difficult it was to purchase a pair of mukluks in Nome. The Eskimos in the area, he learned, refused to make the boots, preferring the white man's shoes. He cringed at the irony of this cultural exchange of footwear. One white local informed him that the Natives who had the least contact with whites showed the best traits, were friendlier, and worked harder.

On October 5, Burg and Hill boarded *Boxer*, a coastal schooner in far better condition than *Good Hope*. For the next two weeks Burg did little else but film on the King, Diomedes, and Saint Lawrence Islands: scenery, landmarks, buildings, churches, ships and small craft, and Native people at work, at home, and at play. When he arrived on the Cape Prince of Wales headlands of the Seward Peninsula, the fall slaughter of reindeer for food had already started. Filming began immediately but was often delayed because of the fierce weather. For hours on end the crack of .30-30 rifles shattered the air.

While Burg realized the undeniable benefits of the successful development of a reindeer industry, both for Native Eskimos and white businessmen, he also commented on the stark gap between the reality of the slaughter and the romantic image of reindeer. He wrote in his travel notes:

> For most the picturesque reindeer is invested with an amount of romance and tradition which our disposition seldom allows to cling to anything. The majesty of their great antlers, the traditions of Christmas which cluster about them, and the medium of poetry and legend thru which comes most of our ideas on the subject have been chief factors in producing this result. We are wont to think of the reindeer not only as a patient beast of service to the fur-clad people of the mid-night sun but as a noble friend to all the world.

Upon arriving back in Nome, Burg and Hill immediately sailed south aboard the *Sierra* to pick up four hundred reindeer at Golovin and transport them to Nunivak Island, where government officials and businessmen at Loman Reindeer Corporation hoped the herd would thrive and increase in numbers. The master had hired Hill as third mate and allowed Burg free passage. Snow was falling when the crew hoisted anchor. Shipboard life had changed little if at all. The smelly diesel engines in the compartment below Burg's bunk rumbled so loudly that he could not sleep much less read or write. He took his work to the mess room where the talk "ran mostly to squaws, court scandals, Tia'Juana, booze, and gambling." The seamen aboard the *Sierra* agreed that Native women were "dangerous to monkey around with" and were only looking for a white man to serve as a meal ticket.

At Golovin, Burg filmed longshoremen loading the reindeer aboard ship. It was a raucous, disorderly scene. He kept the camera rolling throughout the onerous passage across Norton Sound to Nunivak Island. At one point gale winds forced the *Sierra* to seek shelter on the lee side of tiny Besboro Island, a few miles offshore, for three days. At midnight on October 29, the *Sierra* shipped anchor. Hours later Captain Baker summoned Burg to the bridge, where he was greeted with a show of the Northern Lights. "For the first time

I saw the real thing," he wrote. "Reminded me of a great mist curtain full of colors being shaken across the sky." Upon reaching Nunivak Island, Burg spent another week filming.

The *Sierra* passed Cape Ommaney at the tip of Sitka Island along the Alaskan coast on November 20. Another southeastern gale raged, and engine problems caused the ship to flounder. An anxious Captain Baker admitted to Hill that he was unsure of their exact position as they searched for an entrance to the Inside Passage. The reliable Hill came to his rescue. Days later the *Sierra* landed in Ketchikan. Burg and Hill celebrated Thanksgiving on dry land.

During the first week of December, the voyagers arrived in Portland, where the Multnomah Hotel staged a banquet to honor them. Burg's family and friends attended as well as Jesse Sill and his wife. Sill showed the motion-picture film Burg had made of his 1925 canoe trip on the Snake. Burg gave a brief but entertaining account of the adventure, downplaying the heroics. The five-month voyage on the Yukon River—across the Norton Sound to the Bering Strait and back, and the final leg across the stormy North Pacific to Seattle—astounded the audience. Burg shrugged off the adulation but admitted that he had underestimated the hardships of such a voyage. The Yukon had been a wilder, much stranger river than the Columbia, the Snake, and certainly the Yellowstone, Missouri, and Mississippi Rivers. He had left *Song o' the Winds* behind but had brought back two thick river diaries, hundreds of photographs, two thousand feet of film, and two prized qayaqs.

Burg was already planning his next river voyage, but first he needed to begin his seven-thousand-word article for *National Geographic.* Throughout the Christmas holidays he sidestepped the task. He socialized with family and friends, paddled one of his qayaqs on the Columbia Slough, and read *Down the Grand Canyon,* Lewis Freeman's latest effort. Finally he sat down and began a first draft. For the next few days he wandered in a maze of his own design, getting nowhere. He had assumed that his copious note-taking would somehow speed the process. In fact, the vast amount of information overwhelmed him. Determined to settle into a routine, he decided to write as long as he could each day, then visit friends or see a movie in the evening.

By the first week in February, Burg had written eighteen hundred words. He felt that the writing "lacked animation," however. He grew discouraged, complaining to a female confidant that he was a failure. A month later he had completed a handwritten draft of the article but was still not pleased with it, so he reworked the piece. Gradually he found himself willing to admit that the article was getting better with each rewrite. "I really liked the last part for it had running action," he wrote. "Its [sic] good to be through with the story which shows all it takes is work. I have every confidence that it will go over with my pictures." Burg immediately began work on the captions that would accompany his photographs. Bolstered by completion of the article, he crowed in his diary: "I'm going to explore all the rivers in the world. I'll have an outline in my mind for everything I come in contact with for the more we know the better. . . . I'll be able to hold down any job." By May, Burg felt confident enough to send the article and photographs to the editors of *National Geographic* in Washington, D.C.

A year and a half passed before "Today on the Yukon Trail of 1898" appeared in the July 1930 issue. His first *National Geographic* article ran forty-one pages with fifty-three photographs. He received a check for five hundred dollars (approximately $6,400 today), a substantial sum. Upon seeing his name on the famous magazine cover along with regular contributors Frederick Simpich and Alfred Pearce Dennis, he felt a mix of pride and relief. At last he could call himself a writer and photographer who had earned his keep. He could also pay his father for past loans. After a decade of struggle and hard work, Burg had launched a writing and photographic career, beginning what would be a three-decade relationship with *National Geographic*. With *Alaska Wilds*, the silent, black-and-white, ten-minute documentary film he shot on the Yukon for Jesse Sill, he also set course in the emerging field of educational films. At twenty-eight years old, Burg's performance finally matched his ambition.

Chapter 4

DEH CHO:
CANADA'S MACKENZIE RIVER

Midway during his transit of the Yukon River, Amos Burg noted in his diary that he intended to run Canada's Mackenzie River—a bold proclamation given that the Yukon was turning out to be much more difficult than he had anticipated, that he was often hungry and cold, and that he still owed his father money. He certainly had no guarantee that *National Geographic* would accept another article, but he may have been writing his intentions down as a spur, the first step toward realizing yet another epic river voyage. Once the words had been written, there was no turning back. No sooner did he arrive home in Portland after the Yukon trip than he laid out a route for running the Mackenzie: launch on the Clearwater River at Waterways, north of Edmonton, Alberta, in Canada, and float down the Clearwater to the Athabaska River onto Lake Athabaska; then across the southern tip of the lake to the headwaters of Slave River, which emptied into Great Slave Lake; at the southern end of the lake, the Mackenzie River begins its thousand-mile run to the Arctic Ocean. The total distance would be roughly 3,500 miles.

In July 1789 explorer Alexander Mackenzie, on behalf of the North West Company, set out on the river the aboriginal people called Deh Cho (Big River) in hopes that it would prove an efficient water highway to transport furs and goods from the interior to the Pacific Ocean. Instead of voyaging in a westerly direction, the river ran north, debouching into the

Arctic Ocean. At some point on the journey Mackenzie realized that he would never reach the Pacific, and he came to call the Deh Cho the "River Disappointment." By 1825 the explorer's name had become the river's common appellation.

Burg had already forgotten the scolding he had given himself on the Yukon about taking on more than he could shoulder. His plan expanded: after running the Mackenzie River in his canoe, he would hike west over the Davidson Mountain Range into the Yukon Territory. Then he would float down the little-traveled Bell and Porcupine Rivers in a small rubber raft to the Yukon River, where he would board a paddle wheeler traveling upriver to Whitehorse. With the demand for adventure narratives as strong as ever, the chief editor at *National Geographic* gave his blessing to the project. Burg decided to film portions of his voyage. In Portland he rented a Graflex camera and Debrie motion-picture camera and purchased two-thousand feet of motion-picture film. His growing reputation would allow him to sell the rights as well as use the film and photographs in any future speaking engagements.

In June 1929 he landed in Edmonton to prepare for the voyage. He purchased enough supplies for six weeks. His most important purchases, however, were two boats. To carry him the length of the Mackenzie, Burg purchased a new eighteen-foot, ninety-pound, wood-and-canvas Prospector canoe made by the Chestnut Canoe Company and christened it *Song o' the Winds*. The Prospector, designed to fill the gap between the company's Cruiser line (fast and light, but it did not carry sufficient gear for a lengthy trip) and the Freighter (stable but slow and difficult to portage), quickly became a best seller. The canoe was aesthetically pleasing yet rugged enough to withstand the hardships a wilderness river imposed. Able to carry a heavy load, the canoe was maneuverable on rivers as well as lakes and light enough to portage. To achieve these multiple effects, the Prospector was designed with a broad beam (thirty-six to thirty-eight inches), extra depth (fifteen to sixteen inches) at the center of the canoe, a rockered bow and stern, and a round-bottomed hull. It was available in double-ended or transom-stern models to mount a motor. The brochure boasted that it could "run the meanest rapids."

To cross over the Davidson Range and run Bell and Porcupine Rivers, Burg needed something sturdy, compact, and lightweight. He purchased a Sevylor raft, six feet in length and weighing twelve pounds. The raft came with jointed oars that could be broken down and carried in a pack. One newspaper account described it as "similar to the one carried on the Byrd trans-Atlantic flight." The light weight, however, suggests that the rubber material was not as sturdy as the material used for survival rafts by the US Navy. Nevertheless, Burg determined it sufficient for a short river voyage.

In what may have been a burst of intemperate enthusiasm, he had invited Professor George Rebec, head of the philosophy department at the University of Oregon, along on the voyage. He wrote: "I greatly admire Professor Rebec for he is a man of learning and character." The academic had shown a keen interest in Burg's previous adventures, inviting him to dinner at his home, where he questioned Burg about the details of past voyages. Learning of his intention to run the Mackenzie, Rebec expressed interest in coming along. From the start, though, Burg fretted over his choice of companions. Rebec was a sharp departure from the kind of men—Hill, Knudsen, Mullins, even Fogleberry—he had previously voyaged with on the Columbia and Snake Rivers. All had been seasoned sea- or rivermen, relatively young and able to look after themselves.

The sixty-six-year-old Rebec was the quintessential armchair adventurer: strong in knowledge and opinion but short on experience and know-how. He had never camped out much less handled a boat. He also suffered a heart condition. Faculty members had tried to dissuade their department head from making the voyage and failed. Rebec's wife told Burg that her husband had dreamed of an adventure like this all his life. He contributed four hundred dollars (about five thousand dollars today) toward the voyage. What kind of agreement the two men reached remains unclear. Rebec's behavior on the river suggested that he had purchased Burg's services as a guide. Burg's diary comments indicate that he had either misread the nature of their relationship or underestimated Rebec's needs, or both.

On June 16, Rebec arrived in Edmonton from New Orleans. Tired and anxious, the professor immediately attempted to assert himself in the unfamiliar situation, insisting on a strict time schedule once on the river. Burg, knowing the impossibility of such a request, quietly ignored him. Three days later they reached Waterways, the terminus of the Canadian-Pacific Railroad. A light rain fell as the two men unloaded *Song o' the Winds* and their outfit. Late on the afternoon of June 20, the pair pushed off from shore. The rain fell steadily now, tap-tapping the canvas covers on the bow and stern. Burg took to the oars. The steady pull of the river beneath the hull of the boat soothed him: he was home, once again. The river was shallower than he had imagined. He maneuvered his way down narrow channels, bumping over gravel bars and skirting sweepers. For the time being, nothing could dampen his spirits. Even Rebec, nestled beneath the canvas with only his face showing, could not resist the enchantment of beginning a voyage down an unknown river.

That evening they reached the town of McMurray. Burg met a mining entrepreneur named Howells who was leading a party of four young miners bound for the Taltson River. Howells was apprehensive. Two days earlier the party had swamped then capsized their two canoes (which were tied together) on the Clearwater River. The young men had not responded well. Which group needed the other more remains unknown. Burg and Howells struck an agreement to travel together as far as Great Slave Lake. The flotilla now consisted of Howells's skiff *Dorothy* (with a motor) and three canoes.

Squalls plagued the seventeen-mile run to the Tar Island shipyard the next day. Here the steamboats that plied the Athabaska and Slave Lakes during the summer season laid up for the winter. Nineteen-year-old Mildred, the only white girl on the lower Athabaska, was the sole caretaker of the boatyard in her father's absence. The no-nonsense young woman put the younger men to work at various jobs in exchange for river hospitality—food and shelter. She took an immediate liking to Burg. She told his fortune, insisting a tall, dark woman was waiting for him. That evening he accompanied Mildred on a stroll down the beach. "A more active girl I've seldom seen," he later wrote.

The next morning the *Dorothy,* towing the three canoes, headed downriver. The weather was cold and miserable, the scenery of low, rolling hills washed in a dreary gray cast. Thick stands of spruce and birch trees crowded the banks; dirty, misshapen chunks of ice choked the side creeks. Burg passed the time writing in his diary, a brief luxury. The rain came in torrents. By evening everyone was soaked and shivering, except for Rebec, who had found cover beneath the canvas. At a deserted trapper's cabin, the party stopped for the night. Rebec was annoyed. Burg described the situation in his diary:

> The fellows were wet all through, and wanted to stop, but the Doctor, thinking of the long distance yet to be crossed, blew up, quoted

statistics and schedules until Howells promised to get us into Resolution by July 1st. He [Rebec] ended his flight by saying he planned
things, that he was a scientist and not a tramp. He had sunk $400. into
the voyage, and now he expected me to make a marathon out of it
to get him back in the time he had anticipated. . . . Of course I felt
complimented by his trust in coming with me, nevertheless, I realized
all too clearly that I was cramping my summer and running into extra
expense for a fastidious partner, a man whom I must watch, neces-
sitating limitation of the runs to ensure against the cold.

Though loathe to admit it so early in the trip, Burg realized he had made a
poor choice of companions. The next morning a heavy mist hung over the
Athabaska, making navigation touch and go. An air of mystery, even anxiety,
enveloped the flotilla as it drifted downriver. None of the young miners
knew how to read water. The two young men who had the most river sense
ignored Burg's advice. The boats ran aground frequently, forcing the men into
the chilly water. After bragging to the boys of his experience on the Mississippi River as a cub pilot the summer of 1922, Burg was chagrined when he
ran upon a bar and stuck fast.

Rebec's mood eventually lightened. He told cowboy stories and joked
with the younger men. His role as academic authority secure, he gave lectures
on the soil and geography of the river and life at Cambridge and Oxford.
With the pecking order established, the voyagers got along well. On June 27
the flotilla arrived at the delta leading into Lake Athabaska. They motored
tentatively through the maze of muddy, snag-ridden channels only to get lost
and run aground. Local fishermen pulled them off the sandbar and pointed
them toward the Goose Island channel, which fed into the lake. Claiming he
wanted to avoid the squalls and winds that can plague afternoon lake travel,
Burg set out in *Song o' the Winds*. More likely, he wanted time alone.

Avoiding open stretches of water, he aimed for points of land or hugged
the shoreline whenever possible. He slipped in and out of the lee of islands.
When the weather deteriorated, he simply pulled over, tied up to a snag,
and waited. Rowing in the foul weather of the Yukon delta had taught
him valuable lessons. By late afternoon he made a dash for Chipewyan.

Professor George Rebec and Burg met at the University of Oregon when Burg was a student.

"Chipewyan reminds one of South Sea Island villages," he wrote of his arrival. "Harbor landlocked by islands and white sandy beach, with white-washed houses set among the trees that resemble palms." Dizzy from lack of sleep, he curled up in his boat to nap. Late that evening, Howells, Rebec, and the four miners arrived.

They dallied for a day before setting off on the next leg of their voyage for Fitzgerald. By late afternoon they reached the Slave River—wide, sluggish, and straight. On July 2, Rebec sighted the red-roofed cabins in Fitzgerald. They camped at the lower end of town and spent most of the day resting. Initially, Burg decided to portage the sixteen-mile stretch of river below Fitzgerald by truck. The next day he changed his mind, deciding to line and run the rapids. He gave no explanation for his change of heart. Stan, one of the young miners, who regularly ignored Burg's advice, pleaded to join him.

Then Dan, a clerk at the Hudson's Bay Company store in Fitzgerald, asked to tag along. Rebec, Howells, and the rest of the men agreed to meet them downstream. Burg wrote an account of the run:

> Paddling across the mouth of Dog River, we came to our first rapids. Dan took the camera and prepared to snap us lining the canoe over the first fall. Stan's feet skidded on a slippery rock and he flew into the air and landed with a great splash in the mud. I shouted excitedly for Dan to snap the shutter, but Dan was too much of a gentleman to embarrass Stan. A short distance below we had two long carrying places, the second strewn with broken sweeps and decayed rollers, remnants of the Hudson's Bay scow brigades. Mosquitoes with the spirit of a civic welcoming committee clouded the air along the trail and used our necks for landing fields until we launched the canoe below a beautiful basin, into which cataracts poured from several ravines. In three hours we had worked our way to the foot of an island and were trapped by falls. I scouted across the mossy wooded island, seeking another passage. Neither of my two companions had ever ridden such wild water as raged below the island. It was with considerable anxiety that I steered the canoe into the breakers that swept us rapidly toward the brink of a rocky 20-foot drop. In the middle of the river a maelstrom twisted our craft with a suddenness that threw the starboard gunnel beneath the water. The sluggishness of the half-swamped canoe alarmed me. Only the plucky paddling of my comrades saved us from being dashed to the bottom of the falls. We reached a rock island in the nick of time, where two sober-faced pelicans sat watching our performance. Here we camped. . . . the last of our provisions went for supper so that we had nothing left for breakfast. At the Mountain (Rapids) portage, we dragged the canoe over a high hill where Mackenzie had counted off 335 paces. Below Mountain Rapids, with Fort Smith in sight, we came to the Rapids of the Drowned. In 1786 five men and two canoes were lost here while on their way to establish Fort Resolution for Peter Pond. Although the last portage, more than 500 paces long, was on the opposite side of the river, we took the wrong side, as usual, and performed a goat act with the canoe along the steeply

wooded bank, arriving at Fort Smith 28 hours after leaving Fitzgerald. The Mounted Police had sent a canoe upriver to look for us.

The next few days brought more woe than joy for the voyagers. The weather was uniformly miserable. The mosquitoes made stops short and hellish. The meals were unfailingly the same and gradually the portions came up distressingly short, especially for Howells and the young miners. Empty stomachs led to grumbling. Howells bargained for a portion of Burg's and Rebec's provisions, promising to repay them at Resolution. Rebec chafed at the request but ultimately agreed. Whatever goodwill that existed between the two parties was strained. The professor continued to annoy Burg. He did not help with meals, further evidence that the two men had different understandings of their roles. At night Rebec continuously fed the campfire with logs, creating a blazing inferno. Despite his insistence on keeping a schedule, he stood by in the morning while Burg packed up and stowed the gear in the canoe.

The group patched up their differences the night before arriving at Resolution. They were parting ways and now could afford to be generous. "The men had a change of heart," Burg wrote. "They sat together on the bank of the river drinking the last of the coffee and chatting. The crisis had passed. Howells insisted that Rebec give another lecture, something with a 'biblical flavor.'" On July 9 the party landed at Resolution on the shores of Great Slave Lake. The next day Howells and his men departed for the Taltson River drainage. Burg and Rebec remained behind, preparing for the next leg of their voyage. Burg had hatched a scheme. He told his companion that the run across windswept Great Slave Lake in the heavily loaded canoe would be long and perhaps dangerous. He suggested that the professor lay over for a few days, and then book passage aboard one of the local launches to Providence, where they would rendezvous. Rebec embraced the idea immediately and took a room in the local hotel.

Burg set off alone, tracing the southern shoreline of the lake. Free of worry and his demanding passenger, he hoped to make the ninety-mile run to Hay River in two, at the most, three days. The vastness of the misshapen lake astounded him. Although pleased to be on his own at last, he experienced a peculiar physical sensation of his own insignificance. He adhered to the usual antidote: rowing steadily, counting his oar strokes, or breaking into song. By noon, high winds from the northeast produced heavy swells, forcing him to take refuge on shore. He napped in his canoe, then cooked dinner. By evening the winds had died down. He rowed into the northern summer night, arriving at another protected cove around 3:00 AM. Exhausted, he crawled into his sleeping bag in the bottom of the canoe and tried to sleep. Despite the netting, the mosquitoes left him miserable. He had little choice but to continue rowing.

Over the next two days the sun came out and stayed; breezes replaced the winds. The swells ran smooth, green and glassy. Burg cast a line overboard and trolled for whitefish. With nearly twenty house of daylight, he drifted, nodding off occasionally, as if in a dreamscape. After rowing for the better part of an entire day, he arrived at the mouth of the Hay River in the dawn hours of July 14. He lingered, talking with locals and taking notes before setting out for Providence, where he arrived four days later. Rebec was waiting, rested and eager to proceed.

The next morning they pushed off from shore. As the bells of the mission at Providence broke the silence, Rebec asked Burg to stop rowing so they might listen to the sound echo across the water. A haze hung over the points of lands and the few small islands, the residue of inland forest fires. The Arctic Ocean was 925 miles away. It was a fine day for rowing, except for the black flies that swarmed in Burg's mouth, ears, and eyes. At lunch Rebec swallowed a bite of his sandwich and a black fly or two. Without skipping a beat, he turned to Burg and said, "He was a stranger, and I took him in." They stopped for a bath and a nap. That evening they camped on a rocky point near an abandoned Indian camp and ate spuds, sausages, and sea biscuits for supper. Both men agreed it was one of their finest days yet.

On July 22 they reached the fast water of the Mackenzie River. With current and daylight stretching into the late hours, Burg made good time, rowing for nearly thirteen hours. The temperature, in the high sixties, remained pleasant, with light rainfall. At camp that evening, he noticed that Rebec, though trying to be cheerful, looked pale and drawn. Burg set up the tent and helped the older man inside, then prepared soup. The professor had contracted a strain of influenza, possibly a mild case of pneumonia. Anxious about Rebec's health, Burg decided to make a run for Simpson, eighty miles downriver. The next morning he navigated Head-of-the-Line, a narrow corridor of fast, unpredictable water, without incident. Rebec dozed, bundled up in his sleeping bag beneath a canvas tarp. They swept by the mouths of the Jean Marie, Spence, and Rabbitskin Rivers.

The fair weather faded, and squalls blew in. On the evening of July 23, they took a tow from a Royal Canadian Mountie into Simpson, where they remained for the next few days while Rebec recuperated. At some point he broached the subject of returning home early. His illness, he felt, had slowed the pace, making it impossible to complete the journey and still have enough time to get back to his duties at the University of Oregon. He may have also been seeking an honorable retreat from the unanticipated hardships of voyaging. Burg did not disagree. Norman, three hundred miles downriver, would be the most convenient location to catch a paddle wheeler to carry Rebec to Providence, where he could arrange transportation home.

On July 27 the two voyagers departed Simpson. Although Rebec felt marginally better, his condition wavered, and the listlessness made Burg uneasy. In a brief bout of self-pity, he grumbled in his diary: "Will be happy to reach the mouth of the Mackenzie. Wish for a rest at the oars so I could observe and write. Doctor's illness cramps the purpose of my mission." Burg was not feeling well himself. He began to suffer headaches and a general rundown feeling. He also experienced lower back pains, a familiar malady to boatmen rowing from a fixed seat. Midway through the run to Wrigley, he came down with more flu-like symptoms. That night he pitched the tent and put himself to bed without eating. Burg was exhausted. High wind and steady rain combined with their poor condition pinned the two voyagers down for another day. After much effort they arrived in Wrigley. It had taken Burg nearly a week to cover the 150 miles.

Wrigley was desolate, an unwelcoming river town on the verge of collapse. After a day of rest, they departed at 3:00 AM to the sound of howling dogs and a rising sun that set the fireweed aglow, an eerily beautiful scene. A blanket of white mist rose off the river. As the sun rose, the temperature warmed. Rebec napped, Burg rowed. By noon he hoisted sail to catch a following wind. At the mouth of Blackwater River, they ate lunch. Rebec, relaxed and feeling better, reconsidered his decision to leave early, suggesting that he accompany Burg farther downriver. The latter resisted the overture. Time was running short. If he intended to hike over the Davidson Range into the Yukon basin and float the Bell and Porcupine Rivers before the weather turned, he could not afford any more delays. Late on the afternoon of August 3, they arrived in Norman. After a good-natured argument over campsites, they settled on a sandy beach near town. It was their last camp and now Rebec helped Burg "make it as pretty as possible" by clearing away rocks and driftwood. Then the professor scrubbed and washed his clothes in a wooden tub he had found on the beach. They cooked a meal together. Burg had already decided to lay over until Rebec was safely aboard the *Distributor,* the sternwheeler that would carry him upriver.

The next morning brought a surprise. "A large double-ended lifeboat towing two canoes loaded with traps and three silent dogs approached our beach," wrote Burg. The pilot stepped ashore, hitched his lifeboat to a snag, tethered the three dogs, and then, without breaking stride, curled up on the sand in a tattered blanket and went to sleep. When the river voyager awoke hours later, he introduced himself: Hans Roderick. After a long and fruitless struggle as a farmer, Roderick had abandoned his wheat farm on the Peace River for a life of roving along the Mackenzie River. He bragged that he ate

the same food he fed his dogs—Mutt, Brandy, and Sourdough—except for the occasional handful of raisins. He sustained himself by hunting, trapping, and fishing.

That evening as Rebec prepared to board the *Distributor,* teacher and student felt the sting of departure. The voyage had altered their relationship, certainly changed the way they saw one another. Nevertheless, Rebec told Burg how much he enjoyed the trip and thanked him for his effort. Burg replied that they had done well under trying circumstances. "He is much at

Trapper during summer prepares for the winter trap line and deep snows. (Amos Burg photo, 1929.)

home in the world of books," wrote Burg, reflecting on Rebec, "but too much inclined to let little things disturb him in the outer world." As the *Distributor* pulled away from shore, Burg waved goodbye to Rebec, who lingered on deck until his companion was a distant figure on the beach. Both men were relieved, though for different reasons.

Meanwhile, Roderick and Burg had taken the measure of one another and decided to voyage together to Arctic Red River, 385 miles downstream. After a wet, wind-driven night, they loaded their gear the next morning. Burg worked in his usual tidy, methodical fashion, while Roderick threw his kit into the bottom of the lifeboat haphazardly. "Hans is like the country," wrote Burg. "He believes in doing things, and gets them done in a large, rough way." The two voyagers could not have been more different. Under motor, Roderick steered downriver towing *Song o' the Winds*. Burg, seated in the canoe, took advantage of the unusual opportunity to enjoy the scenery and write in his diary. The winds were fair, the sun warm enough to soften his impressions of the seemingly limitless landscape.

The daily demands of river voyaging shaped Burg's writing habits. He often wrote at length in the early morning hours or late at night buried in his sleeping bag. There was little privacy in the conventional sense. His river-flavored style of writing alternated between lengthy descriptions of a scene or anecdote and short, bulleted observations. Occasionally he wrote complete sentences. Like many outdoor writers, he was literally "taking notes" and recording immediate sensations as opposed to writing narratives. Thus a brief one-sentence description of the weather or river could be followed by a peevish declaration of irritability followed by a series of observations on the dietary habits of the old sourdoughs followed by a single isolated historical fact. As the thoughts and ideas cascaded and the inspiration ebbed and flowed, Burg grabbed what he could, lest he forget something. His purpose in keeping a river diary was straightforward: to gather as much information as possible as well as his own personal impressions for the book he one day hoped to write and his *National Geographic* article.

Above Good Hope, the Mackenzie River narrows, pushing its way through seven miles of 150-foot white limestone walls. Midway in the canyon was Ramparts Rapid, a cataract thought to be the most hazardous on the river. Burg photographed Roderick's run from shore and later wrote:

Hans took a glance at the rapid, came back, and said not so bad. He lashed his dogs close to the canoe seats so they could not jump about too much, and swung into the current. The dogs, hearing the roar of the rapids, crouched low in the boat and whimpered. The light was poor for pictures, but I sat down on the point to get something. "Poor Hans," I thought, "and his poor dogs." I had forgotten that Hans was a Viking. With a canoe in each hand, and the tiller between his knees, Hans crowded his power [revved the motor] and shot through close to the line of breakers, his heavily laden lifeboat giving a great leap as it struck the swell above the reef. It was not until I descended that I appreciated his skillful feat in keeping the canoes upright.

On August 15, as Burg and Roderick passed Thunder River, the outboard motor on the lifeboat broke down, forcing them to row to Arctic Red River, their final destination. This was no easy task given the size of Roderick's boat, three barking dogs, and two canoes in tow. Late in the afternoon of the next day they arrived exhausted at the trading post village. Burg rose early the next morning. While Roderick slept, Burg built a fire and made pancakes for his companion. The two voyagers sat on the riverbank side by side, drinking tea and reminiscing over the past ten days. Roderick gave Burg a batch of white fish for his evening meal. He also paid Burg the highest of compliments: an offer to go "adventuring" with him anytime, anywhere. The two men shook hands. Burg set off rowing downriver for Fort McPherson. Roderick made ready to head into the mountains above Arctic Red River to trap.

On his own, halfway to McPherson, Burg noticed that the forest along shore was replaced by thick stands of scruffy willow and alder. The bare expanse of the Mackenzie delta, with its numerous channels and islands, stretched into the distance. Late in the afternoon, he peered into the bag of grub that Roderick had prepared and found two rolls of butter, two cans of baking powder, two boxes of dried apples, two cans of meatballs, a few oranges, and a can of jam. Already he missed his river companion. Nearing the mouth of the Peel River, he stopped rowing and let *Song o' the Winds* drift. Burg had achieved another one of his goals: a transit of the Mackenzie River. Now he had run five major river systems (some more than once)—

the Yellowstone-Missouri-Mississippi (1922), the Columbia (1924–25), the Snake (1925), and the Yukon (1928)—in the past seven years. "This was a big moment for me," he wrote. "There was no life to be seen—only that life I had come to know in the wind that chilled me and in the sun that gave me warmth. In the silence I could hear my watch ticking."

Burg headed up the narrow Peel River to Fort McPherson, his jumping-off point. It was slowgoing against the current, but he was thankful for small mercies: he encountered no wind. He had been at the oars for nearly sixteen hours before stopping to camp below McPherson. The next morning he walked into the village, formerly the Peel River Trading Post, opened in 1840 by John Bell, fur trader and explorer for the Hudson's Bay Company. At the time it was the most northerly of the company's posts. In 1845, Bell had crossed the Davidson Mountains into the Yukon watershed and traveled down the Rat River (later named the Bell) to its confluence with the Porcupine River. That same year he followed the Porcupine to its confluence with the Yukon, being the first European to do so.

Burg had two main tasks at McPherson: to sell *Song o' the Winds* (which was too large to portage over the mountains) and to engage the services of a reliable guide. He sold the canoe to William Firth for seventy-five dollars. Immediately after, he felt the trader had gotten the better of him. Firth did suggest a guide for Burg: Abraham Francis, a Loucheaux Indian. After a meeting, Burg agreed to pay Francis six dollars a day, with fifty cents each for the dogs plus their food. The guide thought they could cross the hundred-mile route over the Davidson Range in five days, if all went well. At noon on August 22 the two men set out in a rainstorm. Francis's dogs carried their provisions as well as Burg's gear and the small inflatable raft. The slippery trail zigzagged through the hummocks and across deep streams.

When they reached camp that afternoon, Burg was soaking wet and hobbling in pain. His right knee, injured years ago in a shipboard accident, was swollen and sore. For the next two days he was forced to walk stiff-legged. He fell behind his guide and occasionally lost his way. Rain turned to sleet and hail. Burg slipped hip-deep into the icy water. His raingear and clothing froze. As the temperature dropped at night, a blazing campfire offered temporary comfort. They spent two more days ascending the eastern flank of the Davidson Mountains. By now the soreness in Burg's knee had become severe.

He soldiered on, snatching handfuls of wild blueberries—a small joy on an arduous climb. Of the physical pain, he wrote:

> I was not without fear of being trapped in this mountain fastness if my leg went bad. It was a dismal outlook for me, in a way, for through the night I suffered great pain. In another way, I am in great spirits: for the ground that we have covered; for having attempted that which I set out to do. (Rather surprised at the driving urge in me that would not let me weaken at any cost.) I would rather perish in McDougall Pass on my way to Bell [River] than turn back. Those are not brave words, now, for I cannot turn back.

On the evening of August 25 they arrived at the summit on McDougall Pass. They ate what Burg described as "a glorious dinner around the campfire with exceptional scenery." Francis pointed west toward the Bell River drainage and the trail descending the mountainside. That night he read from the Bible and offered a prayer of thanks for their success. Burg wrote that he was not much on praying and yet "he did see fit to express the hope that he could make La Pierre House."

The next evening the two rendezvoused with Francis's friends John Martin, Alfred Charley, and their families on an island camp in the middle of a fast-moving creek down the valley. Watching the Native American families, Burg suffered a bout of envy and loneliness. The natural, effortless hospitality of his hosts intrigued him. The adults and older children fussed over the youngsters. They laughed and told funny stories and that evening they sang church hymns, their voices mingling with the gurgle of the mountain stream. It was at times too good to be true. "To be with John Martin and his wilderness friends in this glen of the Rockies north of the Arctic Circle," he wrote, "with their unselfishness and good will toward one another, was more like attending a wilderness shrine or being in the Garden of Eden before the apple got ripe."

Burg spent another festive evening with the two families. The men and women bantered in Loucheaux, laughing at Burg's jointed oars, rubber raft, camera antics, and banged-up knee. Francis suggested that Burg would make a good husband for Mary, John Martin's older daughter. Everyone thought the suggestion hilarious, except Mary. John Martin told Burg that his children became sick and weak when they ate the white man's food in the village. In the mountains they ate caribou and remained strong and active. Anxious to return to his own family, Francis suggested that Alfred Charley guide Burg down the mountain to the Bell River. Burg agreed, and within two days he and Charley reached the river and the deserted compound of La Pierre House, the trading post. Charley gazed nervously as Burg unpacked his small rubber boat, realizing perhaps for the first time that the white man intended to take the small boat down the Bell and Porcupine. Burg paid Charley sixteen dollars for his service and they parted ways.

A fine mist hung over the Bell as Burg rowed downstream on the morning of August 31. The steep, muddy banks rose as high as fifteen feet. Leaden skies and the overhanging sweepers gave the narrow corridor a gloomy feel. The current was paltry, interrupted by short patches of fast water tumbling over shallow gravel bars. The confluence with the Porcupine River lay fifty miles away. Burg wrote that his craft—made by the Sevylor Company—handled better than he expected. At the time the company made small, lightweight rafts for modest recreational use. The flimsy materials and construction of the boat concerned him. The rubber floor of the raft was thin and subject to rips and tears if he ran upon a snag or gravel bar. After a few hours of rowing, he noticed that his port oarlock (made of vulcanized rubber) was wearing thin. Hatchet close at hand, he ran down whichever side of the river had the largest stand of trees. He reasoned that if he had to abandon the rubber craft, he wanted to be near a source of wood to fashion a raft.

In his diary Burg noted the impact of the "profound silence of the river" and that he "lost track of time," which disturbed him. When he reached the confluence with the Porcupine, a day later than expected, he was relieved by the open space—a sweeping panorama of mountains, plateaus, and river valleys. He looked back to the snow-covered peaks of the Davidson Mountains and felt fortunate to be on the final leg of his long voyage: Fort Yukon, his final destination. From its headwaters in the Richardson and Ogilvie Mountains, the Porcupine curls northwest to Old Crow before bending in a southwestern route to its confluence with the Yukon River. There is little or no glacial meltwater feeding the river. Runoff, combined with annual precipitation, is highest in June and July. The Porcupine is roughly a hundred yards wide below the confluence and under normal conditions might be termed a flat-water river. The few Class I rapids occurred in shallow stretches of the river. But the river can present other problems to voyagers in small craft. Fierce upstream winds can generate swells as high as three feet. Precipitation in the high country can cause the river to rise rapidly with little warning, turning the modest current into fast water.

Burg was elated as he rowed down the Porcupine, though. "It was like taking a drink," he scribbled in his diary. The current was swifter than the Bell. The autumn colors—yellows, greens, reds, oranges—of the dense stands of cottonwood, poplar, aspen, and paper birch trees lit up the shoreline. Even a brief downpour did not dampen his spirits. After three hours of rowing, he heard the unexpected sound of a launch coming upstream. It had been two weeks since he left Alfred Charley at the head of the Bell River. Now his eagerness to meet another human being surprised him. The pilot stopped and chatted, then handed Burg a large caribou steak.

Over the next two days, Burg toiled against chilly upstream winds and choppy waves. The chronic pain of his knee injury quieted, only to be replaced by sore hands and an aching back. At times the wind blew so fiercely that the rubber raft stalled or was pushed back upstream. On the afternoon of September 4, he approached Old Crow on the Porcupine River. Local dogs yelped, pacing the shoreline. A Native man pointed at the lone voyager in the strange little boat and waved. By the time Burg reached shore, the village residents, nearly all Native, had lined up to greet him. A police constable escorted him to the home of Corporal Thornthwaite, head of the Royal Mounties, and his wife. Burg was delighted to learn that Mrs. Thornthwaite had discovered fifty-five different varieties of flowers in the area. She had also kept twenty bird's nests under observation in an attempt to track different species. In a moment of candor, she told Burg that she would not know what do if she had to go back to Saint Louis, her hometown.

Burg spent the next four days enjoying the Thornthwaites' hospitality. His rubber raft was the subject of much inspection and sharp humor by local inhabitants. When he persuaded one Native boy to go for a ride in the rubber boat, the rest of the children were beside themselves. As he photographed the Native children, however, Burg was disheartened. He wrote of their schooling:

This village offers a good example of children sent out to Carcross [located near Bennet Lake in the Yukon Territory of Canada] to school. Taken when they are very young. They are taught by teachers, usually from the states, who have never seen an Indian before and are sloppily inaccurate in all things relative to Indian tradition and culture. They think that learning the Bible and A.B.C.'s is the best thing that can happen to any Indian, but this is not a total preparation for life in a cabin or tent on the Porcupine. They come back with a smattering of poor English, hardly able to understand their own families, and certainly alien to them in habits of living. They return from a systemized school where everything is provided for them to filth, squalor, and uncertainty. The schools educate them away from the lives they are to lead, and seek to inculcate more of the white man's point of view.

On the evening of September 7, Burg boarded a launch bound for Fort Yukon, 285 miles downriver. Another shortcut. Upon reaching Fort Yukon, he boarded the last steamer of the season headed up the Yukon River to Whitehorse before the ice-up. He worked unloading coal at Whitehorse, then caught the Canadian Pacific Railroad train over White Pass to Skagway, where he boarded the steamer *Princess Louise* for Seattle. Three days later, Burg arrived in Portland, where good news awaited him. A telegram from the National Geographic Society asked him to give a lecture on his Yukon voyage of the previous year to members at the Washington Auditorium in Washington, D.C., the following spring. It was an unexpected surprise and a major breakthrough. At the time, he would be the youngest presenter in the National Geographic Society's history.

Burg spent the winter of 1929–30 working on his lecture. For years he had given talks around Portland and had proven a natural talent. The stakes, however, had risen: he was not addressing a local audience but the educated and well-heeled elite of the East Coast. He resumed his extensive research on the Yukon River and reviewed his pages of notes, then set out to write a combination lecture and script, the latter to narrate the film. He rented an Ediphone to practice his delivery, attempting to identify what he considered weaknesses in his speaking style. He noted many "speech defects" but thought his humor and enthusiasm would make up for his vocal failings. To sharpen his presentation, he made a handful of appearances in Portland. He also began preparatory work on his second article for the *National Geographic,* tentatively titled "On the Mackenzie Trail to the Polar Sea."

On March 12, Burg presented his "Romance of the Yukon Trail" lecture to an audience of four thousand at the Washington Auditorium. His timing, meticulous planning, and attention to detail paid off, but it was his easy manner and self-effacing humor that quickly won the audience over. Throughout the presentation, he received repeated applause. When stalwart *National Geographic* writers like Frederick Simpich, Maynard Owen Williams, and W. Robert Moore posed questions, he handled them with ease. National Geographic paid Burg the standard fee of $250 (approximately three thousand in today's dollars), plus a bonus.

Perhaps more important, Burg had been befriended by influential people who recognized his talents. Gilbert Grosvenor, president of the National Geographic Society, wrote to James "Bim" Pond, owner of the prestigious Pond Bureau: "It is a pleasure to tell you how much the Washington members of the National Geographic Society enjoyed Amos Burg's motion pictures taken on his canoe trips in the Northwest. His film is of excellent interest and of fine technical quality. It has been well edited and arranged to show its beautiful subjects in a most dramatic style. The Society's audience showed its keen appreciation of this film by repeated applause." On the strength of Grosvenor's recommendation, Pond booked Burg for fifty speaking engagements on next season's East Coast winter lecture circuit. The agency, which handled only the most prominent authors, scientists, and explorers of the day, billed Burg "their latest sensation."

PART II

BEYOND THE
HORIZON

(1930–1949)

Chapter 5

RISING STAR,
EXOTIC CLIMES

In the winter of 1930–31, Burg's name was floated for membership in the prestigious Explorers Club by Bim Pond, owner of the Pond Bureau in New York, and Vilhjalmur Stefansson, the Canadian Arctic explorer, ethnologist, and author. When asked to complete an application, an astonished Burg replied immediately. The elite association, formed in 1904 by a group of Arctic explorers, "sought men who have engaged in exploration, or who have added to the geographical knowledge of the world; travelers who have done some distinctive work, and who have added to the world's store of knowledge concerning the countries they have visited, as for instance, by the publication of a notable book or articles." On March 5, 1931, ethnologist Earl F. Hansen and the eccentrically named Seamus, Chief of Clannfhearghuis, proposed Burg for membership in the organization. Both men wrote flattering letters of recommendation. Hansen, who had traveled to Iceland as well as studied the indigenous tribes of Chile on numerous trips, thought Burg "a splendid chap, very well-liked, and with an impressive record." The Chief wrote: "He is in every way a proper person to uphold the honor and dignity of the Explorers Club and who should achieve new glories to add to its laurels."

A week later, Burg was elected to the club. He was quietly elated to have his name mentioned in the same company as the famous men, some of whom had been his boyhood heroes. Acceptance in the club signaled his arrival professionally, giving him legitimacy as well as access to individuals and organizations that might support future adventures. In the coming decades, the organization would provide inspiration, camaraderie, occasional sponsorship, and a home away from home for the peripatetic Burg. For more than a decade people in Portland had avidly followed his river adventures in *The Oregonian* and other local newspapers. Headlines read "Audience Thrilled by Amos Burg's Canoe Adventure," "Boy Travels 500 Miles in Small Canoe," and "Noted Explorer Will Appear Tonight." Burg had lectured regularly at local schools and service clubs. In early April 1931 eight hundred people crowded into Portland's Neighbors of Woodcraft auditorium to hear his illustrated lecture "The Voyage down the Yukon."

Professionally taken photo of Amos Burg, "adventurer and explorer"

As the film images flickered across the screen, Burg's smooth narration cast a storyteller's spell. He joked that he "always let his companions run the rapids while I operate the camera from the safe shore."

Immediately after his successful speaking engagement for the National Geographic Society at the Washington Auditorium, Burg had traveled to Edmonton, Alberta, to prepare for voyages on the Canoe and Columbia Rivers. His goal was to gather fresh material for his upcoming lecture series. He invited Frank Sparks, a former classmate of his at the University of Oregon, to accompany him. Hungry for adventure, Sparks agreed to pay a share of the trip cost. In early June they arrived at the Columbia Ice

Fields near Jasper Park by horse pack and began photographing and filming scenery and wildlife. A few days later, the filmmaker Jesse Sill appeared on the scene to help. Mentor and student had reached a comfortable business agreement: Burg could use the film in his lectures while Sill, who developed the footage, retained the rights. Sill returned to Portland with five thousand feet of film.

Burg and Sparks packed over to the headwaters of the 125-mile Canoe River near Mount Robson, the highest peak in the Canadian Rockies. They set off down the relatively untraveled river in *Song o' the Winds.* It was fast water—rocky, cold, and crowded with a thick canopy of trees and bushes. Their progress was agonizingly slow. Forced to portage three miles around an impassable section, they reached Boat Encampment, on the Big Bend reach of the Columbia River, exhausted. A trip that should have taken a few days lasted twice as long. After a brief respite, Burg and Sparks started down the river. Burg left no diary of the voyage, his third down the Columbia in five years. Weeks later, he and Sparks encountered the construction of the Rock Island Dam, the first dam to span the Columbia, twelve miles downstream from Wenatchee, Washington. By 1933 the hydroelectric project would be completed. At the same time, preparations for Bonneville Dam at Cascade Rapids, roughly three hundred miles downstream, were in full swing.

Burg and Sparks arrived in Portland in late July. Within a week Burg departed for Jackson Lake, Wyoming, for his second run down the Snake River. Whatever the reason, he did not invite Sparks, choosing to voyage alone in an eight-foot inflatable raft (likely a Sevylor). Easy to line or portage as well as maneuver in the rapids, the raft would have been inadequate to carry any significant amount of camera equipment. The memory of the difficulties he had encountered with *Song o' the Winds* five years earlier almost certainly influenced his decision to take the smaller craft. In Weiser, Idaho, Burg picked up Jack Fletcher, a well-to-do Portland businessman, who brought *Song o' the Winds,* Burg's camera equipment, and more provisions for the run through Hells Canyon. What is considered a "routine" river trip today was for Fletcher a voyage into remote, even hostile, terrain. By early October, the two men had returned to Portland. Fletcher now had bragging rights: he had traveled down the Snake with Amos Burg.

Burg's membership in the Explorers Club bore fruit almost immediately. Dr. William Beebe, the nationally known author, naturalist, and oceanographer, hired Burg as a staff photographer. Burg appears to have been in demand as a photographer: he had been offered positions on expeditions bound for Africa, Greenland, and the North Pole. He thought Beebe's offer the most attractive in terms of salary and publicity. Beebe required that those who worked for him give no interviews or write articles; he earned significant money writing and giving lectures and did not want any competition in the popular press. The conditions of employment gave Burg pause, but the opportunity was too great to ignore.

A year earlier, on June 6, 1930, Beebe and Otis Barton, the inventor of the bathysphere, had made history. After three unmanned test runs, the two men had squeezed into a five-foot-diameter steel ball and were lowered into the Atlantic Ocean off the Bermuda Islands. John Tee-Van, Beebe's assistant, attached an Explorers Club and New York Zoological flag to the hatch. It took twenty-five minutes to reach a depth of 803 feet (134 fathoms)—a world record at the time. They remained under water for a full five minutes before ascending. Four days later, Beebe and Barton descended to the unheard-of depth of 1,426 feet. Newspapers and newsreels across the country ran Beebe's scientific exploration as a front-page adventure story. Beebe did not mind. To attract patronage, he needed all the free publicity he could generate.

In late May of 1931, Burg arrived on Nonsuch Island, Beebe's haven and research center in the Bermuda Islands. Beebe's regulars had already arrived. Salaried John Tee-Van and Gloria Hollister were joined by Jocelyn Crane and other volunteers who came and went throughout the season. Burg's primary photographic duty was to film and photograph the specimens brought up from the sea depths, thus assuring Beebe of an accurate photographic record of the marine life under study. The work began early each morning before the wind rose. The trawler *Gladisfen* trolled the sea bottom a few miles south of Nonsuch Island with a large smelt net, for six hours at a stretch. Once the "catch" was laid out on the decks, the labor of sorting and identification began. Along with her volunteers, Hollister, who held a graduate degree in zoology, collected thousands of specimens.

Three weeks after his arrival on Nonsuch Island, Burg wrote to his parents: "It is a grand school for I am photographing from every angle almost everything from things so small we can scarcely see them to whales.... This is another world not yet explored, the life of small things that we do not see and I can go on with it after I leave here. While people become blasé in beholding the obvious things, this is the world that few have entered." Beebe's assistants also gathered samples from tide pools, which Burg would photograph in his lab. He described their technique: "The tide runs out and leaves these tide pools filled with fish. Tee-Van took a bucket of copper sulphate and sprinkled it in the water which drove the fish to one end of the pool where we scooped them out with nets, Sea snakes, octopuses and a score of highly colored fish are caught in this way and placed in buckets to be carried back to our aquariums on Nonsuch."

Burg discovered a kindred spirit in Tee-Van. Both men, roughly the same age, were intelligent, quick, dryly humorous, and endlessly curious. Like Burg, Tee-Van had not received a college degree, but the academic shortcoming had not stopped him from becoming a competent naturalist and an excellent organizer. Although the work often ran from dawn to dusk, many evenings on Nonsuch Island were given over to rest and relaxation. Around 5:00 in the afternoon, Burg often went for a swim in the warm water of the South Beach cove. In his free time he wandered along the sandy beaches and the trails that ran along the island cliffs. He discovered a rowboat and circumnavigated the island. Impromptu volleyball games and deck tennis broke up the routines. Beebe himself promoted and enjoyed the evening cocktail hour. Once a week Beebe gathered up his team and took them across Castle Harbor in the launch to the Saint George Hotel on Saint George Island for an evening of dinner and dancing. Burg attended but, as he had done aboard ship, abstained from drinking.

In early August, Burg had reason to celebrate. His article on the 1929 Mackenzie River voyage appeared in the latest issue of *National Geographic*. "On Mackenzie's Trail to the Polar Sea" ran nearly thirty pages, containing numerous photos. Burg's initial reaction to the piece was distaste, however, believing the editors had been heavy-handed in their editing. When Beebe unexpectedly congratulated Burg, he was surprised. At times Beebe had been critical of Burg's photographical work.

Despite his initial thrill with the work on Nonsuch Island, Burg was uncharacteristically bored by September. His duties and even the beauty of the island and its undersea life had become routine. He felt lonely, hemmed in. "I think the northwest is the most romantic of all regions on the face of the earth," he wrote. This turnabout may have had as much to do with tedious schedule as with being confined on a small island with people he had come to know perhaps too well. Burg used his diary to make observations he would never speak in public. He thought some of the young women insecure and disapproved of their fawning behavior around Beebe. He noted that the talented Gloria Hollister, Beebe's technical assistant, was unpopular with the other young women who may have envied her favored status. He found Hollister to be demanding, scornful of other's efforts, and constantly in search of the limelight. Burg had also grown ambivalent about Beebe, feeling he had failed to "stand up" to the famous man.

On September 23 he received a telegram from John Oliver La Gorce, vice president of the National Geographic Society and supervisor of the society's numerous expeditions. La Gorce asked Burg if he would consider joining a cruise aboard Julius Fleischmann's yacht *Camargo*, sailing around

Julius and Dorette Fleischmann with their children Dorette and Julius, Jr.

the world from the Bermuda Islands on October 9. The telegram laid out the key details: "nine months three hundred [per] month all expenses believe splendid opportunity Reply." Burg answered immediately, assuring La Gorce that he would be ready when the *Camargo* arrived. Thirty-one-year-old Julius Fleischmann was a well-known businessman, philanthropist, sportsman, patron of the arts, and at the time one of the richest men in the world. Decades earlier, his paternal grandfather had arrived penniless in the United States from Hungary and made a fortune in the yeast business. The rags-to-riches narrative had left a strong impression on Fleischmann.

Despite his high-society status, Fleischmann had a knack for putting people at ease. Fleischmann's nickname was "Junkie," and when asked about the undignified moniker, he explained that he "wandered around the world collecting junk for his museum in Cincinnati, Ohio." On October 7, 1931, the *Camargo* departed New York harbor on the first leg of what would become a yearlong, round-the-world voyage. Accompanying Fleischmann were his wife, Dorette, their two children, his mother, and his mother-in-law. The entourage included a ship's doctor (Dr. Bob Ransdall), a French au pair, and a teacher, charged with the care of the children. Before sailing, Fleischmann had invited two family friends, who had never met one another. Burg was to replace Edwin "Andy" Wisherd, the *National Geographic* photographer, who would remain aboard ship a few more weeks to bring Burg up to speed on the problems associated with developing film in a tropical climate. The *Camargo,* with a crew of thirty-nine, was under the command of Captain C. E. Small.

The *Camargo* reached the Bermuda Islands on October 10. Fleischmann and his entourage toured Hamilton Island by bike and carriage, stopping at the famous aquarium and the Crystal Caves. When they paid a visit to Nonsuch Island across the channel from Hamilton to pick up Burg, Beebe, realizing Fleischmann was a potential donor, took full advantage of the situation. He escorted the entourage around the island. As Burg boarded the *Camargo,* he noted that "he was the envy of the whole staff." It was easy to see why. The elegant, clipper-bowed yacht with the gleaming white hull—built only five years earlier by George Lawley and Sons of Neponset, Massachusetts, at a cost of $625,000 (eight million in today's dollars)—dazzled the eye. With a draft of eighteen feet, the *Camargo* dwarfed every ship it encountered in the South Pacific harbors. At the time the 225-foot luxury yacht was the most expensive in the world.

After his days as an able seaman in the foul-smelling forecastle of aging transport ships, Burg fought disbelief as he entered his large stateroom, "complete with private bath and sixteen faucets on the bathtub and lights with silk painted shades everywhere." Even more astonishing to Burg was his salary: three hundred dollars a month plus all expenses. In 1931 the average annual American income was between $1,300 and $1,500, and unemployment stood at 22 percent.

On the morning of October 12, the *Camargo* weighed anchor. Burg settled in, becoming familiar with shipboard routines and often wandering up to the bridge to chat with Captain Small and the officers. The four-day passage to Port Antonio, Jamaica, was plagued by squalls and rough seas. The less-experienced travelers became seasick and sought refuge to their staterooms. Burg began work with Andy Wisherd, whose assignment had been to keep a photographic record of the voyage for the Fleischmann family album. Fleischmann and *National Geographic* had worked out a copyright agreement. Fleischmann also wanted to incorporate photographs into a book he intended to write about the voyage.

Cameras available to Burg included the latest German-made Leicas (which had only been available since 1925) and a Debrie motion-picture camera. Wisherd instructed Burg on an improved version of the Finlay color photography process, which the *National Geographic* had recently adopted. The process, which could produce a photograph in natural color with a single exposure, had been developed by Englishman Clare Finlay in 1906 but abandoned after World War I. (The Finlay process would soon be replaced by the Agfacolor, then the Dufay process. The real breakthrough would come in 1936, when Eastman Kodak introduced Kodachrome film.)

In Port Antonio, Burg joined the Fleischmann group for a morning rafting trip down the Rio Grande River. It was a one-of-a-kind voyage. Three "captains" propelled their handmade craft down the shallow, eight-mile river with long bamboo poles, a form of punting. Three feet wide by thirty-five feet in length, the rafts were constructed of thick bamboo poles lashed together with strands of ropy vines soaked in water. Passengers sat on a rickety bench toward the stern of the craft as the men steered by striding back

Camargo, at the time the most expensive yacht in the world, at anchor in Hamilton Harbor, Bermuda Islands

and forth, using their poles as a means of propulsion. The fifteen rapids were riffles, more bark than bite. Nevertheless, one of the captains, who learned that Burg too had run rivers, announced that it took three years' apprenticeship to become a proficient boatman. Boatmen the world over like to brag.

By the end of October, the *Camargo* passed through the Panama Canal and entered the Pacific. Wisherd had departed, and Burg had assumed all photographic duties. The *Camargo* anchored in Wafer Bay of Cocos Island, four hundred miles off the coast of Costa Rica. Decades earlier, German treasure-hunter August Gissling had built a simple shack on the island and spent the rest of his life searching for the fabled Cocos Island fortune. Legend held that in the 1820s, Portuguese pirates had hidden the treasure on the island. Among yachtsmen, Gissling's search was almost as famous as the lost treasure. Twice before, Fleischmann had visited Cocos Island, exploring Gissling's derelict huts, fishing in the bountiful waters, bathing beneath the waterfalls, and watching the varied and colorful birdlife. This time he had returned to conduct an informal experiment: to see if domestic fowl could survive on the island.

Burg, Fleischmann, and Dr. Ransdell were astonished when they discovered fresh footprints on the beach. Inside one of the dilapidated huts they found rope, shredded clothing, and the kind of weather-beaten equipment one sees on a sailing ship. Someone had fashioned a makeshift stove of stone and two gasoline tins. Attached to a clothesline was a note:

> Gentlemen, We (3) of us have gone around on the south side of the island to get coconuts as our supply here is very limited. Please stop around to the south of Dampier head and we will see you and you can take us off as our boat is a total wreck. We have been here since April 15 and our supply of nuts and eats are very poor. Thanking you in advance for your kindness which will be very pleasing to us. We remain 3 hungry men trying to get to the Canal Zone. Please do not pass us up. We will return here about Nov. 4 or 5.

Back aboard the *Camargo,* Fleischmann passed the note on to Captain Small, who radioed the US Navy for assistance. Two days later the SS *Sacramento* arrived. After rendezvousing with the *Camargo* in Wafer Bay, both vessels cruised around the island to Dampier Head. A lookout immediately spotted three stick figures along the rocky shore. The captain of the *Sacramento* ordered a motor launch to pick up the survivors. The surf was running high and the rescue boat held off landing. The shipwrecked men could not wait a moment longer. One by one they plunged into the surf and swam toward the rescue boats. When lifted aboard, each of the emaciated men was wearing little more than a grin. Fleischmann invited the three men—Captain Paul Stachwick, age fifty-four; Gorden Brawner, twenty-two; and Elmer Palliser, nineteen—aboard the *Camargo* for lunch and a round of storytelling. Within weeks US newspapers and radio stations had picked up the survival tale. The rescue of the marooned sailors by the famous Julius Fleischmann made good reading across America.

On October 28 the *Camargo* sailed west with the trade winds bound for the Marquesas, 3,300 miles away. Six months of island-hopping proved to be a rich blend of extraordinary privilege and opportunity for Burg. He photographed and filmed in the Tuanotu Archipelago, Tahiti, the Tonga and Fiji Islands, the New Hebrides, the Solomons, the New Britain Islands, and Dutch New Guinea. He visited Timor, the islands of Bali, Java, Sumatra, and Borneo, as well as Manila in the Philippines. In Cambodia he accompanied the Fleischmann family as they explored the lost jungle city of Angkor Wat. They crossed Siam (Thailand) and rejoined the *Camargo* in Bangkok, where the entourage were guests at the Royal Court.

Throughout the voyage Burg allowed the unfamiliar, sometimes strange, customs he encountered wash over him. He drank kava in Tonga and ate unfamiliar food at village feasts. He sought out village elders and shamans to listen to their stories. He admired, if not envied, the skills of the fisherman and their handmade boats, their knowledge of the weather and the sea. He queried the Native women about their basket making, clothing, and jewelry. Burg scowled at the suffocating effects of the missionary churches on the Natives, and bemoaned the loss of their culture. On the more sensitive matters of marriage, sex, and nudity, he seemed to be ahead of his time. He found nothing sinful in Native behavior and much that might do modern people good. Numerous times in letters and journals, he mentioned the adverse effect of "civilization" on Natives.

If there is a difference between bias and prejudice, Burg was occasionally guilty of the former. As on the Yukon and Mackenzie Rivers, he voiced opinions based on assumptions in favor of or against certain behaviors. Although he found humanity on the whole to be "good," he believed there were "bad" people in every group. If he saw the Natives as victims, he also saw them as children in need of education and direction, more so if the tribe was in decline. The solutions, at this time, were far from satisfactory. Inevitably, Burg compared the groups and their customs, concluding some superior to others. Sometimes he romanticized the lives of the people he photographed and wrote about. Whether he believed Western civilization superior to that of the cultures he visited remains a vexing question.

Throughout his time with the Fleischmann family, Burg and Junkie developed a genuine friendship. Both were inquisitive, sensitive men. Fleischmann sought Burg's advice on how to corral the vast amount of information he had collected into a book. He confided in Burg that he had grown tired of reading about the aviator Charles Lindbergh all the time. At one point Burg invited Fleischmann to accompany him down a river, possibly the Yukon. Despite their friendship, however, Burg experienced instances of what could only be called "social inferiority." It is equally possible that he could have misread social cues as well as been made to feel inferior by members of Fleischmann's entourage. Whether he had intended to or not, middle-class Burg had found his way into the highest levels of society. He was grateful for the opportunity Fleishmann had given him but could hardly ignore the immense class difference between them. He occasionally scolded himself for "trying too hard to please." Yet, unlike his relation with Beebe, the friendship between Burg and the Fleischmann family lasted a lifetime.

The *Camargo* made stops in Singapore, Penang, several ports in Sumatra, and the islands of Nias, Ceylon, and Aden before voyaging north to the Red Sea and the Suez Canal. There Burg explored the ancient cities of the Nile valley, photographing and filming the temples, tombs, and pyramids. On the islands of Cypress and Rhodes in the Mediterranean, he wandered through the castles of the Crusaders. In Istanbul, Turkey, his voyage on the *Camargo* ended. At Fleishmann's request, Burg shepherded Grandma Fleischmann across Europe on the Orient Express to Paris and on to London, where they boarded the liner *Majestic* for the journey across the Atlantic. Burg had an entire suite to himself. He guessed it was the first and, no doubt, the last time in his life he would enjoy such luxury. They landed in New York in June 1932.

Upon arriving, Burg returned to Washington, D.C., with a trove of photographs and film. The photographic staff of the *National Geographic* magazine was excited. All parties involved—Burg, Junkie Fleischmann, and John La Gorce of the magazine—agreed that the images could be used by each party as the need arose. Burg's photographic efforts yielded positive results. Portions of the fifty thousand feet of thirty-five-millimeter film he shot were eventually used in a National Geographic film called *Dances of the World*. A dozen or more of his color photographs accompanied an article ("Coconuts and Coral Islands") by H. Ian Hogbin in the March 1934 *National Geographic*. Finally, more than a hundred of Burg's black-and-white photographs, many of them Native portraits, appeared in Julius Fleischmann's 1935 travel book, *Footsteps in the Sea*.

Burg's good fortune continued. La Gorce offered him a fresh assignment: a fourteen-thousand-word article (including photographs) on his home state of Oregon. The piece was to be part of the *National Geographic* commonwealth series. La Gorce agreed to lend Burg camera equipment and the Finlay plates he had used on the Fleischmann round-the-world cruise. He offered Burg seven hundred dollars (including three hundred dollars for expenses) for the article and photos. It was, in effect, a pay raise and a vote of confidence in Burg's skills. Before departing Washington, D.C., Burg spoke with *National Geographic* photo editors. At the time the photography department was considered the best in the nation, with access to the latest techniques and equipment. To smooth the way for Burg, the secretary of the National Geographic Society wrote a letter of introduction on National Geographic stationary, requesting local officials' "cooperation and assistance [for Mr. Burg] in securing material" and ensuring that "the National Geographic Society will be most appreciative of the cooperation and help that is extended."

After visiting with family and friends, Burg spent the summer and fall motoring back and forth across his home state. He filled his three-by-five-inch pocket notebooks with a constant flow of ideas, descriptions, reminders, facts, statistics, impressions, word portraits, addresses, anecdotes, and distances. He had been charged with writing an article about the various industries of Oregon as well as the scenic beauty, but he harbored another view: he wanted the article to convey the pioneer spirit of the working people of Oregon and their attachment to the land. He conducted countless interviews. He visited Warrenton on the northern Oregon coast and spent time with the crab fishermen. In John Day he watched as the local ranchers herded their cattle down Main Street. In Grants Pass he visited the Rogue River and later drove to the coast to view the Oregon Caves. In Klamath Falls the county agent drove Burg around Klamath Lake so that he could photograph the flocks of migrating birds and waterfowl, a stunning spectacle. In Lakeview he sought out ranchers. He ventured into familiar country in eastern Oregon, where he photographed Wallowa Lake, the Eagle Cap Mountains, Hells Canyon, and the Snake River.

Cameras and the cachet of being a *National Geographic* photographer allowed Burg unusual entry into the lives of locals. Farmers, ranchers, policemen, shopkeepers, schoolteachers, farm laborers, fishermen, hotel owners, and their wives—all were eager to talk with the native son. Burg, however, also noted what he considered the provincial attitudes of some of the people he met. "Many of the so-called intellectual people I have met along the road surprise me with their ignorance," he wrote. "They are unaware of the vast phases of life beyond their little ken. Great hordes of people with hopes and fears and aspirations are strangers to them. They know the few people like themselves in their own social strata and think they inhabit a universe."

One of the more fascinating locations Burg visited in eastern Oregon that summer was the recently completed Owyhee Dam on the upper Owyhee River. Begun in 1928, the 417-foot concrete arch gravity dam was the world's highest at the time. The dam, at a cost of six million dollars, was built primarily for irrigation and eventually flooded fifty-two miles of the Owyhee River. Among the numerous national and local dignitaries and businessmen who attended the July 17 dedication with Burg were Ray Wilbur, secretary of interior, and Elwood Mead, chief of the Bureau of Reclamation. Speaking on behalf of President Herbert Hoover, Wilbur stated that the technology used to build the dam would serve as a prototype for another large dam soon to be built on the Colorado River. At the time Burg appeared to have ignored or seen little or no conflict between his passion for rivers and voyaging and the consequences of the construction of large dams. Only decades later did he acknowledge the irony of the situation.

Doors continued to open for Burg. John Bray Educational Films contracted with him to write, direct, and film a travel-wildlife feature. Tentatively titled "Giants of the North," the film placed special emphasis on the brown bears of Admiralty Island, the island the Tlingit Indians called Xotsnoowu, or "fortress of the bears." In August he interrupted his Oregon research to sail north on the yacht *Westwind* to Juneau. Campbell Church Jr., the boat owner and an acquaintance of Burg's from Seattle, accompanied him on the voyage. Initially they cruised Glacier Bay and Icy Strait photographing humpback whales and the spectacular glacial ice. Afterward they made for hundred-mile long Admiralty Island on the shores of Seymour Canal near Juneau. Burg had contracted Al Hasselborg, a well-known local big-game guide, to help him track and photograph brown bears. Self-taught, irascible, and honest to a fault, Hasselborg had worked the backcountry for four decades. Only once in the dozen times he had been charged by a bear had he been injured; it had taken him three days to reach a doctor to dress the wounds. The attack left Hasselborg's right arm partially crippled.

In his tiny, immaculately-kept fourteen-by-fourteen-foot square cabin at the head of Mole Harbor, Hasselborg held court. Burg, a temporary occupant, found himself running afoul of the guide's acute sense of orderliness. When he placed his knapsack and camera gear in front of the "library" corner of the cabin, Hasselborg barked, "That ain't the place for your gear. That's the library. Put your stuff in the gun room, over there," pointing to the opposite corner. Burg picked up one of Hasselborg's books. "Don't mess with those books and get 'em all mixed up," he roared. The fastidious guide explained that the other two corners of the cabin were the kitchen and the dining room. Burg stepped lightly. His host had been long accustomed to quiet, solitude, and plenty of elbow room.

Over the next three weeks Burg filmed two dozen or more encounters with brown bears. One incident was particularly memorable. While filming a large sow and her two cubs frolicking in the bush one morning, he suddenly found himself the object of the sow's ire. The bear charged, stopped, then advanced again. Burg continued to film. When the sow came within twenty-five feet, Hasselborg fired a shot from his .405 over the head of the animal, frightening her off. Burg was badly shaken by the experience. Hasselborg said that he had shot over the sow because of the cubs. Some of today's familiar iconic images of Alaska—whales leaping out of the water, eagles in flight, bears catching salmon midstream— first appeared in Burg's *Giants of the North*. It was the first of his many films about the state that one day would become his adopted home. He sold footage to Paramount Films.

Upon returning to Portland after the Admiralty Island excursion, Burg began writing a rough draft for *National Geographic* magazine as well as making preparations for his second season of lectures. The Pond Bureau had booked him on a fourteen-city tour. While in Washington, D.C., he worked extensively with the *National Geographic* editors choosing and processing photographs and writing captions that would accompany the photographs. Burg was also asked to be the keynote speaker at the annual Explorers Club dinner—an invitation that signaled his rising prominence with the club. He arrived late, wearing a sports coat and tie (typical dresswear for such an event was a tuxedo). The breech of unspoken etiquette was duly noted by a portion of the well-heeled audience. Unruffled, Burg began with an apology and an explanation: "I came in late, and rushed around town to rent a tux before all the stores closed. None was to be had. In the last shop, the owner told me he was sorry, but the last tux had just been rented by the president of The Explorers Club!" The audience burst out laughing.

Throughout the late fall and winter of 1932, he continued to rework his *National Geographic* piece in hotel rooms and train cars. He discovered a methodical way to structure his article-writing. As a photographer, he had always thought in terms of a scene or a portrait. Now he used his notes in conjunction with the scenes he remembered and the associations he drew in his mind to shape a narrative. The next step was to order the scenes in such a way as to create a story people would enjoy. "A Native Son's Rambles in Oregon," his third article for *National Geographic,* appeared in the February 1934 issue. He wove his own boyhood adventures, river voyages, and the history of Oregon into an informative and lighthearted sixty-page travel narrative. He included a full dose of chamber of commerce promotion for Oregon's business community, especially the fishing, farming, and logging industries. The piece contained thirty-nine black-and-white photographs as well as two dozen color images. In a generous gesture, he also included photographs by popular Oregon photographers. *The Oregonian* praised Burg's achievement, estimating that the article (with *National Geographic's* circulation of nearly one million at the time) had been worth approximately two hundred thousand dollars in publicity for the state. Copies of the February issue were hard to find in Portland.

Burg's old teachers at the University of Oregon invited him back to lecture. After one presentation, he attended a gathering of students and teachers at the home of George Rebec, who had accompanied Burg down the Mackenzie in 1929. Always reluctant to speak too much about his future plans, he let slip another adventure he had in the works. One of the students, a Miss Thatcher, spouted, "Why Amos Burg, you're crazy, you're crazy!" Her offhand comments annoyed Burg. "Many people have said that silently and she had a perfect right to," he scribbled in his notebook. "But she has that collegiate 'swellegant' air, kind of a refined wisecracker."

The romantic dreamer, who loved learning, books, and the life of the mind, had shed his youthful naïveté. Around this time he wrote in his diary:

After a man is around this university atmosphere for awhile whose men theorize without action, I grow dissatisfied. . . . The mind with all its education doesn't get a vision bigger than it travels over. It can work out theory but it can't get at the truth of things without living in it. . . . A man living in town gets so he depends on books for his knowledge. When you read too much you lose your power to receive fresh ideas out of space. When you let loose of instinctive knowledge, you maybe lose more than you gain. . . . The world changes fast. The Balinese cling to their [world]. We Americans in everything change rapidly on the surface although remaining pretty much the same basically. The Depression in 1933 has been going on for several years and the latest estimate is 16 million out of work. Chicago owes its schoolteachers 28 million in back pay. Several counties in Alabama have suspended their schools all together. The migrating birds of the Antelope Desert worry little about our turmoil. We justify shooting them or taking the lands of the Indians by classing all these things under natural food or hindrances to progress. As an adventurer one can shift from the centers of depression.

With the publication of two *National Geographic* articles and his successful appearance at the Washington Auditorium in March 1930, Burg had begun the professional career he had dreamed of as an adolescent. Over the next four decades, he worked as an outdoor-adventure writer, photographer, filmmaker, and lecturer. He would go on to write ten more articles for the popular magazine and eventually write for numerous newspapers and magazines. He also penned a well-received column for an Alaskan magazine. Throughout the 1930s he was a regular on the East Coast circuit, presenting lectures (accompanied by film or slides) before such august organizations as the American Museum of Natural History, the Boston City Club, the Brooklyn Institute of Arts and Sciences, the American Geographic Society, and the Philadelphia Geographic Society as well as numerous university clubs, business organizations, museums, and schools. The New York speaking agency representing Burg developed a slate of presentations that included "Voyaging Alaskan Waters," "Our Strange World: Inside Cape Horn," "Across England by Canoe," and "Conquering the Grand Canyon." Whether speaking before a crowd of thirty or three thousand, he remained unflappable, blending entertainment with education in his engaging style of quiet wit and humorous self-deprecation.

Burg had come a long way since the days when the filmmaker Jesse Sill coached him on moving-picture technique and he borrowed camera equipment from nationally known photographers in Portland. His association with the National Geographic organization allowed him to stay conversant with the latest developments in camera equipment and film processing. He took these newly acquired skills to the rivers he voyaged. In the 1940s Burg began a second career in the burgeoning educational film field. His work carried him across the United States and around the world. This experience led to employment as a filmmaker for the Alaska Department of Fish and Game, based in Juneau. Eventually he became the first section leader of the Information and Education branch of the department.

Chapter 6

LAND OF FIRE:
THE TIERRA DEL FUEGO AND
PATAGONIA ARCHIPELAGOS

During Burg's second lecture tour on the East Coast, he found a home-away-from-home at the Explorers Club. He took a room at the nearby YMCA but often spent entire afternoons reading or relaxing at the club in the heart of Manhattan. On any given day, he was likely to find a group of famous men holding court around the Long Table, sipping tea, chai, or coffee. One member described the setting as "architecturally reminiscent of an English baron's estate. The interior featured the same high ceilings, lead windows, and ornate woodwork on both the ceilings and floors. Paintings of exploration from the Arctic to Africa hung on the walls, and artifacts from around the world were displayed everywhere, drawing the eye in for closer inspection." Of his own experience in this unique place, Burg wrote:

> My world became peopled with famous characters. Many afternoons
> I sat at the Long Table listening as I basked in the aura of greatness.
> They were men who achieved. Criticism—only Vilhjalmuur Stepha-
> nsson [the Canadian Arctic explorer and ethnologist] seemed to invite
> it, if only for the opportunity to demolish the theories of his detrac-
> tors. It is not easy to live always in the limelight. Stef was a walking

encyclopedia of the Arctic, a kindly man. Most all the explorers had a powerful propulsion—a hunger that was never appeased fully. Some of the most interesting men were the lesser luminaries like Dr. Clyde Fisher, head of the Hayden Planetarium, who forgot himself in his interest in everything and everybody. I liked them all.

In such a heady atmosphere, Burg hatched another impressive adventure: to voyage the coastal waters of Chile and Argentina—the Tierra del Fuego and Patagonia archipelagos—the fall of 1933. The idea had been sparked by conversations with Stefansson and the ethnologist Earl Hansen, who had spent significant time in both countries studying the indigenous peoples. The unfamiliar archipelagos bordering the west coast of South America were difficult passages. Sudden changes in weather, fierce ocean currents and tides, and isolated stretches of coastline gave the Cape Horn area an unforgiving reputation among veteran sailors and seaman. Most preferred the dangers of the open seas to those of coastlines. Although Burg had worked as an able seaman in his youth, he had little or no experience handling small sailing vessels or navigating coastal waters.

After reading about the Yahgans, the "canoe people" of Tierra del Fuego, Burg appears to have briefly entertained the idea of voyaging in his craft *Song o' the Winds.* John La Gorce at National Geographic questioned whether Burg had given sufficient consideration to the hazards of such a journey in a small boat. Veteran hands at the Explorers Club stepped in and roundly discouraged the idea. Burg took the advice to heart, reassuring La Gorce that he would locate a larger boat. The search for a seaworthy craft, however, would take longer than Burg anticipated. To reach Magallanes, Chile (now Punta Arenas), his jumping-off point, Burg needed to locate a shipping company willing to transport him (and his as yet unknown vessel) along the west coast of North America, through the Panama Canal, and along the east coast of South America to the Straits of Magellan. From Magallanes he intended to voyage south through the Tierra del Fuego archipelago to the Cape Horn region. Afterward he would return north and journey through the Patagonia archipelago on Chile's west coast. Charlie Wheeler, vice president of the McCormick Steamship Company and an old friend of Burg's, agreed to help. He arranged free transportation for Burg to and from South America and sent letters of introduction to all of the steamship company's offices as well as to his personal contacts and government officials in Argentina and Chile. In exchange, Burg would take promotional photographs and film footage of the McCormick Steamship Company's operations.

To secure more financial support, Burg applied for and received Grant Number 98 from the National Geographic Society. The official purpose of the voyage was "to explore and photograph islands and water passages near the southernmost tip of the Western Hemisphere." To this Burg added another goal: "to record in motion picture film and still photography both black and white and color, the tribes of natives that still survived at the southernmost end of the hemisphere. Statistics show that these people are on the road to becoming extinct and that few full bloods will be alive within a generation." The National Geographic Society agreed to provide film and photographic equipment as needed. Burg, in return, would write a ten-thousand-word article accompanied by photographs for the magazine. Burg's color photographs of Tierra del Fuego and its people would be the first of their kind.

Throughout the summer he studied the coastal maps of Argentina and Chile, taking detailed notes about the hazards of coastal navigation and querying any able seamen he knew as well as consulting Captain Alfred Rimer, his former captain and longtime friend. He read voraciously, including such works as W. H. Hudson's *Idle Days in Patagonia,* Benjamin Franklin Bourne's *Captive in Patagonia,* William Singer Barclay's *Land of Magellan,* Charles Darwin's *The Voyage of the Beagle,* and Richard Henry Dana's *Two Years before the Mast.* He also read, more than once, *Sailing Alone around the World,* Joshua Slocum's 1892 account of his solo voyage.

Burg's most pressing tasks were familiar ones: to locate a vessel and a reliable companion. There was little time (or money) to have a boat constructed. He scoured the harbors and waterfronts in Portland and Seattle. On a visit to San Francisco he contacted the Coast Guard Inspector for the Twelfth District (which included the entire coastline north of San Francisco), who suggested Burg look into purchasing a twenty-six-foot, self-bailing Beebe-McClellan surfboat. These workhorse craft, essentially unsinkable, had been used as rescue boats along the Oregon coast for decades. They could ride out the worst of storms and were ideal, with their minimal draft, for anchoring in shallow bays or landing on sandy beaches. Although oar-powered, they could be adapted to carry sail and an auxiliary motor. In Oregon two out-of-service boats were available; the Coast Guard Inspector suggested Burg look at both and then choose one. In Coquille, a small lumber and dairy town along the southern Oregon coast, Burg found the first surfboat lying in the mudflats of the Coquille River. The weather-beaten boat had suffered extensive damage and was clearly beyond repair. In Coos Bay, however, a few miles north, Burg's luck changed. The second vessel, given its age, was in remarkable shape. He placed a bid for forty dollars, a bargain price. Coast Guard red tape delayed delivery for weeks, but finally on July 25 the boat arrived by truck at Superior Boatbuilders in Portland. Time was running short, so Burg reset his departure date for September 15.

Built in 1905 by Fred C. Beebe (no relation to William Beebe, the famed marine biologist) of Long Island, New York, the McClellan surfboats were similar to the *James Caird,* the lifeboat the polar explorer Ernest Shackleton and his men had used in their miraculous eight-hundred-mile voyage across the southern Atlantic Ocean in 1916. The twenty-six-foot, lap-strake surfboat carried a beam of seven feet, a two-foot draft, and a two-hundred-pound oak keel with a removable centerboard. Copper rivets every six inches attached the lap strakes to the oaken ribs. Eight airtight compartments along the decks as well as in the bow and stern served as storage space. The "rescue seats" for the eight men who would typically power the nine-foot oars were also airtight. Sixteen self-bailing ports through the double-bottomed hull were located on each side of the center line. The hardwood gunnels had been covered on the outside with five-inch-thick canvas tubing filled with cork to cushion the boat from normal wear and tear.

Of the many refitting tasks to be completed, a watertight cabin was foremost. It would have to sit forward and be low-lying, provide much needed shelter and storage, and also be able to shed water quickly in high seas. For ease of handling and storage on deck, a short sprit rig with two sails would be mounted through the roof of the cabin. Inside the cabin, where Burg was bound to spend an inordinate amount of time because of the ever-changing weather, living conditions would be cramped and spartan. The bulkhead was reinforced and any suspect ribs replaced. Two simple platforms for bunks were built. The waterproof compartments for camera equipment and film needed larger, waterproof manholes. The cockpit in the aft deck, where the boat would be piloted, remained open and exposed to the elements. Six of the automatic self-bailing tubes as well as a removable steering rudder were replaced.

One hazy Sunday morning in late August, 1933, a small crowd gathered beneath the Saint John's Bridge on the east side of the Willamette River. Bits of ash floated in the acrid air; a smoky yellow pall tinted the sky. Two subjects dominated conversation: the elegant beauty of the recently completed bridge looming overhead and the rampaging forest fire in Tillamook County, seventy miles west. The fire, which had begun on August 26, would burn for a month and blacken more than three hundred thousand acres of coastal forest. At the time the "Tillamook Burn" was one of the worst fires in Oregon history.

As workmen of the Superior Boatbuilding Company begin lowering a small boat by harness into the Willamette River, the crowd of family, friends, and newsmen turned their attention to the freshly painted craft and the two men sitting in the cockpit. Burg and boatbuilder John A. Jacobson were all smiles. The conversion of the surfboat into a sailing vessel was complete. Dorothy Leadbetter Teren, a friend of Burg's, stepped forward to christen the bow of the *Dorjun* with a bottle of champagne, while the crowd clapped and hoorayed. Burg had named the boat after the two Fleischmann children, Dorette and Junior, whose parents he had befriended on the round-the-world voyage aboard the *Camargo* three years earlier. The Fleischmanns had contributed financially to Burg's upcoming voyage.

Although he intended to use sail (and oars in a pinch), an auxiliary motor was an absolute necessity. The unpredictable conditions of the southern archipelagos left little margin for error. He visited Stafford Jennings, who had recently opened an outboard motor dealership and repair shop, embracing the new motor technology patented by Olin Evinrude in 1911. In his shop beneath the Sellwood Bridge in Portland, Jennings himself supervised the construction of the motor well in the cockpit of the *Dorjun* and the installation of the thirty-five-pound, four-horsepower Evinrude.

One urgent problem remained, however: locating a suitable companion. In a voyage this risky, Burg needed an experienced shipmate but could not afford disharmony. Fred "Spokane" Hill, always a favored companion, had

married and was unavailable. Burg had broached the subject with Ellsworth
Kolb, Grand Canyon boatman, author, and filmmaker. Kolb was excited by
the idea but declined, citing family and business responsibilities. Throughout
the summer Burg pursued a number of promising leads, but nothing came
of them. On September 9, only days before he was to depart for San Francisco, he received a Western Union telegram from L. M. Larsen, a complete
stranger. The telegram read:

> Information has reached me that you are sailing for Patagonia for
> exploration purposes [stop] I have spent a number of years amongst
> the Indians of Tierra del Fuego Smiths Channel and the Straits of
> Magellan and only recently returned from a similar expedition [stop]
> Should you need a qualified navigator for that country I offer you my
> services and will sail the *Dorjun* to Punta Arenas or any other places in
> the straits you may desire [stop] I am third officer on SS *San Gabriel
> Quaker Line* leaving San Francisco for San Pedro Tuesday evening
> and sailing from San Pedro Friday for east coast [stop] have very best
> references [stop] Please acknowledge.

Burg made no further mention of Larsen, and the issue of finding a companion remained unresolved. Why he did not pursue Larsen, apparently a well-
qualified candidate, is unknown.

On September 14 he arrived in San Francisco and made his way to Pier
38, where the freighter SS *West Mahwah* was anchored. The only passenger,
he was given a stateroom of his own. (The *Dorjun* had been shipped from
Portland the week before and now was lashed to the aft deck.) Over the
next few days, local reporters made regular appearances, taking photographs
and peppering Burg with questions. It was welcome but time-consuming
publicity. A week later the *West Mahwah,* carrying a cargo of five million
board feet of lumber, departed for Buenos Aires. Standing on the deck of the
ship as it passed out of San Francisco Bay, Burg stared down at the anchored
barges, where construction workers sank pilings into the water. Construction of the Golden Gate Bridge had begun a few months earlier.

Among the officers and crew of the *West Mahwah,* the *Dorjun*'s presence
had not gone unnoticed. Each man had a strong opinion or a cautionary tale.

Like people who worked and lived on rivers, seamen loved to tell tales of doom. Burg remained unconcerned. By the first week in October, the *West Mahwah* was unloading lumber in Puerto Rico. Despite reports of hurricanes, the weather during the voyage had remained agreeable. A shipping agent met Burg and gave him a tour of the island. "I suppose some of the long-faced neighbors have sympathized with you regarding my voyage," he wrote to his parents, "but I can assure you they who have never been further than Washington State, know little about the horn except by hearsay tale. They confuse Cape Horn with Magellan Strait. Sailing ships round the Horn many miles south of the Horn in open seas, whereas Magellan Strait is sheltered [by] inland waters. But the confusion will not be contradicted by me for thereby lies the story."

Over the course of the voyage, Burg shared his plans for his own adventure with the *West Mahwah*'s captain, A. C. Larsen, who thought Burg capable but inexperienced and voiced concern. Even a veteran sailor would face difficulty navigating a small boat single-handedly in unfamiliar waters. Larsen made a generous offer—the services of one of his seamen—agreeing to release the man from duty as well as guarantee passage from Buenos Aires back to the United States. Shipboard gossip spread fast, and six seamen volunteered. After questioning all six, Burg chose Roy Pepper, the least experienced—the trip aboard the *West Mahwah* was Pepper's first. The decision boiled down to the simple fact that Burg liked Pepper. "He could smile with his face full of stinging spray," wrote Burg. "Later I found that he could bake biscuits without an oven and cut his hair with a jackknife." Young, strong, and willing, Pepper combined a can-do attitude and natural competence with an easy-going nature. He did not ruffle easily. Pepper's duties would include mundane shipboard chores, such as cooking, gathering fresh water and wood, and ship maintenance. Later Pepper would write his own description of his duties on the first page of his sea diary, "1st Mate, Steward, Chief Cook, Sailor, Bosun, 2nd Engineer, & Most Anything." Although he was to be paid little or nothing, Pepper accepted the offer without hesitation.

Born in Saint Croix Falls, Wisconsin, in 1914, nineteen-year-old Roy Pepper had grown up under the guidance of his two older brothers, Ken and Chet. The trio had spent hours in and around the Saint Croix River. In the summer they swam, fished, and paddled canoes. In winter they cut wood,

Penquins and Dorjun, *Offing Island*

hunted, and ice-skated. Pepper was used to rigorous, outdoor labor. He had also taken courses in machine shop and photography from his father, a high school teacher. While on board the *West Mahwah,* he had been studying for his radioman's license under the tutelage of his brother Ken. Captain Larsen issued a letter releasing Pepper from duty and agreeing to provide transport back to the United States at the end of the seven-month-long expedition.

In Buenos Aires, Burg and Pepper boarded the *Jose Menendez* to Magallanes. Two weeks later the coastal steamer entered the Straits of Magellan in a gale. Docking the ship was difficult, but unloading the *Dorjun* was a nightmare. High winds, tangled ropes, a faulty engine, and too many captains giving orders in English, Spanish, and Italian turned the operation into a circus. Burg's troubles had only just begun. Once in the water, the *Dorjun* leaked like a rusty bucket. Baked by the tropical sun and out of the water for nearly two months, the wooden planks, deprived of moisture, had shrunk badly. Gear and supplies were hauled onto the decks. The two sailors bailed throughout the night until they collapsed in their sleeping bags the next morning. Outside the rain fell and the wind rocked the boat mercilessly. It was an inauspicious start. "Never have I felt so lonely and downcast with gloomy foreboding," he wrote. "It was the most inglorious launching that has ever been staged."

The next evening a local salvage diver arranged for the *Dorjun* to be hauled from the harbor onto a cradle in the Braun and Blanchard shipyard. On dry land and sheltered from the wind, Burg and Pepper found sanctuary. Once established in the boatyard, the occupants of the *Dorjun* fell into a comfortable routine. Camera in hand, Burg roamed Magallanes, population eleven thousand. He photographed the fire department (with its numerous fire brigades representing several nationalities), the local foundry, the racetrack, and the museum. He received numerous invitations to dinner from locals, where he took portraits of individuals and their families. He also made forays to the outlying sheep estancias and fox farms as well as to the local islands to film and photograph the bird colonies. In his diary he recorded observations of their behavior and habitat.

On Thanksgiving the two mariners celebrated the traditional American holiday. The warmth of their recently purchased wood-burning stove filled the cabin of the *Dorjun*. Burg brought out the phonograph, and Pepper cooked mutton, gravy, potatoes, cheese, bread, butter, onions, marmalade, and cocoa. Waltz music floated through the boatyard.

On December 3, Burg celebrated his thirty-second birthday. The wind was blowing so hard "that the waves on the water could not form," as Pepper described it. "The wind blew water into the air in the form of mist. It was so thick that one couldn't see the ships in the harbor at times." Pepper had proven a good choice. In a letter home Burg wrote: "Roy Pepper, whom the captain paid off the *West Mahwah* to accompany me, has proven to be the wisest choice, for he is not only a good cook, but his disposition is of the cheerfulest under all circumstances. I cannot think of anyone who would be better for such a voyage. He is also water minded."

Captain Arroyo, the marine governor, summoned Burg to his office. From the outset, Arroyo, who spoke perfect English, had made it clear that he was not impressed with the *Dorjun*. He thought the twenty-six-foot lifeboat was inadequate for the rigorous voyage ahead, and he did not want to become involved in the rescue or retrieval of a well-known American with connections to *National Geographic*. Burg countered Arroyo's objections with a rambling recital of the boat's seaworthiness. The salvage diver who had aided Burg on his arrival was summoned and lent the Yankee a boost of much-needed credibility. Gradually the reluctant governor was won over, so much so that he offered the help of the *Micalvi,* a Chilean Navy ship that patrolled the archipelago. Together Burg and Arroyo decided on an approximate date (January 9) and a rendezvous point (in the vicinity of Ideal Bay) where a cache of supplies and gasoline could be delivered to the *Dorjun.*

Arroyo cautioned Burg about two open stretches of water where the small boat would be exposed to the southern Pacific Ocean: the Brecknock reach and the more southerly Wollaston Islands. Weather could turn ferocious, changing from rain, snow, sleet, or fog by the minute. Three-day gales were the norm. Arroyo warned Burg of the infamous "williwaws," the sudden violent winds that roared down the mountain slopes into the bays and channels. Many boats had dragged anchor and run aground on rocky shores of isolated bays, their crew's rescue often a matter of chance and an improvement in the weather. Tides and currents played tricks in the narrow channels. Arroyo suggested that the *Dorjun* carry as much ballast as possible to counter the heavy seas near the Wollaston Islands and to get a larger anchor. Arroyo told Burg the Magellan rule: "Carry one-third more anchor, one-third less sail." By the end of the conversation, governor and voyager agreed that "50% is the boat, but the rest depends on the man." Burg also purchased a dory, the *Cabo de Hornos,* to serve as tender.

Despite this pleasant time in Magallanes, Burg grew restless. The bleak landscape and changeable weather triggered a sense of foreboding, not unusual for him at the start of a long voyage. In these melancholy moods he became increasingly self-critical, voicing past regrets: "At the ends of the earth I am haunted by the promises that I've not kept and the times I've failed and for this reason at night I awaken half-startled and in an agony of mind. In the civilized portions of the world doubts such as these are lost in the roar but down here they stalk forth in the silence. Superficialities are receding and my mind is opened like a door and I look in." One chilly morning Burg summed up his condition from the warmth of the cabin: "It seems strange and yet so natural to be seated here and looking at the shores of the Land of Fire and Dawson Island."

On December 5 the extra film and camera supplies Burg had been waiting for arrived from Buenos Aires. As he and Pepper prepared for departure, the cabin and decks of the *Dorjun* looked, according to Burg, "like a department store counter during a clearance sale." They spent days sorting and stowing gear. Whenever locals dropped by the boatyard, they teased the two Yankees about the length of their stay: Would they ever leave Magallanes? They made trial runs to Elizabeth and Santa Magdalena Island where Burg photographed a vast profusion of wildlife: sea lion and seal rookeries as well as cormorant and penguin colonies. Finally, on Sunday, December 17, the voyagers departed Magallanes harbor, hugging the coastline as they headed southwest to Point Famine where they anchored in an unnamed bay. The next morning Pepper hunted rabbits on shore while Burg hauled his camera gear up 2,600-foot Mount Tarn, the same peak Charles Darwin had ascended in 1834 while on the voyage of the *Beagle*. As Burg wandered the beech forests, flocks of long-tailed parakeets screeched at the intruder. At the summit he was greeted with a stunning panorama of the straits and the snow-clad Darwin mountain range and seven-thousand-foot Mount Sarmiento. The clear weather offered an unusual opportunity to photograph the peak free of clouds. After spending Christmas with the Morrison family on Dawson Island they sailed south along Canal Whiteside until they reached Meskin Canal.

The scenery in the Meskin Canal between Dawson and Wickam Island was equally astonishing. "Terrible and beautiful," Burg wrote in his diary. The sun poked through the clouds. Porpoises chased along side the boat. They encountered their first serious squall. One moment the water was smooth as glass. Within an hour the entire sound was "a smoking maelstrom of fury full of driving hail," according to Burg. An hour later the squall had passed. The *Dorjun* nosed into a quiet bay on Benton Sound. Pepper lifted the Evinrude out of the motor well and rowed several hundred yards upriver, where he anchored within sight of a stream and a twelve-foot waterfall. He named the creek Goose River after an upland goose he later shot and cooked. The meat was hard as concrete, tasteless as cardboard. Burg had set up a temporary lab to develop film by darkening the portholes of the cabin. He washed negatives in the creek. With the saltwater fragrance and the sound of the waterfall, the location was more than either man could have hoped for. Despite the frigid weather, they were reluctant to leave but, alas, the journey called.

Over the next three days the *Dorjun* encountered one squall after another as it worked its way along narrow Gabriel Channel. Pepper thought the

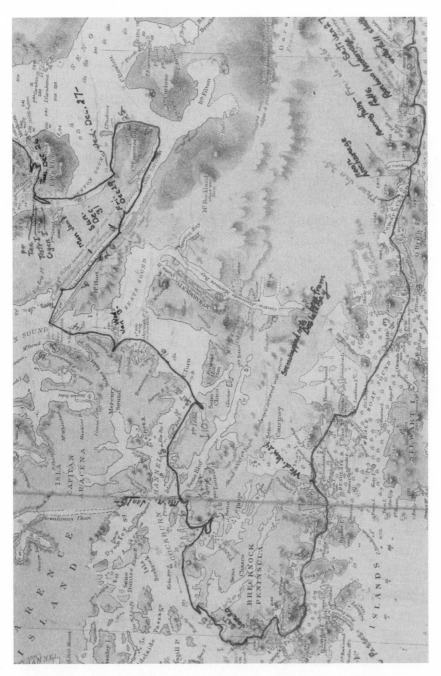

Chart of Burg's Tierra del Fuego voyage with route, handwritten dates, and locations

weather the craziest he had ever seen. Driving rain and fog at times blotted out the shorelines; hail the size of small stones rapped the decks and cabin; snow showers came and went. They ducked in and out of protected anchorages, only to be tormented by the williwaws. Despite foul-weather gear, Burg and Pepper's clothes remained damp, their bodies constantly chilled. Relief came only when they retreated to the cabin, where the heat of the stove provided warmth and comfort.

At the northern end of Gabriel Channel, between Dawson Island and the spindly arm of the Tierra del Fuego landmass, the *Dorjun* was once again forced to seek cover from a gale. As the boat entered the pinched entrance to an unnamed cove under motor, the flood tide and the harsh winds stalled the boat's forward motion. They drifted dangerously toward the rocky shoreline. Burg had never seen moving water behave so ferociously. Pepper thought the effect of the flood tide on the channel resembled nothing less than a raging river during a flood. They maneuvered out of harm's way, barely escaping disaster. The incident served as a warning to the ever-cautious Burg. Once out of danger, Pepper anchored the boat in front of an enormous glacier. Dozens of small waterfalls cascaded into the blackish-green water. When the sun chanced to appear, the glacier flickered like a "million oil lamps," according to

Dorjun *and* Cabo de Hornos *in stream at Dawson Island*

Pepper. Blues, greens, and yellows leaped from the sparkling surface. Danger had abruptly turned into beauty—a pattern the voyagers would encounter time and again.

For two days the temperature hovered near zero; rain gave way to hail and snow flurries. An eerie silence fell upon the scene. They woke one morning to find the *Dorjun* blanketed in snow. On New Years Eve, Pepper went ashore to gather wild marigolds for their supper. Burg cooked a dinner of hotcakes and tea as the waltz music from the phonograph filled the dark night sky. After supper Pepper brought out a couple of candy bars he had smuggled aboard.

Besides securing firewood and freshwater, Burg's most serious concern during the journey was having enough fuel for the Evinrude. To miss the scheduled rendezvous with the *Micalvi* would seriously handicap the voyage. On the morning of January 3, they rounded Anxious Point under a jib sail. The large, northerly swells rolling unimpeded down the open expanse of the Strait of Magellan suddenly turned into irregular white-crested waves. The prevailing winds swung from the east to the south, catching the *Dorjun* midship. Each time the surfboat struck a wave, her port gunnels sank deep beneath the dark water. The aft cockpit was awash. The *Cabo de Hornos,* the flat-bottomed boat they had purchased in Magallanes, wallowed in the wake. Burg fought off the rising fear that the *Dorjun* might roll over. They rounded Squally Point and, with the wind astern, raced for Sholl Bay at the base of Mount Boqueron on Clarence Island. Once at anchor, they ran the *Dorjun* up a rocky creek.

As always, Burg headed for the highest point of land, in this case three-thousand-foot Mount Boqueron, to take photographs. He was gambling on a break in the weather. He had walked a few hundred yards when he collapsed to the ground. After regaining consciousness, he found himself lying in the snow, an intense pain in his lower back radiating up toward his shoulders. Unable to lift himself, he shouted for Pepper, who had been gathering wood. When Pepper finally heard the call for help, he came running to find Burg in agony. With great effort, Pepper walked Burg back to the *Dorjun,* where he covered his shipmate with blankets and spent the next several hours applying hot compresses to his lower back.

For the next three days Burg remained in his bunk with flu-like symptoms. The possibility of missing the *Micalvi* was becoming a reality. Still unwell, Burg insisted on sailing for Ideal Bay, arriving on January 7. He sent Pepper on foot to post a white flag with a note for the *Micalvi* and then retreated to the cabin. He slept long hours, waking to listen to the not unpleasant sound of the rain patter on the roof of the cabin. Staring out the portholes, he lost himself in the scenery and birdlife on shore. The shags "wore worried expressions." The steamer ducks "imitated the sound of a diesel motor late in the night." The terns were the most graceful of the birds in flight; the kingfishers, which Burg considered shooting for a specimen at one point, were the most trusting. He read and kept his diary up-to-date during this time; he also began work on a rough outline for his *National Geographic* article. Pepper checked for signs of the *Micalvi*.

By January 10 the *Micalvi* still had not arrived, a day later than the agreed-upon date. The next morning they ran the *Dorjun* out to the point where Pepper had placed the white flag, only to find that it had blown away. Burg attributed the loss to the carelessness of youth. "He [Pepper] had placed it at such an angle that the wind blew it into a tangle so the *Micalvi* could not possibly have sighted it." They had missed their rendezvous with the *Micalvi*. Even if they conserved their fuel, they would run out before reaching Ushuaia, the largest town in the Tierra del Fuego region, more than two hundred miles away.

After nine days in Ideal Bay, they prepared to depart but not before spending the morning collecting and cleaning mussels for lunch. By mid-morning the wind had risen. After eating the tangy mussels with fried potatoes, they headed for the Cockburn Channel and the Brecknock Peninsula under a light rain. "We have gasoline for 100 miles, whereas we have 200+ to cover," Pepper wrote. "We are being extremely careful of the sailing conditions, anchorages and all, since many people, including the vice-president of the Geographic Society, advised Amos that the trip was too dangerous and that the boat would be wrecked and the expensive equipment and material would be lost. While in Magallanes, I saw many people gaze upon the boat, shake their heads slowly and say, 'It will never come back.' Well—maybe they were right. One little slip down here and we, the boat and everything, won't be worth a snowball in hell."

Visibility in the Cockburn Channel was poor to nonexistent. The sea remained surprisingly calm, the rolling swells carrying the *Dorjun* past the ragged coastline of the Brecknock Peninsula. After their enforced layover, Burg and Pepper were in high spirits. The boat behaved not unlike the porpoises that had raced alongside them a week before. Pepper thought he spotted the trailing smoke of the *Micalvi,* but it turned out to be a whitish streak on the face of a distant cliff. By late afternoon they had covered twenty-one miles and were pleased with their progress. Burg steered through a narrow rocky passage into a well-protected inlet and set anchor. Both men had taken to naming these isolated locations according to their fancy, and occasionally their diaries revealed different names for the same place. That day they agreed, however, and called it Phyllis Bay, after a young Wisconsin woman that Pepper had liked.

Gale winds forced them to lay over the next day. Too much idleness did not suit Burg, who had envisioned a voyage of constant progress, moving from one anchorage to another. He had underestimated just how much the weather would dictate their pace of travel. Pepper remained carefree, even buoyant. He performed the drudge work without complaint, eating and sleeping soundly. The tone of his diaries revealed a good-humored, resilient young man. Burg, twelve years older and in charge, envied his shipmate's boyish enthusiasm.

A break in the weather came on January 20. With no idea how long the window of opportunity might last, Burg decided to continue the run around Brecknock Peninsula. Southwest swells, generated by storms in the Pacific Ocean, rolled unimpeded for thousands of miles before striking the peninsula and the exposed islands, reefs, and islets of the Chilean coastline. The islands—Milky Way and the West and East Furies—were aptly named, thought Burg. He could not afford a navigational error or an engine failure. The situation called for boldness as much as caution. Burg would hug the coastline, ever ready to duck into a safe anchorage if the weather turned.

He worried constantly about one of them being pitched overboard. Even with their life vests, the chance of rescue was slim. In the distance the great swells crashed on islets and reefs, sending up a white curtain of surf and spray that stretched as far as the eye could see. At one point Pepper dropped the sea anchor over the bow as the *Dorjun* was pushed back in the direction of the coastline. After eight hours of touch and go, they reached Tug Bay on Occasion Channel. Wet and exhausted, the sailors were jubilant. The *Dorjun* had performed well. Any anxiety about the seaworthiness of the converted surfboat evaporated for the time being.

Tug Bay was another unworldly anchorage, shrouded in mist and the ceaseless, muted roar of the Pacific. On the higher granite mountains above

Roy at tiller in Desolada Bay

the bay, the vegetation was thin and stunted by the relentless winds. By now Burg had reached the conclusion that the wind was the elemental force he must pay closest attention to. In the Land of the Horn, he wrote, "the wind was King. It bullied the land, the sea, and those who ventured out from shore. Everything bent to the wind." Porpoises patrolled the channel and entered the bay, breaking the smooth surface of the water; large herds of seals barked and waved their heads. If the sun was out, the natural harbor, thick with kelp, burned amber at dawn and sunset. The shoreline was crowded black with edible mussels. They named the anchorage Refuge Bay.

The next morning Burg suffered a scare as he watched Pepper, who had been chopping firewood on shore, nearly fall into the kelp beds while unloading wood aboard the boat. To become entangled in the benevolent-looking kelp, much less the cold water, could be fatal. Pepper, with youthful nonchalance, shrugged at the near mishap. Burg later chided himself for his "mother-hen" attitude. "I watch with the eyes of a hawk," he wrote, "often to the point of ridiculousness." They departed Refuge Bay the next day, in cold, foggy, wet weather. Burg reported in his diary, for the first time, that he "got lost." He had steered for the southeastern tip of Georgina Island instead of the protected passage on the island's northeastern headlands. It is likely that he misread the point of land or coastline he used as a naviga-tional guide. Whatever the reason, he rechecked his plotted course on the map and realized the error.

A fresh northwestern wind came up, allowing Burg to correct his direc-tion, and the *Dorjun* ran down Brecknock Channel, past Georgina Island and the dark stone pinnacles of Tres Pico on Basket Islands, probing for an anchor-age. Cape Saliente, with a view of Desolada Bay, seemed a promising point to anchor for the night. The next morning the sun rose amid a scattering of clouds, casting a rose tint over the water. Northwestern winds brought blue skies and moderate seas. The swells from the Pacific Ocean rolled in, crashing white on the numerous islets and reefs sprinkled around the bay. The *Dorjun* rollicked across Desolada Bay toward Burnt Island, the snow-capped Darwin Range once again rising in the distance behind the island. A school of por-poises followed in the wake of the boat, and all hardship and foul weather was forgotten. By the time they reached their anchorage on Burnt Island, however, the rains had returned. In jest, the men named their latest sanctuary "Conquest Bay." Their enthusiasm was tempered by the fact that they had only three gal-lons of gasoline remaining with which to reach Ushuaia, roughly ninety miles away. Although they sailed and motored sparingly across Whale Boat Sound, they soon were forced to take to the oars. One man handled the tiller while the other rowed.

The pace was sluggish, the physical effort required to keep the boat mov-ing forward against headwinds exhausting. Burg introduced Pepper to river chanteys during this time. Each evening the urgent search for a safe anchorage increased. They could not afford to travel or be caught out at night—they would not use the last of their fuel carelessly. The relentless Fuegian weather affected Burg more than he cared to admit. Night after night he lay in his bunk fretting about past missteps, what he might do to make amends, and how to thank those who had helped him get this far in the journey. Burg and Pepper grew increasingly hungry. The long hours of rowing had sharpened their appetites and provisions were running low, forcing the voyagers to gather mussels and spear crab. An attempt to harpoon a bottle-nosed dolphin failed.

One afternoon as they entered another sheltered inlet, Burg spotted blue smoke rising from shore. He spied a Native hut and two canoes nearby. A single dog paced back and forth, barking. A small child, perhaps a boy, emerged from the shelter. Soon four Indians, the first humans Burg and Pepper had seen in five weeks, stood on shore staring at the *Dorjun*. In his diary Burg wrote:

> [The Natives were] jabbering in a medley of tongues from which we sorted English, Spanish, and Italian words. . . . Four centuries in the track of European voyagers had made these bold beggars linguists. His trousers tattered and ancient, from all appearances might have been discarded by Magellan. A lady's nightcap slouched on the coarse, black hair that hung like thatch over his ears and forehead. In lieu of a shirt, he had laced around his greasy chest a small otter skin which he shifted according to the wind. His blank expression lighted when we passed him tea, tobacco, and matches. . . . The begging Alakaluf is plunder-minded. His wants are endless.

That evening, Burg rejoiced in the day's wonders—mint-green water, snow-capped mountains, and ice-blue glaciers.

> The *Dorjun* leaps like a porpoise in the seas and spray dashes over us," he wrote. "We do not mind. The joy of voyaging is in our blood. . . . One of those rare days there is vigor and inspiration in the sunshine that one can never forget for I shall always feel that I have made a voyage through Paradise. . . . The day's magic is certainly enhanced by the presence of my companion. His mind is clean like the winds. His spirit is free. His ambitions do not torment him for spending time gloriously in the sun. He is a voyager.

The next morning (February 1) they woke early and began rowing along the shoreline of Pia Bay toward Beagle Channel. Ashen skies and icy rain replaced the dawn darkness. Hours later, Pepper pointed to a speck on the horizon. Was it a ship, an island, the face of a cliff? Burg was uncertain. Gradually a plume of smoke appeared—yes, it was certainly a ship, but was it the *Micalvi*? More anxious moments passed, but when the vessel altered course and bore down upon the *Dorjun,* the answer was clear.

Always fastidious, Burg changed his shirt, combed his overgrown beard, and put on his black oxfords. He readied his papers and hoisted the Chilean flag. When the *Micalvi* drew alongside, the crewmen and passengers on deck cheered. The two mariners were taken aback by the enthusiastic welcome. As they boarded the ship, the curious crowd—miners, seal and otter hunters, a geology professor, estancieros, and crewmembers—engulfed them. Everyone wanted to talk to the "Yankees." After much questioning and good-humored teasing, Burg and Pepper were escorted to the wheelhouse. The captain insisted on a toast or two. Meanwhile, the cockpit of the *Dorjun* was loaded with supplies: a gallon of oil, fifteen pounds of potatoes, twenty-five pounds each of salt and flour, and eighty gallons of gasoline, plus photographic supplies from *National Geographic*.

Finally the *Dorjun* was cast loose, and Burg started the engine. Pepper manned the tiller and circled the *Micalvi* one final time to the sound of three loud blasts on the siren and a farewell. Burg snapped his fingers at the wind and said, "To hell with the sail." He laughed as he pointed to the fifty-gallon drum of gasoline. "We had flour—flour for our flap-jacks, flour for our bread, and flour to burn on the stove," Pepper wrote in his log that evening. "Salt—we had enough salt now to start another ocean." No sooner had the two ships departed than black clouds raced toward Pia Bay. The rain swept in, pelting the decks of the *Dorjun*. Urging Pepper to steer toward a point on the eastern side of the bay, Burg paled when he heard the motor sputter and then lose power. Only by repeatedly throttling the choke did he manage to keep the engine running at half speed. Battling a strong tide, the boat struggled to make the entrance to a small bay. At the last instant, Burg signaled Pepper to turn away, as it looked too dangerous after all.

They sought shelter in another cove, but the *Dorjun* pitched wildly back and forth at the anchorage and soon was dragging anchor. Burg immediately went to work on the carburetor, managing to start the engine only to have it fail as they departed their sanctuary. The boat was adrift, as waves crashed over the cockpit and the swells lifted stern completely out of the water, exposing the rudder and the propeller blades. Lacking forward motion, the *Dorjun* slid sideways down the face of the wave into the trough, threatening to broach. Pepper watched as the flat-bottomed *Cabo de Hornos* overturned and the line towing the tender snapped. The tiny boat was swept away. The *Dorjun* tucked into the leeward side of a small headland. Burg leaped ashore and shuttled back along the rocky beach to see if he could locate the missing boat. A torrent of rain and high winds followed him as he crossed a muskeg swamp, trudged through a thick forest, and climbed a headland. On a point above a rocky beach he spotted the *Cabo de Hornos,* tossing and turning in the surf. That afternoon they returned to the cove to retrieve it. The damage was minor.

By evening they were anchored in Olla Cove at the head of Beagle Channel, as the gale continued. Despite the turn of events, Burg joked, "this is our lucky day alright—defective motor, an almost forsaken dory, and one hell of a hard row." He spent the next day taking the carburetor apart again. By poking a pin through the fuel line and blowing hard, he dislodged the cause of the *Dorjun's* near catastrophe—a piece of lint. When he peered out of the boat's porthole on the morning of February 6, Burg knew they would be staying put. Snow had fallen throughout the night, blanketing the surrounding countryside. On the Beagle Channel the windblown snow and the white-capped waves melded together into a whiteout. Travel was impossible, too dangerous.

When the storm passed the next morning, the *Dorjun* hoisted anchor. There were no significant anchorages or glacial bays for the twenty-five-mile-run along the Beagle Channel to Yendegaia Bay and thus little opportunity to escape to safety should foul weather arrive. After two days of slow voyaging, they rounded the northern point of Yendegaia Bay. Pepper steered northeast toward a vertical trail of smoke. The snowy peaks of the 4,400-hundred-foot Pyramid Mountains loomed ahead. As they neared the wooden pier of the waterfront sawmill, a dozen or so young men, none of whom spoke English, greeted the voyagers. The two brothers who ran the local mill insisted that Burg and Pepper share meals with them.

On the morning of February 11, Pepper and Burg set sail for Lapataia Bay. The black cliffs of the Beagle Channel with the white breakers crashing at their base made for an ominous-looking landscape. Five hours and fifteen miles later, they dropped anchor at deserted Lapataia Bay, their first port of call in Argentina. A police corporal hailed the *Dorjun* from shore. The formalities of entering Argentina were brief, the hospitality immediate. With freshening winds out of the southwest, they ran due east between Estorles Island and the mainland of Tierra del Fuego. When they rounded the northern end of the Ushuaia Peninsula that evening, the clouds broke apart and shafts of sunlight pierced the channel waters. Pepper stood on the decks of the *Dorjun* searching for a water trail through the glistening kelp fields. A triumphant Burg steered.

An hour later, they dropped anchor alongside a beach outside of Ushuaia. Climbing a hill above the beach for a view of the lights, Burg wrote that night: "I looked long at the World's most southerly town with a thrill in my heart worth all the trouble and hardship in getting there. In celebration of our conquest we had fresh milk, potatoes and beans which proved to be such a heavy diet that I went to bed uncomfortable and regretting that I had eaten so much." Tucked away from the prevailing winds of the Beagle Channel by the Ushuaia Peninsula and shielded by the snow-covered spires of the Martial Range, Ushuaia was a mariner's delight. The natural harbor was safe and accessible, and with the colorful waterfront buildings and snow-covered Mount Olivia towering above the horizon, it presented a picturesque scene, an invitation to linger.

News of the arrival of a photographer for *National Geographic* spread quickly. Curious visitors trickled down to the waterfront, waiting to be invited aboard the *Dorjun*. For nine days the voyagers dallied in sunny Ushuaia. They slept soundly, without worry, and graciously accepted every invitation to tea, lunch, and dinner, as much for the social opportunities as to slow the drain of their dwindling funds. In town, Burg relished the flower gardens of the residents, a sight that at first struck him as strange "at the ends of the earth." For a week he worked in the prison photo laboratory, training the prison photographer in the latest Rochester method of portraiture. In exchange, Burg was allowed to use the facilities to develop his negatives. The prison was one of the primary economic mainstays of Ushuaia. Of the political prisoners Burg wrote, "Fierce dignity, overbalanced poise of exiled Napoleons, a nonchalant scarf coiled around the neck and flung over the shoulder, mustaches trimmed to an exactness and twisted martially with the fingers. The exiled politicos, exiled because they belonged to the wrong party, become naturalists, geologists, mountaineers, authors, fishermen. They give the town a cosmopolitan air." Pepper made friends easily and began to pick up rudimentary Spanish phrases. Burg interviewed numerous residents of Ushuaia, seeking background information for his article. He hit pay dirt, however, when he met Martin Lawrence, the son of missionaries, who had spent his entire life in the area. Lawrence readily agreed to share his extensive knowledge of the dwindling Yaghan, Alakaluf, and Ona tribes. Their conversations filled pages of Burg's notebooks.

Before European colonization in 1880, the population of aborigines in Tierra del Fuego was estimated at 11,500. The early European settlers, in their search for gold, timber, and grasslands for their sheep herds, gradually pushed the tribes out of their traditional hunting areas, making an already precarious existence even more difficult. The inevitable clash of cultures resulted in warfare. Stern competition with whale and seal hunters, professional killers hired by farmers to "shoot on sight," military campaigns, contagious disease, and famine had taken their toll on the population. The nomadic Onas, the "foot Indians" of the region, lived in the interior forests of Tierra del Fuego. They roamed in small groups hunting the guanaco, their main source of food. They avoided white men at all costs and rarely traveled beyond their hunting ranges, except perhaps to steal sheep. Lawrence laughed at the rumors that the Onas took scalps of intruders or lost travelers. "Nonsense!" he told Burg. Over time the Ona population had declined from 3,600 people to 60 or 70 Onas by the time Burg appeared on the scene.

Lawrence was more familiar with the Yaghans, the "canoe people." They inhabited the islands and both sides of the Beagle Channel and the adjacent channels as far south as Cape Horn. In decades past, they moved from camp to camp, often living aboard their bark canoes for weeks at a time despite the harsh conditions. When not traveling, they pitched wigwam-like shelters in isolated nooks on shore. Few Yaghans, Lawrence told Burg, followed the old ways. Alcohol consumption contributed to ill health as well as to marital and family discord. Tuberculosis spread quickly among entire families who lived in damp close quarters in wigwams covered with burlap or small, drafty wooden shacks. In Darwin's time the Yahgans had numbered three thousand. In 1884 a measles epidemic reduced the tribe to fewer than a thousand people. By 1908, a mere 170 individuals remained. When Burg arrived, just forty-three Yaghans, including those of mixed ethnicities, could be counted.

The Alakalufs, four of whom Burg had briefly encountered in an unnamed bay earlier in the voyage, ranged along the west coast of Chile, from the Gulf of Penas south to Brecknock Peninsula. Although they primarily used bark canoes, Lawrence recalled finding a dugout canoe twenty-nine feet in length and three feet in depth with wooden oarlocks and primitive oars. Trees of that length were few and exceedingly difficult to locate. The Alakalufs, Lawrence pointed out, were far more assertive than other tribes. At times the Yahgans and the Alakalufs had warred and occasionally intermarried. Neither tribe ventured inland, he told Burg. The devastation the whites had inflicted, both intentionally and otherwise, on the two tribes had been severe. Population decline of the Alakalufs had been as spectacular as the Yahgans: from roughly 3,500 at the time of Darwin's visit, only 150 remained in 1935.

In 1520, Magellan, the first European to visit the area, had noted the fires (and the smoke) running for miles along the channels of the archipelago. He feared the local tribes were waiting to ambush his men once they landed. He was correct. Although the Yahgans often built these blazing fires to keep warm, they also used them to signal their people to gather when intruders were at hand. After initial encounters with European ships, the Natives realized the value of the cargo they carried. They began to lure sailing ships onto the rocky coastline with their fires to salvage the wrecks. Hence the name Tierra del Fuego—Land of Fire.

Lawrence arranged the necessary introductions for Burg to the remaining members of the Yahgan tribe who inhabited nearby Isla Navarin, offering practical advice on their social customs. He agreed to store Burg's spare equipment until his return and pay for all provisions and fuel for the voyage to the Horn. The gesture, generous beyond measure, left Burg speechless. Lawrence suggested that Ken Williams, who lived on Isla Navarin and knew the waters of the Cape as well as any man, might accompany Burg and Pepper on their journey. He warned the voyager to make the most of the remaining good weather, not to dally taking photographs that could be made on the return journey.

Yahgan girl at Murray Narrows on Isla Navarino

On the morning of February 22, the heavily laden *Dorjun* weighed anchor and sailed southward across the Beagle Channel for Isla Navarino. Streaked with clouds, the sky looked ominous; the wind carried a familiar chill. Upon landing, Burg spent the next three days photographing Yahgan tribe members; he made a point of taking a portrait of each individual. Most of them had settled into a sedentary life. Burg asked some to dress in their Native garb and to reenact "the old ways." He discovered one Yahgan family who still lived the nomadic canoe life of their ancestors. Domingo, his wife, and seven children had recently returned from a six-month voyage through the southern archipelago. One evening Burg camped with them, photographing and taking notes. As a goodwill gesture, he brought his phonograph into the family wigwam for an evening of entertainment. Even Burg, despite good intentions, could not escape decades of Yaghan suspicion and mistrust. "The phonograph concert was, to Domingo, merely a white man's trick to rob him of something," Burg wrote. "He let the fire go down, chilled us into departing."

After sailing through Murray Narrows, the *Dorjun* entered the mouth of the Rio Douglas on Isla Navarino. Formerly a mission station, it was home to the Estancia Rio Douglas, the most southerly sheep ranch in the world as well as a haven for seamen and otter hunters who had run into trouble. The mission itself lay a mile upriver on the south bank. Ken Williams, who had just returned from seal-hunting, greeted Burg and Pepper with enthusiasm. He earned a living scrimping by—raising sheep, hunting otter, and sealing—and remained as nomadic as the Yaghans' ancestors. When Burg asked if Williams was interested in guiding them, he jumped at the opportunity. Burg later wrote of the guide "his learning was not so broad in scope but he was deep and original with a great personal courage that made him master of his environment."

The party sailed south to Hoste Island. Burg and Pepper ate mussel stew that night and gossiped with Williams and his Native friends. Early the next morning, the *Dorjun* voyaged along the eastern shore of the island toward the Hardy Peninsula. The weather quickly deteriorated, with winds from the south rising fast. Williams predicted that the black clouds over the Hermite Islands would reach them in two hours. He tended the sails while Pepper steered. Off Cape Webley, Burg caught his first glimpse of the Atlantic and Pacific Oceans. He quipped that now all 230 million inhabitants of the Americas were astern.

Near Packsaddle Island, the squall Williams had predicted struck with ferocity neither Burg nor Pepper had ever experienced. Burg steered southeast, making for Cape Hall at the northern tip of Gravy Island at the head of the Wollaston Islands. Late that afternoon he saw the blue conical-shaped peaks of the Wollastons rise and fall on the horizon, then disappear in the driving rain. The *Dorjun* bucked the current for hours before reaching a protected cove. The next morning they woke to howling winds. Outside the whitewashed reef, the sea was black with hillocks of smoking foam and waves crashing as far as the eye could see. The three men gulped down their breakfast and prepared to depart for better-protected Seagull Anchorage on Bayley Island. Another full-force gale was closing in, and Williams delayed sailing, only to change his mind moments later.

As the *Dorjun* beat her way out of the kelp-laced harbor, the Evinrude motor sputtered and died, the prop entangled in kelp. To check the boat's drift, Williams placed an oar at the stern and tried to scull the boat out of harm's way; Burg hoisted a sail. A combination of seamanship and good luck allowed them to clear the point. The eight-mile run to Seagull Anchorage was daunting. With Williams steering, the *Dorjun* ran before a violent sea, the northwestern winds blowing spray and hail into their faces. The massive swells blotted out the shoreline. The cockpit filled with seawater, soaking Williams at the tiller. The giant swells lifted the stern out of the water as it mounted the crest of a breaking wave only to send the boat hurtling down the steep dark face of the next wave.

As the wind roared and shifted directions without warning, Williams and Burg alternated steering. Williams's time-tested approach to foul-weather sailing was blunt and direct. To hesitate in a harsh environment was to risk injury or worse. He never carried a compass and never wore a lifejacket. "Who," Williams wondered aloud, "would want to stay alive any longer than he had to in this unforgiving water?" He steered "head up" to meet each swell, anticipating its size and direction with nonchalant skill and confidence; he carried no more sail than he felt necessary. More often than not, the *Dorjun,* with one rail in the water, seemed on the verge of capsizing. Burg, now at the tiller, shouted at Williams to let out more sail or reef the sail all together; either Williams did not hear the order or he ignored it.

Fearful of being blown out to sea, they continued on a close tack to the coastline of Bailey Island. Although he marveled at Williams's grace under pressure, Burg was unsettled by his apparent foolhardiness. Burg's mixture of caution and boldness, a key to past successes, contrasted with Williams's experienced but impatient approach. Worrying that the boat might capsize, Burg released the sail. The *Dorjun's* port rail lifted out of the water. The sail boom snapped and fell overboard. Williams, who by now had gone below decks to warm his frostbitten hands, emerged on deck. He gave Burg a scornful look "that would have withered a cornfield." They finally reached the entrance to Seagull Anchorage, and Williams guided the boat through the narrow passage between two reefs, steering into the wind before dropping anchor.

So fierce were the winds and the torrents of rain that the crew hunkered down for the next three days. Pepper estimated the winds at seventy miles an hour. Their supply of fresh water and firewood ran low, requiring that two men go ashore in the tender at least once a day. The water they collected had to be strained to get rid of the dirt and moss. Pepper wrote: "It is irritating, here day after day, wind howling through the rigging, waves slapping the boat, the wind swinging us from side to side, and having to go out. . . . Only 600 miles from Antarctic Circle, where [Admiral] Byrd is at the present moment. We are closer to Byrd than anyone else in the world. The weather is terrible here, and down there—huh!—the poor devil." Naval officer, aviator, and polar explorer Rear Admiral Richard Byrd was the first to reach the North Pole and the South Pole by air. Controversy over his claim to have reached the North Pole, however, continues to this day.

In the cramped cabin the three men made the most of their confinement. Pepper prepared the evening meal while Burg wrote in his diary. With Strauss's *The Blue Danube* playing on the phonograph, the talkative Williams spun one harrowing yarn after another. Once he had been stranded on Horn Island alone for seventeen days; another time he had nearly been swept out to sea in a gale rounding the tip of Hermite Island in a *chata* (boat) smaller than the *Dorjun*. That night Williams slept on the aft deck beneath a pile of sheepskins, indifferent to the weather. Burg suspected that Williams had complained to Pepper about Burg's lack of nerve while steering the *Dorjun*. He wrestled with Williams's unspoken insinuation, readily acknowledging the guide's superior skill and experience, and that he was "more or less" the pilot of the *Dorjun* at this point in the journey. But Burg doubted if Williams had ever fully imagined what it would be like for three men to be adrift in a gale.

Morning blue skies, an unfamiliar sight, lightened the mood. The *Dorjun* ran through Washington Channel like a teenager on a joyride. At sundown the men anchored in a protected cove at the base of 2,200-hundred-foot Mount Hyde on Wollaston Island. The following morning Burg and Williams loaded camera equipment on packboards and started for the summit in the dark. Soon they were probing a dense forest of gnarled beech trees bent and twisted by the relentless winds. Two hours of bushwhacking brought them to the loose volcanic rock of the talus slope. Far below, Burg spotted the *Dorjun* safe in the cove, "a speck of hospitality in the wastes of land and sea." Mindful of the weather, they climbed until they reached a narrow rocky ridge beset by fog. At 9:25 AM they emerged atop the summit of Mount Hyde, their vision temporarily obscured. When the weather did clear, they were greeted with a breathtaking panorama of the most southern islands of the Horn—Hermite, Deceit, Herschel, Hall, and the brown mass of Horn Island itself. Burg lived for such moments. He shot still photographs and filmed a 360-degree sweep of the islands.

Williams erected a cairn and without a word rose suddenly and started down the mountain. Burg lingered, standing silently before what he described as "the scene at the end of the earth." Banks of windswept clouds and mist advanced and retreated. Once again, he felt himself riding the current of historical voyaging. Cape Horn, Drake's Passage, and the meeting place of the two great oceans lay beneath him. Magellan, the English sea captain Sir Francis Drake, and Robert Fitzroy, the captain of HMS *Beagle* during Darwin's famous voyage of (1831–36), had voyaged these same waters. Four hundred miles beyond the horizon lay the otherworldly terrain of Antarctica. Burg later called this a supreme moment.

On the evening of March 7, the *Dorjun* reached Isla Navarino across the channel from Ushuaia. Williams returned to his estancia, and Burg and Pepper holed up in the warm cabin of their boat. For the next five days they relaxed, visiting Williams and sharing meals. Pepper played poker with the men who worked the sheep ranch. With the journey to the Horn behind him, Burg allowed himself the deep contentment of a difficult journey completed. He even managed to come to terms with his apparent "lack of spine," writing in his diary: "I forgive myself for my cautiousness in caring for the boat and equipment and for the strong desire to bring all back safely and without disaster, for forgiveness should be first in one's own soul."

On the morning of March 13, the *Dorjun* crossed the channel and lay anchor in the Ushuaia harbor. While Burg prepared for the next leg of the voyage aboard a Chilean navy ship in the Patagonia archipelago off the west coast of Chile, Pepper remained aboard the *Dorjun* with time on his hands. Within the month, he and the boat would be transported by an Argentinean freighter to Buenos Aires, where the *West Mahwah* would transport both back to the United States.

The obstacles Burg and Pepper faced—logistical, financial, personal—on their voyage throughout the Tierra del Fuego archipelago had been formidable. With no prior experience, they had navigated the twenty-six-foot *Dorjun* through an unfamiliar and dangerous maze of coastal waters. They had witnessed stunning beauty and endured daily hardship. The harsh weather and desolate landscapes at the southern latitudes were known to "drive men to despair and beyond," but the two sailors had gotten along remarkably well. A friendship developed that held steady for five decades, a testament to each man's character. Pepper later married Helen, one of Burg's nieces. "I simply cannot recall any surly or cranky words that were said between us for all those months," Pepper later wrote of the experience. "Considering our quarters, weather and all, it was remarkable."

On April 26, 1935, Burg departed Ushuaia for Magallanes aboard the *Micalvi* to continue his assignment for *National Geographic*. Upon reaching Magallanes, Burg boarded a Chilean training ship on a monthlong, thousand-mile voyage to film and photograph the Patagonian and Chones archipelagos on the west coast of Chile as far north as Puerto Montt. The voyage through the Chilean archipelago was, according to Burg, "one of continuous grandeur." Fresh scenery and less hostile weather, the comforts of the ship, and the company of seafaring officers made for a pleasant voyage. Captain Arturo Young made every effort to accommodate Burg, giving him ample opportunity to interview and photograph the nomadic Alakalufs. Burg continued to marvel at the tribe—their seamanship, the construction and seaworthiness of their canoes, their way of life.

He arrived back in Magallanes on June 23 and rented a large room in town for fifteen dollars a month (including coffee in the morning and two daily meals) to continue his research while waiting for a ship home. When he was not accepting numerous dinner invitations or going to watch Tom Mix films in the evening, he holed up in his room working up an outline for his article. He read everything available about the region and continued to interview locals. In total, Burg had taken more than five hundred color plates, a thousand black-and-white negatives, and twelve thousand feet of motion-picture film.

The National Geographic Society contacted Burg with an unexpected offer: Would he be interested in shooting color photographs of the major cities in Brazil, Venezuela, and Colombia on his return voyage to the United States? If he agreed to take the assignment, money, film, and a letter of instructions would be waiting for him at the American consulate in Buenos Aires. Burg considered the offer to be his first genuine photographic assignment for the magazine, one in which his photographic work would not be subsumed by the demands of writing an article. He had always thought of himself as a professional photographer first, a writer second. The assignment was evidence that the photo editors back in Washington, D.C., approved of his work. A week later Burg arrived in Buenos Aires, where he picked up his film, money, and instructions. For the next month he roamed the city, discovering that the *National Geographic* name carried considerable cachet among the governmental agencies, especially the tourist ministry, whose head was quite willing to accommodate a visiting American photographer.

In mid-August he boarded the freight ship SS *West Camargo* bound for Los Angeles via Barbados Island in the Caribbean, where he laid over for a month before heading to Caracas, Venezuela, and Cartagena, Colombia, to complete his photo assignment. After landing in Los Angeles in late November, he wrote to his parents, asking them to keep his arrival quiet to avoid reporters from the local newspapers. When he finally reached Portland, he was greeted with unexpected good news: the *Dorjun,* shipped months before, was resting on the wharf at the Superior Boatbuilding Company beneath the Saint John's Bridge in Portland, awaiting his arrival.

Chapter 7

YANK IN A CANOE

By the time Burg returned to the United States from Tierra del Fuego in 1934, the decade-long debate about where (not if) to build dams on the Columbia River was over. Two years earlier, President Franklin Roosevelt had authorized construction of Grand Coulee Dam on the Columbia as a Public Works Administration project. By August 1933, excavation at Grand Coulee, Washington, had begun, employing hundreds of men. With national unemployment at 25 percent, Roosevelt needed to show the public he was doing something to ease the burden on working people. The dam would eventually spawn a vast network of dikes, canals, siphons, and smaller dams called the Columbia Basin Project—and significantly more employment.

Downriver, near the town of Cascade Locks, Oregon, the United States Army Corps of Engineers had begun construction on another major project, the Bonneville Lock and Dam. Its main purpose was to generate cheap electricity and improve river navigation. The notorious rapid that had given Burg problems would be eliminated, once and for all, by 1938. While William Finley, a pioneering wildlife photographer and Burg's friend, raised questions about the impact of the dam on salmon, most people, including Burg, wondered what the fuss was about. Decades later, Burg explained: "In the thirties the public—and even the builders—had little idea of the consequences a dam might have on a salmon run. But this is understandable. In the still unspoiled, boundless spaces of the West, the water and land resources seemed limitless and inexhaustible. The lessons of environmental damage were still to be learned." The Columbia Burg had known as a teenager and a young man was in the early stages of a decades-long disappearing act. A string of reservoirs stretching from Portland to the Canadian border and beyond would turn desert into farmland, fast water into flat water, and adventure into recreation. Voyages like Burg's would no longer be possible, much less imaginable. His romance with rivers would be tested.

Burg had been on the go for a decade. Despite his passion for adventure, he always looked forward to returning to the family home. His brothers and sisters, many who lived in the neighborhood, now had families of their own. Among his nieces and nephews, news of their famous uncle's arrival inevitably created a stir. Along with neighborhood children, they crowded into the basement of his aging parents' home to watch films and listen to Uncle Amos spin heroic tales of voyages to faraway places. In the old neighborhood Burg renewed acquaintances and friendships. He visited his old haunts, including the Columbia Slough, and had little trouble persuading friends to accompany him on short day-trips on the Columbia. His diaries of the period are conspicuous for the absence of any mention of courting, girlfriends, or a desire for a long-term relationship.

Although he no longer struggled to make a living, Burg had no guaranteed income. Throughout the spring of 1935, he continued to accept numerous invitations to speak at local high schools and chamber of commerce luncheons as well as at the University of Oregon, where he lectured to full houses. The Portland-based Pope and Talbot Lumber Company hired him "to film every trestle, culvert, dock and bridge from Vancouver, B.C. to San Diego," in an effort to promote the use of creosote-treated Douglas fir. Another unexpected source of revenue came with the publication that year of Julius Fleischmann's *Footsteps in the Sea* by G. P. Putnam and Sons of New York. Fleischmann, who had hired Burg as trip photographer on a round-the-world cruise aboard his yacht *Camargo* in 1931, used dozens of Burg's photos in his book.

During the Christmas holidays, Burg also worked with Elaine Bennett, a radio announcer for station KXL in Portland, on the finishing touches of her radio script for her upcoming interview with him. Bennett thought the material so interesting that she had argued, to no avail, for an hour-long show.

At 7:30 PM on January 8, 1936, Burg and Bennett went on the air from the Multnomah Hotel. From the start the two personalities hit it off, seesawing back and forth with their commentary. Bennett played it up, gushing about "the adventuring nomad, the explorer into the unknown and the gentleman at home anywhere in the world." Burg, who rarely took himself seriously, toned down the radio melodrama. After Bennett's effusive introduction, he replied, "Elaine, if I didn't hear my name mentioned I'd be very much afraid I'd walked in on the wrong program."

During the half-hour presentation, Bennett pitched her guest numerous questions about his childhood, early days aboard transport ships, various river voyages, and his work with the National Geographic Society. More revealing than the biographical sketch of Burg's life, however, were his own observations about the path he had chosen. He dispelled the stereotypical idea that the life he led was free of work. "Some think mine a vagabond's life," he said. "But it takes almost unlimited hours and a great amount of money that must all be earned. . . . In the field time is limited and I'm always feeling under pressure to get things done. Scooping up information takes a tremendous amount of hours. If you have a country or a people to portray, the job is almost endless. 16 or 17 hours a day for a whole year is not uncommon. Therefore, you must like what you do." He spoke forthrightly about his philosophy of travel, whether on a river or in a foreign country.

> If a person is not kind and considerate, nor sympathetic, natives any-where will seem like thieves and rogues. What we see wherever we go is a reflection of what we are in our own hearts. . . . Through life, Elaine, there seems to run a sort of universal language of feeling. When you learn that language you feel you are kindred to all things. I love Portland and will always come back here, but the world is no longer a matter of towns and cities. The whole world is your town. I am at home anywhere. When I really leave home, I'll have to go to Mars or the moon. The world is home and the winds that blow are just the electric fans working. . . . I'm always experimenting. You might call it extending the period of adolescence; so I don't come to a point where I feel things are lost or that I have stopped growing. My purpose is to continue my quest until it focuses on some one task.

A week after the radio interview, Burg headed back East. Months earlier, he had pitched a fresh idea to the editors of *National Geographic*—a voyage aboard the *Dorjun* along the Inside Passage of British Columbia and Alaska. His reputation now carried enough weight that the magazine editors tentatively agreed to the project. They suggested that when he arrived in Washington, D.C., he visit the offices to finalize the details. Nearly a decade had passed since Burg and Fred "Spokane" Hill had made the same voyage in *Song o' the Winds,* then tacked on another 1,200-mile run on the Columbia for good measure. He assured the editors that the Inside Passage had never been filmed nor photographed in its entirety. He proposed the voyage to begin in Seattle, Washington, and end at Glacier Bay, where the naturalist John Muir had ventured decades earlier.

In early April, Burg visited the *National Geographic* offices. When Gerard F. Hubbard, an illustration editor and a relative of one of the society's founding members, expressed an interest in the voyage along the Inside Passage, Burg invited Hubbard and his wife, Joanne, to accompany him. It was a friendly gesture as well as an effort to cut costs. Burg's friend and former shipmate Roy Pepper would also join them. During the winter and spring lecture tour, Burg had stopped in Saint Croix Falls, Wisconsin (Pepper's hometown), to appear on stage with Pepper two nights running at the local theater. The lecture—"Voyaging Fuegian Seas for Cape Horn"—had kept the full house spellbound. After the show Burg had invited Pepper along, and of course the adventure enthusiast could not resist the offer.

Pepper arrived in Portland in early May and immediately

LEE KEEDICK presents

AMOS BURG

MOTION PICTURES OF UNSURPASSED BEAUTY.

In a Lecture about his Latest Adventure
VOYAGING
FUEGIAN WATERS
to CAPE HORN

After his Tierra del Fuego voyage Burg became an even more popular presenter on the East Coast lecture circuit.

went to work on the *Dorjun*. After two years of neglect and Oregon weather, the boat needed attention. He sanded and painted the hull and made numerous small repairs and additions, including constructing a "collapsible darkroom." Burg ordered a new sail, a canopy for the stern, and a radio receiver set. He also purchased a new engine and charts of the 1,200-mile coastline. He had the *Dorjun* shipped to Seattle and on June 21, Burg and Pepper sailed north out of Puget Sound for the San Juan Islands. The relatively mild weather triggered fond memories of the miserable days they had spent together in the Tierra del Fuego archipelago.

Upon arriving in Ketchikan, the Hubbards joined Burg and Pepper for a ten-day voyage along the Inside Passage. Afterward, they continued their vacation aboard one of the coastal steamer ships. Little is known about Burg's voyage in the *Dorjun* along the Inside Passage. Although an inveterate diarist, he either failed to keep a diary or it has been lost. Although he casually mentions keeping copious notes for his planned *National Geographic* article, these have also gone missing. Only newspaper clippings and a handful of letters provide a patchwork account. The proposed four-month voyage stretched into six, and Burg shot hundreds of panchromatic photos and four thousand feet of motion-picture film. Whatever the reason, however, his proposed article never appeared in *National Geographic*.

The following spring, Burg received an assignment as a freelance photographer to cover the coronation of King George VI with two *National Geographic* staff writers. Months earlier, Edward VIII, George's older brother, had abdicated the throne to marry the twice-divorced American socialite Wallis Simpson. An international scandal erupted. Burg, ever-ready to seize an opportunity, had approached the editors with a novel idea for an article: after the coronation he would make a four-hundred-mile voyage on the Grand Union Canal System from London to Liverpool. He guessed correctly that a "Yank in a canoe" would strike a chord with both an American and an English audience. The canal journey would be a far cry from the whitewater of the Columbia and Snake Rivers and the turbulent coastline of Tierra del Fuego.

Burg had cut a deal with Electrical Research Products, Inc. (ERPI) to film the voyage as an educational program for American schoolchildren. Spurred by the introduction of talking pictures, ERPI (a subsidiary of the American

Telephone and Telegraph Company) had been formed in 1929 to develop "nontheatrical" films for the classroom. Company executives accepted Burg's proposal. He had arrived on the scene at an opportune time and would work for the company off and on for the next decade. In May 1937 he sailed from New York aboard the ocean liner SS *America* for England. In the cargo hold of the ocean liner was *Song o' the Winds*.

In the days before the coronation ceremony, Burg wandered the crowded streets of London, camera in tow, soaking in the sights and sounds of the bustling metropolis. He tagged along on the practice marches and processions and back at the Marble Arch Hotel, mixing easily with the locals. The voyager, who often fled the confines of society for the sanctuary of nature, relished the spectacle. History was in the making, and Burg literally had a front-row seat. On May 11, the evening before the coronation, he stationed himself and his camera on a platform in front of the Queen Victoria monument near Buckingham Palace. Already the crowds overflowed the sidewalks, parks, and roadways. Realizing that he might not be able to reach his perch on time if he went back to the hotel, he had no choice but to spend the night on the platform. The next afternoon seven million people jammed the parade route. They were in a celebratory, raucous mood. The procession lasted for hours. Burg relished the pomp and circumstance and the march of the military units of the British Empire—the Royal Canadian Police, the Bengal Lancers, the British Guard, and other smaller, lesser-known units. Late that afternoon he headed back to his hotel, a trip that normally took fifteen minutes lasted nearly two hours.

Burg had initially invited the son of his benefactor Charlie Wheeler, vice president of the McCormick Steamship Company and an old friend of Burg's, to accompany him on the voyage. In late June, however, Burg marched off to the United States consulate in search of an alternate. Charles Jr. had been a no-show. Burg scanned a list of stranded young Americans who had "run out of funds" and were available for "work." He decided on Harry (no last name was provided). At their first meeting, Harry agreed to accompany Burg as far as Birmingham, roughly half-way, but no farther. Another week passed before Burg secured a pass for the journey and the all-important lock key from the Grand Union Canal Company. Upon viewing seventeen-foot *Song o' the Winds,* one official curtly informed the American that a vessel that size would not be appreciated along the crowded waterway.

Burg, as usual, smiled and shrugged. He and Harry spent one day shopping for camping equipment and provisions. On July 1 they paddled away from the Regent's Canal Dock. Burg would later write, "With Yankee emphasis on speed, we expected to launch our canoe and get under way immediately. But no Grand Canyon rapid ever looked more formidable to me than that basin, a seething cauldron of shipping activity."

At the start of the Industrial Revolution, London's various canal systems had been a viable alternative to the muddy, deeply rutted roads that bogged down the transportation of raw materials, goods, and machinery in and out of the city. When the railroads appeared, canal use waned and the "ugly ditches" disappeared behind rows of hedges. In the 1920s, however, overburdened roads and rail lines revived interest in the waterways as a cheap alternative. The Grand Union system, linking eleven old (and often failing) canal systems, had only been completed in 1925. Burg was amused to find himself paddling flat water through the heart of London's industrial district—there was not a rapid nor a mountain in sight. Canal travel was not without perils, though. He and Harry dodged barges and tugs, ignoring the glares and teasing of longshoremen and boat operators. From river level the industrial cityscape looked numbingly uniform. If Burg carried a map, it did him little good. Whatever directions he received were either deliberately misleading or wrong. He could not find the lead out of the bustling Grimsby Dock Basin and was forced to retreat.

The next morning Burg and Harry set out again. Three hours of paddling and more poor advice from shipyard workers left the two voyagers in Paddington Basin, only eight miles from their starting point. It was hardly the pastoral countryside he had hoped for. New dangers awaited. Without warning a shower of dirt clods descended on the two voyagers. The canal water danced with divots. Burg ducked, but Harry took a direct hit. On the banks above the canal stood a group of smiling boys, hands clutching more ammunition. The men paddled out of range, as dirt clods followed in their wake. Later a bobby explained the local sport: a canoe with two live Americans, he suggested, was an irresistible target. Burg was forced to agree.

Lacking a current, they paddled into a headwind for the better part of the next day. Harry was not pleased. At increasingly regular intervals, they were forced ashore to tow the canoe. They passed villages, thatched cottages, tidy gardens, green fields, canal-side pubs, and a landscape that harkened back to another age. Industrial England, with its grimy, noisy factories, was left in the wake. Burg began filming and taking notes in earnest. He had entered the English countryside of his imagination. He also began to encounter the fabled canal boats. Beyond London, these barge-like vessels (sometimes called "quick-boats," "fly-boats," or "family boats") were powered by diesel engines instead of being towed by horses. Seventy-two-feet long and seven-feet wide, the boats traveled in pairs. The lead boat, called the "motor," towed the rear boat, the "butty."

Burg felt a kinship with the canal people. For nearly two hundred years the canal boatmen and their families had lived a nomadic existence, part of English society but suspect, insulated from the mainstream. The job of moving freight was handed down from father to son. Families intermarried, babies were born on board, and children attended school sporadically, if at all. The hours were long, the labor hard, though improved with the advent of diesel engines. In the near past there had been such a dearth of canalmen that a half million tons of cargo had been refused in a single year. Panicked owners searched the London docks for deepwater sailors to captain the boats. Roughly five thousand seamen, along with their wives and children, were hired. One Grand Union Canal boatman told Burg they disliked being referred to as "water gypsies," a term in common use at that time.

Life on the canal was not without its simple pleasures. When the weather was fine, the scenery along the canal could be enchanting, at least in the countryside. Dairy and meat products could be purchased at below-market price from local farmers. The decorative folk art on the boats, largely developed during the Victorian period, continued to evolve. Independence, freedom of movement, and the sense of an enduring community was strong. Although he had been forewarned about the canal people's reticence toward strangers, Burg, paddle in hand, used his curiosity and innate modesty to win some over. The families, many of whom had heard about the "Yank in the canoe," were equally curious. Whenever possible, Burg tied up to the barges, ate lunch, and chatted with the boatmen. Occasionally he was invited aboard, where he gleaned information and anecdotes from conversations with talkative wives.

Women and children played an integral part in the operation of the barges. Boatmen were more or less their own boss, but their wives had an equal voice.

Life on the canals had its small pleasures.

On board the women ran herd over their children, insisted on domestic cleanliness in their small cabins, oversaw school lessons, helped with boat maintenance, kept accounts, and literally directed canal traffic. The toddlers, prone to wander on the decks of the canal boats, often had to be lashed to a rain barrel or crate to keep them from plunging overboard. One mother informed Burg that only the week before, one of her children had been pitched overboard and drowned. "The older women at times are well set-up," he wrote, "competent and self reliant and have a cheerful countenance. Others whose husbands put them on a par with the horse have tired backs and trigger tempers from work and children and arguing. When quarreling the women are like black panthers speaking canal dialect."

The older children, often girls, were sent ahead on foot or bike to crank open the gate with their lock key. "They mature early, a girl of fourteen often passing for twenty," wrote Burg. "Some are clumsy walkers, others are lithe as panthers in their movements. Theirs is a hard life with a routine dictated by daily steering or the movement of cargoes. I am beginning to feel closer to them than to the landsmen who watch from the bridges and hangs over his gate as we go by. Most of them [the canal girls] have dirty faces reddened by wind and sun." At one lock, two boats arrived simultaneously. Right-of-way generally belonged to the first boat in sight. Burg witnessed one hilarious incident, which he recorded in his notes: "In this case the wife on each craft claimed precedence. Bickering in unintelligible Midland accents, both demanded right of way and both jammed the noses of their vessels into the mouth of the lock. Thomas Henry, of the fourth generation of Cutlers, shook his finger at the one whom he considered in the wrong. At last, one of the husbands, tired of the wrangling, shouted to the captain of the other boat: 'Come on, man. Let's go 'ave a mug of beer and let the ladies settle it.'"

After fifty-six locks Burg and Harry reached the Tring Summit, an elevation gain of 393 feet above the Regent's Canal Dock, where they had embarked. Over the coming days, they paddled through the hedge-shrouded, stone-walled canals Burg called "green aisles, like secret corridors in a strange land." The weather was often cloudy, rain not far behind. Like all rivers, the winds seemed to only blow upstream, at times forcing Burg or Harry to tow *Song o' the Winds* from the bank. They pitched camp in farmers' fields and shopped in the local villages. Burg, never one to refuse lunch or after-noon tea, boasted of a record-setting "24 cups of tea and 16 pieces of cake in one day." Weekends brought hikers, fisherman, and cyclists to the paths alongside the waterway as well as a steady stream of visitors to camp. Burg spent many evenings walking the countryside while Harry's enthusiasm for the voyage waned.

At Blisworth Tunnel one of the canal boats towed *Song o' the Winds* through the two-mile tunnel, at a cost of two shillings. One of the boatmen explained to Burg the ancient method of "legging," a laborious technique of canal boat propulsion. Before diesel engines became available, pairs of horses had towed the boats. The longer tunnels along the canal, however, lacked towpaths. While the horses were walked around, bargemen hired young men from the local village as "leggers," who lay on their backs atop the cabin of the boats and used their legs to push against the roof of the tunnel, inching the boat along the canal. It took three hours to pass through the Blisworth Tunnel; Burg's tow had taken thirty minutes. Upon emerging from the tunnel, the bargeman's wife dropped the towline, leaving Burg and Harry on their own.

After topping Knowles Summit in a rainstorm, they descended into the industrial heart of Birmingham. The bleak landscape along the canal—miles of slag heaps, sooty factories, and shipping businesses—reminded Burg of a scene from a Dickens novel. A bright moment arrived when the factory girls leaned out the windows of the nondescript buildings, waving handkerchiefs as they launched slips of paper with their names and addresses. They hoped the voyagers would send them a letter or even a photograph.

At Wolverhampton, just beyond Birmingham, Harry departed. Burg arranged for another American traveler to replace him. Nineteen-year-old "Steve" (the last name is unknown) arrived from London, fresh and eager to paddle to Liverpool. Burg and his new companion entered the Shropshire Union Canal at Autherley Junction. The canal ran northwest through storybook pastoral settings to Nantwich and Chester. Horse-drawn barges outnumbered the diesel-powered ones. The two voyagers drew constant hails from shore. Wherever they stopped, small crowds gathered. At one stop a local schoolmaster brought his charges down to the canal, where Burg and Steve had camped. Burg delivered an impromptu lesson on the history and geography of river voyaging in the American West. The boys sang "Home on the Range" in their broad English accents.

Burg's dairy entry for July 21 registered a new awareness: England, a small country with a large population, made for crowded spaces. Wilderness rivers in the United States had offered a sense of space and freedom of movement that he now realized he had taken for granted. "Wilderness freedom, of firewood, water and ability to shout at the top of your lungs is lacking," he wrote. "There is always a house in sight or someone looking down from a bridge or a fisherman just around the corner or two children leaning over a fence to stare still harder. But the rain has made a garden of England."

Near the city of Chester, Burg ran afoul of the lock system. He let water into an already full lock, causing a small torrent to sweep into a barnyard of pigs. The local tender was not amused. Nine miles below Chester, *Song o' the Winds* passed into the Manchester Ship Canal. The great harbor entrance leading to the Irish Sea was plainly visible. It was on to Eastham, where they passed through the last and largest ship locks into the wind-tossed Mersey River. A flood tide carried Burg and Steve onto Liverpool. Two companions and twenty-five days later, Burg had completed one of his more unusual river voyages.

The film *Canal Children of England* was the start of numerous collaborations between Burg and ERPI over the next decade. Despite the travel and difficult logistics, he loved the work. He had achieved relative economic stability in a field where paychecks, though large, were few and far between. After the voyage, Burg rented an automobile and spent another month filming in northern England, Scotland, and Wales. When he returned to New York in early October, he spent the next few weeks visiting friends and associates at National Geographic. Close to Thanksgiving, he returned to Portland and took up temporary residence at his parents' home. While he was at work on his article, his account of the Tierra del Fuego voyage, "Inside Cape Horn," appeared in the December 1937 issue of *National Geographic*.

Throughout the winter Burg spent countless hours aboard the *Dorjun* at Gaults Harbor, outside of Portland on the Columbia River. Like most sailors, he felt a strong emotional attachment to his boat. It had served him well under difficult circumstances. Now the craft provided a home away from home, a sanctuary on the water. On rainy days he lit a fire in the stove and read or worked on his articles. One chilly morning, Burg picked up the February issue of *The Saturday Evening Post*. The opening lines of the first article stopped him in his tracks: "Great adventures seldom have a press agent. The thing is done first; the world hears of it later." "He Shot the Colorado Alone," a magazine article by Portland writer Robert Ormond Case, was a stirring account of a single-handed voyage through the canyons of the Green and Colorado Rivers. Gas station attendant Haldane "Buzz" Holmstrom, from Coquille, Oregon, had covered the 1,100-mile voyage in fifty-two days in a boat he had built himself. On Thanksgiving Day of 1937, Holmstrom had nudged his boat against Boulder Dam.

By the spring of 1938, Boulder Dam (in 1947 the name was changed to Hoover Dam to honor the president) had been in operation for nearly three years. The 726-foot dam was the largest concrete structure and electrical-generating station in the world. The dam had also backed up the river for 115 miles of the Colorado River to a depth of five hundred feet, creating the largest human-made body of water in the world, Lake Mead. Burg was excited. Nearly a decade had passed since he had run a major western river.

A transit of the Green and Colorado Rivers would complete the goal he had set as a naïve teenager. First, however, he had to find Buzz Holmstrom and persuade him to join forces.

Ambition, curiosity, an adventurous spirit—these character traits carried Amos Burg away from the world of women for decades. Although conventional notions of marriage were never a serious consideration for him, relationships with women, whether romantic or platonic and however fleeting or long-lasting, remained vitally important to Burg. He had given his heart to the river and forged an unusual career that kept him on the move, but he enjoyed and continued to seek out female company. Many women were attracted to the romantic gentleman-voyager who always managed to stay just out of reach. Those who understood Burg, appreciated him and expected no more; others ended up with broken hearts. Many of the traits that attracted them to Burg doomed any long-term relationship.

While his father and older brothers went off to work, young Amos Burg grew up in a household of females. As a child, he was shy, observant, and anxious to please. By his late teenage years, he was keenly aware of the sacrifices both of his parents had made in an effort to raise a family. As a young boy, he saw his mother's contribution firsthand. Not unlike many men of his generation, he placed his mother, Annie Burg, on a pedestal and later compared possible mates to her. Vera, his older sister, was a life-long confidante. Mabel, his other sister closest in age to him, had been a reliable ally.

During high school, Burg dated numerous young women. He routinely fell in and out of love, recording his missteps, observations, and hopes in his diary. He fretted, equivocated, and plainly got carried away. His heart was fickle and hungry. In one diary entry he reviewed some of the girls: Bernice (candy eater); Sadie (frivolous minister's daughter); Mae (kisses free for all); Dollie (too much powder); Norma (of my own heart, the only one?); and Alice (lack of respect for her mother). Throughout his college years, it was the same. Few women met Burg's standards.

When pretty, dark-haired Marie began to date Andrew Yunkers, a friend of Burg's who had accompanied him on some of his shorter voyages on the

Columbia, he wrote: "I told her I envied Andrew. Marie asked me what I was going to do. I told her I was going to canoe down a river. She said she hoped I got a good partner. I said that I wished I'd seen her before Andrew did. She promised to write me my letter. I wonder who she likes best. Andrew is the better man but it's according to what type of life attracts her, a canoe or a dentist chair."

Early on, Burg had pinpointed a conflict between the emerging arc of his life and the joys and responsibilities of conventional marriage. This conflict would not be resolved for decades. He voiced his true desires in another diary entry: "If I ever get a girl I want one that will stand hardships or real fun in the winds, rains, snows, and the so-called disagreeable [parts] that make life really worthwhile." During the early years of his long-distance river voyages, there is little in his diaries about women. At some point Burg realized he could not have both, and he made his choice. As he entered manhood, he became more circumspect in his diary entries concerning his relationships. It is clear, however, that he had both romantic and platonic relationships with women until he married in 1958 at the age of fifty-six.

Chapter 8

BURG'S EXPERIMENT: THE GREEN AND COLORADO RIVERS

In the spring of 1924, Amos Burg had attended a lecture by Colonel Claude H. Birdseye, chief engineer of the United States Geological Society (USGS) in Portland. He had already run the Yellowstone-Missouri-Mississippi Rivers (in 1922) but had yet to launch his first Columbia River transit. The subject of Birdseye's lecture was the survey river trip he had led through the Grand Canyon the previous year, only the ninth since Major John Wesley Powell's voyage in 1869. Burg came away impressed. If the Colorado River was not already on his list of rivers to run, he added it then.

Six years later, as a newly elected member of the Explorers Club, Burg had met a handful of "the fraternity of Grand Canyon voyagers," a loose-knit group he had long admired that included the daring Kolb brothers, Emery and Ellsworth, and World War I veteran, businessman, and would-be film-maker Clyde Eddy. Of the numerous conversations he had at the Long Table in New York, however, the ones he valued most were with seventy-seven-year-old Frederick Dellenbaugh. In 1871, Powell had invited Dellenbaugh, then eighteen, to become a member of the second Powell Expedition. He was brought along as "trip artist," assistant topographer, and general river handyman. The voyage left a profound impact on Dellenbaugh. Later he wrote two well-received books about the experience, *The Romance of the Colorado River* (1902) and *A Canyon Voyage* (1908). The old voyager's firsthand accounts of the pioneering journeys sharpened Burg's already keen sense of river history. Once again, he was floating on historical currents; he understood that his own voyages linked him to a larger narrative. Dellenbaugh encouraged Burg to make the Colorado River voyage as soon as possible.

After the Powell Expeditions the first wave of men to run the Colorado —mining and railroad entrepreneurs as well as surveyors and members of the USGS,—were looking for economic opportunities. For hermits, trappers, and hardscrabble miners who found their way onto the Green and Colorado Rivers, it was often a matter of a way of life as well as the slim chance of striking it rich. In these remote areas, knowing how to row a boat and navigate rapids was a necessity. Gradually a new kind of adventurer, men with an eye for beauty and a thirst for adventure, emerged. Some had the means and time to make extended voyages. By the time Burg arrived on the scene, the idea of adventure as pleasure and challenge, if not enlightenment, was well-established but hardly available to the general population. For the most part, the Colorado River remained a mysterious, if not hostile, environment, best viewed from the rim.

The Grand Canyon cast a powerful spell on this group of men. It was an idiosyncratic group—loners, scientists, local residents, doctors, onetime visitors, government surveyors, and wealthy businessmen. Tourists they were not; neither were they explorers or adventurers in the strictest sense of the word. Most were individuals looking for a challenge. The Grand Canyon provided the opportunity to test themselves. Some took the task seriously, others less so. The idea of setting records and establishing firsts emerged. Grand Canyon had captured their imaginations, if not their souls. The entrepreneurial spirit resurfaced. Perhaps, one or two boatmen thought, people would pay to go down the river. Even women might enjoy the experience. People who ran the river were viewed as brave, even heroic, individuals. Burg was part of this "new wave" of adventure-seekers.

Burg wrote to Holmstrom: "Your voyage down the Colorado floored me." The compliment was genuine. He saw his fellow Oregonian's voyage in historic terms. After a brief summary of his own background, Burg suggested that they team up for a voyage the coming summer. It is unclear whether Holmstrom, whose recent fame made him uncomfortable, had heard of the well-known Amos Burg. Nevertheless, he replied within days of receiving the letter, and he was coming to Portland.

Haldane "Buzz" Holmstrom was born May 10, 1909, in a logging camp on Schofield Creek, a tributary of the Umpqua River in the coastal mountains of southern Oregon. At an early age he worked with his father building wooden boats, a necessary means of transportation on the roadless, isolated coast. Eventually the tight-knit family settled on a farm outside of Coquille, Oregon. Holmstrom attended high school in town, where he played football and excelled in his schoolwork. After graduating, he took a temporary job at Ed Walker's gas station. Boatbuilding and running rivers, however, were his preference. He had twice run the Rogue River in southern Oregon and completed a three-hundred-mile solo voyage down the Main Salmon, the "River of No Return," in Idaho. His single-handed transit of the Green and Colorado Rivers in the fall of 1937 had thrust him into the national spotlight. In the *Saturday Evening Post* article Holmstrom admitted that he only decided to go alone after his friends, at first excited by the voyage, had backed out. He felt he had no choice.

In early March 1938, the lanky, dark-haired Burg met his future voyaging companion for the first time at Gaults Harbor on the Columbia River. Holmstrom, eight years younger, was a solidly built man, short with a firm jaw and an open countenance. He was losing more hair than he liked but carried himself with a quiet confidence. The fastidious Burg could not have helped noticing Holmstrom's unkempt appearance. Although time revealed that both men had clearly different personalities, their similarities were many and strong. Both were modest individuals with a wry sense of humor, their Scandinavian backgrounds much in evidence. Each was close to his family (especially his mother) and valued his personal friendships. Both prided themselves on their ability to get along with people. In Coquille, locals claimed that Holmstrom "never met a stranger he didn't like." Neither man was married. Burg and Holmstrom had each fallen under the spell of rivers in their adolescence. They had harbored vague dreams of somehow making a living on rivers. Burg, with the financial backing of his father, had come closer to realizing this ambition than Holmstrom. The struggle of both men to obtain adequate money to fund their voyages was ongoing. If Burg had run his numerous trips on a shoestring, Holmstrom had run his on a thread. All evidence suggests that the two Oregonians hit it off instantly.

Burg pitched a bold plan: Why not combine their resources and know-how to recreate Buzz's solo voyage on film? Holmstrom knew the two rivers, and would serve as de facto "guide." He also had a ready audience. His river voyage, only months old, had captured the nation's attention. Whether Holmstrom liked it or not (he didn't), his name was now known across America. Burg—writer, filmmaker and photographer—had the know-how and equipment plus the necessary contacts in the film industry and at *National Geographic* to make their joint effort a money-making venture. He would be responsible for planning and logistics, as well as securing cameras and film. Although they would split camp chores, Burg's main responsibility would be to produce a top-rate film and photographs.

Burg queried Holmstrom about his expectations for their joint venture. Holmstrom's ambitions appeared modest and perhaps uncertain compared with Burg's: he had long sought escape from the humdrum job of pumping gas in a small town. The overwhelming reception of his Grand Canyon voyage by the public had widened his horizons. Provided their trip was successful, Holmstrom wanted to take a booth at the upcoming World's Fair in San Francisco. With a few photos and his famous boat on display, he would tell the story of his epic voyage. He hoped to make enough money to finance his next adventure—preferably another long river voyage. Burg thought the plan plausible. Holmstrom also mentioned a desire to write an account of his solo journey. He even had a title: *Lone Voyager.* Holmstrom had another goal he did not mention at the time to Burg: to run every rapid on the Green and Colorado Rivers. On his previous voyage he had portaged or lined, with much difficulty, four major rapids. No one, as far as Holmstrom knew, had run every rapid on the two rivers.

Both men agreed they would share the initial costs as well as any profits from the film. Holmstrom, of course, would keep any money he made at the World's Fair. Burg encouraged Holmstrom to go to work on his book immediately, offering to contribute photographs to complement the text. Any profits from *Lone Voyager* would be Holmstrom's. Burg also agreed to forego writing a *National Geographic* article so as not to compete with Holmstrom's book.

Time was short. As usual, Burg's plan was ambitious. Instead of launching from the town of Green River, Utah, the normal jumping-off point for river travelers, they would launch from the lakes in the Wind River Range above the town of Green River, Wyoming, the first week in August. If they reached their final destination, the Gulf of California, they could claim to have run the entire length of the two rivers—certainly a first. The August date offered three advantages: low water to navigate rapids (especially through Cataract and Grand Canyon), photographic opportunities during the fall, when the seasonal lighting produced spectacular scenes, and ample time to reach their final destination before winter weather set in.

Holmstrom would row his handmade fifteen-foot wooden boat, a craft that had served him well on his previous trip. What of Burg? He needed a lightweight boat, one he could carry his camera gear in safely, maneuver in the rapids (and portage or line when necessary) with ease, yet sturdy enough to take a beating. He made no mention of taking *Song o' the Winds*. Given the size and number of rapids in Cataract and Grand Canyon and Burg's own skill level, a voyage in a canoe would have been hazardous. It is likely that he never gave the option serious consideration. Neither did he appear to seriously consider voyaging in a wooden boat like Holmstrom's. Three factors— lack of time and money, the skill necessary to pilot a wooden vessel, and the cargo of expensive camera equipment Burg would be carrying—likely contributed to his decision.

Burg came up with an alternative to traditional river craft. Although there was considerable controversy (including lawsuits) surrounding the development of vulcanized rubber, Charles Goodyear is generally credited with the invention. About the same time Goodyear received his patent in 1844, however, Englishman Thomas Hancock also received a patent. In the late 1840s one-of-a-kind inflatable boats had been used by British naval officers for Arctic exploration. At roughly the same time the American explorer Lieutenant John Fremont and inventor Horace H. Day had developed a crude inflatable raft for use on the Platte River in Wyoming. General George Cullum had introduced an inflatable boat made of rubber-coated canvas during the American Civil War. The boats were often used for ferrying supplies or troops *across* rivers. They were easily punctured and hardly suitable for running whitewater. Vulcanization—the chemical process for converting uncured natural rubber into more durable materials by adding sulfur or other "curatives" brought inflatable boats to the next stage of development. The material was sturdy and reliable. In France and Great Britain, two companies (Zodiac and RFD, named after founder Reginald Foster Dagnall) began developing the first modern inflatable "life rafts" for use at sea. The US Army and Navy had made use of similar crafts.

By the mid-1930s Burg had made an imaginative leap: the sturdy life rafts, by virtue of their ability to bounce off and slide over rocks, would make excellent river craft. Another decade would pass before the use of inflatable rubber rafts on whitewater rivers would catch on. A small wave of post–World War II river runners across the West realized the utility of Navy surplus rafts and began trying them out. The boats were cheap, easy to transport and repair, and best of all they bounced off rocks. River running was in its infancy. In another ten years these same individuals would turn their avocation into businesses, introducing "wild" rivers to a wider, paying audience.

The potentially contentious issue of leadership never came up between Burg and Holmstrom. Both men had a history of avoiding conflict and certainly direct confrontation. Each had much to offer to the joint venture. Burg wrote to Holmstrom: "There is only one thing I desire most and that is to come off the river your friend and to remain one. Otherwise, I shouldn't like to take it." Each kept river diaries. Burg's prose was detailed, occasionally flowery and high-minded as his enthusiasm got the better of him; Holmstrom's letters and diary entries tended toward sparseness with sporadic bursts of heart-felt sentiment.

In early May, Burg boarded the train for Akron, Ohio, home of the B. F. Goodrich Tire Company. His benefactor, Charlie Wheeler, had arranged a meeting with a Mr. Asfall, a personal friend and an executive vice president of the tire company. Asfall summoned one of his engineers from the aeronautical division to listen to Burg's proposal. No one had ever tried to construct an inflatable rubber boat for whitewater. He thought the vulcanized rubber material more than sufficient to withstand the rigors of a whitewater voyage but was unsure of how to fabricate such a boat. He agreed to provide Burg with as much material as needed, but he pointed the voyager to Air Cruisers, Inc., in Bayonne, New Jersey, for the boat's construction. At the time, Air Cruisers was known as a supplier of flotation devices for the US Navy.

At Air Cruisers, oddly enough, Burg was greeted with skepticism. Production managers and workmen were less than eager to take on the task of a onetime project. They had reason to be reluctant. Burg had no proper designs or specifications drawn up. After hours of negotiation, he persuaded company officials to take on the job. He spent another week explaining in detail what he wanted. An article in the 1958 fall issue of *American White Water* magazine suggested that the raft cost $1,500. Air Cruisers promised to deliver the boat by train to Portland, Oregon, in early August, four months away. Burg returned to Portland with a sense that things were moving in a positive direction. Unfortunate news awaited him, however. His seventy-five-year-old father had been diagnosed with cirrhosis of the liver and other health complications.

On July 22 the workmen at Air Cruisers began production on Burg's raft. They estimated the project would take a week. They immediately ran into problems, some due to soaring summertime temperatures in the factory. A series of delays followed, and in late July, Burg wrote to Holmstrom that his rubber boat was *probably* being shipped at this moment. (It was not.) Buzz believed they had another problem, though: the growing publicity surrounding Norman Nevills's trip through Cataract and Grand Canyons. Nevills, of course, had commercial ambitions. Working out of Mexican Hat, Utah, he had previously taken small groups of friends and the occasional tourist down the San Juan River. On June 20, however, he had launched (to much fanfare in the press) three boats from Green River, Utah. Of the four paying passengers, two were women: forty-year-old professor of botany Elzada Clover and twenty-four-year-old Lois Jotter, Clover's lab assistant. Nevills hardly needed to point out the fact that they were the first females to attempt such a lengthy voyage down the Colorado. If successful, Nevills Expedition would be off and running as a commercial enterprise.

Burg reassured Holmstrom that he need not worry about the publicity Nevills or anyone else was receiving. The attention would fade by October. "Start writing your book," he encouraged Holmstrom. "Write down all the occurrences on your former trip. Make the outline complete and then fill in with this voyage's observations. Your book will be strengthened enormously on this second voyage." National interest in Holmstrom remained strong. He continued to receive a stream of letters from admirers, armchair adventurers, and would-be river runners. He gave a series of interviews on the radio. *Ripley's Believe It or Not* planned to feature him; the Explorers Club notified the reluctant hero that he had been accepted as a member. This kind of attention—the praise of his peers—Holmstrom relished.

The question of finding a distributor for the yet-to-be-made film remained unresolved. Burg wanted to promote the Holmstrom film as an adventure documentary as well as place it in the weekly newsreels at local theaters. In a July 25 letter to Holmstrom, he wrote that he had found "a firm in New York who will pay me a thousand dollars for a few hundred feet which will take care of our expenses." Burg brought much of his own camera equipment and rented the rest. He proposed taking two black-and-white thirty-five millimeter motion-picture cameras. The film would have to be specially packed in waterproof tins. To shoot still photographs, Burg carried two, perhaps three, Graflex cameras.

By August 4, Burg's boat still had not arrived in Portland. Realizing the voyage would be delayed, he decided to have it shipped to Green River, Wyoming. In the meantime he would rendezvous with Holmstrom in Salt Lake City. As the days ticked by, Burg grew anxious and could wait no longer. On August 19 he arrived in Salt Lake City, ten days after Holmstrom, who had been staying with Russell "Doc" Frazier, a local river runner and Grand Canyon history buff. Frazier introduced Burg to Julius F. Stone, who had descended the Colorado River in 1909 on the first "recreational" trip with hired guide Nathaniel "Than" Galloway. Stone, an Ohio businessman, had sent Holmstrom a five-hundred-dollar contribution in support of the upcoming trip. Holmstrom, in turn, had named his boat *Julius F.* Burg had named the as yet unseen rubber raft *Charlie* in honor of Charles Wheeler, who had donated two hundred dollars to the expedition.

After a day of preparation, they set out for Green River, Wyoming, in Holmstrom's car and boat trailer. They arrived at Maher's Covered Wagon Auto Camp outside of town within twenty-four hours. Two days later freight men for the Union Pacific unloaded a wooden crate containing *Charlie*. There would be no "test runs" for the yellow raft. Burg had called

Burg photo of Green River Lakes in the Wind River Range; Buzz Holmstrom sits in the foreground.

this creature of his imagination "an experiment in Colorado River voyaging." The raft measured roughly sixteen feet in length, five feet at the beam and weighed eighty-three pounds (in contrast to the 450-pound *Julius F.*). Twenty-six separate airtight compartments, inflated with two-and-a-half pounds of air, would allow *Charlie* "to float on a dew drop," boasted Burg. According to the Goodrich Company, the boat could float five thousand pounds of gear. A laconic Holmstrom joked why anyone would want to row something that heavy through a rapid. In the bow and stern, watertight compartments sheltered Burg's personal gear, camera equipment, and film.

Anxious to get under way, they hired Jim Maher to transport them 125 miles north to the Green River Lakes. On the evening of August 25, Maher dropped his passengers off on the shores of lower Green Lake, altitude eight thousand feet. A late summer chill laced the air. Squaretop Mountain dominated center stage of the dramatic scene. To the east stood White Rock and to the west, Tabletop Mountain. Beyond this stunning vertical stone cul-de-sac, the Green River rises in the snowfields of Garnett Peak. Burg took numerous photographs of the scene. Originating in Wyoming, briefly jogging east into Colorado before bending west into Utah, the Green is by far the largest tributary of the Colorado River. A significant part of the river, the fourth-longest in North America, flows 730 miles in a southerly direction to its confluence with the Colorado. It courses through mountains, across basins, and down numerous canyons. Far downriver in Desolation Canyon, the normally green water turns a silt-laden brown in spring and summer. In fall and winter the river's color stays true to its name.

After months of tedious preparation and maddening delays, the two Oregonians pushed their boats into the placid waters of the lake on the morning of August 26, nearly a month behind Burg's original departure date. He flew the New York Explorers Club's burgee, a triangular pennant with the number eighty-three on it, to signify the eighty-third expedition the club recognized. Bands of clouds floated above the tree line, enveloping the base of the mountains. Overcast skies threatened rain. Burg and Holmstrom, accustomed to Oregon weather, remained unfazed. A local observer might have been surprised, even alarmed, as the two men rowed slowly across the lake that morning in their dissimilar boats to learn they were bound for the Gulf of California. The yellow raft would have appeared especially unsuitable for the task ahead. Already *Charlie* lagged behind *Julius F.*, rowing on flat water would be a chore, and how the boat would handle in large rapids was anyone's guess. A fisherman or ranger might have also wondered how *Julius F.* would manage in the shallow, rocky web of creeks and side channels that meandered through the high country before forming the main stem of the Green.

Of Green River Lakes, Burg wrote in his diary: "Ascended river toward Continental Divide where snowfields & glaciers feeding source of river visible. Cooked lunch on bar making photos head of Green River. Our noon camp nearly 8,000 feet elevation, one of continent's highest watersheds in the primitive area of Wyoming National Forest. Typical glaciated geography, ice streams, snowfields. Lateral moraines and crevices. 1:00 PM paddled down lake for Gulf of California arriving lower end Green River Lake 3:30 PM. Camped above lake in lodgepole pines." Below the lakes, the initial ten-mile stretch of river ran shallow and boulder-ridden, the perfect testing ground for Burg's rubber boat. *Charlie* bumped and slid its way downstream with little consequence, allowing him a margin of forgiveness not available to Holmstrom, who worked mightily to keep *Julius F.* off the rocks. Concerning

Holmstrom's extraordinary boating skill, Burg wrote:"The *Julius F.* did things a wooden boat can't do."

Over the next two days they struggled. Logs and debris blocked the channels. Holmstrom bumped from rock to rock, hitting so hard at times that Burg thought serious damage inevitable. With Burg's help, they manhandled *Julius F.*, already leaking badly, across rocky shoals. *Charlie* slid over the shallows, but Burg encountered barbed wire fences strung across the river in several places. In one instance the vulcanized fabric of the raft was torn. He had yet to fit it with a rowing frame and proper oarlocks, which made rowing arduous and clumsy. Upstream winds further slowed their progress. They had underestimated the labor the upper Green River demanded.

To compound the difficulty, the endless meandering and braiding of the river left the two men backtracking upriver to find a through channel. Burg joked to Holmstrom that their success was measured in how few rocks hit. "To reach Green River City on schedule," he proclaimed, "the river must quit this foolish meandering." Nearly seven hours later they reached Daniel Bridge, covering roughly eleven miles, a snail's pace. With a storm rolling in, they slept on their boats under the bridge that evening.

The rain continued the next morning, turning the side creeks into raging torrents flooding the Green with debris. The river rose three feet and turned a muddy yellow. Talk of reaching the Gulf of California ceased. A disappointed Burg hiked into the town of Daniel and called Jim Mahar, who agreed to come and get them. They spent three days at Mahar's auto camp, making the most of their retreat. Holmstrom made repairs on the bottom of his boat and painted the hull red so it would stand out in photographs. He helped Burg construct a wooden rowing frame for *Charlie*.

At Burg's invitation Phil Lundstrom, a Portland friend, arrived in Green River. Lundstrom had sculled for the Oregon State University Rowing Club and had explored the lower reaches of the Columbia River in his motor cruiser. Not only was he comfortable around water, he had worked as a commercial graphic artist and cartographer in Portland. He knew his way around cameras. In him, Burg had gained a genial companion as well as an able waterman. Down-to-earth Holmstrom joked that "a trio of square headed Scandinavians" were about to head downriver. Lundstrom had also designed the postcards that served as Burg's personal communication to family and friends as well as publicity announcements for newspapers and radio stations. He planned to write daily snapshots of their voyage—a hundred words at most—and mail them to San Francisco from a handful of locations along the river. To lend the cards an air of authenticity, he decided to have the postcard postmarked from each location. Once they reached San Francisco, a secretary would type the daily chronicle on the back of the postcard and send them out.

On September 3 the three Oregonians launched in a downpour. A small crowd of locals and reporters stood shivering on the soggy shore. Holmstrom carried Mahar in *Julius F.*; Lundstrom and a female reporter for the Associated Press rode with Burg for the short celebratory float down to Green River, where they dropped off Mahar and the reporter. Amid the hubbub, Burg began filming Holmstrom. By 1:30 PM the town lay in their wake. "The adventurous voyage and my dream of fifteen years has actually begun," Burg wrote. "A thousand cataracts lay between us and Boulder Dam."

Two days later they reached Flaming Gorge, where the Green River deserts the flat sagebrush plateau ands cuts abruptly through the heart of the Unita Mountains. The scenery changed dramatically. It was "like entering a huge open castle gate," Burg wrote. They passed through nearly rapid-free Horseshoe and Kingfisher Canyons without incident. The melodic song of the canyon wren followed them downstream. Burg got terribly sunburnt, and all three men suffered from frequent upset stomachs likely due to their drinking water. Nevertheless, they enjoyed themselves.

At thundering Ashley Falls, their first major rapid, Burg admitted to a case of nerves but made the run without incident. They pitched camp at Dutch John Draw. On September 8, Lundstrom's birthday, Holmstrom concocted a cake recipe out of fifteen unlikely ingredients. Burg described the frosting as "a cross between wall paper paste and an omelet." Deep in the heart of Red Canyon, they encountered their second major cataract—Red Creek Rapid. The previous year Holmstrom had portaged around it, a Herculean task for one individual; this time he was quietly determined to run the rapid. Both Burg and Holmstrom made successful runs, their choice of routes and styles dictated as much by their craft as their experience. Lundstrom described the scene; "There seemed no possible way of running boats through safely, but Buzz and Amos are undaunted and each selected a different course, certain that his was the only way and the other's was suicidal. Buzz took the deeper channel through crashing breakers, while Amos preferred the shallow, sliding over many boulders on the way. Both came out without a scratch." Lundstrom thought Burg's craft "showed to advantage" in this type of water.

A storm was coming, so the party camped for the night at Beaver Creek (Camp #14). Burg wrote in his diary the next morning: "5:15 AM & still dark when I peeked under the tent flap and the roaring storm was over. The jagged rim of canyon cliffs were etched against a sky sprinkled with stars and blue evening darkness. The feathery pine limbs above were like peacock tails. This moment I am in the arms of earth & sky & stars and feel like one of them. And Buzz stirring the batter sees with wondering eyes & expresses his love for the dawn."

As the trio passed through the Gates of Lodore on September 10, the temperature reached one hundred degrees. The historically minded Burg pointed out "the clump of mountain cedar where Butch Cassidy and Oregon's Harry Tracy had shot and killed Sheriff Val Hoy for trailing them." He mentioned other serious events that had taken place downstream at Disaster Falls in 1869. Major John Wesley Powell had lost one of his boats, much-needed gear, whiskey, and supplies in the early days of their trip. Two of his men had nearly drowned. In 1936 the amateur boater Tony Backus, traveling alone, had abandoned his boat at the same location. Under an overcast sky Holmstrom and Burg ran the impressive rapids at Disaster Falls and Triplet Falls. *Charlie* hung up on a rock at Triplet, forcing Burg out of his boat and onto a nearby rock to push it free. Nevertheless, his modest confidence rose. After two weeks on the river, the advantages of rowing an inflatable raft were undeniable.

Although the dangers of Hell's Half Mile needed no further description, Holmstrom could not resist teasing Burg about the difficulty of the run. Burg had already decided to line and portage his raft (for the first time) for a portion of the rapid. After portaging the cargo of *Julius F.* to a point along the rocky shore, Holmstrom executed a flawless run. Upon entering the lower half of the rapid, however, he struck a rock so hard that his boat seemed to groan. It had stopped abruptly, shuddered, and then tilted up on one side as the water rushed by. Only fast work by both Holmstrom and Lundstrom avoided a turnover. Lundstrom later claimed that he had never heard a sound that made his stomach churn like that before.

When the voyagers neared the head of Whirlpool Canyon, peals of thunder and flashes of lightning ripped the sky, followed by a deluge of stinging rain and hail. Drenched and cold, the three boaters huddled beneath an overhanging ledge for a few hours, watching and listening to the raw display of Nature's power. Side canyons flooded, turning the main channel of the Green River a dark chocolate. Dozens of waterfalls poured like liquid ribbons off the towering cliffs, carrying fresh soil and small boulders that crashed and ricocheted down the canyon walls onto the slopes. Thunder and boulders played a stunning duet. Spooked deer scrambled up the slopes for cover. The rain turned the river surface into a smoky mist. That evening Holmstrom built a huge bonfire to dry their clothing and gear. The blaze nearly drove them out of camp.

A short distance above Jensen, Utah, the trio were greeted by a group of excited residents who hailed them from shore and insisted that the two boats tie up to the same tree Major Powell had anchored his boats to in 1869. Burg could hardly contain his enthusiasm for this idea. That afternoon they rowed into Jensen, completing the first leg of their voyage. According to Burg's calculations, after three weeks on the river they had traveled nearly four hundred miles, run ninety-seven rapids, and passed through seven canyons. They were a mile above sea level. Holmstrom had quietly kept a count of his own. He had run three of the four rapids he had lined or portaged the year before. The last rapid he had portaged—Lava Falls—lay weeks away and hundreds of miles downstream. The two voyagers got along famously. "Our thoughts, coming out of simplicity and awe," wrote Burg, "filled us many times a day with a deep earnestness. I felt humbly that Buzz and I were as one in understanding. We never sulked, nor did we argue too unintelligently, even when under the utmost strain."

A steady stream of visitors washed through the front door of Aunt Atta's Hotel in Jensen, where the voyagers had taken rooms. It was time for a shower and home-cooked meals. Curious locals came to gawk at Burg's raft, which sat out on the front lawn. Burg mailed off his first batch of postcards, mindful of keeping their voyage in the public eye. After five days in the limelight, both Burg and Holmstrom were restless. Lundstrom had departed for Portland to go back to work. On the morning of September 18 they restocked their provisions, readied their boats for departure, and launched downstream. Strong upstream winds, ovenlike temperatures, and swarms of flies and mosquitoes made the rowing onerous. Burg, at a disadvantage in the sluggish rubber raft, reckoned that he needed to maintain a rate of forty strokes a minute to keep up with Holmstrom. The team spent four days crossing the Uinta Basin.

At Camp #26 on Green River, Burg recounted the events of September 23 in his diary. They were close to MacPherson Ranch, "where a colt scampered about the yard. No one home but we made a ranch story in pictures. Mormon style house cut of stone by mason brought in for the job. Wood corrals. Irrigation has made flat as green as a park." The men "borrowed" seventeen apples from the ranch and "beat a grunting hog to a melon." Later that evening Burg wrote, "A voyageur could scarcely make such a voyage without becoming a student of astronomy. I lay for a long time in my sleeping bag gazing up at the stars in their courses. The night breeze brings tales and whispers them through the sage and willows." Gray Canyon had been "not so striking as Desolation [but] Requires experience and good boats to run 3 of rapids this stretch. Buzz is as accurate as knife thrower." They had landed opposite Gunnison butte, with Gunnison Valley lying before them.

On the morning of September 24, Burg and Holmstrom landed under the bridge at Green River, Utah, and pitched camp. Word of their imminent arrival had preceded them. Rivermen from all over canyon country showed up to welcome and, in some cases, take the measure of the two river runners and their boats. Norm Nevills drove up from Mexican Hat; Don Harris, one of Nevills's boatmen, came down from Salt Lake City, as did Bert Loper, a miner, veteran boatman, and jack-of-all-trades. A prickly character, Loper thought Burg's rubber raft "a new-fangled contraption," later announcing to anyone who would listen that "the next time they heard about these guys would be in the obituary column." Local rivermen, like those familiar with the Big Bend reach on the Columbia, harbored proprietary notions about the Colorado and Green Rivers.

For all the bonhomie among Grand Canyon rivermen, there was also competition and petty squabbles, as in any self-selected group. Burg never quite fit in with this group and appears to have made little effort to do so. His manner—low-key, modest, but self-assured—could be misinterpreted. He had traveled the world, visited exotic locations, and mixed with the elite of the exploratory and adventure world. By the time he ran the Colorado, he was something of a celebrity himself. His extensive travel and invaluable camera equipment, not to mention the cost of his raft *Charlie,* gave the appearance that he was well-off. More often than not, Burg plowed his earnings back into equipment, travel expenses, and the next voyage. Later, his need for an assistant to help with camp chores and camera work on the river would raise eyebrows. A sense of ownership inevitably affected those who had worked in, made their mark on, or arrived before the next wave of rivermen on the Colorado River. Burg, a newcomer and late on the scene, may have presented a threat with his reputation, his yellow raft, and his ambitions to make a film. Next to homespun Holmstrom, he looked like a city slicker.

One evening after the crowds had departed, Holmstrom casually remarked that the Grand Canyon would be a good place to do away with a person. Burg, unsure if his friend was joking, later wrote that he was alarmed not by the comment but by Holmstrom's tone and manner. He did not press the issue. In the face of later events, he would ponder Holmstrom's remark on the banks of the Green River for the rest of his life.

With Lundstrom back in Portland, Burg needed another "voyage assistant." The work in camp, coupled with the demands of filming and picture taking, were simply too much for one man. The success of his film depended in part on finding a reliable, hardworking companion. More important, he and Holmstrom needed someone they could get along with for the next month and a half. This person would have to know, or learn quickly, how to handle a boat, cook a meal, and operate a moving-picture camera. A sense of humor would not hurt either.

Enter Willis "Bill" Johnson, a twenty-seven-year-old Mormon coal miner from Thistle, Utah. He had tired of working in the Bingham Canyon Mine outside of Salt Lake City for low wages that went mostly to the company store. He had come to Green River and found work picking cantaloupe and watermelon. The money was not much better, but he enjoyed the sunshine and open air. When he heard about two "river fellas" preparing to go down the river, he made a beeline for their camp. He was upbeat and good-natured. What sealed the deal for Burg, however, was Johnson's penchant for storytelling. He began a yarn each time he visited the camp but never finished. Holmstrom later joked that they only took him along so they could hear the end of his last story. Burg, the history buff, was intrigued by Johnson's claim that his grandfather had worked for Brigham Young, the Mormon leader and founder of Salt Lake City.

The newly formed trio set off on the morning of September 28 for the confluence of the Green and Colorado Rivers, 120 miles downriver. They rowed south across dry, wide-open Gunnison Valley. Johnson straddled the forward deck of *Julius F.*, seemingly at ease despite the upriver furnace winds and the fact that he was headed down an unfamiliar river with two strangers. Burg insisted on stopping at Dellenbaugh Butte, in honor of the man who had encouraged him to make the trip. Frederick Dellenbaugh had died three years earlier, in 1935, at the age of eighty-two. By the time they entered Labyrinth Canyon the next morning, Johnson had proved himself a capable oarsman, taking a turn at the oars of both *Julius F.* and *Charlie.* The sixty-mile reach of river weaved back and forth on itself, offering lengthy stretches of flat water and a seemingly endless number of spectacular vistas. Blue-black and brown desert varnish coated portions of the sandstone cliffs. Rapids were few and insignificant, the water warm, shallow, and silty. For the first time Holmstrom rode with Burg, even set his hand to rowing the raft.

Burg took full advantage of the photographic opportunities, stopping often to shoot still photos of scenery that left him in a state of wonder. Under his tutelage Johnson began operating the motion-picture camera and proved a quick study. They visited Hell Roaring Canyon to photograph the signature of Denis Julien, the mysterious French trapper who had scratched his name in rock a century before. A short while later downriver, the pair climbed a hillside to explore the ruins of a rock shelter that had reportedly been used by the western outlaws Butch Cassidy and the Sundance Kid but may also have been used, because of its superior location, as an Indian lookout.

That night Burg slept fitfully. He had listened to the world news on the radio in Green River, which likely informed his dreams. In his October 2 diary entry he wrote: "I had dreams of a Europe in flames. Today Hitler had threatened to march. But rain, winds, heat or a mad dictator willing to risk the doom of Europe couldn't alter the fact that canyons lay before us & that Boulder Dam must be reached and the voyage done. My deadline was November 1st for another job."

They passed through Stillwater Canyon and on the morning of October 3 landed a half-mile above the confluence of the Green and Colorado, the head of Cataract Canyon. Major Powell had named Cataract for its succession of treacherous rapids. Burg and Holmstrom set out to climb to the rim, while Johnson stayed behind to keep an eye on the boats and prepare dinner. In his bare prose style, Johnson wrote, "This is very beautiful here at the junction. One river is red and other brown." Burg and Holmstrom hauled a bulky load of camera equipment on the 1,200-foot climb. Three hours later they were rewarded with a breathtaking panorama of the canyon country. A landscape unlike any other he had witnessed, Burg described this "land of standing rocks" as "dome-shaped

Willis Johnson joined the Holmstrom–Burg river expedition in Green River, Utah, and proved an able, worthwhile companion.

and pinnacled, weird and fascinating in shape and color. From overhanging rock shelves we gazed down & watched the swirling waters of the Green and Colorado Rivers mingle. Limitless leagues of silence. Far to east merging with sky is the group of eruptive snow-clad Sierra La Sal Mts. Blue and mysterious in the enchantment of distance. To the west the orange cliffs."

Like schoolboys, Burg and Holmstrom shouted to Johnson on the canyon floor, who heard them clearly and waved back.

"Graveyard of the Colorado" is an apt name for forty-mile Cataract Canyon. During extreme spring runoff the chain of twenty-seven rapids (named prosaically numbers 1 through 27) in a sixteen-mile reach become one fast, unpredictable, and nearly continuous rapid. Historical high-water flows have ranged from 40,000 to 112,000 cubic feet per second. Boils and whirlpools grow in size and ferocity, pools and eddies disappear, the river is choked with debris, and eddy fences (the border between fast-moving downstream water and slow eddy water) rise to three feet or more. Numerous "explosion" waves, laden with silt, grow in height (from fifteen to twenty-five feet) and behave erratically and shift position. Standing waves make a hollow, grinding sound and when they strike a wooden boat or raft, it is with unexpected force. Boats of all sizes routinely flip and can be washed downstream, along with their occupants, for miles. At the same time, "keeper holes" in the trough of a wave have been known to trap boats and swimmers, recycling each for inordinate amounts of time. Modern boatmen have nicknamed certain rapids and specific parts of rapids in this stretch with more evocative labels: North Sea (#7), Mile Long (#13–20), Ben Hurt (#20), and Big Drops I, II, and III (also known as Little Niagara, #21–23).

Burg and Holmstrom, like most other boatmen of their generation, avoided these extreme high-water events by running in summer and fall, when river flow was falling. United States Geological Survey records show that the combined flows of the Green and Colorado during the first week of October 1938 ranged from 5,000 to 8,500 cubic feet per second—in other words, low water. Although the rapids of Cataract were less ferocious than they could have been, Burg and Holmstrom faced other difficulties on the river. If they got into serious trouble, they were on their own. A timely rescue was out of the question; a hike out of the canyon would be a major undertaking.

At low water, Cataract runs pool–drop–pool–drop, allowing sufficient time above each rapid to position a boat for the run but, more important, time to correct position if one has misread the entry. Many of the rapids are crowded rock gardens with deceiving approaches, sharp drops, and twisting routes. Slab-like boulders choke the narrow channel; coffee-colored water (masking rocks just below the surface) is harder to read than clear water. The silt-laden waves, while smaller at low water, continue to jump around and carry considerable punch. Scouting some of the rapids requires time-consuming hikes along shore. A mistake—a flip and a raft washed downstream, or especially in Burg's case, the possibility of "wrapping" *Charlie* around a boulder with the full force of the current pinning the boat—would have had disastrous consequences.

On the morning of October 4, Burg and Holmstrom rearranged their boat-loads, putting emergency food in Burg's boat and much of the heavier gear in Holmstrom's. Burg was tense. As he rowed to Spanish Bottom, the first major rapid, the muddy brown water made a strange hissing sound on the bottom of his boat, which only increased his sense of foreboding. How would he perform? Could his raft handle the rapids? "I studied each rapid for its intrinsic difficulties," he later wrote. "Then they did not disturb me." Holmstrom showed no visible signs of distress, a fact Burg appreciated. At Spanish Bottom, Holmstrom, with Johnson clinging to the deck of *Julius F.,* steered for the deep water in the middle of the cataract. They crashed into the murky holes and sharp waves, exhilarated and awash in brown river water. Johnson wrote that Holmstrom "made it look too easy. The boats were tossed about like two chips. I rode lying down on the stern deck and would get soaked at every huge wave and so would Buzz for many waves came clear over into the boat. We were wet all day."

Early on, Burg recognized that following Holmstrom's chosen routes would be perilous. He worked *Charlie* along the shore, lining when necessary at the head of the rapid, navigating the slow water on either side of the main channel afterward. Burg had taken stock of his raft, realized its limitations, and adapted his technique. He erred on the side of caution. In 1869 Major Powell had portaged a majority of the rapids in Cataract Canyon. Done correctly and with enough manpower, lining around a rapid is preferable to portaging a boat. In terms of labor and the possibility of injury, however, both endeavors are time-consuming and not without risk. The hazards inherent when lining a boat arise from a potential combination of possibilities: clambering over a rocky, slippery shoreline; lines becoming tangled; the boat drifting too far out into the current, pulling the person onshore into the river or forcing him to let go of the lines as the boat is pulled downstream. A runaway boat can swamp or be carried away, a boatman's nightmare.

With rain and thunder threatening, the trio camped at the head of notorious Mile Long Rapid that afternoon. They had traveled eleven miles into the heart of Cataract Canyon, running twelve rapids without major incident. Although jubilant, they remained apprehensive. "It roars so loud it can be heard for a great distance," Johnson wrote of the canyon. "It has never been completely or successfully run. It took the Nevills Expedition four days to go a fourth of a mile. They had to portage all their boats around it. Buzz had to portage it also when he was alone but he is going to try and run it this time. It looks pretty dangerous."

Mile Long Rapid is composed of eight closely spaced rapids (#13–20) which at high water effectively become one rapid. At low water, rapid #15 (known as both Capsize and Hell-to-Pay Rapid) becomes a demanding run, requiring a series of maneuvers. After a lengthy scout the next morning, Holmstrom navigated the series of rapids in what Burg described as "clear-cut and skillful as usual." He and Johnson had worked their way downriver, filming portions of Holmstrom's run and lining or running portions of Mile Long. Two miles downriver, Big Drops Rapid awaited, perhaps the most notorious stretch of whitewater on the Colorado River at the time.

Although there is flat water between Big Drops I, II, and III, the routes through the individual rapids are anything but obvious. When Holmstrom claimed he had deciphered a water trail through the cataracts, Burg and Johnson were surprised. Without a word, he pushed off from shore, the wind blowing sand and river spray in his eyes. Burg and Johnson held their breath and watched as Holmstrom weaved his way through one rapid after another, making it look deceptively easy. It was oarsmanship of another order, built more on a deft touch, quiet courage, and imagination than on physical strength. But Holmstrom was not immune to mistakes. As the trio battled headwinds throughout the afternoon, he twice struck rocks, causing enough damage to require repairs.

Burg ran the upper half and lined the lower portion of Dark Canyon Rapid. Then he set up cameras to film what would be one of Holmstrom's more spectacular but flawed runs. The ace boatman uncharacteristically lost control of *Julius F.* and drifted sideways into a crashing wave; Johnson was nearly thrown overboard. The boat filled with water, washing helplessly downstream until Johnson was able to bail it out.

On October 8 the voyagers rounded Mille Craig Bend, passed through Narrow Canyon, and entered Glen Canyon. Ahead lay 165 miles of steady rapidless current and subdued natural beauty. They spent the next week floating lazily downriver, soaking in the sunshine and silence. There were more photographic opportunities for Burg. Water seepage through the porous sandstone had caused tapestry-like designs and green vegetation on the thousand-foot sandstone walls. Sulfur springs along the shoreline stained the rocks in bright hues of color. The weather cooperated, and sandy beaches made for spacious, comfortable camps with inspired views.

Burg had rejoiced when he heard on the radio at the Chaffin Ranch that Hitler had not marched. Ever the world citizen and romantic idealist, he reflected grandly on his place in the world. He wrote on his daily postcard:

> I am of the earth. London, Paris, Rome, Berlin, Vienna, Prague are a part of my vast possessions and I shouldn't like to see some maniac destroy them. More and more I should like for my mind to reach out and embrace the earth with neither prejudice nor division, to become part of the vast stream of humanity in this inexhaustible living World. I believe this to be the road to understanding and peace, and while I poke into the nooks and crannies of the Colorado and for long hours at night my mind explores these possibilities, ideas inspired a great deal by my contact with the National Geographic Society.

With a cold wind blowing upstream and the sun behind the canyon walls, the voyagers broke camp at Meskin Bar and started rowing the morning of October 14. They passed Lees Ferry that afternoon and camped upriver from Navajo Bridge, the walls of the canyon rising above them. After seven weeks and 950 miles, Burg and Holmstrom were poised to enter 62-mile-long Marble Gorge, the first section (from Lees Ferry to the confluence with the Little Colorado) of the Grand Canyon. Both men were excited, eager, and quietly confident. Burg felt he had met the challenge of Cataract Canyon.

Just before noon on October 16, the trio launched. The temperature was sixty degrees, hardly summertime weather and certainly not enough to counter the chilly waters of the Colorado. Night temperatures dropped considerably, with lows in the high thirties. The upstream wind continued unabated, tearing at the river's surface and raising white-capped waves. If rowing was difficult for Holmstrom, it was misery for Burg in the soft-hulled *Charlie*. Soon they approached Badger Rapid at Mile 6. Mileage in the Grand Canyon is measured from Lees Ferry, that being Mile 0. Today's Grand Canyon river runners use a rapid rating scale of 1 to 10, which varies at each rapid depending on water levels: very low (1,000–3,000 CFS); low (3,000–8,000 CFS); medium (8,000–16,000 CFS); and high (16,000–35,000 CFS). Estimates of the water level Burg and Holmstrom encountered in October 1938 suggest medium, at 10,000 CFS.

Holmstrom positioned himself above Badger Rapid, inching his way down the tongue by pulling upstream against the current. He entered on the right side of the marker rock in the middle of the river and with a push of the oars glided through the crashing waves effortlessly. Burg held to his cautious routine, lining *Charlie*, with the help of Johnson and Holmstrom, midway down the left shore. He then ran the lower section of the rapid. Three miles downstream, he lined the raft along the right shore of Soap Creek Rapid before running the lower section. Afterward he shot black-and-white photographs of Holmstrom while Johnson, who had become a proficient cameraman, operated the motion-picture camera. They made camp below the rapid.

When they woke the next morning, temperatures had dropped to near freezing. They waited for the sun to creep over the rim and then started downriver. The voyagers encountered series of whirlpools and erratic, moving water that seemed to follow no pattern. The river current toyed with *Charlie*, stalling

Burg in Charlie *in the Grand Canyon*

the rubber raft, sending it surging forward toward the limestone walls, only to bring it up short. Burg could do little but hold on. Later he downplayed the incident. Johnson, however, wrote: "We almost lost Amos and his rubber boat today. His boat is too flexible and half the boat was sucked straight down into a strong whirlpool. It is a wonder the rubberized fabric it is composed of didn't rip for there was a terrific strain put on it. It is very tough though."

Burg lined House Rock and North Canyon Rapids. Large waves below North Canyon repeatedly swamped the raft. Holmstrom ran everything, as he had intended at the outset of the voyage. Floating through Marble Canyon, Burg experienced an abrupt change in mood, not unlike earlier episodes in Tierra del Fuego. "The descent through this dark chasm with no place on shore for footings in a flexible rubber boat is anything but reassuring," he wrote. "As we go along the walls are hard and grim in aspect which bodes danger and inspires caution. . . . Sometimes comes the sense of imprisonment and that there is only one way out." He was not the first, and certainly not the last, boatman to be momentarily overwhelmed by the size and scale of the Grand Canyon.

The next morning they ran 36-Mile and President Harding Rapids successfully. At Nankoweap Rapid (Mile 52), the three voyagers officially entered Grand Canyon National Park. Burg called the scenery "splendid desolation." They ran Kwagunt and 60-Mile Rapid without incident. That afternoon they camped on an island at the mouth of the Little Colorado. During a haphazard run through rock-strewn Hance Rapid the next morning, Holmstrom punched a hole in *Julius F.* Later he admitted to being in a hurry, a violation of one of his own rules. Burg, with Johnson's help, lined his raft along the rocky left side. Below Hance, the river narrowed and the rocks along shore changed in shape and color. They had entered the Inner Granite Gorge, the deep heart of the Grand Canyon.

At Sockdologer Rapid, Holmstrom and Johnson, perched on a cliff above the rapid, stood ready to film Burg's run. It is a dramatic scene—the exploding train of oversize waves rushing through a narrow portion of the gorge, the canyon walls rising vertically from the water's edge, the bellowing noise of crashing water. It was a difficult, if not impossible, rapid to line or portage. Burg's yellow raft swept down the smooth tongue and vanished in the troughs of the towering waves, appearing for an instant as it topped the crest, only to disappear again. "The waves are at least 20 ft. above the trough,"

Johnson observed, "and are about 35 or 40 feet crest to crest." It was a spectacular run, standing *Charlie* on end, and Burg was mightily pleased with his effort. Holmstrom and Johnson followed with an equally thrilling run of their own. A mile downriver, however, Burg, in the lead, nearly turned over when he entered what Holmstrom described as "a small one [wave] but deep troughs and reverse angling waves."

At noon on October 21 the three boatmen spotted the Kaibab Suspension Bridge downriver, a welcome sight. They had been forced to line Burg's boat around 83-Mile Rapid. Then *Julius F.* caught a wave sideways, forcing both Holmstrom and Johnson to leap for the high side to keep the wooden boat from rolling over. After passing under the bridge, they landed at a beach above Bright Angel Creek. The recent near-misses, combined with the anticipation of their arrival, left the three voyagers wet and worn-out. Burg and Holmstrom climbed to the South Rim the next day to pick up mail and send off more film. In his daily postcard, Burg wrote: "The publicity man here for the private concession had us eating sumptuous meals at Phantom Ranch and via radio citing our preference for their feather beds to canyon rocks. Their exploitation amuses us as we comment upon the unreal quality of sand in our beans down on the bar. They offer neither beans nor feather."

That evening Holmstrom and Burg hiked back down to the river. Burg had not anticipated how much their brief visit offriver would affect him. "Under other circumstances Grand Canyon [South Rim] might have been delightful," he wrote, "but the manufactured tourist atmosphere jolted us too much after the magnificent realties of the Canyon."

By the time Holmstrom and Burg arrived on the South Rim, the photographer and Canyon icon Emery Kolb was well aware of their film project and he was not happy. Emery, along with his brother Ellsworth, had been the first to make a motion-picture film of their run through the Grand Canyon in 1911. In August 1914 they coauthored an article for *National Geographic*. They had also served as guides and boatmen on the 1923 USGS trip through the area. Emery felt a strong proprietary interest toward the Grand Canyon, especially concerning photography and filmmaking. By the time Burg appeared on the scene, Emery had been showing his Grand Canyon film daily in his studio for nearly twenty-five years. Although Burg had met Ellsworth Kolb and had felt comfortable enough to invite him on his Tierra del Fuego voyage in 1934, Emery thought Burg a "Johnny-come-lately." The relations between Emery and the two Oregonians remained chilly.

Burg and his generation of river runners were not yet vexed by the paradox that would ambush modern-day adventurers: that their articles, lectures, books, photographs, and films as well as the promotional work they did for railroads, steamship companies, and government agencies inevitably generated publicity that drew more people to the places they loved. Neither Burg nor Holmstrom could have imagined themselves as forerunners of the river running "industry" that would arrive five decades later.

Burg spent two more days transcribing his river diary to mail off to his secretary in San Francisco. Holmstrom and Johnson wrote letters home, warning family members not to believe the wild exaggerations that they read in the press about their voyage. Holmstrom made repairs on *Julius F,* and by October 25 he was miffed with Burg. "We have stayed two days longer than we at first intended," Holmstrom wrote, "as Amos has done a lot of writing, but we will start tomorrow for sure." To Johnson and Holmstrom's relief, they launched the next morning. At Horn Creek and three miles downstream at Granite Falls, Burg lined his raft down the left shore while Holmstrom ran through the formidable rapids in spectacular rides. After only one previous trip in the canyon and without the benefit of conferring with experienced boatmen, Holmstrom was in a class by himself. The trio camped at the head of Hermit Rapid, after traveling a mere eight miles that day, with the freight-train roar of the river ringing in their ears.

Burg had called *Charlie* an "experiment." After seven weeks on the river, he now had a solid idea of what the rubber raft was capable of. It excelled in shallow water, bumping over rocks when it could not dodge them, maneuvering in and out of eddies with little worry over damage. Flat-water rowing was slow but not a terrible handicap unless the wind began to blow upriver. The raft could handle medium-size waves (five to eight feet high) reliably well. Large crashing waves and turbulent, "squirrelly" surface water and whirlpools, however, presented the inflatable with difficulties. "Amos's boat was tossed by waves with such speed and force," wrote Johnson, "that Amos was tossed at least a foot up from his seat. This has happened several times." Burg explained the phenomenon:

> It should be explained that every morning in the coolness of the canyon walls, I pumped *Charlie* up to where his pontoons were rigid. As morning passed on the river the heat expanded them and I had to start letting out air to take care of the expansion. By noon they were still rigid. By 2 PM the air began to cool and the pontoons begin to sag. By 4 o'clock they were flabby, but I'd tell myself no use pumping them up now we will soon be in camp. Several times we ran into some real breakers and *Charlie* was not rigid enough so he buckled.

With Johnson's help, Burg lined Hermit Rapid along the left shore. After running Sockdolager, his decision to line the straightforward but towering waves of Hermit was surprising. They set up the cameras to film Holmstrom. With its rigid wooden hull, *Julius F.* rode the rapid high and handsome. Two-thirds of the way through, Holmstrom was knocked out of his seat and lost his oars. He drifted sideways through the remaining tail waves, taking on river water and getting pushed around. It was a stirring run on camera but not one an oarsman like Holmstrom appreciated. The trio ran Boucher Rapid nearly without incident. Midway in the rapid, Holmstrom lost control of his boat, and below Tuna Rapid, Burg found himself in trouble. "Amos in the rubber boat was hurled against the cliff," Johnson wrote. "His oar was forced out of the oarlock and he was held there by the current for a moment. If the water had been boiling down instead of up, he would surely have been sucked under."

Looking ahead to Turquoise Rapid, Burg was anxious. He later wrote in his diary: "Viewed this with anxiety and it took several recitations of Ulysses calling upon his comrades 'To shove off and smite the sounding furrows' to arouse enough shaky kneed courage. At the foot of the rapid intrepid Buzz complimented this performance and added soberly, referring to *Charlie*, 'That thing isn't safe.'" But the river was not done with Holmstrom either. At Ruby and Serpentine Rapids, *Julius F.* swamped, washing overboard Holmstrom's sweater and map. For the third time he struck a rock, this time in Waltenburg Rapid. After repairing the three- by eight-inch gash, Holmstrom estimated that he had enough materials for only one more hole.

Burg's short film Conquering the Colorado *showcased Holmstrom's superior rowing skills.*

On the afternoon of October 29 the voyagers left the Granite Gorge behind with a visceral sense of relief. The river widened and the canyon walls retreated, offering panoramic views and a moment to relax. Burg relaxed perhaps too much, as the waves in Forster Rapid nearly turned over his raft. Afterward, he pulled over to recoup his strength on a beach in the sunshine. Feeling listless and faint, Burg had fallen ill from drinking water at Crystal Creek. That afternoon they camped at the head of Dubendorff Rapid, one of the more difficult and technical rapids on the Colorado. The cataract was long, littered with boulders, rocky bars, and huge tail waves that looked deceivingly small from a distance. The entry was misleading, making it easy to get lost in the watery maze. Holmstrom studied the rapid, committed a route to memory, and pushed off from shore yet again. He made it look easy, while Burg and Johnson spent considerable time lining *Charlie* downriver.

After a long day's row made more difficult by slow water and a steady headwind, the voyagers approached Lava Falls (Mile 179) on October 31. "Purity of blue heavens & sunset tinged clouds above the canyon," Burg wrote, "were like looking upward into another world." Since Vulcan's Anvil, a mile upriver, they had been listening to the growl of the famous rapid develop into a thunderous bellow. The noise was nerve-wracking, throwing off aural premonitions of disaster. The trio made camp on the left shore and scrambled over the boulders to scout the rapid they had heard much about. The unfamiliar scale of the setting—the wide open sky, the distant rims, the mass of black basalt rock that covered the cliffs on the right shore, an oversize side canyon on the left—as much as the rapid itself made Lava Falls daunting. One quick look at the rapid on the afternoon of August 24, 1869, had convinced Major Powell to portage. His men had taken three hours to lug their boats around the rapid.

It was a strangely hypnotic scene. The beauty and danger of the rapid intertwined, one masking the other, each beckoning. Spanning the river from bank to bank and with multiple entry points that seemingly led nowhere, the smooth, harmless flat water slipped over the falls and sent up a fine mist that looked not unlike smoke. If order reigned above the rapid, all was chaos below—boulders, ledges, swirling eddies, back water, churning shape-shifting rapids, black holes, green patches of smooth water, boils. Standing on shore, Burg and Holmstrom would have heard the river roar, grumble, grind, hiss, whine, trickle, whoosh, and even, for an instant, relent into silence. Sounds layered within sounds. The rocky shoreline would have felt like it was rumbling beneath their feet. Of Holmstrom's decision to run Lava Falls the next morning, Burg wrote, "at breakfast Buzz admitted half-bashfully like a school boy bringing an apple to a teacher that he would run."

After lining *Charlie* along the left shore and portaging the gear and provisions that Holmstrom's boat had been carrying, Burg and Johnson set up cameras on both sides of the river. After much study Holmstrom had deciphered a route. By now he had grown increasingly anxious. He rowed across the river to the right shore to wait. At 10:00 AM he signaled that he was ready.

Today's boatmen have numerous advantages when preparing to run Lava Falls. Commercial and private river runners are likely to have deep reservoirs of experience. History is also on their side, but the knowledge that hundreds of boatmen have successfully run the rapid lessens the anxiety only so much. More immediately comforting is the location where boatmen gather to study the rapid. The

Black Rock, the balcony-like perch overlooking the maelstrom on the right shore, offers a panoramic view of the rapid as well as a visceral sense of the river's power. The perch can hold as many as a dozen or more boatmen and passengers. It is here that the tribal nature of modern-day river running is most evident. Boatmen glean information, gather their courage, and focus their energy. Nerves are calmed, confidence boosted. Burg and Holmstrom had only themselves to rely on.

Since entry is everything in a rapid like Lava Falls, the approach is studied as thoroughly as the rapid itself. Markers (a rock or ledge) on the river above the rapid, the invisible pull of the current, upstream wind, the glare of the sun are pointed out, allowing the boatmen to imagine his or her position on the river and where he or she will enter the rapid. More experienced oarsmen pass on information and anecdotes; to lessen the growing tension, ill-timed jokes are not uncommon as a boatman points to a wave or draws in the fine dust atop the outlook with a stick. Rookies need little reminding that it is one thing to locate a route through a rapid from a perch above (where the view, though oblique, is panoramic). It is quite another thing to be on the river in the boat looking downstream at a watery horizon, where all the markers appear to have changed shape and migrated to a new location.

If the meeting on the Black Rock boosts confidence, floating down to the horizon lip of Lava Falls tears away at it. One feels small, isolated, and alone, no matter how many people in the boat or how many years at the oars. Hearts race, stomachs turn, muscles tighten. Excitement is leavened with fear. Rowing becomes a manifest act of faith and imagination as much as physical skill. Often, the least experienced boatmen can watch a run or, once on the water, slip behind a fellow boatman and follow, but not too exactly, the path of the boat in front. The comfort of knowing that a boat or two will be downstream waiting to help out is immeasurable.

Today there are many boatmen, both men and women, who row as well or better than Holmstrom. But the solitary nature of his endeavor, coupled with his modesty and humility, make Holmstrom's boating accomplishment unique. He remains a much admired figure among river runners in the Grand Canyon and rivers of the West. To Burg's credit, he recognized Holmstrom's talent early on.

Days later a reporter from a Salt Lake City newspaper interviewed Holmstrom about his run. "I didn't know what went on. I would swear I didn't dip an oar," he told the reporter. "I felt as if I were in a nutshell and some all power-ful hand reached out and guided me through the rapid. How long I was in there I don't know. I never hit a rock nor did I pick up a drop of water. I can hardly wait to see the movies to see what really happened. I might have lost consciousness for all I know." By the next day, however, his exhilaration gave way to contentment as it dawned on the three voyagers that their adventure was coming to an end.

They departed Diamond Creek in the early morning. The ever-thorough Burg noted that they had sixteen rapids to run in thirteen miles. Both boats had taken a beating, *Charlie's* hatches leaked continuously; Holmstrom thought *Julius F.* would need a new bottom. As they drifted into the calm waters of Lake Mead that evening, the sound of the river disappeared. Lava Cliff (which some rivermen believed to be as formidable as Lava Falls), the rapid Holmstrom had run the previous year, had disappeared beneath the rising waters of the lake. On November 3, Burg wrote his final postcard, from Camp #57 on the Colorado, after running the final breakers into calm lake waters and pitching camp:

> Dangers and triumphs over, our freedom is ecstasy. The river flows by in silent majesty. On this beach I taste a moment of perfect peace. Tomorrow we row out of the westerns portals of Grand Canyon to Grand Wash Cliffs to Boulder Dam, and our canyon voyage will become a memory. But the fascination of these hazardous steps in the drama of human endeavor is I hope only prologue. For like Ulysses "my purpose holds, to sail beyond the sunsets and baths of all the west-ern stars . . ." And in the end to say "I am part of all that I have met."

Seventy-four days after departing Green River Lakes, the trio arrived at Boul-der Dam on the morning of November 7. They were greeted by a small crowd—Johnson's family, Holmstrom's aunt and uncle, newspaper reporters, dam workers, and passersby. Holmstrom was in fine spirits—he had become the first man to run all the rapids on the Green and Colorado Rivers. Johnson, who later admitted that he had been "bitten by the river bug," had become famous, if only briefly. Burg, the world traveler, had completed his goal of

Burg and Holmstrom near the end of their 1,100-mile voyage

running all the major western rivers in the United States. He had navigated an inflatable raft the length of the Green and Colorado Rivers and through Grand Canyon—the first to do so. Another decade would pass before inflatable rafts would appear on the rivers of the West.

Burg ranked this voyage as his finest river adventure. "The grandest trip with the best partner I ever had," he wrote of Holmstrom. In a letter Holmstrom returned the compliment: "Amos wears well & I liked him better all the time." Holmstrom drove north to Coquille and a hero's welcome. Burg returned to Portland and a family crisis. At the beginning of the summer, his father had been diagnosed with cirrhosis of the liver. As fall approached, his condition, exacerbated by other health problems, had deteriorated. Although the disease is often caused by chronic drinking over a long period of time, there is no clear evidence that Burg's father suffered a drinking problem. If he did, it was a well-kept secret within the family. However, the younger Burg's decision to become a virtual teetotaler invites speculation.

Burg's diaries and letters do not mention his father's illness, a strange omission for a faithful diary writer and dutiful son. In his youth he had been keenly aware, at times embarrassed, that his hard-working father had financed his river adventures and college education. Now, in a time of need but perhaps at his father's insistence, Burg had been floating the Colorado River. In the early hours of December 1, Amos Burg Sr. died at the family home on Dekum Street. The doctor, a friend of the family, listed the cause of death as "acute occlusion of the heart." Two days later, the younger Burg turned thirty-six.

After the holidays Burg headed back East. Whatever deal he had struck before the trip, he soon learned that neither Paramount Studio nor Warner Brothers was interested in his Colorado River film. He contacted Lowell Thomas, the well-known radio announcer whom he had met at the Explorers Club, for advice. Thomas made arrangements for Burg to meet with producers at 20th Century Fox Pictures. "Personally I'm pretty sick about some aspects of the deal," he wrote to Holmstrom. "It wasn't sold to the best advantage because I had to acquire the experience as I went along. I spent exactly two-and-a-half months on the salesmanship job, a month of which was spent in cutting at the Fox studios here. The anxiety was terrific because I used up all my funds and had to borrow to keep going. Just at the end of the rope I made the deal. They took 800 feet which leaves 8,000 feet."

Throughout the winter of 1938–39, Burg worked on *Conquering the Colorado,* a title that made both Burg and Holmstrom cringe. The heads of the Fox publicity department had insisted on the heroic-sounding title. Burg continued to correspond with Holmstrom, reassuring him that the project was moving along. He had been prepared to preview the short film at a February 2 presentation for the National Geographic Society at Constitution Hall when the date was pushed back. According to Burg, the reason for the delay was "because of Mme. Curie for whom I graciously stepped aside. At least the Geographic said it was gracious co-operation."

Burg complained to Holmstrom that he had a bone or two to pick with Richard Neuberger, a wealthy Oregonian and influential columnist for *The Oregonian* who had written a lengthy account of their voyage. While in Portland, he had read the proof sheet of the Neuberger article and felt he had been misrepresented. Reputation, for Burg, counted a great deal. In a letter to Holmstrom, he wrote: "Did you see where he made me out to be a killer of deer and that you were 'visibly disturbed' and vowed you'd live on bacon and beans rather than kill any of God's Woodland creatures. When I think of all the information I've given that guy on the western rivers for his articles and the poor light in which he'd put me to get a story. . . . Maybe I pass information the wrong way. . . . Dick is not a river runner but he cashes in on the experience of others."

Since the death of his father, Burg wrote two or three times a week to his mother, Annie Burg, often enclosing a check for expenses. "Don't try to cut on the grocery bill or expenses because it doesn't pay," he reassured her. "As partners we are going to get along just fine. Please write and let me know how much you need. . . . It is necessary to do everything possible here so that I'll get as much money for us as possible."

On February 16, Burg presented *Conquering the Colorado* to an audience of three thousand at Constitution Hall in Washington, D.C. His editing of the dynamic footage he and Johnson had shot made the film a visually crisp, well-paced, and exhilarating story. He had eliminated most of the footage of his raft *Charlie,* focusing the film on Holmstrom instead. Burg knew his audience. The thundering musical soundtrack and the dramatic narration combined with Burg's prose cast the modest Holmstrom in heroic garb. The audience responded enthusiastically. Months later the ten-minute film showed in movie theaters throughout the country and around the world.

Burg and Holmstrom each received approximately six hundred dollars, an amount that fell well below their expectations and likely their break-even point. In the coming years, unsubstantiated rumors made the rounds in the small world of river runners that Burg had somehow cheated Holmstrom out of his fair share. Decades later, when Burg heard of these accusations, he was dismayed and hurt. He and Holmstrom were not the first, and certainly not the last, to try to turn a profit from a river voyage. "What I wanted was to show Buzz's lone trip for what it was—a heroic historical conquest," he later claimed. "I felt the documentary extolling his bravery and super-man performance would give him a sense of accomplishment that would spur him on to something else."

On July 1, 1983, we—seventeen passengers, six boatmen, a cook, and a cook's helper in five wooden boats and a raft—launched from Lees Ferry, a day late of our scheduled departure. The river had reached historic high levels never seen before. As local and national news of events on the river unfolded, we boatmen had spent the previous week in a whirlpool of anxious debate, excitement, and indecision. Do we go or not? What was the degree of risk involved? Was the river simply too dangerous for inexperienced passengers, not to mention ourselves? Cancelling the trip would mean refunding considerable sums of money, although management had offered the passengers a trip the following season if they wanted to bail out of this one. None had accepted the offer.

The stage had been set the preceding spring in the high country of the western intermountain region, when the snowpack for the winter of 1982–83 had increased dramatically in the final months of the season. In late May another major snowstorm struck, followed by a hot spell and an unusual amount of rain. The result was a snowmelt runoff that caught the Bureau of Reclamation engineers and dam operators in Salt Lake City and at Glen Canyon Dam by surprise. Fearing the unthinkable—that Glen Canyon dam might be breached—dam bureaucrats gave the order to release as much water as possible through the eight generators and the never-before-used diversion tunnels to slow the rising water of Lake Powell. As a last resort, four-by-eight-foot sheets of marine plywood were attached to the spillways at the top of the dam to buy time and increase the reservoir's capacity.

The release of so much water caused havoc for boaters in the Grand Canyon. Rumors circulated of an eighteen-foot oar-powered raft somersaulting end over end for minutes while being trapped in the "new hole" at Crystal Rapid (Mile 98). Four thirty-seven-foot motor rigs (large pontoon rafts weighing about five tons) overturned at Crystal, pitching ninety people into the river. One person died and fifteen others suffered injuries ranging from severe bruises to broken bones. A fifty-six-year-old man floated ten miles before being rescued. Upside-down motor rigs drifted like ghost ships downriver for days before they could be anchored to shore, awaiting retrieval. The river was littered with recreational flotsam—cushions, orange lifejackets, white coolers, five-gallon gas and water containers, yellow waterproof bags.

On June 28, Grand Canyon park superintendent took the unprecedented step of closing the Colorado River to boat traffic. Planes flew over the canyon, dropping fliers to those already on the river and unaware of the danger at Crystal Rapid. The next day, however, the superintendent opened the river. Increasing pressure from outfitters may have had something to do with his decision. Now each river company would have to decide for itself whether or not to run the river. Our company decided to go ahead with the trip.

When we launched from Lees Ferry, the Colorado River was running at 87,000 cubic feet per second, three times what any of us dory boatmen had ever seen. The river raced at an estimated eight miles an hour, higher, we later learned, in narrower reaches in the canyon. One boatman questioned: "What are we doing here?" Our flotilla was swept mercilessly downriver. We had run this river countless times, but now it looked strange, unfamiliar. Woody debris that once rested above the waterline floated along shore and circled in eddies stretching for hundreds of yards. The current behaved erratically, surging and boiling one moment, deceptively smooth the next. Eddies, landmarks, and sandy beaches had disappeared under the high water, the towering walls of the canyon seemed to have shrunk. The river smelled of desert soil and uprooted vegetation,

When we arrived at Badger and Soap Creek Rapids, both sizable rapids that deserve respect, they too had disappeared, replaced by a river that looked like a giant, bank-to-bank sluice-box far more dangerous than any of our passengers realized. If anyone fell in the water, he or she would be instantly swept downriver, making rescue difficult. Our passengers (three or four per boat), usually excited and talkative on the first day of a trip, gripped the gunnels, waiting silently for instructions.

The water continued to play tricks on us—trapping and spinning a dory in a whirlpool as the main current, two to three feet higher, raced by. It was an unnerving visual reminder of the river's force. The next dory would close in, and just when a collision seemed imminent, the trapped dory was released. Other times the current sent a boat racing downriver out of sight. If the boatman was lucky, he or she might find one of the few patches of slow water and wait. Our typical practice of keeping one another at a safe distance but within sight proved impossible in these conditions. The river gnawed at our communal confidence while the passengers searched our faces for signs of reassurance. At camp that evening we boatmen closed ranks, uncertain of our next step. Should we continue the trip? Evacuate the passengers as soon as possible? What were the risks? Was the river even too dangerous for experienced boatmen? There was no clear consensus or solution, so we continued downriver, reluctantly.

The defining moment of the day-old trip occurred the next morning at Twenty-Four-and-a-Half Mile Rapid. Normally we scouted the rapid, but with the water fast and no place to land, we were forced to run cold. There was no way to avoid the rapid, whose waves had grown in size and ferocity. The first four boats—the *Colorado, Roaring Springs, Emerald Mile,* and the raft—had wild, stomach-churning rides but made it through, more by luck than skill. Midway through the rapid the next dory, the *Flaming Gorge,* stalled in a cavernous hole, shuddering violently as it tried to climb the face of the wave two, three, four, five times before sliding back down into the trough, stalling and then turning over. The furious motion was unlike the slow-motion gracefulness that often characterizes a dory when it flips. Our worst fears were realized: bodies in the fast-moving river, three passengers, our cook, and a boatman.

Bobbing like dolls' heads, they were flushed downriver. The overturned dory followed, crashing along shore before being spun back into the current. They washed through Twenty-Five Mile Rapid, and now the roar of Cave Springs Rapid signaled more trouble. Somehow the boatman managed to gather his passengers and with much effort right the boat. They climbed back into the boat only to discover that one of the oarlocks had been sheared off. Unable to pilot the dory with one oar, he drifted helplessly before another waiting dory managed to throw a line to the *Flaming Gorge* and tow the dory and its exhausted passengers to shore at the head of Cave Springs Rapid.

At camp that evening the mood was somber. Passengers gathered to discuss the day's events and comfort those who were shaken by the experience. The cook had her doubts about continuing the trip, as did some of the boatmen. The crew debated the possibilities: abort, evacuate, or continue downriver and hope for the best. The next morning we headed downriver. The following afternoon at camp we reached a decision. We would evacuate anyone who wanted to leave at Little Colorado (Mile 61) the next day. Two people who had been in the *Flaming Gorge* took up the offer.

We radioed for a helicopter evacuation the next day and asked the park rangers to tell our company manager that we wanted a twenty-two-foot snout rig with a motor to run ahead of our dories, waiting at the foot of rapids or anywhere else we deemed necessary in case the flotilla ran into trouble again. The snout rig, with two inflatable tubes and a metal frame platform, was smaller and far more maneuverable than the behemoth thirty-four-motor rigs that plied the river. The river was too dangerous to run without support.

We laid over another day at Nankoweap (Mile 53). People rose late, sat by the riverside sipping coffee, watching the river race by. For the first time people laughed and joked. They read, napped, and made small talk as they wiggled their toes in the warm afternoon sand. Some hiked up the nearby cliffs to granaries for a better view of the river. At dinner that evening we toasted the departing passengers and lit fireworks to celebrate the Fourth of July. The next evening our support boat, piloted by two smiling fellow-boatmen, arrived. The remainder of the trip, though not without moments of urgency, was a more relaxing voyage for both passengers and crew.

Chapter 9

BOATMAN, FILMMAKER, SPY: THE MIDDLE FORK AND MAIN SALMON RIVERS

R ussell "Doc" Frazier, who had greeted Amos Burg and Buzz Holm-strom with enthusiasm when they stopped in Salt Lake City on their way to Green River, Wyoming, the previous summer, invited the two Oregonians to join him on his next trip down the Middle Fork of the Salmon River in Idaho. Burg, who liked Frazier and was keen to run another western river, had accepted the invitation immediately. With the popularity of *Conquering the Colorado* in mind, he now suggested filming the trip; Frazier agreed. Burg had another reason to join the trip: no one, as far as he knew, had ever taken a rubber raft down the Middle Fork. Holmstrom, initially keen on the idea, later declined. He had accepted an unusual offer to guide a wealthy female client cross-country from Oregon to New York by river—a herculean task given that he would have to travel upriver on the Columbia and the Snake. When Burg asked Frazier if Willis Johnson could join them, he readily agreed.

As his plans took shape, Frazier told Burg and Johnson to meet him in Ketchum, Idaho, the third week in June 1939. The Middle Fork, fed by snow-melt, should have enough water by then. On June 23 a Blaine County land agent wrote to Frazier, who had arrived in Ketchum days before: "The water is right. Grab your boats and come!"The next morning Frazier, Burg, Johnson, the writer and amateur Western historian Charles Kelly, and members of the self-proclaimed Colorado River Club (boatbuilders and rivermen Frank and Gib Swain, storekeeper Bill Fahrni, and Hack Miller, a journalist with *Deseret News* in Salt Lake City) loaded four freshly painted boats onto trailers and drove to Bear Valley Creek, elevation six thousand feet, west of Stanley, Idaho. They spent a cold night by the river and launched the next morning.

The 105-mile Middle Fork, located on the north flank of the Saw-tooth Mountain Range, was known for its isolation, natural beauty, and near-continuous rapids. In the past decade only a handful of people had run the river for pleasure. Frank Swain, accompanied by Gib, rowed the *Rimrock*; Fahrni manned the oars of the *Also Ran*; Miller was in *Polly B.*; Frazier, with Kelly aboard, captained the *Stefansson,* named after the Antarctic explorer. The carefree group was primarily interested in having a good time and not overly concerned about damaging their boats. Hitting rocks, swamping, and turning over—it was all part of the fun. If they lost or destroyed a boat, they would go home and build another. Johnson, elated to be back on the river, rode with Burg in *Charlie.* The yellow raft drew curious stares from the Utah boatmen, as did Burg himself, dressed in his signature outfit: leather oxfords, khaki pants, long-sleeved shirt with tie, sailor's cap. It was hard to know what to make of the boat or the gentlemanly Burg.

Frazier and Frank Swain had found a way to satisfy their mutual interest in running rivers. City-bred Frazier, trained as a doctor, financed and organized the river trips, paying for provisions and the construction of the boats; Swain, from Vernal, Utah, built the boats and acted as lead boatman. They had had mixed success on the Middle Fork. Two of their three previous trips (in 1935 and 1937) had been aborted, the latter due to a combination of high water and poorly constructed boats. In 1936, however, they had managed to complete the second documented run of the Middle Fork and Main Salmon Rivers to Riggins, Idaho. Frazier wanted to repeat that run, then continue down the Lower Salmon to the Snake River and Lewiston, Idaho—a 375-mile voyage.

The high mountain river was fast, cold, and rocky. Within an hour of departing, the party pulled ashore. The *Rimrock,* Swain's boat, was leaking like a sieve, the other boats less so. Having come from a desert climate, the boats had not

Rescuing a sinking boat, not for the last time

absorbed enough moisture to swell the seams between the planking. The men plugged the gaps as best they could with rags and strands of rope. Their troubles had only just begun, however. When they were not bouncing off rocks, the river runners were dragging their wooden boats over shallow gravel bars. It was rough, time-consuming labor, hard on both the boats and the men, who slipped repeatedly into the icy water. But Burg's experience was different. As Kelly reported in his diary, "Burg's boat floats over everything." After *Charlie,* river running on the Middle Fork would never be the same again.

That afternoon they camped near Marsh Creek. Frazier found the two wooden boats they had abandoned two years earlier just where they had left them. At the time Frazier, who had had a few drinks, had become so frustrated with the boats' performance that he threatened to take an ax to them. To everyone's surprise, the weathered boats were in decent shape. Gib Swain was assigned the *Blue Goose.* Johnson, who had pined for his own boat, took command of the *Deseret News.* He immediately broke an oar, though, then lost control of the boat in a small rapid. The open boat washed up on a rock, turned on its side, and filled with water. It took all hands to heft it off the rock and drag it to shore for repairs. Johnson was mortified. They had covered a scant seven miles. Burg, who had filmed the action, "stepped out of his rubber boat with his shoes dry," as Kelly noted.

There was more trouble the next morning. A couple of miles above Sulphur Falls (today's Dagger Falls), Miller had wedged the *Polly B.* fast between two large boulders. It quickly filled with water. Manhandling the boat, they punched a one-square-foot hole in the bottom and watched it sink. They scrambled to unload the gear, most of it soaked. A chastened Miller now rode with Gib Swain. The flotilla portaged their gear around Sulphur Falls and camped early. That afternoon Kelly filmed Burg lining *Charlie* over the upper set of falls. Burg then ran the lower section without incident. "Amos has plenty of nerve," Kelly wrote. Burg's experience on the Green and Colorado Rivers, coupled with studying Holmstrom's technique, had improved his rowing.

Once below Sulphur Falls, the Middle Fork proper begins its ninety-five-mile run to the Main Salmon. The first fifteen miles of the snow-fed river (with a gradient of thirty feet per mile) runs fast and shallow through the narrow canyon. The rapids are near continuous and demand constant attention. By the sixth day of the trip, Johnson—his face swollen from a tooth that Frazier had pulled and ragged from lack of sleep—rode with Burg. The inexperienced Kelly took a turn at the oars of *Deseret News*. Moments later, he drifted into a logjam and pinned the boat. Kelly and Miller wrestled to free the boat from the tangle of fallen logs and debris. Kelly took an ax to a large branch on the downstream side and started to work on an upstream log. Suddenly the boat lurched free, and Miller found himself pitched into the fast water. Kelly followed him into the river, while the unmanned boat drifted downstream and stuck fast on a rocky shoal.

By now, the entire group was suffering a variety of ailments: tick bites, sore lower backs, an eye infection, a mild case of hypothermia, upset stomachs, perhaps a hangover or two (except for Burg, who did not drink). The next morning the group encountered the first of two major rockslides blocking the river, the result of heavy rainfall the previous summer. The first required lining and heavy lifting, an exhausting task no one looked forward to. A mile downstream they encountered the second landslide, which forced them to stop and scout. Frank Swain took charge, successfully piloting all the wooden boats through a narrow, rocky passage.

It had not gone unnoticed by the Swain brothers that Burg had brought along a tent that Johnson helped him erect each evening. Johnson, who had worked with Burg in the Grand Canyon the year before, knew that the tent was not a luxury but a necessity. Burg used it to clean his camera equipment and to load and unload film. "One grain of sand on the camera's pressure plate can put a scratch in a thousand feet of film," he wrote. Nevertheless, his reputation as a river prima donna had taken hold.

At Velvet Falls the men had successful runs. For several miles the river and the boats melded in effortless harmony. Fishing was fruitful. Kelly, who had a reputation as an abrasive personality, got along well with Burg. He enjoyed their conversations. Both men were well-read, articulate, and had traveled extensively. There was talk of collaboration on a book about rivers. The boaters' good fortune ran out below Soldier Creek (Mile 12). Frank Swain broke an oar, lost control of *Rimrock*, and crashed into a rock. Fahrni was knocked from his boat and ended up clinging to a rock midstream before being rescued. Whether they cared to admit it or not, these members of the Colorado River Club and their boats were taking a beating. Initially skeptical of Burg's rubber raft, the Swain brothers grudgingly acknowledged that *Charlie* might be the right boat for a river like the Middle Fork.

No sooner had they launched the next day (July 1) than Miller punched another hole in the bottom of *Polly B.*, forcing the fleet ashore for repairs. They lined one rapid after another. At Pistol Creek, Johnson filmed Burg making a seemingly effortless run. That evening Kelly wrote that he was "too sore and tired to enjoy anything." On July 3 they landed at Crandall's Ranch (Mile 66). Mishaps that day were limited to one runaway boat that drifted for a half-mile before they caught up with it. No matter—the sun was out, the water forgiving. They fished the river and ate cherries from the Crandall's orchard. Seventy-three-year-old Mrs. Crandall, who had not been out of the canyon in ten years, visited the men after supper. That evening rain fell, the first of the trip.

The next afternoon the flotilla rowed through Haystack Rapid (Mile 67.5), the beginning of Impassable Canyon. The riverside trail ended, the canyon walls rose, and the skyline narrowed. An unseasonably cold rain followed the boaters. Although the runs were straightforward, the rapids were increasingly frequent. The voyagers camped at the mouth of Parrott's Creek, near one of Earl Parrott's cabins, and later they visited with the sixty-eight-year-old hermit. Burg wondered aloud why Parrott always carried a pistol. If he fell on the trail and broke a leg, Parrott explained, he could shoot himself.

Frazier and Frank Swain held counsel with the other boatmen. Instead of trying to reach Lewiston, Idaho, they decided to end the trip at Riggins, roughly eighty miles downriver. They were behind schedule, and the men (as well as their wooden boats) were worn-out. By noon the next day the fleet entered the Main Salmon, the famous "River of No Return." At Salmon Falls Rapid, Frazier broke an oar. Johnson got caught in the backwash of the falls and nearly overturned. Below the rapid, however, as Kelly described it, there was "plenty of water now, easy going." The sun was out; the temperature climbed into the nineties. The river regained its dazzling green color. Along the shoreline thick forests and white sand beaches made for inviting camps. They covered thirty miles before pitching camp near John Cunningham's ranch.

Trouble and inconvenience continued to plague the trip. At Big Mallard Rapid, Burg lost an oar and had a wild ride. Johnson almost capsized. Fahrni nearly washed out of the boat in which he was riding. The next day (July 9) Miller swamped the *Polly B.* and had to be rescued by Frank Swain. Farther downstream, after failing to stop and scout a rapid, the *Stefansson* hit a wave sideways and turned over. Frazier and Kelly went for a swim. Burg, following behind, made it through but was irked that he had failed to get a photo. The Swain brothers volunteered to run the biggest waves at Carey Falls to allow Burg another photographic opportunity. Frank nearly flipped but managed to come out right side up in the tail waves. His younger brother was less fortunate. The *Blue Bottle* stalled in one of the larger waves and turned end over end. Gib disappeared beneath the whitewater. When he finally popped up, everyone laughed nervously.

The voyagers battled hot upstream winds all the way to Riggins, the temperature soaring to 109 degrees in the shade. Upon landing in town, they sorted gear, loaded their boats, and went their separate ways. Kelly later wrote: "Everybody is glad the trip is over." Plain-spoken Johnson made an equally telling entry in his river diary: "We may have rubber boats next year for they add to the thrills of boating, but it will be hard to have a more thrilling or enjoyable trip than this one we have just finished. Although I believe . . . open boats can be taken on through, it will be much better to have rubber boats, for Amos Burg has proven them to be far superior to any other kind of boats even though a person will have his share of upsets if he isn't on the alert all the time."

World War II slowed recreational river voyaging to a trickle on the Middle Fork of the Salmon and western rivers in general. As cheap surplus rubber rafts became available after the war, experienced and especially novice river runners returned to the river. In 1946, Oregonian Ruth Hindman piloted her rubber raft down the Middle Fork—the first woman to do so. She repeated the feat the following year. The door to the joy and excitement of river running had opened to a wider audience. With the growth of commercial river companies, each decade witnessed explosive jumps in the number of people floating the river every season: twenty-five in 1949; twelve hundred in 1965; forty-five hundred in 1975; and nearly nine thousand in 1990.

Throughout the summer Burg negotiated with Paramount Pictures. Company executives were now eager to purchase the footage of the Middle Fork voyage. Confident that he could produce an exciting river film, he boldly asked for more money than he thought he could get. The eager Paramount executives agreed to his price. Burg titled the film "Seeing Is Believing." After his Middle Fork trip, he reached the Christiansen Ranch in Modoc County, California, to begin work on another assignment for ERPI, the educational film company. They wanted him to film a working ranch. When he heard that there were numerous creeks and rivers near the Christiansen Ranch, Burg brought along a lightweight rubber raft to make day trips.

With the financial good news, Burg wrote to his mother back in Portland, reassuring her that money, for once, would not be a problem. "I don't want you to worry about the property Mother," he wrote. "We could work something out together. I've always come home no matter how far I've gone away and you will always be my first interest." By Christmastime in 1939 he had returned to Portland. He visited with longtime friend Captain Oliver P. Rankin and his wife, Gertrude. Rankin had just retired from an eighteen-year career as a Columbia River Bar pilot. Age and failing health had convinced Rankin that it was time to let go of the *Solace,* his treasured ketch. He offered to sell the boat to Burg at a bargain price. Half in jest, he declared that if Burg would not purchase the *Solace,* Rankin would sail the boat out over the Columbia Bar and burn it. Burg accepted the generous offer. After talking with Rankin, he renamed the boat *Endeavour,* after the vessel of their favorite explorer, Captain Cook.

After the holidays Burg headed back East. One afternoon he was summoned to the Explorers Club to be interviewed by club member Seward Cramer, the editor of a volume of adventure stories (tentatively titled "Through Hell and High Water") by club members that was to be published the following year. Cramer wanted Burg to give an account of his and Holmstrom's 1938 voyage through the Grand Canyon. Burg, mindful of his place in Grand Canyon history, was glad to oblige.

ERPI offered Burg another plum assignment: to make three films for their Children of the World series. *Children of Japan, Children of China,* and *People of Western China* would be used in schools to promote goodwill among nations. In March 1940 he boarded the *Tatsuda Maru* in San Francisco bound for Japan. Upon his arrival in Tokyo, government officials viewed him with suspicion and kept him under surveillance throughout his stay. Relations between Japan and the United States had grown increasingly thorny. Despite his initial misgivings, however, Burg set out to win over the Japanese he encountered. In an effort to please his hosts at Japan's Department of Tourism, he accepted numerous speaking invitations. When he made a cultural gaffe, he immediately summoned his head guide, Mr. Nishinohara, to repair the damage and explain where he had gone wrong. At their first meeting, Nishinohara had been polite but standoffish. Burg later wrote in his diary: "Americans in foreign countries have the unhappy habit of making unfavorable comparisons [between the United States and Japan]." He scolded himself for his coarse American habits: "The delicacy of manners and gentle politeness made me resolve to refine some of my barbarian ways." He was also aware of the Japanese sense of superiority over their Asian neighbors. "In subtle ways," he wrote, "they let me know that Japan was about to embark on a great mission in East Asia."

Although the Department of Tourism extended Burg their full cooperation, the filming of *Children of Japan* was not without problems. Each location

During his travels in Japan and China, Burg reached across cultural barriers to make friends.

and scene he shot had to be vetted by a succession of officials. The need for consensus among officials slowed the process to a crawl. Burg bit his tongue. After completion of the film, he presented it to an audience of Tokyo city bureaucrats, and they responded enthusiastically. In a gesture of appreciation, Nishinohara staged a large farewell party for Burg. Twenty-five officials from the tourism department attended. Serving Burg, according to Nishinohara, was the loveliest geisha in all of Japan. Usually Burg avoided alcohol, which he considered "a deadly poison for the lonely traveler," but that evening he relaxed his code. He answered every toast of sake from his hosts with one of his own. When he woke the next morning, he found himself stretched out on the floor of the hall where the party had been held in his honor. The lights were mercifully dim. "The cleaning lady had my head in her lap and her right hand on my head," he wrote. "In her other hand she still held her mop."

In early July 1940, Burg sailed aboard the *President Taft* from Kobe, Japan, to Hong Kong. He took up temporary residence at the Hong Kong YMCA. His immediate problem was how to safely reach the Chinese mainland. Only a week earlier, Japanese pilots had shot down a China National Airways plane with passengers, a Chinese co-pilot, and an American pilot aboard. At China National Airways the clerk informed him that the airlines flew only in bad weather, to avoid Japanese attacks. "How bad is bad?" Burg asked. The clerk replied: "Well, a typhoon is ideal, but we'll settle for less, provided it's real cloudy."

Seventeen days passed before he received a late-night call summoning him to the airport. On the rocky flight across the China Sea, Burg asked the pilot of the DC3 how he knew where he was, given the absence of lights and radio guidance. The pilot smiled—he flew by the stars when he could, he said, but if he could smell Canton on his left, he knew he was on track. In the early morning hours the pilot landed on a gravel bar in the Yangtze River at Chungking (now Chongqing). No sooner had Burg reached his hotel when the whine of the air-raid siren filled the air. He took cover in a bomb shelter, the first of twenty-one bombing raids he experienced during his stay in China.

The three-hundred-mile journey to Chengdu, where Burg would be based, was long, dusty, and uncomfortable. He arrived exhausted at a small village to spend the night, only to be shaken down for a fee by a group of local toughs. In Chengdu he stayed with missionary teachers at West China Union University. While working on *Children of China,* he also filmed newsreel stories of the bombing of Chinese cities and reservoirs by the Japanese—a fact that pleased Chinese officials. For his next film, *People of Western China,* he roamed as far west as the foothills of the Himalayas. By the end of the summer he was bound for San Francisco aboard the SS *President Pierce.* En route, in Kobe, Japan, officials detained him once again. After lengthy questioning about his trip to mainland China, he was released by the Japanese officials. When he learned of his arrival back in the States, Charles Wheeler, Burg's friend and benefactor, threw a lavish dinner party for Burg at his San Francisco home.

As the United States's relationship with Japan continued to sour, Burg found the demand for speaking engagements about the Orient on the upswing. In 1941 he was invited to be the keynote speaker at the Explorers Club dinner at the Waldorf Astoria. At the speakers table he found himself seated next to John D. Rockefeller, a leading patron of exploration. Burg lectured and showed his film *Chungking to the Himalayas.* The toastmaster was Lowell Thomas, the well-known writer, radio personality, and world traveler. A relentless self-promoter, Thomas was best known as the journalist who made the British Army officer T. E. Lawrence (Lawrence of Arabia), a household name with his film *With Allenby in Palestine and Lawrence in Arabia*. Thomas, who had always been impressed by Burg's performances, invited him to present his Cape Horn film before the Motion Picture Exhibitors of America, where he rubbed shoulders with such luminaries as Eleanor Roosevelt and Dale Carnegie. Afterward, Thomas persuaded Burg to speak at the Dutch Treat Club, a social as well as a literary and illustrative arts venue that had attracted the likes of writer Robert Benchley, poet Ogden Nash, and political cartoonist Rube Goldberg.

Before introducing Burg, who was to speak on his 1938 Colorado River voyage, to the Dutch Treat Club audience a few nights later, Thomas pulled him aside. Former president Herbert Hoover was in the audience. "For God's sake Amos," Thomas implored, "call it Hoover Dam, not Boulder." After Hoover's failure to be reelected in 1932, a controversy over the naming of the dam had erupted. Not until 1947 would the issue be resolved, when Congress restored the original name—Hoover Dam. Burg began his speech by noting that he and Holmstrom had traversed eighteen canyons in two small boats over a period of seventy days before reaching the Hoover Dam. He continued in this vein, taking every opportunity to thread the former president's name into his narrative. By the end of Burg's presentation, Hoover wore an ear-to-ear grin. He sought out Burg afterward, congratulating him on the finest dinner speech he had ever heard.

Pleased with his work in the Orient, the ERPI producers assigned Burg two more films—*Alaska, Reservoir of Resources* and *Eskimo Children*—Burg was delighted. He now had the opportunity to voyage the Inside Passage. It would be *Endeavour's* first lengthy maiden voyage. Captain Rankin had purchased the thirty-six-foot lifeboat in 1929 as surplus and had it converted to a ketch rig by a Finnish shipwright at the Wilson Boatworks in Hammond, Oregon. To make the trip worth his while, Burg secured an assignment with *National Geographic*, persuading the editors that an article chronicling *Endeavour's* voyage would be a sure hit. He also agreed to film and record the folklore and music of the Eskimo, Native, and Caucasian people he encountered for his friend Dr. Vilhjalmur Stefansson of the Bureau of Ethnology of the Smithsonian Institute and the American Folklife Center, a branch of the Smithsonian and the Library of Congress. Besides traveling the Inside

Passage, Burg planned on visiting the Alexander Archipelago, Prince William Sound, the Bering Straits, and the interior of Alaska. He would travel by boat, plane, train, and dogsled.

Burg approached Willis Johnson with an offer of work. Johnson, who had come a long way since first captivating Burg and Holmstrom on the banks of the Green River with his yarns, had never been to sea. He had proved a competent cameraman and a reliable companion. Burg agreed to pay Johnson fifty dollars per month plus expenses and a bonus if the filming went well. Before heading west, Burg spent two days at *National Geographic's* photo lab in Washington, D.C. He met with the staff to learn more about color techniques with the new Kodachrome film.

By mid-April, he had returned to Portland to prepare for the trip. For the first but not last time, Burg took on passengers to defray costs. He had entered the charter boat business. On June 20 two young women and their chaperone arrived at the docks in Seattle from San Francisco. They were to accompany Burg and Johnson on a three-week pleasure cruise to Ketchikan. The itinerary included fishing, sightseeing, isolated beaches, numerous ports of call, including a handful with outstanding hotels and shops, as well as land excursions and visits with the local inhabitants.

For the next two weeks Burg guided *Endeavour* north through the maze of coastal waterways. Birdlife was abundant; porpoises trailed alongside the boat. There were numerous sightings of gray whales breaching and spouting. Early one morning Johnson roused the women from their sleep. Nearby, a pod of orcas (Johnson called them "black fish" or "tigers of the sea") performed acrobatics. For the most part the weather cooperated. Sheer forested cliffs, morning fogs, waterfalls, snowcapped peaks, blue glaciers at the tail end of the inlets and channels, the silence—the endless variety of the coastal landscapes left Burg's passengers tongue-tied. When they were not picnicking and sunbathing on a sandy beach, the three women hiked the trails of the small islands at which they anchored, discovering fields of wildflowers and small pristine lakes. They helped with the daily routines, including cooking. They stopped at the small coastal villages and towns (for supplies, socializing, and respites at hotels) as well as abandoned canneries and Indian villages, where weathered totem poles stood guard. When they anchored for the evening in a particularly striking cove or bay, Burg often took the women out in his canoe-turned-tender,

Song o' the Winds. By July 3, *Endeavour* was anchored in Ketchikan harbor. The women departed. All parties appear to have been satisfied with the voyage.

During the layover in Ketchikan, Burg learned of the death of Captain Rankin and immediately wrote to Mrs. Rankin: "Every moment that I am aboard her [*Endeavour*] I become more grateful for the loving care and honest wood and construction that went into the creation of this noble ship. I know that I shall never feel that I own her for she will always belong to Captain and you, but I shall try to be worthy of this trust you have put in me by allowing me to sail *Endeavour* again to sea."

For the next month Burg and Johnson shuttled back and forth between Ketchikan and Juneau. In Petersburg, Burg took photos of a large fox and mink farm. They motored up the Stikine River to explore the mining towns along the shoreline. Back in Ketchikan they spent a week filming at a local school, the Ketchikan Spruce Mill, and the numerous canneries whose operations were in full swing. In the fertile Matanuska Valley Burg and Johnson gaped at a twenty-eight-pound cabbage in the vegetable garden of one old-timer. By the end of August, Burg was bound for Seward aboard an Alaskan Steamship Company vessel. Johnson remained in Juneau, living aboard *Endeavour*. He found work at the Alaska-Juneau Mine outside of town.

Working on behalf of the American Folklife Center, Burg recorded twenty-six twelve-inch discs of interviews, accordion performances, recitations, narratives, and songs. He interviewed Harold Wood, a Seventh-Day Adventist, about his experiences as a boat-traveling missionary doctor in southeastern Alaska. One disc contained songs and recollections by Arndt "Lonesome Pete" Pederson of Meyers Chuck (forty miles northwest of Ketchikan), whom Burg had befriended two decades earlier. There were recordings of birdcalls, church hymns, and Native American myths. Five discs contained an interview about the recent adventures of Paul Satko, an unemployed welder from Richmond, Virginia, and his family aboard the "Ark of Juneau." Satko had built a boat that even he admitted "looked kind of whacky" and trailered it across the country to Tacoma, Washington, in 1939. He planned to pilot the boat along the Inside Passage to Juneau and then homestead in the Matanuska Valley in the interior of Alaska.

Just as the sea and the rivers of Alaska had caught Burg's imagination, now the snow-covered interior beckoned him. With a shooting script in hand (written by Jim Brill of ERPI), Burg roamed the state filming and shooting photographs. His *Reservoir of Resources* called for a panoramic view of the state and its natural resources. In late October, the work complete, Burg returned to Juneau, where he planned to spend the winter aboard *Endeavour*, writing his magazine article for *National Geographic*. Not long after arriving in Juneau, he was invited to speak at the monthly Chamber of Commerce luncheon at the Baranof Hotel downtown. He delivered the tales of his travels down rivers and around the world in his usual self-effacing, humorous style. Of special interest were his comments on the war between China and Japan. Burg said he could not decide who he was angrier with, the Japanese or the Americans, when he realized that the Japanese pilot's planes were propelled by American gasoline while they dropped American scrap iron on Chinese cities. He was no longer uncertain when on Sunday, December 7, 1941, he heard the news of the Japanese attack on Pearl Harbor on the radio. He was aboard *Endeavour* at the time. He was not surprised by the discouraging news.

Late in February 1942, Burg sailed alone for Seattle. He had numerous obligations, including a stop in Portland to visit his ailing mother and speaking engagements on the East Coast. Upon reaching Seattle, he placed *Endeavour* in dry dock storage. Four years passed before he sailed aboard his ship again.

ERPI offered Burg more film work, and in the spring of 1942 he traveled back and forth across the United States for a four-film series on the country's different regions (*Far Western States, Northwestern States, Middle States,* and *Southwestern States*). He carried a weathered set of the Encyclopedia Britannica with him, claiming the background reading gave him the historical context he needed to make sense of each region.

At forty-one and with numerous injuries, Burg was hardly military draft material. His South American travels and background, however, yielded an unexpected opportunity to serve his country. The Ethno-Geographic Board at the Smithsonian Institution asked to use the photos he had taken during his 1933–34 Tierra del Fuego voyage. Burg readily agreed, and the board turned copies of the photos over to the US Navy and Army and the Office of Naval Intelligence. The photos included views of ships, shipping facilities, industry, towns, and cities along the Straits of Magellan as well as the coastlines of

Argentina and Chile. Next the Office of Strategic Services (OSS), a forerunner to the Central Intelligence Agency (CIA), came calling. For some time the US government had suspected Argentina of aiding the Axis powers. Not until 1945, when Allied victory in Europe was imminent, did Argentina and Chile declare war on Germany and Japan.

In January, Portland's chief of police performed a routine background check on Burg and wrote a "clearance" letter to the OSS. Arthur Canfield, Burg's family doctor, reported that he was in sound health, physically and mentally. Upon arriving in Washington, D.C., Burg received a series of typhoid vaccinations as well as a smallpox vaccination. In wartime it was not unusual for *National Geographic* to lend the services of their overseas writers and photographers to the US government. Burg never revealed the exact nature of his government assignment, however. It is unlikely that government officials in Chile and Argentina knew of his activities. He did say that he had been warned that if he got into any trouble, the US embassy would deny that he worked for the OSS. Burg joked that the need for secrecy gave him indigestion.

Upon returning to Washington, D.C., in September 1943, Burg received another choice assignment from ERPI. Already scripted by the company writers, the as-yet unmade films would present a summary view of the Caribbean West Indies, Central America, Colombia, and Venezuela, including geography, history, and economy. It was an unexpected opportunity to voyage Colombia's Magdalena River. Although he would travel as a passenger on a paddle wheeler for the journey, not exactly an exploratory adventure, he applied to the Explorers Club to carry their flag. The club granted his application, issuing Flag #111. Burg also sold the idea of an article about the journey to the *National Geographic* editors.

In early December he landed in Cuba. He spent the next two months exploring the remoter regions of Central America. Small aircraft were the only means of reaching these areas, including the Mayan ruins he wanted to photograph. He spent many anxious moments, one eye on the gas gauge and the pilot, the other scanning the forest for a patch of ground to land on. If landing was hair-raising, taking off was akin to near-death, according to Burg. The "airfields" were so small that before take-off the tail of the plane would be yoked to a tree at one end of the runway. The pilot then revved the engine to maximum RPM before someone on the ground cut the line with a machete. The plane barreled down the runway at full throttle to increase the safety margin of clearing the jungle canopy.

In February, Burg flew from Panama to Bogotá, the high-altitude capital of Colombia. He spent the next few weeks traveling the countryside by rail and boat. After stays in Bogotá, Popayan, Cali, and Buenaventura, Burg boarded the sternwheeler *Jesusita* in Puerto Berrio for the five-hundred-mile journey to the coastal town of Barranquilla on the Caribbean. The thousand-mile Magdalena River rises in the Cordillera Central of Colombia, flowing effortlessly through a roughly fifty-mile-wide fault-block valley before spilling out on a broad alluvial plain. There the Cauca River joins it and the Magdalena winds north toward the sea. Although eight hundred of its thousand miles are navigable and the Magdalena was the main transportation route in Colombia at the time, the area along the river was sparsely settled.

As a passenger aboard the *Jesusita*, Burg could not help but draw comparisons between the river pilots of the Magdalena and those of the Columbia, Yukon, and Mississippi Rivers. They were more alike than different. From the decks of the *Jesusita* he watched as dozens of bamboo rafts and hand-hewn dugout canoes piloted by Natives on their way to market with fish, platanos, rice, and pineapples to trade plied the river. The rafts, upon landing, were dismantled and the bamboo sold as fence posts and building material for houses. He spent a few days in Barranquilla, the end of his voyage, before making the three-hour journey by road to Cartagena. He wandered the historic city, visited the sights, interviewed officials and Cartagenians, took photographs, and watched tankers being loaded with Colombian oil at Mamonal, a few miles south of the city. The oil flowed from hundreds of wells of the De Mares concession in the Magdalena Valley, 334 miles away. The same pipeline paralleled the Magdalena River.

By the time Burg reached Washington, D.C., in late June, he was suffering a variety of illnesses. He felt unusually tired and suffered constant headaches, diarrhea, and an unruly stomach. The doctor diagnosed dysentery. Months of travel had drained his cash reserves. He spent the next two and a half weeks holed up in a stuffy apartment in Washington, D.C., writing his article for *National Geographic*. Once completed, he thought it the worst he had written, a clumsy failure. Leo Borah, an editor at the magazine, disagreed. He told Burg that "Cruising Colombia's Ol' Man River" was the best he had written. With rest, Burg's health steadily improved. Then he learned that he had been elected to the Board of Directors of the Explorers Club along with Dr. Roy Chapman Andrews, Dr. William Beebe, Admiral Richard Byrd, and his river-running friend, Russell "Doc" Frazier.

Burg decided it was time to return to Hells Canyon on the Snake River. He had no trouble finding companions. When his old friends Charlie Wheeler, Pat Patterson, and Doc Frazier heard of his plan, they jumped aboard. By mid-September 1944 the four men were camped on the banks of the Snake near Huntington, Oregon. Seventy-five miles downstream lay Hells Canyon. Although a river trip through Hells Canyon is considered routine today, in 1944 few people traveled the mile-deep gorge with recreation in mind. Considered remote, hostile country, Hells Canyon, with its string of what would be classified as Class V and VI rapids, was simply too dangerous.

Patterson, who had let Burg moor *Endeavour* at his waterfront home near Seattle, brought a skimpy six-foot rubber raft of dubious quality—hence the name *Junior*. Frazier rowed an aging twelve-foot canvas-covered wooden boat he labeled *Patches*. Burg, of course, rowed his *Charlie,* with Wheeler as a passenger. By modern standards the boats were inadequate for Hells Canyon. Burg and Frazier had the most experience in the group. A lighthearted mood prevailed; the men were on holiday. They launched downriver and immediately lost track of time. Soon Frazier and Patterson had disappeared. Burg and Wheeler pulled over and waited. Eventually the two river runners arrived, both riding in the bathtub-size *Junior* with *Patches* in tow. In Bayhorse Rapids the rotting wood-and-canvas boat had stuck a rock and torn a hole in the hull. Frazier spent the afternoon repairing the boat.

The next day Frazier purchased a fourteen-foot wooden boat from a local ferryman near Homestead, Oregon. He was delighted with the craft, but Burg thought the boat poorly designed. An inexperienced but willing Wheeler was given command of *Patches*. Burg led the cheerful flotilla down the river. Running the rapids was viewed as a straight-ahead-take-it-as-it-comes undertaking. *Junior* took a beating, folding up regularly and turning over, pitching Patterson into the water. Wheeler, in the larger craft, fared marginally better. Under a warm September sun the voyagers lined their boats around Kinney Creek, Squaw Creek, and Buck Creek Rapids. At Thirty-Two Point Rapid, the overloaded *Patches* nearly sunk. Frazier's wooden boat broke away while being lined and crashed through the rocks to the foot of the rapid. The hull of the boat was so badly damaged that Frazier used towels and socks to bandage the gaps. The men also lined Wild Sheep and Granite Rapids.

The trip settled into a leisurely pace. It was a far cry from Burg's earlier, more adventurous exploits, but he did not mind. He remained enthusiastic, enjoying his companions and his return to Hells Canyon after fifteen years. He surprised many of the old-timers who lived along the river with impromptu visits. By day nine the flotilla was far behind schedule. After lining Rush and Sluice Creek Rapids the next morning, they rowed downriver as fast as the current would carry them. Late that afternoon a US Army search plane swooped down the canyon so low that Burg could see the pilot waving. Burg gave the pilot a thumbs-up. When the men had failed to show up in Lewiston on time, Wheeler's family and business associates had informed the Army, which sent a rescue plane to search the area. Newspapers in San Francisco had reported Wheeler gone missing in Hells Canyon. Burg joked that while he, Frazier, and Patterson had been delayed, only Wheeler had been "lost."

Upon arriving at Pittsburgh Landing, Wheeler arranged for a small airplane to fly him and Patterson back to Portland. The four men had gotten along splendidly. They agreed to run another river together next season. Burg and Frazier continued downriver to Lewiston. That winter Burg wrote to Wheeler: "For myself in Hells Canyon, at first I was a little bewildered. I had been away from the vast thoughts that voyaging on a clean river brings that I felt as though my mind was trying to break its way out of a cocoon. I am only sorry that I did not have a couple weeks more on the river; it would have done my mind a lot of good."

Upon arriving in New York at the end of January 1945, Burg rented an apartment on Riverside Drive overlooking the Hudson River from a member of the Explorers Club. He would spend the next fourteen months there. His first order of business was to find a physician. Ever since a shipboard fall aboard the *Dorjun* years ago, he had experienced intermittent back pain. He had also had bouts of listlessness. Burg discovered he had contracted malaria during his travels in South America. He spent the next few weeks recovering.

As his health improved, he sought refuge in the Explorers Club writing and researching his latest film projects. He took celestial navigation courses at the local maritime school with the vague intention of getting his deep sea license. To keep cash coming in, he found himself photographing and filming set-ups at the posh stores on Fifth Avenue, including Macy's and Lord & Taylor. Burg's unfashionable clothes and battered camera equipment unsettled what he called the "suave and glossy haired" clerks. He thought he would be better off "among the crocodiles on some jungle river."

In March 1946, Burg began his annual migration back to the Pacific Northwest. En route he ventured off to Wisconsin for eight weeks to make a film for ERPI called *Milk*. Upon reaching Portland, he spent time with his mother, Annie Burg, who was in the early stages of undiagnosed cancer, now under the care of Burg's sisters, Vera, Mabel, and Annabelle. After reassurances from his sisters, a worried Burg set off for Seattle. Nearly four years had passed since he had left *Endeavour,* his beloved boat, in Lake Union under the care of Pat Patterson. The boat needed attention and Burg was eager to begin the overhaul. He had set a June departure date for another voyage north along the Inside Passage. He began making lists, ordering provisions, and planning an itinerary. He struck another agreement with *National Geographic* for an article and photographs.

As preparations for the next trip neared completion, Burg received shocking news. In May 1946 thirty-seven-year-old Buzz Holmstrom, his companion on their 1938 Grand Canyon voyage, had died on the Grande Ronde River in northeastern Oregon, where he had been working as lead guide for a government survey party. Burg, like many others, was stunned when he heard that his friend had apparently shot himself. He recalled, how-ever, Holmstrom's peculiar comments at their camp in Green River, Utah, eight years earlier. The family and most of the people in Coquille vehemently denied that Holmstrom was capable of such an act. Many in the small fra-ternity of river runners as well as Holmstrom's family and friends felt it must have been an accident or something worse. For the next year they pursued an investigation of possible homicide. Nothing came of it.

Perhaps the most provocative response came from one river runner who voiced the opinion that Holmstrom's suicide was a result of friction between Burg and Holmstrom over the financial failure of their joint venture. The charge was that the famous river runner had killed himself out of shame that he had not stood up to Burg for cheating him out of a fair share of the money. Burg was stunned that anyone would make such a connection. The charge that he deliberately cheated Holmstrom was farfetched. A misunderstanding, if there was one, may have arisen for any number of reasons: rising and unanticipated costs involving the film processing, poor communication, high expectations, poor bookkeeping. Could Burg, who spent months working on the film without pay, have paid some of his own bills out of their communal funds? Perhaps.

The behavior of Burg and Holmstrom after their historic Grand Canyon voyage suggests that they remained friends. Burg carried on routine correspondence with Holmstrom, who visited him in New York during and after the war years. (Holmstrom had enlisted in the Navy and been trained as a ship's carpenter for P.T. boats in the Pacific. Later he signed up for another tour of duty in Europe but arrived too late to see action.) The two men had talked of making another river voyage together at some point. After his friend's death, Burg communicated regularly with Holmstrom's mother, sister, and brothers. They had nothing but good things to say about Amos Burg.

Out of respect for Holmstrom's family as well as a result of his own natural reticence, Burg said little publicly about his friend's death at the time. "Most of the poetry of Buzz was in Buzz," he wrote. "Interested in birds and animals. Intense, simple. He wanted to get close to life. Buzz was so complicated it finally got the best of him. Every time I talked to him I felt I was arrogant and boastful. He had the common touch." Decades later, Burg aired his deeper views on Holmstrom's untimely death. In a 1983 letter he began with a cautious admonition: "I think it would be a mistake to speculate to Buzz's detriment on any aspect of Buzz's character we could not be sure about." He supposed that his friend "could have had mental complications we did not know about, especially during and after the war for he was a sensitive man." Burg offered his thoughts on the easygoing Holmstrom's character:

> I thought several times how tough and uncertain it would be to spend a winter with Buzz if he had no way to unleash the tremendous energy that drove him. Buzz, like Amundsen, Shackleton, and Scott needed a great challenge—something as formidable as the Grand

Canyon. When that challenge was met and he drifted back into easy everyday living, it was like hitching a Percheron to a baby carriage. For that reason, although fully aware of the tremendous difficulties in a Hells Canyon ascent, I did not discourage him. Buzz, I felt, needed another canyon, something to exhaust his energies. I had asked myself what role this man with a boiling volcano inside him could play in the humdrum of ordinary living. Will he blow up? When he is relegated into a backwater, what will he do?

For his own part, Burg rarely faltered in terms of charting his next move. For all his idealism and adventurous romanticism, he had forged a career out of hard work, dedication to craft, unquenchable curiosity, and quiet ambition. By the spring of 1946 he had been on the go for nearly thirty years. He was a successful writer, photographer, filmmaker, and lecturer. He remained unmarried, a consequence of his nomadic lifestyle. At forty-four, Burg was about to return to his first love: the sea.

In June 1946, Burg headed north aboard *Endeavour* for the Georgia Straits, in the lee of Vancouver Island. Two decades had passed since he and Fred "Spokane" Hill voyaged south along the rugged, weather-bound archipelago of the Inside Passage in the *Song o' the Winds*. It was a dramatic yet well-protected waterway. To the west the peaks of Vancouver Island stood as sentinels, slowing the incoming storms from the Pacific. To the east the rugged, forested coastline was interrupted by the inviting mouths of inlets—Jervis, Powell, Desolation—and dozens of smaller, lesser known waterways. Viewed from the decks of *Endeavour,* the scenery was fluid, ever-changing—the shifting color of the water, the abundance of wildlife, the acre-size islands, waterfalls whose ribbons measured in hundreds of feet. Dense forest crowded to the edge of steep black cliffs. Towering inhospitable peaks of ice and snow coupled with serene, inviting coves, the mix of fresh- and saltwater, and the unruly meeting of tides and rapids. The shades of green, gray, silver, and black were intoxicating. Burg, voyaging alone, found himself lingering at overnight anchorages.

At infamous Yaculta Rapids, where a narrow rocky passage played havoc with the tidal bore, the thirty-six-foot *Endeavour* was rendered helpless by a fierce ebb tide. Instead of waiting or hugging the shore in search of back eddies like the Native trawlers, Burg chose to run down the middle of the fast water. The crosscurrents and tide spun and tossed *Endeavour* around like a toy boat in a wading pool of frenzied children. In the midst of the chaos, the unflappable Burg was thrilled by the sight of dozens of bald eagles perched on the branches of a tree on an island in the middle of the rapids, "their white heads standing out against the green branches like popcorn balls on a Christmas tree."

Five weeks into his voyage, Burg rendezvoused in Prince Rupert, British Columbia, with the Taylor family in their thirty-four-foot cabin cruiser. He was to guide them, from *Endeavour,* as they traveled the Inside Passage. Although he had largely given up the chartering business, he continued to be a magnet for fellow travelers and less adventurous souls. Dick Taylor, however, was an experienced sailor, fisherman, and boatbuilder, who needed little looking after—a fact Burg appreciated.

Burg continued to collect stories. He heard one tale about a trapper-fisherman who watched his fishing boat head up Cleveland Passage one morning with no one at the wheel. The fisherman jumped in his tender and followed. The boat zigzagged (but never near to shore) before he realized that a whale, which had become entangled in the fishing boat's anchor line, was towing the boat. The trapper-fisherman caught up and managed to cut the boat loose. The whale kept twenty-five fathoms of rope and the sixty-five-pound anchor.

During the winter of 1946–47, Burg lived aboard *Endeavour* in the Ketchikan harbor. He had another stroke of good luck when EBF (ERPI had been sold to the University of Chicago, which renamed the company Educational Britannica Films), invited him to shoot five films in Europe the following spring. The films would continue the popular Children of the World series he had shot in 1940–41. It was an offer not to be refused. As Burg prepared to depart for Europe that summer, his article "*Endeavour* Sails the Inside Passage," with twenty-one photographs, appeared in *National Geographic.* It was his tenth piece for the magazine. In July he boarded the *American Importer* in New York, bound for Liverpool. As an able seaman he had carried his set of encyclopedias around the world. Now he was working for the company that produced them.

The next few months Burg roamed the English countryside. The EBF script called for a film highlighting various sections of Britain's recovering postwar industries—steel, coal mining, shipping, agriculture, fishing, forestry, textiles, and ceramics—as well as the daily life of the average English family. He noted in his diary being unnerved by the experience of crawling along a twenty-four-inch-wide coal seam hundreds of feet below the ground with his camera and lights. The result of his efforts was the 1947 film *British Isles.* By Christmas he was filming in the village of Torremolinos on the southern coast of Spain. He joked that "there were no automobiles available, so my assistant and myself had to transport the little leading lady of six and the leading man, same age, on the handles of our bicycles." From Torremolinos he traveled the Iberian Peninsula, covering the interior of Spain as well as Portugal.

By summer of 1947 he was exhausted. Long hours, language barriers, lack of sleep, stomach bugs, the unfamiliar Spanish food, and continual stress—left Burg chronically ill. Forced to stop work for three weeks to recover, he pondered larger issues in his letters home:

> Our government is trying to make friends with these countries and the films that I am making create international good will and understanding by presenting these countries and their people in schools and colleges through the US and in 18 different languages in other lands. One wonders why more money is not put forward for such work if it is so important, but few people seem to realize the importance of fighting for peace. It has always been our policy to fight and win a war, then fold up into isolation until the next war. With this European Recovery Plan the United States has abandoned its habitual crisis statesmanship and is really doing something to preserve peace before war comes. . . . I just feel better in my conscience utilizing my feeling for the world and humanity this way.

Upon recovering from his illnesses, Burg returned to England, where he began work on the film *English Children* in the city of York. In London he took in the sights, including a visit to the Royal National Lifeboat Institution (RNLI) at 42 Grosvenor Gardens. Both of his boats, *Dorjun* and *Endeavour,* had once served as rescue craft. Impressed by the exhibits and photographs at the RNLI, he decided to write an article for *National Geographic.* His status as a regular contributor to the famous American magazine persuaded a young assistant curator to "loan" him thirty-seven original photographs (ranging from 1890 to 1948) of the coastal rescue boats. It was an astonishing breech of institutional protocol.

When the RNLI publicity secretary learned what the assistant had done, he was shocked then panicked. He sent the assistant out into the street to find Burg, but it was too late. The invaluable photographs were gone forever, and Burg never wrote his lifeboat article. Only after Burg's death decades later were the photographs returned. Charles and Ellen Campbell, Burg's Juneau neighbors, had purchased his house, discovered the photographs, and realized their value. When the Campbells appeared at the RNLI in Poole, England, photographs in hand, the curators were astonished and grateful.

After spending the better part of three years in Europe, Burg returned to New York in January 1950. He had grown tired of living out of a suitcase. In May he drove across the country to Portland. He would never again return to the East Coast or Europe. Burg decided to retrieve the *Dorjun* from the mudflat on the Columbia, where it had washed up during a Memorial Day flood in Vanport, a housing development near Portland, two years earlier. He enlisted longtime friend Andrew Yunker to help him. They borrowed a flatbed trailer, hoisted the sorry-looking *Dorjun* out of the mud, and transported it to Yunker's home outside of Portland, where it remained for the next decade, much to the dismay of Yunker's wife, Neita.

Amos Burg's enthusiasm for journeys to faraway places remained undiminished. Yet his notion of adventuring had undergone a change that was inevitable. His work now dictated the places he traveled to and the schedules he followed. He was no longer free to roam at will, to set off on a months-long voyage. An established professional with solid contacts and a reputation to uphold, he was essentially a freelance photographer, writer, filmmaker, and lecturer. As World War II came to an end, the money Burg earned, though substantial at times, often went out faster than it came in. He continued to finance a portion of his projects, to cover his living and travel expenses, to shoulder the costs of routine maintenance of his boat *Endeavour,* and to send checks to his mother. His easygoing manner belied his discipline and drive.

Although a regular contributor to the *National Geographic* and EBF, Burg now competed with another generation of writers and photographers. His moment in the limelight at the prestigious East Coast venues had passed. His successful lectures ("Across England by Canoe," "Inside Cape Horn," "Voyaging Alaskan Waters," "Conquering Grand Canyon," and "The Enchanted Islands") had been based on months of shoestring travel, thorough research, and weeks of painstaking preparation. He sensed, correctly, an impending shift in tastes and appetites of the American public and began to lecture on the West Coast, closer to home, at far smaller venues. Now middle-aged, Burg found himself gravitating toward Alaska, not yet a state and absent the romantic label "the Last Frontier," which would draw an entire generation. He held steady to his internal compass, which led him to bear the sacrifices of a life on the move in pursuit of natural beauty while trying to make a living doing what he loved in the outdoors.

PART III

COMING ASHORE

(1950–1986)

Chapter 10

RETURN VOYAGES:
THE BERING SEA AND THE
YUKON RIVER

In August of 1950, Burg boarded *North Star 2* in Sitka, Alaska. The five-
thousand-ton freighter was preparing for the last and longest of its three
annual voyages for the Alaska Native Services—a three-month, eleven-
thousand-mile loop of the Gulf of Alaska, the Bering Sea, and the Arctic
Ocean. During the voyage the freighter delivered supplies, machinery, and
other vital goods to forty or more isolated coastal villages stretching as
far north as Point Barrow. The ship also dropped off and picked up students, teachers, and field supervisors at various locations, and served as a
floating hospital, equipped with a full-time nurse, a sick bay, and an x-ray
clinic. Burg's assignment was to chronicle the journey in another article for
National Geographic. Two decades had passed since he, along with his buddy
Fred "Spokane" Hill, had voyaged along Alaska's coast filming the reindeer
and caribou herds for their producer Jesse Sill.

As *North Star* glided out of the harbor past the island of Japonski (across
the channel from Sitka), where the Alaska Native Services Hospital was
located, nurses waved white bed sheets from the third-floor windows. The
long-established custom signaled farewell and a safe journey. Captain Charles
Selenjus steered a southerly course across the Gulf of Alaska for the Aleutian

Islands. At eleven knots they could expect to reach Dutch Harbor at the tip of the Aleutian island chain in ten days.

During Burg's years working with *National Geographic*, the magazine's continued success was based on a reliable formula: clear, simple prose, a swift narrative, an abundance of facts, and lots of photographs. The articles tended to be lengthy (a fifty-page article was not uncommon). The editors aimed for a readable and recognizable style, and tens of thousands of American and overseas readers subscribed. The editors rigorously avoided controversy or partisanship. Critics suggested that the magazine's scrupulous neutrality made for bland, repetitive stories, numbing the readers to more important issues. Some accused the magazine of painting an unrealistic picture that seduced readers with its storybook narratives.

Burg had learned early on what the *National Geographic* editors wanted—a positive, uplifting, noncritical storyline about people in faraway places—and delivered precisely on that vision. Two recurring themes emerged from his work: the plight of the indigenous people and the conservation of natural resources. But he was no crusader. In the postwar decade, popular environmental movements had yet to come into existence nor was there any large-scale effort to protect Native rights. In his early writing, Burg never pointed a finger, advocated solutions, or attempted to rally an uninterested public. Indeed, the magazine editors would never have allowed such advocacy. He did, however, have his ear to the ground.

Burg had spoken often of the need to treat people of foreign countries, especially indigenous groups, with dignity and respect. In his published articles and private letters, he frequently inserted his observations on the condition and treatment of indigenous people, as well as the behavior of those who exploited the natural world. These facts could be ignored but hardly denied. Over the coming decades, he gradually raised his voice in defense of rivers, wilderness, and the people who lived with them.

On the fourth morning of the *North Star's* journey across the Gulf of Alaska, the freighter entered the channel between the Shumagin Islands and the Aleutian peninsula. Burg awoke to a scene that he later wrote "was so beautiful it was heartbreaking." The sun was shining; the wind had ceased. The unexpectedly fine weather and the protective arm of the Aleutian chain had turned the coastal waters of the Gulf smooth as a mill pond. He half expected to see a couple out for a Sunday row. To starboard, the stark, treeless islands rose sharply out of the green sea like a parade of dry land mountain peaks. Puffy white clouds scudded through a disarmingly blue sky. In the distance 8,900-foot Pavlov Volcano belched a column of black smoke through the clouds.

Selenjus steered as direct a course as possible, determined to avoid the worst of any future weather the Chukchi and Beaufort Seas were likely to offer on the return voyage. Once across the shallow Bering Sea, *North Star* discharged tons of freight at Hooper Bay before moving on to Saint Michael, gateway to the Yukon interior. Few ships made Saint Michael a port of call. Passengers and crew came ashore; thirty or more Native children boarded the tug to visit the shipboard clinic for chest x-rays. Tuberculosis sapped the health of the coastal tribes.

On August 22, *North Star* crossed into the Arctic Circle. The next morning the ship anchored fifteen miles offshore, as close to land as the shallow water of Kotzebue Sound would allow. A tug towing a barge arrived to pick up passengers and freight for the first of numerous shuttles across the featureless expanse. On the return trip to town, the tug's engines failed and the boat ran aground, not for the last time. Seven hours passed before passengers set foot on Kotzebue's main street—a narrow, deeply rutted, and thoroughly

Hooper Bay Natives visit North Star.

muddy track. A cacophony of yips, barks, and growls of the packs of dogs greeted them. An indescribable stench—born of dog, fish, and seal odors—permeated the town. The baying and screeching of the ill-treated dogs set the visitor's teeth on edge. Electricity, potable water, and sleeping accommodations were in short supply, as was decent food. The sole restaurant had no regular operating hours. The passengers found the behavior of the Eskimos jaded, as they played to the tourists and their pocketbooks. Burg later noted that the non-Native locals, while polite enough, feared the Communists were about to cross Bering Strait at any moment.

Tired and wet, Burg was rewarded with a visual spectacle. A thousand or more Eskimos, their tents crowded at either end of the town, had gathered for their annual end-of-summer rendezvous. They had come from the coastal villages as well as the inland rivers to visit with family and friends, exchange gossip, court, feast, gamble, drink, and trade. Racks of drying salmon and beluga whale meat, known as "Eskimo chocolate," lined the crowded waterfront. "Wandering along Kotzebue's waterfront," he later wrote, "I could view the life of the town and acknowledge the heart-warming smiles of the Eskimos. . . . The native's cheerfulness especially confounds those who share the common belief that happiness stems from security, material possessions and a kindly climate, none of which the Eskimo count among their dependable assets."

A week later *North Star* weighed anchor. After a brief stop at Wainright, the freighter made the short run to Barrow, Alaska's northernmost town, 340 miles north of the Arctic Circle, with a population of about a thousand. Barrow was hard on the eyes. Without its winter cover of snow and ice, the town was enveloped in a sea of mud and debris. After four days of near-constant labor, 3,500 tons of offloaded freight lay scattered about the beach. *North Star's* numerous stops at isolated, often impoverished, villages offered Burg a window into Native life along the coastline. Some villages thrived, due to a combination of geography, strong leadership, and a tenacious hold on traditional ways while taking what was suitable and available from the white culture. Other villages suffered, pulled apart by poverty, isolation, and disease, unable or unwilling to adapt.

On September 15 the clearing weather offered Burg a rare sight: a panoramic view of the Bering Strait. To starboard lay the headlands of Russian

Siberia, the Kamchatka Peninsula; to port was the ragged coastline of North America and Cape Wales. Between the two lay the fifty-three-mile long strait named after the Swedish navigator and explorer Vitus Bering, who was working for Peter the Great when he made the discovery in 1741. Nothing satisfied Burg's poetic sensibilities more than encountering dramatic landscapes with historical significance.

North Star made a stop in Nome on the return voyage. In the once rollicking seaport town, two hundred or more Inupiat Eskimos waited to board the ship to return to their villages on King and Little Diomedes Islands. In June, with the channel ice free and the weather improved, the entire village had made the eighty-mile passage to Nome in their umiaks, where they spent the relatively warm summer months trading, fishing, longshoring, purchasing provisions, and selling their exquisite ivory carvings to tourists. By October the threat of weeklong fogs and an early ice pack made their return voyage to the islands in their umiaks too dangerous. They waited for *North Star* to ferry them across the channel.

As the ship approached King Island, the silhouette of a stark rocky mountain peak jutted up out of the sea. It was difficult to believe anyone lived on this vertical landscape, much less throughout the winter. Roughly two-and-a-half square miles in size, the island was bare, steep, and treeless. Pinnacles, like earthen ribs weathered by wind, rain, and ice, slanted at peculiar angles; a cluster of white toy houses atop toothpicks perched precariously on the mountainside. The rocky shoreline offered no landings. The entire scene was framed and at the same time diminished by an immense sky and the surrounding sea. The haunting, harshly beautiful place drew long stares from the passengers aboard *North Star*.

Burg took a keen interest in the King Islanders' boats. "Admired the simplicity and sturdiness of the Aleut umiak or skin boat," he wrote in his diary. As the men lowered their craft over the side of the freighter, he filmed and photographed the operation. The flat-bottomed boats were reminiscent of other traditional boats he had seen throughout his world travels. The King Island umiaks generally ran thirty to forty feet in length and seven to nine feet at the beam. Lightweight and with a shallow draft, these boats enabled a small number of men to land on and depart from shore. One umiak could carry as many as twenty-five barrels of oil or forty passengers with gear safely across the strait.

Burg visited King Island in 1950. By 1970 the Native population had moved to Nome, Alaska on the mainland.

Indeed, the added weight combined with the flat bottom and buoyancy made for a stable, seagoing craft capable of lengthy voyages, even in foul weather.

An umiak's construction depended on the communal efforts of both men and women. After being treated, the skins of walrus or bearded seal were meticulously sewn together by the women, then soaked and swollen to seal the seams until waterproof. Native women were embarrassed if they saw anyone working grease into a seam to staunch a leak, which suggested that their work had been inadequate. The finished skins were then stretched over a wooden frame, usually made of driftwood spruce—a durable, flexible wood that cost the Natives nothing. Umiaks were sturdy and easy to repair. Burg could not help drawing comparisons between the umiaks and his own "inflatable," his trusty *Charlie*.

Camera in hand, he followed the procession of islanders as they mounted the steep path to their vertical village. A steady parade of dogs and children darted along the narrow cliffs, oblivious to the heights. Seabirds wheeled overhead. The dogs, he wrote, "were sleek and fat from feasting (all summer) on the gulls, auklets, puffins, murres, and kittiwakes that nest in the cliffs." He spent two days exploring the maze of narrow trails and makeshift stairs, ladders, and wooden walkways that connected the village. Bundles and crates littered every available space between the shelters. Walrus and seal skins used as rugs and sleeping material swung on thick clotheslines. The weathered shelters of the King Islanders were constructed of shipping crates and driftwood, resting on stilts and clustered close together on the barren and rocky forty-five-degree slope. The backs of the shelters faced north against the cliffside, away from the weather. The "front door" was the size of a small window through which an adult in winter clothing might slip through, if careful, leaving the icy wind behind. A turn-of-the-century Catholic Church and school, built by the Bureau of Indian Affairs, dwarfed the islanders' shanty homes.

Hunting, the mainstay of the King Islanders, could be perilous. The previous season, Burg learned, three experienced hunters had been carried out to sea on an ice floe. Either they had not heard or had failed to heed the warning siren the lookout onshore had sounded when foul weather approached. Before a rescue boat could reach them, two men froze; the third man survived, his toes later being amputated. Legends and myths handed down for generations claimed that the ancient King Islanders had not crossed over any land bridge from Asia but had always been "people of the sea." This implies that they were from the South Pacific.

The scene on King Island was as powerful a tableau of Native Alaskan life as Burg had ever encountered. Perched on a mountainside from which there was no escape during the long winters, the King Islanders literally lived life "on the edge," as close to the unforgiving conditions nature imposed as one can get. In 1959 the Bureau of Indian Affairs closed the King Island School, forcing those families with children to relocate on the mainland. A decade later the island was uninhabited and remains so to this day. King Islanders return each year by boat to hunt and gather, continuing their traditional way of life.

Winter was closing in. After a week's stay at Gambell and Savoonga on Saint Lawrence Island, Captain Selenjus weighed anchor and pointed *North Star* south across the Bering Sea toward Sitka. Burg had been at sea for nearly three months and voyaged more than ten thousand miles. He had a trove of photographs and film and a brimming notebook. On the last leg of the voyage, from Seward to Sitka, *North Star* bucked headwinds and a ferocious, three-day storm. Finally, just before Thanksgiving, Mount Edgecumbe appeared on the horizon and within a few hours Burg stepped onto the dock in Sitka harbor. Two years passed before his article "*North Star* Cruises Alaska's Wild West" appeared in the July 1952 issue of *National Geographic*.

Another *National Geographic* assignment awaited Burg upon his return from the Gulf of Alaska voyage. When the editors decided to put out a commemorative edition celebrating the Yukon Gold Rush of 1898, Burg was the obvious choice as author. He hurried back to Seattle from Sitka to outfit his treasured ketch *Endeavour*. He took twenty-four unhurried days, traveling alone, to reach Juneau, where he began preparations for his next assignment.

Skagway was a far cry from what it had been when Burg and Hill had passed through on their way to the Yukon in 1928. The town, Burg thought, now resembled a Hollywood western movie set. Nevertheless the train journey over White Pass to Bennett was as breathtaking as ever. Determined to trace part of the actual river voyage of the Gold Rush stampeders, Burg purchased a dilapidated dory, *Klondike III,* at Bennett Lake. He set out with a companion, thinking it a novel way to reach Whitehorse, but the boat leaked so badly that upon landing in Carcross, he left it behind and boarded the train to Whitehorse. There he decided (whether by design or spur of the moment) to paddle a Freightliner canoe down the notorious stretch of the Yukon above Whitehorse, which included Miles Canyon and Whitehorse Rapids. He convinced two locals to accompany him. In late summer the low-water run was less hazardous, a fact that the ever-cautious Burg took into consideration.

Miles Canyon was as emblematic of Yukon River history as any location on the river. In the early days of the rush, more than a hundred boats and numerous lives had been lost in half-mile-long Whitehorse Rapids. Dozens of other boats had capsized or been severely damaged, leaving the fledgling stampeders stranded. In the face of mounting deaths, the Northwest Mounted Police instituted a number of precautions. They assigned a number to each boat and collected the names of the occupants so that in the event of a fatal mishap, next of kin could be notified. Women and children were encouraged, and eventually ordered, to walk around the rapids; gold-rushers were encouraged (then ordered) to portage their supplies and gear—a time-consuming endurance test that few tolerated well. At one point boats were not allowed through Whitehorse Rapids without an experienced pilot.

Burg's run would be broadcast over the Whitehorse radio station. By the time he and his companions launched their canoe at the head of Miles Canyon on September 14, dozens of people had gathered along the cliffs to watch. At Whitehorse Rapids the Yukon River narrows to three hundred feet and swings to the right on a blind curve between basalt cliffs twenty to thirty feet high. At river level it is impossible to anticipate what is coming. Near the bend the cliffs begin to close in, and by the end of the rapid the river narrows yet again, to forty feet. At high water the volume of constricted water picks up speed and turns into a deafening, turbulent mass. Burg described the river as "turning on its edge." Burg and his companions, however, crashed through the rapid, waving at the crowd on shore, without incident. Not a few were disappointed in the successful run. They had hoped to witness some river drama.

After a few days in Whitehorse, Burg boarded the sternwheeler *Casca,* one of a handful of vessels remaining in service, for the run to Dawson. The era of the sternwheeler and the unique river life it bred was coming to an end. At the turn of the century, the stately craft had carried gold seekers, fishermen, adventurers, ministers, hustlers, trappers, woodcutters, bootleggers, troublemakers, eccentrics, and those on the lam. By the 1920s the stern-wheelers ferried tourists, businessmen, and government officials to Dawson and beyond. Like so many other travelers, Burg had been seduced by the elegant boats—their boxy, familiar lines, the subdued majesty of the wheel-house, the sound of the whistle, the trainlike comfort and soothing views, the great sweeping motion of the paddle wheel. He had marveled at the navigational skills of the pilots, their feats of memory on a river that changed on each run, their well of river lore, and their sharp wit. Although he rationalized the loss of these magnificent boats as part of the cost exacted by progress, in his heart of hearts Burg mourned their demise. His own youthful adventures on the Yukon were intimately linked with the vessels. He found solace in the thought that he was making a photographic record of the boats for future generations. They would not be forgotten.

Pushing a steel barge loaded with freight, *Casca* set off across Lake Laberge. Burg joined Captain Bill Goodlad in the pilot house. Downstream pillars of smoke curled up into the sky. Careless trappers, Goodlad suggested, were responsible for the forest fires. Twenty-four miles below Carmacks lay Five-Finger Rapid, named for the five channels created by four large, snag-covered islands of basalt that spanned the river. Because of its narrow passage and contrary currents, the infamous rapid remained a formidable obstacle for *Casca*. In olden days downriver runs were considered dangerous; upriver runs worse. When strong rogue winds blew, veteran skippers routinely delayed their passage, fearful that their large boats would be driven onto the cliffs. Only one channel was navigable: the thumb of the hand on river right.

An admiring crowd gathered in front of the wheelhouse as Goodlad sounded the bell signaling full-speed ahead, steered the craft into position, and without the slightest hesitation ran through the claustrophobic passage. It was all over in a minute. Burg swore he could have reached out and run his hand along the rock wall. The next morning *Casca* arrived in Dawson, the only vessel at anchor besides a motor launch. In 1898, five decades earlier, hundreds of stampeders' boats of every size and shape had anchored along the crowded waterfront.

Dawson, like Skagway, disappointed Burg. The shopkeepers, their survival at stake, catered to the tourists' desire to hear tales of the American West, Alaskan-style, and to brush shoulders with a gaudy, little understood past. Myth had replaced hard facts. Only the unruly growling of the Klondike River on the south side of town hinted at the previous frontier vitality, thought Burg. Despite coming face-to-face with these changes, he wrote optimistically of the town's future in his *National Geographic* article. His mood changed once he reached 4,250-foot King Solomon Dome—the highest, most accessible viewpoint outside of town. The historic panorama of the Klondike Valley and the famed creeks (Gold Bottom, Dominion, Last Chance, Eureka, El Dorado, Sulphur, Little Blanche, and Bonanza) were part of American history, for better or worse.

Burg's article "Along the Yukon Trail," appeared in the September 1953 issue of *National Geographic*. Upon returning to Juneau, he received news from one of his sisters that his mother's health was declining. But when he wrote home telling her that he was considering returning to Portland, his mother urged him to stay in Juneau and continue working. Annie Burg, surrounded by her family and friends, would want no less.

Now fifty-one, Burg took a job—his first salaried position—as a seasonal patrol officer with the US Fish and Wildlife Service in the Slocum Arm region of the Alexander Archipelago, north of Sitka. Traveling aboard *Endeavour* from spring through fall, his primary duties were to deliver supplies to the fish guard camps and to discourage fish pirates from illegally netting fish. The work was not without danger. At times the pirates openly challenged the patrol officers, who were not popular in the waterway towns and hamlets. Nevertheless, Burg thoroughly enjoyed the work. It offered natural beauty, freedom to roam, solitude, and a regular paycheck. The abundance of wildlife so close at hand—brown bears, bald eagles, salmon, whales—was invigorating. He also enjoyed visiting the old-timers who manned the fish camps. After decades of making pitches, meeting deadlines, and living out of his suitcases, Burg felt at home in this environment. He resurrected his old seagoing habit of carrying a phonograph and a set of *Encyclopedia Britannica* aboard ship. He spent three seasons working as a patrol officer.

In the early 1950s, Burg's decade-long relationship with EBF came under threat. The new vice president of product development informed him that the company would no longer offer Burg projects based on a contract. This would force him to carry the costs of filmmaking without any guarantee that his project would be accepted. His returns would now be based on a royalty basis. Questions about the quality of Burg's work, based on mediocre sales of one film (*Norwegian Children,* one of the "Children of the World" films), arose. Loathe to admit it, Burg was stung by the slight. In a letter to EBF he wrote:

> While making your films I was bombed 23 times in Chunking [Chongqing], ate bird's nest soup in Chengtu [Chengdu], endured bored and "board" in an Eskimo igloo on the Bering Sea, flew over Mayan ruins in Central American Jungles and drank copious amounts of possibly infected unpastuerized milk in a Spanish sanitarium, going in with one ailment and coming out with four. All this time you bigwigs of ERPI and E.B., fathers of the American educational film, supported me to the limit and received me hospitably with gracious friendliness into your homes.

No one from the company had alerted him to the seriousness of the "problems" with his film. "You mentioned the need for a 'new look' in my technique," he continued. "What I needed was not silence, but for you fellows to say, 'Listen Dumbo, this and that and so and so.' I had been filming far continents away from any advice whatsoever." For the time being, Burg's relationship with EBF was put on hold.

It is likely that Carolyn Warren had heard of Amos Burg, the bachelor-adventurer living aboard *Endeavour,* before they met. The divorced mother of two grown children, she had moved from Milwaukee, Wisconsin, to Juneau in 1951 to take up a position with the Veterans Administration. She also made her first forays into local politics, unafraid to speak out on issues important to her. Given the size and isolation of Juneau in the 1950s, and the fact that neither Burg nor Warren drank, it is easy to imagine their meeting each other at some social event or through mutual friends. In any case the pair began to socialize together, had informal dates, and agreed to keep in touch through letters when the freespirited Burg was on patrol or one of his adventures. Tight budgets and caution may have circumscribed the beginning of their relationship. Warren was a churchgoing Methodist; Burg, of course, was always coming and going but rarely to and from church. She had never met anyone like him. Another seven years passed before the elusive Burg felt ready to make a commitment to Carolyn.

While on a lecture tour in California in the fall of 1952, Burg received more news of his mother's deteriorating health. This time he returned to Portland immediately, and on October 15, eighty-six-year-old Minerva Ann Burg died, her family at her side at their home on Dekum Street. Although the doctor listed pneumonia as the cause of death, she had been suffering from some form of cancer for three years, likely more. In the immediate months after his mother's death, Burg became involved in an intense yet brief relationship with a woman named Ruth. Intelligent, articulate, and independent, she had been previously married. In the safety of this relationship, Burg revealed that his mother's death had rocked him more than he anticipated, bringing up memories of his childhood and youth as well as his long absences in pursuit of his career. In his grief he turned to Ruth for comfort. She in turn poured her heart out to Burg, who had always been a good listener. Both were wary of commitment, but Ruth fell in love with Burg. Kind, handsome, courtly, interesting, adventurous, and a bit mysterious, he was also uncatchable. Initially he seemed to reciprocate Ruth's feelings but then retreated—his customary pattern over the decades.

In the spring of 1955 the director of the Alaska Department of Fisheries (ADF) asked Burg if he was interested in a temporary position with the department—to head an Information and Education section that did not yet exist. The director emphasized the word "temporary." The section would play a key role in shaping the Alaskan public's (and the Lower 48's) view of the department and Alaska itself. He wanted an individual with a winning personality and public relations experience. He thought Burg was his man. Later Burg joked, "At fifteen, I retired; at fifty-five, I got my first real job."

B urg, who had remained devoted to his mother throughout her life and supported her financially after his father died, was devastated by her death, especially because his sisters—Vera, Mabel, and Annabelle—had encouraged him to remain in Alaska working. He likely felt a spasm of guilt for not being more available during her lengthy illness. Throughout his childhood and youth, he had looked to his father for guidance, approval, and financial support. In his mother, however, he was assured of unconditional love and affection as well as gentle encouragement to follow his star. In an interview late in life he said, "My mother, she gave [us] love; she didn't give advice, she gave [us] love. The fact that I received this great love all my life was the difference."

On his early sea voyages and river trips, he wrote detailed, lengthy letters to both parents, and often to his mother alone, assuring her that he was safe. It was a habit—a letter a week to his mother—that he continued throughout his life. She was known to send jars of jam and handmade candy to her seagoing and river-running son. She relished his adventures and the fact that he had made his way in the world as a photographer, writer, and lecturer. Burg, for all his wandering, was firmly anchored to the home his parents, each in their own way, had created.

Chapter 11

THE SAME RIVER TWICE:
THE MACKENZIE REVISITED

No man ever steps into the same river twice,
for it's not the same river and he's not the same man.

—Heraclitus, Greek philosopher

For forty years Amos Burg had been on the go—living out of a sea bag or suitcase, sleeping in forecastles, his canoe, aboard *Endeavour,* or in hotel rooms around the world. In 1956 he began work for the Alaska Department of Fisheries (ADF) in a windowless office in a rambling wooden building on the Juneau waterfront. It was a decidedly informal, relaxed environment. As long as tasks were completed in a timely fashion, little attention was paid to time clocks. Although he was initially responsible for making promotional and educational films that highlighted Alaska, Burg's responsibilities increased over time, ranging from managing the film storage and editing rooms and responding to letters from the public to giving talks to schools and organizations and acting as editor of the fledgling department newsletter. He often worked out in the field for weeks at a time, filming the scripts a staff member or research biologist had written. Most employees at the ADF regarded themselves as pioneering professionals in their various fields, the leading edge of a movement to both use and protect Alaska's natural resources.

Alaska was approaching a prolonged period of significant change, accompanied by controversy and upheaval. After statehood the federal bureaucracy was replaced by a state bureaucracy, the military presence continued to grow, and tourism, to the dismay and horror of some Alaskans, became a major source of income. In the 1960s idealistic, earnest youths would flock to Alaska in hopes of finding a northern but chilly Eden. The battle to move the state capital from Juneau inland continued, off and on, for decades. Juneau itself would see more growth than many of its citizens liked. The Alaska National Interest Land Conservation Act (ANILCA) as well as the Alaskan Natives Claim Settlement Act (ANCSA) thrilled some and angered others. Oil discoveries on the North Slope had the same effect. Growing population, increasing wealth, the demands of Native Alaskans, an influx of newcomers, and the environmental movement would profoundly alter the social and economic landscape and with it the definition of what it meant to be an Alaskan. Myths as well as longtime special interests would be challenged. The uniquely American notions of unlimited progress and frontiers, two concepts that Burg had grown up with and embraced, would come under fire.

Over the coming decades, Burg became increasingly aware that his early river voyages were a thing of the past, that a young person could no longer set off down the river of his or her choosing on a whim without bumping into a dam or having to get permission from some agency. Progress had brought undeniable benefits, but now he questioned the cost, once hidden, of this distinctly American ideal. Had we built far too many dams? Had we forfeited something intangible? He continued to argue for the value and health of free-flowing rivers beyond their commercial and utilitarian aspects. Modest and self-effacing, he became an unlikely hero, as much for his link to the voyageurs of the past as his heartfelt convictions about rivers.

Burg made three films for the ADF in quick succession. The first, *Quest for Better Fishing,* took him to the Kitoi Bay Research Station on Afognak Island, south of Anchorage in the Gulf of Alaska. There he filmed attempts to improve and expand the salmon runs. He also filmed the herring spawn near Craig on Prince of Wales Island. It was a wild, raw scene, the milky-white water churning with spawning herring as seals and sea lions competed with gulls and fishermen for their share of the catch. Burg's second film, *Valley of the Kings,* was filmed in Taku Inlet near Juneau. He followed fish biologists Robert Parker and Bud Weberg up the Taku River into Canada as they monitored the fish and their habitats. He spent a month in the backcountry, dodging bears while shooting ten thousand feet of film as well as hundreds of photos for the twenty-seven-minute film. The two biologists brought back humorous tales about Burg, who gained a sturdy reputation among the men in the field as a thorough professional and a dependable companion. He was also an excellent campfire storyteller with a lively wit and something of a dandy, with his fisherman's cap, long-sleeved shirt and tie, and khaki pants.

Teamed with James Brooks, a wildlife biologist, Burg filmed *White Whales of the Bering Sea.* (Brooks would eventually go on to become director of the Alaska Game Division and later commissioner of the Alaska Department of Fish and Game.) During the shoot Burg found himself inadvertently drawn into a local natural resource controversy. Brooks had been sent to Bristol Bay to determine whether the beluga whales feeding on the salmon were hurting commercial fishing. The vivid movie, with Brooks narrating, produced irrefutable results: the beluga did not overfeed on salmon. The local fishermen scoffed. Brooks had a difficult time convincing them that the impact was minuscule.

When in town between field assignments, Burg saw more of Carolyn Warren, whom he had met in the early 1950s when he was living aboard *Endeavour.* Both were social and enjoyed mixing with people. Each had a sense of humor—Burg's dry, gentle, but mischievous; Warren's voluble and direct—and they played well off one another. As the relationship developed, Warren provided Burg with comforts he had given up to pursue his career: stability and intimacy. Warren gained the company of a thoughtful man and entrance into his exciting world of adventure. She admired Burg for doing something important for Alaska. Burg took Warren on *Endeavour* for day outings. She refused his invitation for lengthy, overnight voyages. Women of her generation did not risk the appearance of impropriety, especially in a town the size of Juneau.

After four years of courtship, Warren was clearly taken with Burg. His feelings, though genuine, were slower to emerge. By October of 1956, however, talk turned toward marriage. Since she lived in Ketchikan, where she held a temporary job as a secretary for the US attorney, they corresponded by letter four or five times a week, attempting to work out the details of a middle-age marriage (Burg was fifty-four, Warren forty-five). The letters were affectionate, complete with pet names, advice, and constant concern over one another's welfare. After years of living on their own, they fretted over work, where they would live, the habits each might have to alter, and, of course, money. Warren's nest egg was the profit she made from the sale of her home in Milwaukee. Burg's largest asset was *Endeavour*. Both adults had steady jobs with nearly guaranteed incomes. Still, another two years passed before they exchanged vows.

On June 2, 1958, Carolyn Warren and Amos Burg were married in a private ceremony at Warren's home near the Governor's House in Juneau. Burg's close friend Walter Soboleff, a Tlingit tribal leader and Presbyterian minister, performed the ceremony. Burg claimed he had finally "come ashore." The Burgs planned to build a home on Douglas Island across the Gastineau Channel from downtown Juneau and towering Mount Juneau as soon as possible. A month after their wedding, the US Senate and House of Representatives passed the bill recognizing Alaska as the forty-ninth state. Official statehood arrived on January 3, 1959, when President Dwight Eisenhower signed the bill. The territorial Department of Fisheries was now known as the Alaska Department of Fish and Game (ADFG).

Warren took a new job with the Alaskan Highway Department. For the next few years Burg continued to roam the state with his cameras. He produced a steady stream of films for the ADFG, fifteen in all. Most were shot in sixteen-

On June 2, 1958, Amos and Carolyn were married in Juneau by Burg's friend Walter Soboleff, a Tlingit tribal leader and Presbyterian minister.

millimeter color film and lasted thirty to forty minutes. To supplement his income, he worked as contributing author to the second volume of *Marine Atlas*. Complete with charts and illustrations, the *Atlas* covered the coastline of the Inside Passage from Port Hardy to Skagway. He also began writing a column for the *Juneau Alaska Empire*, "Mushin' along Alaska Trails with Sourdough Sam," about the people of Alaska past and present.

Twelve years had passed since Burg's last *National Geographic* article, so when he received an unexpected letter from Gilbert Grosvenor, first president and onetime chief editor of the magazine, he was delighted. Grosvenor explained that he had been unable to mention Burg (and others) in his celebratory article, "The Romance of the National Geographic," which had recently appeared; there had simply been too many articles to choose from and Grosvenor had been forced to narrow the range to the early years of the magazine, 1899–1920. "I feel very badly that I could not recognize men like you," he wrote, "because you did not come along with your wonderful work until beginning in the 1930's. . . . I recognized your talent when you were a very young man, and I am very proud that I had a part in getting your experience and observations permanently recorded." Any concerns Burg had about his reputation or place in the history of the famous American magazine were assuaged.

More kudos for Burg arrived. Alaskan governor William A. Egan wrote to congratulate Burg on his films, which he thought "presented a more effective picture of Alaska than many of the professional travelogues now in production." When Burg presented his new film, *Juneau, Alaska's Capital City* (produced for the Alaska Territorial Centennial), to his hometown audience in January 1966, he received a rousing ovation. Calls to show the film throughout Alaska flooded in. Not long after, the Juneau Rotary Club selected Burg as "Man of the Year," citing his talks to schoolchildren as well as his work with the Sons of Norway and the Tlingit Indians, whose ceremonial dances he photographed. These photographs were later used to establish a scholarship fund for young Native Americans.

Despite the well-deserved attention and a busy schedule, Burg experienced moments of wistfulness. The days of hopping aboard freighters or launching *Song o' the Winds* when he pleased, disappearing for months at a time, had passed. He reconciled himself to aging by reflecting on his youthful voyages. After decades of not keeping a regular diary, he returned daily to the comfortable medium to express his thoughts and feelings on nature, marriage, growing old, and spiritual matters. Loathe to admit it, he struggled through blue periods. Few, if any, of his numerous friends or associates witnessed these episodes. Carolyn tried to comfort him by suggesting possible multiple causes—diet, inactivity, the long Alaskan winters—as well as various remedies. Burg had another cure in mind: a river voyage.

In the summer of 1967, sensing that changes were coming to the ADFG, Burg decided to take a much-needed unpaid leave of absence. He began laying the groundwork for a lengthy river voyage: retracing his 1929 journey down the Mackenzie River to the Arctic Ocean. Determined to make the trip pay for itself, he developed a theme to pitch to *National Geographic*: old voyager returns to the rivers of his youth. In the article he would write about the changes that had taken place on the Mackenzie over the past forty years. What would take him by surprise, however, were the changes that had taken place within himself.

His proposal was rebuffed. One editor wrote: "This is a highly ambitious plan and does you credit. However, all three of us have now reached an age when perhaps we should leave these strenuous undertakings to others." Besides, the editor continued, "we have several North Country projects in the works or in prospect and thus have no real need of such a story or film at present. For all these reasons we feel we must decline." The editor hoped that Burg would not be "too disappointed." If Burg was stung by the refusal, he was hardly deterred. He had already placed an order with the Chestnut Canoe Company in Frederickton, Canada, for a nineteen-foot V-stern freighter canoe. He could not help reminding company officials that the boat's name was *Song o' the Winds*, not *Song of the Winds*.

Vic Bracher, an old friend and an executive at the Remington Arms Company in Cleveland, Ohio, jumped at the opportunity to accompany Burg. The two men had known each other since their student days at the University of Oregon. At one time or another, Bracher had worked for the Oregon State Game Commission filming antelope in the remote Hart Mountain Reserve, developed and constructed an underwater camera for filming the migration of the Pacific salmon, and floated stretches of the Rio Grande River in the Big Bend area of Texas as well as the North Fork of the Flathead River in Montana. He was an able companion.

On May 23, 1968, the two "ancient mariners" launched *Song o' the Winds* into the icy, silt-laden waters of the Athabaska River, near the town of the same name. The headwaters of the Athabaska, one of the five main tributaries of the Mackenzie, lay roughly five hundred miles to the southwest in the Rocky Mountains near Jasper. That morning the river was wide, deep, and running swift with snowmelt. A dozen or so of the town's inquisitive residents hailed the pair as they set off. Besides oar, paddle, and sail power, Burg had brought along a six-horsepower Johnson engine, an indispensable piece of equipment on a lengthy voyage. The Arctic Ocean lay two thousand miles downstream, a daunting distance.

Burg noticed that *Song o' the Winds* carried far less freeboard than he liked, the result of the considerable amount of gear and provisions they had brought. He hated to think he had left anything behind but was bemused by what his six-page list had wrought. Once upon a time he had traveled light, taking only necessities, scraping by, and relying on the generosity of strangers. Awash in gear he once considered a luxury, Burg joked that he and Bracher "had spent six months figuring what to take instead of what not to take." A few miles downstream a pall of acrid-smelling smoke enveloped the river. They had not reckoned on the dozens of forest fires burning in the back-country, the result of lightning strikes. Cinders and ash wafted through the hazy air. Their nostrils burned and their eyes stung. Bracher kept a close eye as embers fell into the interior of the canoe.

The construction of the rail line to the upriver town of Waterways in 1925 had left the two-hundred-mile stretch of the Athabaska virtually unin-habited. Exaggerated tales of the hazardous rapids kept outsiders away. Mean-while, a handful of recreational boaters floated the river as they pleased. With the diminished human traffic, Burg and Bracher found wildlife abundant along the riverbanks. Burg reported sighting moose, deer, caribou, fox, river otter, mink, beaver, and black bear. Bracher's list of bird sightings included sandpipers, plover, sandhill crane, bald eagles, osprey, American white pelican, cormorants, grebes, herons, loons, and geese.

After three days the canoeists stopped to visit Dick George Nauman, one of three permanent residents living along the Athabaska, at Pelican Portage. They had traveled a hundred miles. Nauman, a large, bearded man, made little effort to engage with them, but Earl Kay welcomed them. Kay, who lived a few miles below Pelican Portage, trapped for a living, averaging about $1,400 a year, more money than he could spend in a decade. He agreed to help the men portage around the formidable Grand Rapids, a day's journey downstream. The mile-long rapid fell thirty-four feet in the first half-mile through sandstone channels choked with six- to ten-foot boulders made of conglomerate rock containing pieces of petrified logs.

It took the better part of three days to portage around Grand Rapids. Burg downplayed the danger and hard labor. He wrote "Waterways" in his diary, but the town was now called McMurray, and more than that had changed. Thirty-eight years before, when Burg had launched from Waterways, serious interest in developing a refining plant to separate the oil from the sands had been brewing for a decade. At the time he had noted in his diary the asphalt-like substance along the riverbanks. Bitumen, the raw hydrocarbon found in the oil sands, had once been used by local Native Americans to patch their canoes. The Alcan Oil Company had only recently begun bulk-testing the oil-rich sands at nearby Fort McMurray. A few hundred people lived in the area near the confluence. In 1968 the Great Canadian Oil Sands (now Suncor and Syncrude) plant opened. The population climbed to more than two thousand. Three years later it would reach seven thousand, and by 1980 thirty thousand people lived at the confluence of the Athabaska and Clearwater Rivers.

At McMurray the boatmen restocked and mailed letters. Once back on the river, Burg set the oars aside and fired up the Johnson motor. The first day they passed historic Fort McKay, thirty miles downstream, where Burg noted more changes. The Canadian Department of Transportation had erected beacons to mark the numerous braided channels. Even the river charts Burg had purchased had been upgraded. He found it hard to complain about the improvements.

Traveling at a leisurely place, it took five days to reach Lake Athabaska. At the marshes above it the two men dragged *Song o' the Winds* through the shallows. Near Lobstick Island they restarted the Johnson and cruised into Fort Chipewyan to restock. Despite the sluggish current on the Slave River, the two men took to the oars. By afternoon, *Song o' the Winds* was wind bound. They were glad to have brought the motor. Thirty miles downstream the Peace River entered the Slave River, where the current picked up. They ran the fast water of Primrose and Demicharge Rapids. At Wood Buffalo

Park the voyagers spent several days filming the largest herd of buffalo in North America.

The Slave River made for easy boating, except for the seventeen-mile reach between Fitzgerald and Fort Smith. Over that distance the river fell 109 feet through a corridor of granite, creating four virtually impassable rapids: Cassette, Pelican, Mountain, and Rapids of the Drowned. For centuries the series of cataracts had proved an intractable obstacle to the Indian tribes of the area as well the first white explorers and traders. Smaller vessels with skilled boatmen had been able at times to make the run. But they could not carry enough cargo to justify the risk. River lore suggests that the last known successful run of Mountain Rapid occurred in 1921, when a local farmer and part-time boatman Louis Mercredi shot the cataract in a free trader's scow. Eight years later Burg, while running portions of the notorious stretch of water, had wisely elected to portage. By the time he finished the dangerous stretch, he was behind schedule and the Mounted Police had sent a canoe upriver to search for him.

Burg had no compunctions about trucking *Song o' the Winds* by road to Fort Smith. Upon arrival, he and Bracher pitched their tent on a bluff above the river. Flocks of white pelicans floated lazily over the water. Upstream they could see the white-capped waves of Rapids of the Drowned. At night they fell asleep with the tumult of the river in their ears. They had been out nearly five weeks. Bracher, who had business obligations, reluctantly returned to Cleveland the next day. Burg was on his own.

After a few more pleasant days at Fort Smith, he set off down the river, determined to complete the voyage to the Bering Sea. Seven miles below town, he passed Belle Rock, which marked the end of the portage road around the rapids. With the completion of the Mackenzie Highway to Hay River, the warehouses and wharves along the river had been abandoned, discarded relics of an age when the river had served as a transportation route, when people had lived and worked and taken their recreation along the river. Farther downriver at Cunningham, Burg found more weather-beaten storefronts, decaying sawmills, and boarded-up trapper's cabins. He experienced a wave of nostalgia.

Below LeGrand Detour, a sweeping bend on the Slave River, he met an agricultural employee who worked for the Canadian government raising various kinds of hay to see which species would have the highest yield. Burg was surprised by his eagerness to engage the man in conversation. He realized that he had become increasingly lonely. "I, who had longed for wilderness solitude," he wrote, "now searched the shore hungrily for signs of human habitation. I just thought it would be nice to have someone to talk to for first-hand yarns and inquire about the country through which I was passing."

Nights on the lower Slave turned into sleepless ordeals. At 11:00 PM the northern sky was awash in light. In the hopes of avoiding mosquitoes, Burg anchored offshore, and although he covered the cockpit with a tarp, a swarm inevitably found its way in. Insecticides proved useless. He set off the next morning exhausted. The wind rose steadily; waves splashed over the gunnels. There were more abandoned sawmills and a river with no fellow-voyagers or riverside hermits. The next night proved no better. He anchored out from a midstream island, but by 2:00 AM he was on his way downstream. Lightning and dark thunder clouds rumbled overhead. As he motored in the gray darkness, rain began to fall. The shoreline flashed by. After two days with little sleep, Burg felt anxious and miserable.

As he approached Great Slave Lake, whitecaps rippled across the lake as far as the eye could see. He briefly debated attempting a passage, then anchored at the mouth of the Resdelta Channel. It was a blessing in disguise, and he laid over for two days. The weather turned warm and the scenery was spectacular and strangely reassuring. Burg began to relax. With the mosquitoes at bay, he read Emerson, his longtime favorite author, and his gloom vanished. "It was a soul-lifting experience watching the pageant of days from sunrise to sunset with no need to voyage or do anything but drink it all in," he wrote. "During those two days I once again became a universal spirit."

On the third morning of fair weather, Burg set out along a wind-sheltered delta onto Great Slave Lake. When he rounded Mission Island, he was greeted by mild headwinds and choppy but manageable waves. He started the Johnson motor, bound for Resolution. There the recently completed road to Hay River proved irresistible. Burg loaded *Song o' the Winds* onto a truck and arrived at the once isolated village in a couple of hours.

Hay River was booming. Perched on the northern spur of the Mackenzie Highway, the town served as the shipping port and distribution center for all goods and equipment bound for the villages and oilfields in the Arctic.

Burg thought the scene chaotic, likening it to the Gold Rush. Mountains of freight crowded the waterfront; tugs and barges scrambled for position along the narrow waterway. Larger tugs pushing four or five steel barges headed north down the Mackenzie. He learned from questioning locals that the town had a reputation for rowdiness. Wherever men on the move—construction workers, railway men, tugboat operators, deck hands, oil rig roughnecks, longshoremen—gathered to spend money and drink, trouble followed. Up in Yellowknife, a man in a drunken rage had stabbed seven people. The victims survived but the perpetrator received a mere three months in prison. The river culture fostered by the early riverboat captains that Burg had so admired was now disappeared.

Burg met his old friend Bill Goodlad, who had been a pilot on the Yukon when Burg and Fred "Spokane" Hill came downriver forty years earlier. When the sternwheeler era on the Yukon ended, Goodlad had moved to the Mackenzie and now captained the tugboat *Pelican Rapids*. He readily agreed to give Burg a lift to Fort Simpson. Early on the morning of July 14, they departed Hay River with six small barges in tow. The sun was shining and light winds ruffled the surface of the southern end of Great Slave Lake. Except for the swarms of sand flies, it was an auspicious start. They arrived at the headwaters of the Mackenzie before a deep-red dawn the next morning.

Above Fort Simpson the Liard River spilled a torrent of mud and driftwood into the green waters of the Mackenzie. The *Pelican Rapids* nudged its way through the debris and hauled into the muddy banks. For a mile or so downstream the two currents—one clear, the other muddy brown—remained separate. Burg spent two days in Fort Simpson, an orderly, attractive river town. After saying good-bye to Goodlad, he motored *Song o' the Winds* into the swift current of the Mackenzie, bound for the towns of Wrigley and Fort Norman. At Wrigley he purchased provisions and five gallons of gasoline from the Hudson's Bay store.

Thirty miles above Fort Norman, Burg anchored *Song o' the Winds* midstream in a clear-running side creek. It was a tranquil setting. The fresh cold creek water he drank was delicious. He ate a satisfying meal and relaxed while the canoe swayed back and forth in the mild current. A crisp breeze kept the mosquitoes at bay. "While getting water," he wrote, "I observed a mud streak thru the water, traced it to the bank and there was an otter slide into the water. The scene about me is full of wood lawn beauty. I think of Carolyn and how deeply I love her. I've never felt so deeply before."

At Fort Norman, Burg was greeted by a young Royal Mounted Police officer. Holding to tradition, he offered Burg a cup of coffee and queried him for details about his journey. Burg was warmed by the old custom. That evening he motored downstream to Norman Wells under the spell of a tantalizing sunset that cast rainbow hues over the river. He was pleased with his progress: 150 miles in an eighteen-hour day. "River very quiet—Now that I am here," he wrote in his diary. "Yesterday River and I became one." He hopped aboard the *Dumit,* a survey and buoy tender boat, on July 21. He had arranged passage with the Canadian Department of Transportation in exchange for shooting film footage. Transportation aboard a large vessel allowed him to greatly expand his film coverage of the area. The captain invited Burg into the wheelhouse, where the views were superior. The *Dumit* made stops at Ramparts, Fort Good Hope, and Little Chicago.

Above Arctic Red River he briefly entertained the idea of abandoning the boat for *Song o' the Winds* for the final run into Unuvik, but then he thought better of it. He grudgingly conceded that he had bitten off more than he could chew. "My role is not that of a long distance voyageur," he wrote. "It is more the short assignment I'm fitted for. Don't care for the long voyage. Athabaska to McMurray just right. Then one's interest and energies can be at their height." His return to the Mackenzie had triggered a bout of soul-searching. He had come with expectations, some obvious, others less so: to escape office politics, to revisit the scenes of his youthful adventures, perhaps to capture some of the excitement and magic he had experienced as a young voyageur, free of conventional duties and responsibilities.

Although it is clear that Burg experienced moments of communion with the river, he also suffered conflicting emotions—loneliness, homesickness, a bout of anxiety, a sense of loss, nostalgia—that surprised him. At times he had wished that the trip was over, a notion that had rarely occurred to him as a young, unencumbered voyageur. He missed his wife. Burg's unrest may also have been exacerbated by any number of physical causes: dehydration, irregular diet, lack of sleep, the stress of piloting *Song o' the Winds* alone. The river voyage that was to recapture some of the wonder and joy of his youth had forced him to recognize an indisputable fact: he was aging. The old voyageur's stamina could not quite match the arc of his imagination or his memory. Burg would not stop running rivers, but he would be forced to redefine his love affair with the river.

A week later Burg arrived in Inuvik, the sky thick with the acrid smoke of a tundra fire. Situated on high ground along the East Channel, the town served as a vital river post and clearinghouse for all shipping to the Arctic region. Local boosters called the town the "new modern metropolis of the Mackenzie Delta." Burg stored his canoe and gear in a warehouse in Inuvik and crossed windy Kymallit Bay aboard the *Dumit* to the Inuit village of Tuk-toyuktuk. "Tuk" also had become a busy port. Tugs and barges unloaded their cargos onto the oceangoing ships that distributed the supplies and equipment to the Alaskan and Canadian oil fields.

Burg's own voyage came to an end upon his return to Inuvik. Summit Lake in the Richardson Mountains, where he had planned to launch his canoe for the next leg of his journey into the Yukon watershed, was enveloped in smoke from a tundra fire. All aircraft in the area had been commandeered to carry firefighters from the local villages into the interior. The Bell River, he learned, was running extremely low. Dragging and portaging *Song o' the Winds* over rocks and gravel beds would be hard labor for a man Burg's age. He accepted his fate with equal amounts of relief and disappointment. He had been out nearly nine weeks.

The following summer Burg returned to Aklavik, across the Mackenzie delta from Inuvik, with his friend Joe McLean, the mayor of Juneau, and McLean's wife, Isabel, and son, Duncan. It was the kind of boating companionship Burg enjoyed—a small group who loved the outdoors as much as he did and could take care of themselves. He would be following in the historic wake of the voyageurs. The men of the Hudson's Bay Company had paddled freight up the Rat River and then portaged their trading goods over McDougall Pass to the Bell River. They navigated their boats down the Bell to the Porcupine River, trading with the local Gwich'in tribes for furs until they reached Fort Yukon. At 480 miles, the trade route down the three rivers into the Yukon Valley matched Burg's intention to scale down the length of his trips.

Burg hired an Eskimo youth to accompany him and the McLeans as far as Old Crow at the confluence of the Bell and Porcupine Rivers. The young man would help with the camp chores and assist Burg with lining *Song o' the Winds* over the rocky shallows. After two days of preparation, a Northern Airlines Otter flew the river runners and their equipment to Summit Lake, which straddles the border between the Northwest and Yukon Territory watersheds. There the group began the onerous task of portaging their canoes and equipment a half-mile across the tundra to the Little Bell to launch. Ten- to fifteen-feet wide at best, the muddy, steep-banked river ran fast through a dry, windless canyon. A mile or two downstream the current picked up. Although the river was thick with schools of grayling and arctic char, there was no time for fishing. For most of the afternoon the river runners found themselves shoving, lifting, and dragging their heavily loaded canoes through the rock-strewn channels. By sunset the next day they reached the confluence with the Big Bell.

The 180-mile river was a welcome change. The mountains retreated; stands of birch and spruce crowded the shoreline. Swift-flowing and wide, the Big Bell drew fresh winds down the river corridor that drove the mosquitoes and black flies away. Bursts of rain followed the voyagers. At evening camp Burg had hopes that his Eskimo guide might regale them with Native tales of life along the river, but the young man had little to say except: "River very crooked." Burg joked to the McLeans that he was paying the young man about thirty dollars a word.

After a week the group reached the Porcupine River. Hundreds of yards wide, stamped with gravel bars, clear water and a fast-moving current, the river was a delight. Small herds of caribou roamed the shoreline. The weather improved; the only drawback for Burg and company were afternoon headwinds that made paddling a task. Another three days brought them to the town of Old Crow, the only permanent settlement on the Porcupine. The McLeans ended their journey and returned to Juneau. Burg paid off his guide. He would voyage the final 285 miles alone. He thought it would take four, at the most five days.

The first day Burg motored downriver, entering the upper Ramparts region of the Porcupine River. Purple and brown cliffs, ranging from three hundred to five hundred feet high, and oddly shaped rock formations bordered the thirty-five-mile canyon. Mist turned to rain, followed by patches of sunshine interrupting the procession of clouds—typical Alaskan weather. Upstream, winds ruffled the swift water. The colors along shore danced to the tune of the shifting weather. Burg stopped at Rampart House, the once busy HBC post where the Porcupine River crossed the International Boundary into Alaska. The site was deserted, overgrown with fireweed and raspberry bushes chest high. The store, the Anglican Church, and the Northwest Mounted Police post were gone; the few remaining log cabins in shambles. Burg lingered. When he had passed through in 1929 he had enjoyed the hospitality of a white man and his Native wife. Supper had consisted of unsalted meat, prunes without any juice, and jam and tea served "in a spirit that would have enabled me to eat anything." In 1947, he recalled, the last resident had left. An unexpected bout of melancholy swept over Burg. He had not expected his memories to bring sadness. An inescapable sense of time passing dogged the old voyageur.

He set himself a daily routine. At night he ate and slept in his canoe close to the water's edge. He read Emerson, always a balm when he felt lonely. At nightfall he lay in his sleeping bag and listened to the sounds of the river until he fell asleep. In the morning he did not dally. An early start met quiet, no headwinds, the sense of a new day with possibilities. At lunch he let *Song o' the Winds* drift, trying to catch the rhythm of the rivers of his youth. "One learns the necessity of knowledge if he is to interpret the passing wilderness scene," he wrote. "Rock formations, trees, fish, birds, insects; all this without knowledge is a closed book. Each day my exultation increased by constant reminders that life is indeed a miracle when one lives face to face with Nature, as every hour yields its tribute of delight."

Burg passed through the lower Ramparts and entered the Yukon Flats region. The Porcupine now split into numerous channels, many of them deadends. Burg pushed ahead and eventually found his way to the mouth of the Yukon, four miles below Fort Yukon. On day twelve of his solo journey, he motored up the muddy river and found his wife, Carolyn, waiting on shore. The two-thousand-mile voyage he had begun the previous summer was complete. He summed up his experience by quoting the newspaper columnist Hal Boyle: "It is awakening in a sleeping bag at midnight on the river shore, surrounded by all the awesome glory of the universe, and talking your heart out to that lonesome stranger, God."

Back in Juneau, Burg returned to work to find the ADFG in upheaval. The new commissioner continued to reassure him that his job was secure. Initially,

Burg seemed satisfied with the arrangement. He remained busy, with to-do lists that were as long as they had ever been: write and edit newsletter, organize a series of lectures for the Glacier Visitors' Center, meet with personnel department, order film, prepare budget cost and logistics of his next film, and of course keep up with the voluminous correspondence. The honeymoon was short. "These days seem to be coming to a close," he wrote, "even the job itself. But I'll do my best and a miracle might happen."

In September the new commissioner had written a piece in the department newsletter blasting his predecessor for a poorly run operation. Although Burg recognized the validity of some of the complaints, he thought the piece intemperate and counterproductive. He was hurt by the indirect but public criticism of his work as head officer of the Information and Education department. He recognized that although he had always been a quick study, he had never been a professional manager. In the early, pioneering days of the department, it had not mattered. The managerial duties of the Information and Education officer, however, had been expanding over the past decade. Public relations was no longer simply a matter of answering letters or giving speeches. Burg admitted that the increasing workload gnawed into the time he preferred to spend filming, writing, and taking photographs.

In 1970, Burg was gently moved out of his managerial position and appointed assistant editor of *Alaska Fish and Game*, an in-house publication that was expanding and would eventually become a glossy bimonthly magazine for the general public. He began writing a regular column, "Campfire Reflections." More storyteller than magazine columnist, Burg weaved his own experiences into his subject matter—Alaskan history, the behavior of bears, the courage of wildlife biologists, profiles of sourdoughs, the need to protect the environment, advice to newcomers. His stories usually carried a moral or cautionary warning. His photographs of Alaskan Natives were regular features for the back cover of the magazine. Over the next fifteen years his column became increasingly popular, serving as a mainstay for the magazine in good times and bad.

While Burg navigated a changing work environment, his wife charged into local and state politics. After nearly two decades in Alaska, Carolyn Warren Burg had become a voluble activist for a number of causes. Some viewed her as a pushy firebrand; others admired her willingness to speak out. Her initial foray into activist politics had begun in the early 1960s with the "Save Our Capital" campaign. For decades, politicians and businessmen from the interior of Alaska had argued for the relocation of the state capital, preferably to Anchorage or Fairbanks. Juneau, they complained, was simply too isolated. They cited lack of access to decision makers, transportation costs, and time delays. In the first forty-two years of statehood voters faced ten ballot measures dealing with moving all or part of the capital.

Carolyn had developed an interest in becoming a lawyer while working as a stenographer with the US State Attorney in Ketchikan in the late 1950s, and began taking correspondence courses. She now used her amateur's knowledge to articulate an anti-relocation position in local court, where she appeared numerous times. During one session her passion got the better of her and she was held in contempt of court for talking back to the judge. He sentenced her to an overnight stay at the Juneau Correctional Institute. Her daughter Nancy came to pick her up the next morning.

While working for the Alaska Highway Department (AHD) throughout the 1960s, she had spearheaded a statewide anti-littering campaign. In her zeal she used the copying machine and other resources at the department for campaign publicity, actions that ran counter to state policy. When her supervisor asked her to stop, she ignored the request. In 1967 she retired. Some local residents speculated that she was forced out of the Alaska Highway Department. Burg, who was by temperament nonconfrontational, cringed at his wife's behavior but comforted her nonetheless. Later she received a state award from Governor Egan for her work on the anti-littering campaign. Despite these professional successes, she suffered a crisis of confidence. In search of a consuming cause or belief to satisfy her considerable energy, she quit the Methodist Church in the late 1960s and joined the Bethel Assembly of God Church, an evangelical denomination.

Meanwhile, Burg struggled to understand the shift in cultural attitudes that by 1970 had reached isolated Juneau. An unfamiliar, even unruly, crowd of young nature-lovers and back-to-the-woods advocates had arrived in town. Disheveled in appearance, they had what a usually tolerant Burg would have called "loose morals." Some passed the harsh test of an Alaskan winter and remained, but most moved on. One newly hired young copywriter showed up barefoot for work. "It seems strange a man will handicap himself with long hair and a scraggily beard," Burg wrote. "When I see a man with hair down to his shoulders, I feel certain revulsion. I ask why? Because he looks like a female."

Burg had grown quietly and increasingly disenchanted with his working conditions. At seventy, he still hankered after the freedom of movement of his youth. He wanted to cruise the Inside Passage in *Endeavour* with Carolyn. He spoke about returning to the rivers—the Snake, the Columbia, the Colorado, and the Salmon. He made lists of projects. He also fretted—about his health, his weight, office politics, and the mountain of memorabilia stored in his shed. For the first time he voiced a serious interest in retirement. A state pension and Social Security combined with freelance work might carry him and his wife comfortably into old age. In January 1974 he gave a six-month notice to his employer. On June 17 friends and colleagues gathered at the Baranof Hotel in downtown Juneau to pay tribute to Amos Burg. The mood of the crowd was warm, lighthearted, and celebratory. Governor Egan presented his longtime friend with the Alaskan meritorious achievement award. Burg had worked hard on his acceptance speech. The enthusiastic crowd needed little encouragement when it came to applause. Burg was one of their own.

Although I was unaware of it, my last trip as a working guide in the Grand Canyon occurred in August 1988. Any intimation that a time would arrive when I would (or should) move on had never arisen. From the moment I first pushed off from Lees Ferry a decade earlier, I fell in love with the place, smitten beyond words. It was as if I had stumbled into a stone cathedral with a river running through it that had been awaiting my arrival. Never had I been so certain that I belonged to a place, or that Grand Canyon was where I would stay.

In the off-season I pined for my life on the river. Jobs and relationships were fleeting, mere interruptions of a more important voyage. At the start of each winter I had trouble sleeping indoors. Where were the stars? Those sounds the river made? That particular musty river smell? What of the melodic call of the canyon wren or the bickering conversation of the ravens? The laughter of my fellow boatmen? Once I settled down, I dreamed about the river so intensely that in my twilight sleep I felt my wooden dory rocking beneath me. For months I played the waiting game, my gaze firmly fixed on the day I would return to the canyon. I was an unapologetic, river-loving, mystical, capital "R" romantic westerner with what we boatmen jokingly call B.D., "boatman's disease"—a chronic longing for the river. Everything else shrank in comparison.

With so much of their heart and identity wedded to the canyon, the seasonal void caused some boatmen to suffer "river blues," bouts of depression, and what today is called "substance abuse." When my son Jake was born in May 1989, I knew I would not return to the Colorado River that season and that likely my days as a full-time canyon boatman were over. My wife was glad to hear that. I had sufficiently grasped the idea of fatherhood and figured it was time to move on. As a result, I underestimated the river's hold. Thus began a period of heartache more severe than any seasonal river disorder I had experienced.

Spring brought an unexpectedly deep sense of loss, both of place and identity. It crept in like a flood tide washing over me. I had abandoned my old seasonal rhythms, the freedom of movement, the excitement that always accompanies the start of another river voyage, my place as a boatman in Grand Canyon. Though I knew better, in my more restless moments I sometimes asked myself, "For what?" I missed so many things, concrete and ineffable, dramatic and commonplace: the easy camaraderie of the crew, middle-of-the-night flashfloods, rapids that changed over time, epic side-canyon hikes, passengers who conquered fears and some who underwent spiritual transformations, summer storms, sleeping on my boat at the river's edge, morning coffee, the marker-wave at Crystal Rapid, boat wrecks and flips, waterfalls during the monsoon season, heartbreaking natural beauty, the playfulness the river provoked, my hard-earned knowledge of the 280-mile Colorado. Would I ever get over the river?

Never completely but one day, without warning, my memories of Grand Canyon, once colored by loss, turned warm and consoling, the raw material of stories my son and newborn daughter Gwen would soon demand to hear.

Chapter 12

A VOYAGEUR'S LAMENT

Nancy Long wanted her first video interview to be a success. The novice videographer's search for a fresh, compelling subject had yielded little to her satisfaction, however, and time was running out. She casually mentioned her predicament to the station engineer at the local public TV station in Juneau where she volunteered. He suggested that she talk to a chiropractor in town who had told him about a patient he was treating. This patient had, among numerous adventures, run all of the major Western rivers in the 1920s. Long called the chiropractor, who gave her the phone number of Amos Burg. Although Juneau was a small town, the name was unfamiliar to her. After casual research on Burg revealed that he might well be a subject far more interesting than she could have hoped for, Long called.

Carolyn Burg was initially reluctant when she heard Long's pitch for a profile piece on her husband's life as an adventurer. At eighty-two, he was not well and had been bedridden for weeks at a time. Long added that the piece would appear on the popular *Rain Country* TV program, which covered the people and places of southwestern Alaska. Carolyn, always protective of her husband's reputation, was pleased that someone was interested in him. She reconsidered, thinking that Amos might enjoy the conversation. She would talk to him. The next day Carolyn called Long back. Burg would be glad to speak with her, but Carolyn made it clear that the interview would have to be brief, no longer than an hour at most. If he was feeling unwell that day, it would be postponed until a later date.

On a spring afternoon in 1984, Long set up her video equipment in the Burgs' crowded front room overlooking Gastineau Channel. She tried to mask her nervousness. Introductions had been brief, pleasant. Although she had further researched Burg and had a list of questions, her octogenarian subject, sitting in his armchair covered in a blanket, appeared fragile. She needed at least an hour's worth of taping to gather enough material for the seven-minute segment. Would he be able to hold out that long? She explained to the Burgs what she hoped to achieve. Once filming began, Long's worries vanished. Burg was a born storyteller. With a gentle, melodic voice, he launched effortlessly into a series of anecdotes about his life and past river adventures. Exuding warmth, Burg was clearly comfortable in front of the camera.

As he pondered the past, his face registered a range of emotions from amazement to wistfulness. As the interview progressed, his memory remained remarkably sharp. He recalled long-ago incidents in detail, the character of his river companions, and he even quoted verse from the English poet Lord Tennyson. By the end of the interview Burg, who had clearly enjoyed himself, was tired. The interview had exceeded Long's expectations. The Burgs invited her to return, and over time a friendship developed. A few months later Alaska Public TV aired the piece. Like many young, adventurous people in Juneau, Nancy Long found herself profoundly affected by her friendship with Burg. Four years after his death in 1986, she received a grant to make another documentary about her friend. The half-hour documentary, *The Journey of Amos Burg*, appeared on Alaskan Public Television on December 3, 1992, and was later nominated for a regional Public Broadcasting award.

A month after retiring from the Alaska Department of Fish and Game in 1974, Burg set out for the Navajo reservation in New Mexico. Charlie Wheeler, his longtime friend and chairman of the board of Navajo Forest Products, asked him to produce a documentary about the economic benefits to the Navajo people of sustained-yield forestry. Burg spent the next two months in the Chuska Mountains of northeastern Arizona filming the ponderosa pine lumbering operations. He fretted about the quality of the film. Although he was unsatisfied with how the film turned out, *Wealth from the Navajo Forest* was well received by Wheeler and the other board members. "We all (are) more interested than ever in the industrial prospects for the Navajo people as a result of the viewing," Wheeler wrote.

Later that summer Burg took another freelance film assignment in the Brooks Range of Alaska's North Slope. He spent two weeks crisscrossing the Colville River delta of Prudhoe Bay, taking both land and aerial shots. In 1968 ARCO and EXXON corporations had discovered oil in the area. Construction of the eight-hundred-mile Alaskan Pipeline to carry oil to Valdez, the northernmost ice-free port, was under way when Burg arrived in the area.

"Campfire Reflections," Burg's column for *Alaska Fish and Game,* continued to grow in popularity. He ranged over a wide variety of subjects, and in the January–February 1974 issue he returned to his favorite author, Ralph Waldo Emerson. Burg had carried a worn copy of Emerson's essays with him on the Yukon and Mackenzie River voyages in the 1920s. "For in Emerson's time, which we love to reflect upon as the good old days," he wrote, recalling the poet's lifelong influence, "the nation was confronted with the chilling problems of slavery and civil war. However, while he could be deeply shaken at times, nothing could alter Emerson's belief in the goodness of the universe and he was buoyed up all his life by his faith that nature and man could be trusted and that a sublime and friendly destiny guided the human race. Emerson believed in the oversoul of which everything living was a part and parcel of God." Despite this Emersonian Christianity, Burg occasionally attended services with Carolyn at her Pentecostal church. Over time he developed a genuine interest in the faith itself.

He liked and respected the assistant pastor of the Pentecostal church, Don Brown. Soft-spoken and low-key, Brown enjoyed spending time outdoors. Because his sermons carried none of the usual fire and brimstone preached by other Pentecostal pastors, Brown had drawn an atypical group into his congregation—loggers, fishermen, big game guides, roughnecks, truck drivers. They were not the types to be won over by threats or what Brown called "fluffing up" the message of Christianity. Belief in Jesus Christ did not necessarily mean attending church every Sunday or relinquishing a way of life. Brown, in the idiom of the times, was "a man's man," albeit a gentle one. Burg was comfortable with the rituals of the Pentecostal congregation, even when witnessing members experiencing the "gift of tongues."

In the small, isolated town of Juneau, the Burgs and the Browns became friends. In the summer of 1975, Amos invited Don and his teenage sons to accompany him, along with Carolyn's son-in-law and grandson, on a canoe trip on the Yukon River from Whitehorse to Carmacks. Drifting down-river had always been conducive to conversation for Burg, and now was no different. He and Brown had more in common than either had suspected. They ranged over a variety of subjects—Burg's past adventures, the beauty of nature, human relationships, the existence of God, conventional religion. This would not be their last trip together.

Burg had long prided himself on his health and physical stamina. Over the years he had suffered his share of injuries and illnesses—malaria, food poisoning, chronic knee damage, recurring back problems—but he had always recovered in good form. It came as a shock when, in 1976, doctors at the University Hospital in Seattle announced that he would need triple-bypass heart surgery. They suggested that his arteries were likely to become clogged again within five years—not an encouraging diagnosis. That spring Burg entered the hospital. The operation was successful, but his lengthy recovery forced him to slow down considerably. Once back in Juneau, Carolyn fussed over her husband, making sure he adhered to his diet and took his heart "rhythm" pills. She screened visitors so that his afternoon naps were not interrupted. Burg had not counted on spending his retirement in an easy chair or being taken care of.

While recuperating, he began making plans for a "recreational voyage" down the Yukon River the summer of 1977. He sent anticipated participants in the journey a page of "Voyaging Notes," with the caveat "Suggestions Only." His range of friends had always been eclectic, and he liked nothing better than bringing along people (with families) who did not know each other to share the river. The party this time numbered twenty, including Pastor Brown's family and the well-known Alaskan artist Rie Muñoz. In 1951, the year after Burg had visited King Island, Muñoz arrived to teach school to twenty-five Island children. The flotilla included canoes and rafts, propelled by engines, paddles, and oars.

On August 2 the group made ready to launch from Whitehorse at noon, hours behind schedule but in bright sunshine. Despite the teenagers' high spirits, a relaxed atmosphere prevailed. Many in the group were meeting for the first time; all assumed that "a friend of Amos's was a friend of mine." The de facto leader was dressed in his traditional river outfit: long-sleeve shirt (often with a tie and vest) khaki pants with cuffs, leather oxford shoes, and a weathered Greek fisherman's cap. Easily manageable by the average boater, the 240-mile run to Carmacks had become an increasingly popular stretch of river. On this morning, however, it remained relatively free of people. After ten miles the group camped at White Rock Camp.

Around the campfire that evening Burg charmed his fellow voyagers with tales of his own adventures down the Yukon. Others recited a series of Robert Service poems, including "The Shooting of Dan McGrew," "The Spell of the Yukon," and the group favorite, "The Cremation of Sam McGee." In the morning Burg blew his horn to signal a wake-up call. After breakfast Pastor Brown led devotions, a habit that was repeated each morning before launching. The flotilla covered eighty miles, camping near the wreckage of the *Casca,* the same sternwheeler Burg had traveled aboard (while marveling at Captain Bill Goodlad's skill as a river pilot) more than two decades before. The following evening, the voyagers camped at a beach near where the Teslin River enters the Yukon—Hootalingua, the once-thriving sternwheeler repair area. That evening the fishermen in the party caught enough grayling and pike to feed the entire group. With an abundance of driftwood, they built a blazing campfire and enjoyed more of Burg's stories, more singing and laughter. Late that night the Northern Lights appeared.

The next morning the flotilla stopped at Steamboat Island, three-quarters of a mile downriver. Burg had a secret to show them: he led the group through overgrown brush and past a stand of trees to an unexpected sight—another abandoned, derelict sternwheeler, hidden from river view. It was a strange but exciting experience to step back in time, especially for the younger river voyagers. Back on the Yukon, Burg pointed out the woodcutter's camps he had passed in the 1920s. Something he would not have seen fifty years earlier was the odd-looking vessel that floated by the group—a log raft with a small tent carrying a group of partially clad young women and long-haired men. At mile 147, Burg and company camped on a swath of sandy beach on one of the islands. The mosquitoes disappeared. Someone named this ideal location "Amos Island." The women bathed in a nearby creek.

After a breakfast on the final morning of the trip, the group floated five hours before passing under the bridge at Carmacks. By any measure, the trip had been a success. Burg was pleased, especially since everyone promised to return the next year. Back in Juneau, he immediately began planning two river trips for the following summer: a much anticipated run on the Snake River through Hells Canyon and a return to the Yukon. He wrote to the Explorers Club in New York requesting to carry one of the club's expedition flags. Three decades had passed since he last attended a club dinner.

In early February 1978, Burg arrived at Seattle's University Hospital for a routine health checkup. Throughout the winter he had suffered chronic pain in his lower back, abdomen, and groin area. After testing, the doctors diagnosed prostate cancer. (It may not have come as a surprise. In a letter to a friend he had written, "He [the doctor] had operated on me 12 years ago for prostate.") The doctors advised him to begin radiation treatment immediately. He remained in Seattle for the next three months, living frugally, seeing friends, reading, churning out letters daily, and taking short walks whenever possible.

During treatment Burg struck up a friendship with Dr. Clifford Lee, his radiologist. When he mentioned his upcoming river trip through Hells Canyon, Lee expressed an interest and Burg immediately extended an invitation. He also invited Don Brown and his family, writing to his old friend:

> Since I made the last voyage down the Snake three dams have been built, Brownlee, Ox Bow and Hells Canyon making 92 miles of continuous lakes. Hells Canyon is a concrete slab 395 feet above the river. It sets in the river near Squaw Creek. Below it is still 110 miles of wild river stretching to Lewiston. Only the prolonged fight by conservationists saved the rest of the canyon from being drowned as power interests have been fighting to construct the 670-foot High Mountain Sheep dam which would create a lake 52 miles long. As power shortage grows the energy advocates may win so your sons should see this great wild river while its waters are still alive. Fishing below the dam is fantastic—24 species of fish still live in the wild waters including white sturgeon and small mouthed bass.

As the weeks passed, however, the effects of the radiation treatment took their toll on Burg. His buoyant optimism wavered. He retreated from socializing, but when he felt well enough, he began attending churches throughout the city. He made occasional appearances at Lee's Chinese Baptist Church and St. Luke's Episcopal Church on Twenty-second Avenue in Seattle, where people from different walks of life and faith attended: businessmen, working people, the poor, Roman Catholic nuns, Baptist ministers, Lutheran and Assembly of God pastors, Catholic priests. When able, he attended services at Brown's Bethel Assembly of God Church in Chehalis, Washington.

Burg summed up his search for spiritual solace: "A church is a church and that one will be my church tomorrow." Given the lengthy time period he was in Seattle and the cost involved in traveling from Juneau, Carolyn remained at home. Of his spiritual quest, he wrote to her:

> Worship is a very personal thing and our relation to God should not
> be dictated by another, even a wife. People are alienated over religious
> beliefs. I think my relationship with God is personal and a very good
> one and constantly growing but in my own way. Freedom to worship
> in our own individual way is one of the great tenets of the Constitu
> tion. I love going to church with you because we share it together,
> but I'm not only a Sunday 11:00 to 12:00 worshipper as many are. I
> don't think religion should be argued about and fought over bringing
> death and misery as it does in Northern Ireland and Israel. I think it
> should be lived by each of us in our own individual way throughout
> every working day. I love you.

At the end of April 1978, Burg finished with his treatments at University Hospital. He was anxious to return to Juneau and prepare for his Snake River voyage.

On a warm July morning in 1978, Burg and his river companions stood on the launch ramp below Hells Canyon Dam, readying themselves for their voyage. Anticipation rippled through the group. Upriver, the ten-year-old dam rose implacably skyward, undeniably impressive. The river remained in the shadows of the towering canyon walls, racing by rambunctiously, a trace of its old spirit still evident. The canyon air—arid, warm, and pine-scented—was unfamiliar to the Alaskans on the trip. Among the group of eighteen were Carolyn Burg, Clifford Lee, Don Brown and his family, and Roy Pepper, Burg's companion on his trip to the tip of South America in 1934, and Pepper's son, Randy, and his children.

As the group prepared to launch, Randy mentioned to his father that Burg appeared a bit unsteady on his feet. They would need to keep an eye, not too close, on their fellow voyager. If he suspected he was being looked after, Burg would have been irked. He had planned to bring *Charlie,* the rubber raft he had piloted on the Green and Colorado Rivers in 1938, the Middle Fork and Main Salmon Rivers in 1939, as well as the Snake River in 1944. After four decades, however, the raft's condition was suspect, having suffered the normal wear-and-tear and been stored in Burg's shed through numerous Alaskan winters. Instead, he brought his twelve-foot Avon Redshank with a square stern for a motor mount. It was better suited to the Yukon River. The size of the Avon also limited how much gear Burg could carry. To remedy that problem, he had purchased an eight-foot Sevylor to tow behind the Avon. This boat was ill-suited for the fast water of Hells Canyon. Ever in good humor, he summed up the inferior quality of his water trailer as a "one-rock" boat. Carolyn would ride with him, and the other three boats included two sixteen-foot Campways and one seventeen-foot Havasu raft.

United States Geological Society records showed river flows of 17,000 cubic feet per second for July 5. Over the next few days the river (due to water released from the dam) would fluctuate as high as 22,000 cubic feet per second, relatively high but not unusual water for experienced boatmen familiar with the river. As they floated downriver, Burg watched as other excited groups of rafters passed them by. Since the late 1960s, recreational river running had exploded in popularity. In summer it was not unusual for three or more trips a day to launch on the Snake, a floating population of fifty to seventy-five people. Provided each trip moved downriver at a regular pace, contact would be minimal and the illusion of an uncrowded river might be maintained. The spell was broken by the growing number of upriver jet boats.

Burg had mixed feelings during his return voyage to Hells Canyon. There was no denying the beauty of the mile-deep canyon or its ability to inspire wonder and excitement. The impact of the dam, however, had been enormous. Notorious rapids he had run or lined years ago were now buried beneath sparkling green reservoir water; once numerous sandy beaches pocketed amid the rocky shores had disappeared; the ubiquitous "bathtub ring," the result of daily dam releases, stretched for miles.

Wild Sheep Rapids, one of the two remaining major rapids on the Snake, lay six miles downstream. The party, arriving late in the afternoon, decided to camp above it. The next morning they scouted from the left shore. Aware of the Avon's limitations (in the short distance from the put-in, the Avon had taken water over the tubes at an alarming rate), Burg decided to line his boat around the first large protruding boulders and slip along the left shore past the rapids. Despite many helping hands, midway through the effort the Sevylor swung out into the current and overturned. Burg's gear and provisions got a thorough soaking before it was pulled to shore. Towing the toylike raft had been a mistake.

Randy Pepper ran the rapid first, making a successful left-of-center run, followed by his father, Roy. A few minutes later Don Brown, a novice oarsman, drifted down the tongue of the rapid but misread his position. As the raft turned sideways, Brown, with his two teenage children aboard, took a lateral wave from the left shore and immediately flipped and washed downstream. The recovery took longer than expected, and the Browns were forced to spend the night separate from the rest of the party. The following morning, they reunited. At Granite Creek Rapids, Randy once again led, followed by his father, and Brown. All made successful right-of-center runs. Burg, with help, lined his Avon around the rapids. At a lunch stop, he confided to Randy that he was worried about keeping up with the group. If the Avon overturned, he (and Carolyn) would be in a precarious position. Burg's radiation treatment months earlier had weakened him more than he cared to admit. Randy suggested that Burg ride with him for the remainder of the trip. He reluctantly agreed. They rolled up the raft and stowed it, along with his gear, in Pepper's raft. Everyone, including Burg, breathed easier.

That evening they pitched camp at Saddle Creek. Brown noticed that Burg was unusually quiet. Acknowledging the need to ride as a passenger was a smart move on Burg's part and good for the group as a whole. Nevertheless, it was a humbling moment. Burg was disappointed with himself. He had made a number of poor decisions: the Avon raft was clearly unsuitable for a river the size of the Snake; towing the flimsy Sevylor had been a fool-ish idea; he had lugged far too much gear; and most disappointing, he had overestimated his ability to row his own raft. He had to ask for help. He also had trouble navigating the rocky shoreline and side creeks. In his diary he wrote:

> Lost my sense of balance. Kept falling down on slippery rocks. Even when I didn't slip I'd fall over. Once down had a hard time getting up. My final fall was at a small creek below Johnson's Pass. It struck halfway across the str [stream] & had moss on the lower edge. I leaped and stepped on the moss. The next instant I was flat on my side in the creek. . . . Rolls of film and a thermometer flowed out and down-stream—I never noticed the loss at the time. I lay there unable to move. Finally enlisted my full strength & crawled out of the creek.

Burg was not one to brood for too long. Summoning old river remedies to counter the blues, he kept busy. He ignored any physical discomfort he experienced riding on Randy's raft and resumed his role as storyteller and guide, pointing out places he and his guide the moonshiner John Mullins had stopped on their historic 1925 voyage.

When asked later about this six-day trip down the Snake, Burg claimed that it had been a success. Carolyn had relished the visit to the river where her husband had voyaged as a young man and made a name for himself. Clifford Lee had been delighted. The Pepper family was game for another trip. Pastor Brown now had a river yarn to spin about his flip in Wild Sheep. Burg's experience on the Snake had also left him cautious and introspective. He abhorred the idea of being a burden to his river companions; yet, he had plainly needed their help.

Regardless of his physical condition, a month later he set out to run the Yukon River again. One obstacle after another threatened to end the trip before it began. Several people dropped out at the last moment. When Randy Pepper's converted school bus broke down on the way to Whitehorse, the trip was delayed four days. Eventually Burg and Carolyn were joined by Randy, his wife, and their four children as well as his father, Roy. The original goal of reaching Dawson to attend the Discovery Day celebration on August 13 was set aside. They would float to Carmacks instead.

On the morning of August 5 the diminished fleet launched from White-horse under an overcast sky. The steady drizzle turned to intermittent rain. Randy and his family rode in their seventeen-foot Havasu; Roy had rented a nineteen-foot Grumman canoe with a sail rig; Burg, with Carolyn riding midship beneath a tarp, piloted his favored Chestnut canoe, *Song o' the Winds*. Each vessel carried an outboard motor. As they motored toward Lake Leb-arge, the rain increased. Burg, in an unusual lapse, had not brought sufficient raingear. Soon he and his wife were soaked and shivering. Then the motor failed, forcing Burg to paddle the last few miles to camp. He was in a bad way when he arrived and quickly retired to the dry comfort of his tent.

The next morning the voyagers were greeted by more dismal weather. A lake crossing looked problematic. No one argued when Randy suggested a layover day. Rest, meals, a steady fire, idle chatter, the comfort of a tent would mend dampened spirits. Burg remained in his tent napping and read-ing. When the afternoon sun appeared, Roy and Randy spread out a tarp and tinkered with Burg's outboard motor, then cleaned out his canoe. Burg remained ambivalent about these gestures of friendship. "Yesterday in the cold and wet I thought they were unfeeling," he wrote, "but they are truly full of kind deeds."

Practical jokes on the river lightened the mood. One evening as Burg tried to light his ancient camp stove, Roy offered to help. Instead of lighting the stove, however, he picked up the battered piece of equipment and hurled it into the lake. Burg stared in disbelief; Carolyn was flabbergasted. Roy then retrieved a new stove from a waterproof bag in his tent and presented it to his old shipmate. "Time for a new stove, Amos!" Laughter filled the campsite. Over the next two days, the three boats rode a following sea to lower Lake Laberge. The weather improved; to the west lay the Saint Elias Range washed in sunshine and blue skies. They passed between Richtofen Island, known for its abundance of wildflowers in early summer, and the western shore of the lake. The next day they made a run down the Thirty Mile River section of the Yukon to Hootalinqua. Swift and clear, the river cut through a narrow corridor. Wind-carved hoodoos stood like sentinels on the cliffs above. Burg grew animated as he recalled the river names: Dog Crossing, US Bend, John-

Burg and Roy Pepper share a joke on the Yukon, 1978.

son Island, Anchor Bar, Casca and Tanana Reef, Rocky Point. Arriving at the
mouth of the Teslin River on the evening of August 8, the group camped on
the island they had camped the previous year.

To make the thirty-five-mile run to Big Salmon, the voyagers lashed
the two canoes to Randy's raft and set off downstream, arriving ahead of
an incoming storm. Rain delayed their departure the next morning. Burg
retreated to his tent, where he grumbled uncharacteristically in his diary:
"Sure be glad to arrive in Carmacks (70 miles downstream). . . . The voyage
will be over and we will be back in our van on the 21st (of August)." That
afternoon they stopped at Little Salmon to visit the "spirit houses" in the
old Native cemetery. Constructed over graves, these doll-house-like "cabins"
(with windows) contained the personal effects of the person buried there.

Early on the afternoon of August 11, the flotilla spotted the Tantalus Butte
Coal Mine on the east side of the river. As they passed under the highway
bridge above Carmacks, Burg yarned about the final journey of the sternwheeler *Keno* to Dawson City two decades before, when the top deck and
the stacks of the ship had to be removed to clear the bridge. Engineers had
failed to make allowances for the height of the steamboats. An era had ended.
At Dawson City, the *Keno* was converted into a museum. In jest he drew

comparisons between the paddle wheelers and himself. Poor weather, physical discomfort, his growing awareness of his dependence on others—all may have contributed to Burg's complicated emotions. "Been a nice trip," he wrote, "but I probably shouldn't have taken it in my state of health."

If anyone could fully appreciate Burg's historic river voyages, it was river historian Cort Conley. In high school he had become fascinated by the history of the western fur trade, especially the trappers and voyageurs who freely roamed the West on foot and by river. While attending law school at the University of California at Berkeley, he took a "Western Americana" history course that later caused him to rethink his career goals. While Conley pursued his law degree, he held a series of jobs during the summers that brought him face-to-face with the West of his imagination: stints as a fire lookout and a backcountry packer in the Sierra Mountains; a backcountry ranger in Teton National Park in Wyoming; and a taste for river running on the Green and Yampa Rivers in Utah. Although he received his law degree, Conley never practiced law.

In 1972 he moved to Idaho to run pack and river float trips on the Main Salmon River. Working as a guide, he soon discovered that although the oral tradition of storytelling along the Main Salmon remained strong, no one was recording and collecting river stories. He set out to remedy the situation, reading the available literature (which was scant) and in the off-season searching local and university libraries for firsthand accounts. He built a web of contacts—outfitters, guides, old-timers, librarians, rangers, local residents, even passengers—and started doing interviews. The amateur historian had discovered a rich tributary of neglected Western history: the tales of boatmen, past and present, and the people who lived along the river.

As Conley's research expanded beyond the Salmon River, the name of Amos Burg continued to pop up. Burg, he learned to his delight, was still alive. Numerous people suggested to Conley that the old river runner would never talk to him, but Conley obtained Burg's address in Juneau and in fall 1978 wrote to request an interview. Conley, along with coauthor Johnny Carrey, had recently published *River of No Return,* a guide to the Main Salmon. The previous year their *The Middle Fork and the Sheepeater War* had also come out. The writing team was presently at work on another guidebook, *Snake River of Hells Canyon.* Conley wanted to include an account of Burg's 1925 voyage with the inimitable John Mullins. To his surprise, Burg replied immediately, inviting Conley, who had relatives in Seattle, to visit him at the University Hospital the next time Burg was in town for a checkup.

In the meantime, a steady correspondence between the two men developed, with subjects ranging from favorite rivers and river history to the difficulties of writing and publishing. Burg appeared to thrive in these exchanges, recalling in increasing detail his interactions with individuals, among others, like the miner, moonshiner, and river guide John Mullins; the Hells Canyon homesteader Cy Bullock; and fellow Oregonian Buzz Holmstrom. Of his most recent Snake River trip, Burg wrote in a letter to Conley: "The dam had changed the river greatly. The beautiful bars had been washed away confining the river with rock walls." (Indeed, many old-timers had once considered the camp at Steamboat Creek the most beautiful river camp on any western river.) In another letter he wrote: "Had a series of dreams last night—all unhappy ones. Had to do with the terrible dwindling of the natural Columbia I knew as a boy. The clutter and over-running of the lakes, sloughs and river bottoms once a paradise, devastating to the spirit."

Conley soon realized that Burg's famed Snake River voyage of 1925 was only one of many epic river journeys. When he asked for more stories, Burg responded enthusiastically with accounts of trips down the Columbia (1924–25), more on the Snake (1930), and others along the Green and Colorado Rivers (1938) and the Middle Fork/Main Salmon (1939). A year later Conley showed up at the Seattle hospital with his tape recorder. Burg, undergoing a round of radiation treatment, was delighted to have a river man as a visitor. He shared with Conley his popular "Campfire Reflections" columns. Conley, in turn, kept Burg up-to-date on the finishing touches of his latest guide book. Shoptalk led to discussions of a collaborative effort. Although he had often resisted the idea of writing an autobiography, Burg now hinted to Conley that he might, with help, take up the task.

At one time Burg had suggested a collaborative writing project to his friend R. T. "Skip" Wallen, a wildlife biologist and staff artist at the Alaska Department of Fish and Game. Wallen had heard many of Burg's river and sea adventures and had frequently encouraged him to write a memoir. He thought Burg's account of his voyage aboard the SS *Katia* in 1920 the most exciting. Initially he agreed to take notes and then write a rough summary based on Burg's diaries and reminiscences, after which Burg would take over. Five or six chapter summaries later, however, Wallen realized that the old man had no intention of taking over the project. Burg had joked, "I can hardly wait for the next chapter to see what happened to me."

Throughout late winter and early spring 1980, Burg had corresponded with Randy Pepper about Pepper's Main Salmon River voyage. He assured Pepper that he was coming, but after visiting his Seattle doctor in June, Burg had to write and say he would not be able to make the trip after all. He would do whatever he could to help with the planning. The appearance the same month of *Snake River in Hells Canyon,* Conley's latest guide book, soothed the sting of being left behind. Conley's thumbnail sketch of Burg's 1925 voyage through Hells Canyon ran four pages, and Burg's contribution to Conley's section on Buzz Holmstrom also pleased him.

In September, however, the aging voyageur suffered another setback. X-rays revealed that his prostate cancer had spread to his bones. Over the next four years he returned often to Seattle's University Hospital for treatment. During the periods when his condition improved, Burg forged on. Although he rarely took *Endeavour* out any more, he enjoyed doing routine maintenance on it. He began to consider selling his beloved craft. "Campfire Reflections" remained the highlight of *Alaska Fish and Game* magazine. Regardless of how he felt from one day to the next, Burg continued to plan for the next river trip.

Burg made his final river trip on the Yukon before health problems made such voyages impossible.

In July 1980 the Burgs spent three weeks traveling through the lake country of the upper Yukon River. Burg brought his twelve-foot Avon raft as well as his canoe *Song o' the Winds* for fishing and idle floating. The weather remained warm and sunny, the scenery splendid. With time on their hands, they lingered at their lakeside camps enjoying "sunrises, sunsets, and the glorious pageantry of the heavens." The couple arrived back in Juneau relaxed and refreshed. The following summer they made a short trip down the Yukon River with friends. It would be Burg's last river voyage.

In the spring of 1982 a small gathering of young, adventurous people, many of whom had worked with Burg at one time or another at the ADFG, began meeting at Burg's house on Saturday mornings. Regulars included fish biologist and boatbuilder Fritz Funk, writer and editor of *Alaska Fish and Game* Mark Kissel, and Skip Wallen, whom Burg had tried to coax into ghostwriting his autobiography. Carolyn liked nothing better than playing host to the weekly get-together. She delivered a steady flow of crepes, sausage, and coffee to the table, and insisted everyone not skimp on the toppings—jelly, butter, sugar, honey, cinnamon. The river of talk turned from one subject to another—adventure, boats, sea journeys, charging bears, sourdoughs, famous explorers, fierce weather, good books, Alaskan politics, and companions best left at the dock. Burg relished the company of the younger, like-minded voyagers. They in turn savored Burg's tales and the chance to rub shoulders with a link to a past that seemed more adventurous, less encumbered. The so-called Endeavour Breakfast Club became a regular event, one that Burg looked forward to in the coming years.

Mindful of Burg's efforts to organize his voluminous materials and his place in river history, Conley urged him to place *Charlie* in a museum. Conley worried that the raft, although stored in Burg's damp outdoor shed, would deteriorate after too many more harsh Alaskan winters. Burg tentatively agreed but dallied. He considered placing the boat with the Oregon Historical Society in Portland or the Columbia River Maritime Museum in Astoria at the mouth of the Columbia River. Conley sympathized with Burg's desire to keep the inflatable raft in his home state but argued persuasively that it should be placed closer to the Grand Canyon, where tens of thousands of people who visited the South Rim each year would see it, thus assuring Burg's role in Colorado River history.

Burg relented, but when Conley first approached officials at the Grand Canyon Museum on the South Rim, he was dismayed by their lack of interest. He next turned to the Utah State Historical Society in Salt Lake City, where Gary Topping, manuscript curator and an Oregon native, was enthusiastic. In early 1982, Topping wrote to Conley: "The raft, which was the first one to be taken through the Grand Canyon, is of great historical significance, and we would feel honored to be chosen as its repository." Topping contacted Burg, and within a month had won him over. By April, the Burgs had signed the release form and sent the boat to the Utah State Historical Society. "Any sand you find in the craft is from Hells Canyon," Burg joked to Topping. "I left it just as it came off the river." Burg was referring to his 1944 trip with his friends Charles Wheeler, Doc Frazier, and Pat Patterson. He had also sent Topping a copy of his 1938 Colorado River diary. In response, Topping wrote:

> I spent quite a little time with it, for it is a remarkable document that all river historians would do well to become closely acquainted with. I call it remarkable because of its poetic evocation of wind, water, and stars, and its focus upon the challenge, the tragedy, and the humor of man's experience with this tremendous country. So many river journals are prosaic accounts of mileage traversed, rapids run, and water volume, with little of the human element, the emotional response called forth by a great river expedition. I also appreciate your constant self-deprecating admiration for Holmstrom's great skill with a boat in fast water—a welcome change from the egotism so prevalent in river literature.

With his raft *Charlie* now in safe hands, Burg decided to sell his cherished *Endeavour* as well, a decision made easier by his friendship with Fritz Funk. Funk had long admired the *Endeavour* and Burg knew he would give the boat the attention it needed. In July 1982 they reached agreement on a sale price of fifteen thousand dollars with little haggling. Although he mourned the loss, Burg was relieved. *Endeavour* was in good hands. Funk was an excellent shipwright. *Song o' the Winds* would serve as Burg's last vehicle for adventure on the shallow channels and rocky beaches around Juneau.

Meanwhile, Conley had been working behind the scenes with the Western River Guides Association to pay tribute to Burg at their 1983 annual meeting in Salt Lake City. A combination of business, river politics, and partying, the boatmen's rendezvous drew guides and outfitters from throughout the West. Burg wanted to attend, but in January he underwent gall bladder surgery, which kept him in the hospital for six weeks. At the meeting the next month Burg was inducted into the organization as an honorary member and presented with a plaque for "early and significant voyages on American rivers."

By fall he felt well enough to begin the road trip that he and Carolyn had postponed the year before—retracing his Snake and Columbia River voyages. They drove up the Columbia Gorge in their late model Pinto, the subdued Columbia at their elbow. Burg pulled over numerous times to point out landmarks and the location of rapids now underwater. Above The Dalles Dam he showed his wife the flat stretch of placid water where Celilo Falls, "the Niagara of the West," had once roared like thunder. Experiencing an unexpectedly visceral sense of loss, he later wrote: "Although the great benefits derived from harnessing a river for electrical power and irrigation are undeniable, the incredible folly of blotting out Celilo Falls by The Dalles Dam is incomprehensible. It took countless millions of years for the creative forces to produce

In 1982 Burg sold his beloved Endeavour *to his friend Fritz Funk.*

such a masterpiece of power and beauty to inspire and uplift the human soul, yet man flooded and destroyed it without a qualm.... So it was all the way up the Columbia, a sad journey for me, pointing out what was there before the natural force of the river was drowned by 18 dams."

The river road trip began on this somber note, but they continued on to Ontario, on the dry, eastern edge of Oregon, and picked up the Snake River on their way to Pocatello, Idaho. The couple stopped at markers for the Oregon Trail and upon reaching Salt Lake City, they visited Topping and his family. Topping took the Burgs to the Utah State Historical Society building to see *Charlie* and later drove Burg out to Tooele, Utah, to visit with Burg's old friend Willis Johnson. Unfortunately there would be no reunion, as Johnson was nowhere to be found.

The Burgs headed north to Jackson Hole, Wyoming, traveling roughly 150 to 200 miles a day, stopping at 3:00 in the afternoon to ensure that Burg received enough rest. They found the resort town bustling with traffic, tourists, and shops. He thought the area "romantic and surprisingly unspoiled, but it is a place of make-believe like a Disneyland. In the summer it is flooded with tourists, all with more money than I have." Traveling along the Snake River to Jackson Lake, he spotted groups of day-trippers paddling the river. He stopped to point out locations to Carolyn where he had camped or had a mishap. Memory piqued, the stories flowed: Harry Fogleberry's heroics and foolishness; the generous hospitality of Slim "Bacon Rind" Hossman; the wreck of *Song o' the Winds* below Hoback Junction; the spectacular mudslide that had stoppered the Gros Ventre River and created a lake. Despite the traffic, the scenery in the Grand Teton Valley remained as spectacular as ever.

After two weeks of exploring, the Burgs turned west again, following the Snake River across the arid swath of southern Idaho. They stopped at Hells Canyon Dam. By the end of October, the couple arrived back in Juneau. Burg was in a reflective mood. He wanted to write about what he had seen on his river road trip. In February 1984 his article "A Voyageur's Lament" appeared in his "Campfire Reflections" column in *Alaska Fish and Game* magazine. Reader response was positive and overwhelming. He received numerous phone calls and letters praising his plea for preservation of natural wonders, especially those in Alaska. His words carried weight: he was arguably the last living person to have run such free-flowing rivers as the Columbia, Snake,

Yukon, and Mackenzie. Burg did not argue against dams per se so much as the reckless willingness to build one after another at the cost of the very things that inspired and made us uniquely American. He issued a cautionary warning. Rivers carried not only commerce and produced electricity, but also our history and poetry. The way we treated rivers, he argued, revealed our national character.

After pointing out the natural losses caused by the Hells Canyon Dam, Burg wondered if those who advocated for dams had suffered any remorse. He thought not. At the conclusion of the article, he worried aloud about the welfare of his adopted home, Alaska. He suggested that Alaskans were capable of making the same mistakes as those made in the Lower 48, and they might learn from them. "When one views the senseless destruction wrought on rivers in the name of industrialization," he wrote, "the need to study every value and possible alternative before construction becomes apparent." He wrote:

> Unlike my early canoe voyages, when I was the only voyageur on thousands of miles of river, America today is becoming water-minded again. More and more canoeists and kayakers take to our rivers. Thousands of would-be voyageurs fill the rosters of the National Park Service, waiting their turn to float down the Salmon, Snake, Green, or Colorado Rivers. The lineup is so long that it may take years for a prospective voyageur to make a booking. Rivers, once free and uncrowded, now have limited entry. Inevitably, these voyageurs and commercial river outfitters will soon move northward to Alaska, attracted by the Yukon, Gulkana, Taku, Tanana, Kuskokwim, Colville, Iditarod, Noatak and Kobuk Rivers. Alaska could well benefit from this outdoor invasion in terms of tourist dollars. But primarily, the state should see to the protection and preservation of the streams and rivers that will make all this possible. We have plenty of bad examples.

He voiced his concern about the growing wave of people who used the river for recreation, their impact on the rivers in what had once been pristine, uninhabited, even lonely stretches of river. Would not the wilderness experience be compromised, if not spoiled, by too many people in one place at one time? And yet who would protect these rivers and the natural beauty and sanctuary they offered?

Burg's health continued to seesaw. His periods of well-being were like shrinking islands in the path of the rising river of ill health. In March 1984 he wrote in his diary: "I feel no pain, but of course, I take pain pills. I feel the presence of the bone cancer." By April he had turned to the specialists in Seattle at the Fred Hutchinson Cancer Institute at Swedish Hospital in an attempt to stem the spread of his cancer. He stayed a month and regretted missing the warm Juneau summer.

Back at home Burg, when he was able, seized the moment. He kept up on his correspondence, sometimes writing as many as three or four letters a day. He gave a talk before the Gastineau Historical Society and began researching an article on the Yukon steamboats for the next edition of *Alaska Fish and Game*. He wrote his old friend Bill Goodlad, the Yukon River pilot, with two pages of questions. He made plans to accompany the Peppers down the Big Salmon River in the Yukon Territory. He was also making progress on organizing his large cache of papers and memorabilia for the Oregon Historical Society, which was anxious to have his collection. When the Alaskan Sportsman Council honored Burg with its "Conservationist of the Year" award for his contributions to the Alaska Fish and Game Department, he accepted an invitation to dinner at the Baranof Hotel in Juneau.

In an attempt to cope with his failing health, Burg sought refuge in reflective reading. The subject matter varied: Dale Carnegie and Norman Vincent Peale on the power of "positive thinking," Dostoyevsky's *The Writer's Diary,* the work of his old companion Ralph Waldo Emerson, and the Bible. He continued his lifelong habit of making lists of aphorisms and advice from the books he read. He jotted his own bits of advice in his diary, as if to reassure himself: "In 81 years nothing really bad has happened that wasn't rectified. I will banish this fear." As he reviewed the arc of his life, his buoyant optimism sometimes floundered, his wistfulness giving way to regret. "In looking back on my life," he wrote, "I can see where I missed many opportunities not only to build my name and make money, but simply to do things right—to be a good friend."

On the fiftieth anniversary of their Tierra del Fuego voyage, Burg wrote to Roy Pepper, his former shipmate aboard the *Dorjun*, enclosing a check (the amount is unknown) for "services rendered." Initially Pepper, nearly seventy at the time, was taken aback by the gesture. An exchange of letters followed and Burg eventually revealed that he felt that he had shortchanged the young sailor for his help aboard the *Dorjun*. In Burg's moral universe it was time to make amends. Pepper, who had always held Burg in high regard, was deeply touched. Although Burg's letters pertaining to this have been lost, Pepper's reply reveals much about the character of both men and the remarkable nature of their voyage.

Complete strangers and novice coastal sailors, Burg and Pepper, thrown together in a small boat under difficult, even life-threatening, circumstances, had managed well. Pepper responded to Burg:

> It['s] suddenly apparent to me that you and I have been suffering from the honorable thoughts about the Cape Horn trip. At least it seems that way to me. I felt that the trip was wonderful and so did anyone that I ever talked to about it—or ever heard of it. Everyone thought that I was very fortunate to have such an experience especially at the age of 19. They also thought that it was fortunate to have at least St. Croix Falls and myself recognized in a world wide magazine. I always tried to not make any waves about it in bragging fashion. Not because I was not secretly proud about it—it just was simply not my style. As far as I was concerned with you and the monetary situation—it did not enter my mind. It entered other people's minds—not mine. I just felt that I had been repaid many times over to just have been on the trip without being "charged for it!" In fact I lost several nights sleep over the fact that I owed you money for dumping the four and a half horse Evinrude into the Ushuaia Bay in full view of the southern Argentine Navy. . . . Regarding the Cape Horn trip, I feel that you and I got along very, very well together. We did not always have the best of food; we had our share of Cape Horn gales and storms for days on end. In between we had the endless rain. This we had to endure in quarters that were very small. In fact a modern queen bed would be far bigger than the entire area where we slept, dined, cooked, washed, wrote, dressed and other incidentals. I simply cannot recall any surly or cranky words that were said between us for all those months.

Considering our quarters, weather—and all it was remarkable. . . . So Amos, I think you and I have been suffering from the same things. Namely that we both think we owe each other something. There is only one way to resolve this dilemma, and that is to recognize the fact that you and I are about the two best fellows that we have ever met. Our thoughts are mutual, our wishes toward each other are mutual, and our appreciation of each other is mutual. When I got your letter with the check on our Horn 50th anniversary I felt bad at first, and then very good. Bad because I felt, gosh, now I owe Amos more than before. Then I thought—by golly he must feel the same toward me so that made me happy. At first I felt like returning the check, but then I knew that would not please you. So I am keeping it, Amos, and I plan on buying a new set of special jointed, unbreakable adjustable oars for my 16 foot rubber boat. I would like to put on the blades—"Song of the Wind." There is only one trouble about our mutual admiration society—we should have been together on more trips that just the one to the Horn and to Alaska. When we came through Grand Canyon last year I tried to visualize your first rubber boat trip through the canyon a couple of years after the Horn. Your first mate would have made that one with you had he not run away with your niece. As we came down the canyon and came to the mile post page with your name on it as the first rubber boat. We discussed it generally until Randy brought up the Horn trip and intimated that I should have made this trip 50 years ago.

By the summer of 1985, Carolyn felt she could no longer look after her husband without help. She hired a hospice care nurse to come to the house once a week. The nurse took a shine to Burg, often visiting on her day off. To relieve Burg's pain, his doctor had prescribed a "mint cocktail" composed of methadone, Vistaril, and liquid Tylenol. With the arrival of the Alaskan summer, Burg began each day reciting portions of his favorite verse. Most were poems about the sea: John Masefield's "Sea Fever," A. E. Housman's "Home Is the Sailor," and, of course, Tennyson's "Ulysses" and "Crossing the Bar." He followed with a series of simple exercises and breakfast. When he was not reading, writing letters, or making another list for an impending river voyage, he took pleasure in the view from Gastineau Channel. Burg became an enthusiastic birdwatcher, which suited his penchant for making lists.

Often he slipped into a half-sleep reverie, allowing his memory to run scenes like the lantern slide shows he had presented to enthusiastic audiences across the country: a smiling young man paddling *Song o' the Winds* with Fred "Spokane" Hill down the silt-laden Yukon; steering the *Dorjun* with Roy Pepper past glaciers along the Beagle Channel in Tierra del Fuego; rowing *Charlie* through the rapids of the Grand Canyon with Buzz Holmstrom and Willis Johnson; and setting sail on *Endeavour* through the Inside Passage.

On his birthday in December 1985, he wrote: "We celebrated my 84 years as a space traveler on the good ship Earth, I thought I could hear the distant roar of the breakers on the bar, but as before they grew faint and I could no longer hear them. That's the way it is with this type of cancer; you can win battles but not a war." He carried on his correspondence, advising a friend on everything he needed to know to make a trip on the Yukon River. He wrote weekly to Conley, clarifying details of his numerous river voyages and offering support for Conley's projects. As the warm days of spring approached, Burg's condition deteriorated and he was hospitalized. News of this quickly spread throughout Juneau. Over the next three weeks he received a stream of visitors. He told one that he traveled daily in his mind, reliving his old voyages. On June 11, shortly after midnight, Amos Burg's final voyage ended.

A memorial service was held in Portland on June 27, 1986. As Burg had requested, Carolyn brought her husband's ashes back to his hometown on the Willamette River. She asked Pastor Don Brown, who had run the Snake and Yukon Rivers with Burg and counseled him during his long illness, to officiate at the service. Cort Conley, whom Burg had looked upon as a kindred river spirit, delivered the eulogy. After the service Carolyn and Conley drove to the Multnomah Channel near Sauvie Island to spread Burg's ashes. Conley launched the rowboat, rowing downstream stern first. It was a sunny day and Mount Hood stood in the distance, bathed in blue. As Conley rowed, he asked Carolyn about an idea he had been pondering: to spread some of Burg's ashes over the Western rivers he had run throughout his life. She agreed immediately. They drifted farther downstream before Conley opened the box with Burg's ashes, stretched over the bow, and poured a portion into the river.

On Conley's way to Idaho, he stopped in The Dalles, Oregon, to spread a portion of Burg's ashes at Celilo Falls. Later that summer, working as a guide on the Snake and Main Salmon, he repeated the gesture. The following spring, Conley voyaged on the Middle Fork and left a handful. He sent his sister, who lived in Alaska, a packet of ashes to sprinkle along the Yukon River. Another summer passed. Conley canoed a portion of the Missouri River and continued the pilgrimage. In the coming years, he enlisted fellow river guides and friends to carry Burg's remains to rivers Conley had not reached—the Green, Colorado, Yellowstone, and Mississippi. One river remained.

In September 2002 thirty-year-old river guide Jim Norton drove north across the US border onto the featureless plains of Alberta province. On the passenger seat beside him was a wrinkled envelope sent by Conley containing the remaining ashes of Amos Burg. Norton, who previously had never heard of Burg, had been enlisted to deliver the contents of the envelope to the Mackenzie River. Between river trips on the Middle Fork the previous summer, Norton had read everything he could get his hands on about Burg. He had become increasingly curious about the early river runner. Much about the

peripatetic voyageur felt familiar—the adventurous spirit, the insatiable curiosity, the love of the river, the struggle to make a living. Upon reaching the mouth of the Great Slave Lake, where the Mackenzie River begins its long push to the Arctic, Norton had a change of heart. At camp that evening he came across a note Burg had scribbled about the location of the "Mother of All Rivers." He pulled out a tattered map of Canada's Rocky

Amos Burg—writer, filmmaker, photographer, sailor, river voyageur (December 3, 1901–June 11, 1986)

Mountains and traced the Mackenzie River with his finger back to Great Slave Lake, up the Slave and Athabasca Rivers into the Columbia ice fields in Banff National Park.

Two days later Norton arrived at Banff and after a snowy night in his tent at the foot of the Athabasca Glacier, he began hiking up the glacier. He spent most of the day ascending snowy slopes and ridges, finally reaching a point high above the valley floor by midafternoon, where he was greeted by a panoramic view of towering mountain peaks bathed in swaths of fog rising up from the glacial valleys. Norton emptied the envelope, one handful of ash after another, into a small, icy pool. After nearly two decades, the river pilgrimage to honor Burg was complete. As evening descended, Norton began the long trek back to camp ahead of an incoming storm.

Amos Burg, the last voyageur, would have approved of his final resting spot.

As I drive along the narrow two-lane gravel road toward our put-in below Hells Canyon Dam, the placid green surface of Hells Canyon Reservoir shimmers in the morning sunlight—a slender belt of flat water stretching for twenty-five miles. The water reflects the surrounding scene—the brown hillsides crowded with sagebrush and bitterbrush, the scattered stands of ponderosa pine and Douglas fir, the rugged crags of once-distant mountaintops, the blazing blue sky overhead. A lone water-skier carves a stitch of white in the emerald cloth of the lake. Two hundred or so feet beneath the silent waters, great rapids once churned and thundered. The weathered wooden sign posted in the dry rock gullies along the road say as much—Kinney Creek, Squaw Creek, Buck Creek, Sawpit Creek, Steamboat Creek. I can almost see Amos Burg and the overconfident John Mullins in their canoe, paddling downriver. I pretend I can hear the deafening roar of the rapids, feel my stomach twisting in knots as I line my boat up behind *Song o' the Winds* to make the run. Afterward, I feel relief mixed with satisfaction.

In the spring of 1978 I rowed my first raft through Hells Canyon. It was a small training trip, three boats in all. More accustomed to ocean waves (that move toward shore) than river waves (that remain in place), I somehow managed to find my way through Wild Sheep and Granite Rapids. During my first two seasons I ran what we boatmen called "The Snake Express"—six-day trips, one- or two-day turnaround, and back out again, nine, ten, a dozen trips a season from May through September. And so it is highly likely that I was on the river when Burg launched his final voyage on July 5, 1978. Perhaps we passed one another on a stretch of flat water and exchanged small talk the way river runners do. It is a possibility I enjoy, a serendipitous moment laden with rich meaning: we are fellow boatmen, bound together by the river, part of the flow of time.

Burg, then accompanied by family and friends, had come back to reunite with the river. Thirty years later I am doing the same, part of an aging tribe of ex-professional boatmen, cooks, and their families who have been making dory reunion trips on the rivers of the West since 1992. Like salmon we return to the fast water of our youth, bound together by the river and ancient memories.

Appendix 1. Chronology

1901–16   Born in Portland, Oregon, on December 3, 1901, to Amos and Minerva Ann ("Annie") Burg, the sixth of eight children; attends Woodlawn Grammar School; discovers the Columbia Slough and the Columbia River.

1917   Serves as a bellboy on the coastal steamer the *Rose City*; enters Jefferson High School in September but drops out at the start of the new year to go to sea; begins to make numerous three- to five-day solo voyages up and down the Columbia, from The Dalles to Portland and Portland to Astoria; begins to keep "voyage" diaries.

1918–20   Ships out as a deck boy, an engineer's cadet, an ordinary seaman, and an able seaman aboard the vessels SS *Ventura*, SS *Katia*, SS *Waikiki*, and others; travels to the South Seas, Europe, Asia, and around the world; meets Fred "Spokane" Hill, a river companion who becomes a lifelong friend, aboard SS *Waikiki*; begins to show an interest in photography and writing magazine articles.

1920   First lengthy voyage along the lower Snake and Columbia Rivers (from Lewiston, Idaho, to Astoria, Oregon, 450 miles) in his canoe *Song o' the Winds* (with Hill); ships out on SS *Egeria* for Sydney, Australia.

1921   Serves as a quartermaster aboard the coastal steamers *Rose City* and *Beaver*.

1922   Ships out on SS *West Kadar* for the Orient in June, begins a 135-day, 3,800-mile canoe voyage down the Yellowstone, Missouri, and Mississippi Rivers; writes first magazine article.

1923   Returns to high school and eventually receives his diploma; ships out on SS *President Madison* to purchase goods for his fledgling import business.

1924   Enters Navigation School in Portland to qualify for officer's deep-sea license; launches *Song o' the Winds* at the headwaters of the Columbia River in Canada in October; arrives in Astoria, Oregon, in early January 1925, as the first voyager to complete solo transit of the 1,243-mile river in a canoe.

1925   Enrolls in a winter term at Oregon Agricultural College (today's Oregon State College) in Corvallis but drops out and does not return; in June departs for Jackson Lake, Wyoming, to begin transit of the Snake River, with Harry Fogleberry; becomes the first known canoeist to complete the 1,078-mile voyage.

1926   Enters the University of Oregon to study journalism; voyages the Inside Passage (with Hill) from Skagway to Vancouver, British Columbia;

portages his canoe (via railroad) from Seattle to the headwaters of the Columbia River to repeat the 1,243-mile voyage to Astoria.

1927   Returns to the University of Oregon; elected editor of school newspaper; continues to ship overseas to purchase more goods for his import business; runs Oregon's McKenzie River.

1928   Launches *Song o' the Winds* (with Hill) from Lake Bennett on a five-month, two-thousand-mile voyage of the Yukon River to the Bering Sea; films the voyage and the caribou migration; continues the voyage on government schooners to islands in the Bering Strait and locations along coastal Alaska; his article and photographs ("Today on the Yukon Trail of 1898") appear in the July 1930 issue of *National Geographic*.

1929   Accompanied by university professor George Rebec (for a portion of the voyage), completes the 3,500–mile transit of the Mackenzie River (via the Athabaska River, Lake Athabaska, Slave River, and Great Slave Lake) to the Arctic Ocean; treks over the Davidson Range to float the Bell and Porcupine Rivers to the confluence with the Yukon River; his second article ("On Mackenzie's Trail to the Polar Sea") appears in the August 1931 issue of *National Geographic*.

1930   Begins East Coast lecture tour for the Pond Bureau; presents lecture in Washington Auditorium before four thousand members of the National Geographic Society; in June, descends the Canoe River from Mount Robson in British Columbia to the confluence with the Columbia to photograph and film the area; continues voyage to Portland, his third transit of the river; in August, launches on the headwaters of the Snake River, his second transit of the river.

1931   Continues Midwest and East Coast lecture tours; elected member of the Explorers Club in New York; in June, joins world-famous William Beebe, naturalist and deep-sea explorer, as staff photographer on Nonsuch Island in Bermuda; in October, sails aboard the yacht *Camargo* on a nine-month, around-the-world voyage as photographer for multimillionaire Julius Fleischmann. Burg's photographs appear in Fleischmann's book *Footsteps in the Sea* (1935) and in "Coconuts and Coral Islands," an article by H. Ian Hogbin that appeared in the March 1934 issue of *National Geographic*.

1932   Begins work on "A Native Son's Ramble in Oregon" for the February 1934 issue of *National Geographic*; sails to Admiralty Island in Alaska to film *Giants of the North* about Alaska's brown bears.

1933–34   Sails *Dorjun*, a converted surf-rescue boat, through the Tierra del Fuego archipelago with Roy Pepper to study, photograph, and film near-extinct indigenous tribes; makes first color photographs of the area; begins work on the article "Inside Cape Horn," which appears in December 1937 issue of *National Geographic*.

1935–36   Produces commercial films for Talbot Lumber Company; explores the Inside Passage from Seattle to Glacier Bay in *Dorjun*.

1937   Sails to England to cover coronation of King George VI for *National Geographic*; paddles a canoe through the English canal system, from London to Liverpool; films *Canals of England* for ERPI classroom films; writes article "Britain Just before the Storm" for the August 1940 issue of *National Geographic*.

1938   Completes the 1,100-mile voyage of the Green and Colorado Rivers through the Grand Canyon with fellow Oregonian Buzz Holmstrom; becomes the first to pilot an inflatable raft (*Charlie*) of his own design down both rivers; films the re-creation of Holmstrom's solo journey the year before; *Conquering the Colorado* is nominated by the Academy for best documentary in 1939; Amos Burg Sr. dies.

1939   Purchases the thirty-six-foot *Endeavour* from Captain O. P. Rankin; in June, accompanies Dr. Russell Frazier and others down the Middle Fork and Main Salmon Rivers in Idaho in *Charlie*, the first inflatable raft to make the voyage; films the voyage (*Seeing Is Believing*) for Paramount Pictures; films *The Cattlemen* in California for ERPI classroom films.

1940   Sails to Japan, Hong Kong, and China to begin filming the *Children of the World* series for ERPI.

1941   Delivers keynote address at the annual Explorers Club dinner; continues work for ERPI, sailing *Endeavour* to Alaska to film *Alaska, Reservoir of Resources* as well as to make the first folklore recordings for the Music Division of Library of Congress; also films *Eskimo Children*.

1942   Travels the United States filming a regional series for ERPI, sponsored by the State Department; his photographs appear in the September 1942 issue of *National Geographic* accompanying the article "Strategic Alaska" by Ernest Gruening, the territorial governor of Alaska.

1943–44   Reports for a special undercover wartime assignment in Argentina and Chile; films in Central America, the West Indies, Colombia, and Venezuela; descends the length of the Magdalena River in Colombia aboard a river steamer; his article "Cruising Colombia's Ol' Man River" appears in the 1947 issue of *National Geographic*.

1945   Films for ERPI as well as department stores (including Macy's and Lord & Taylor) in New York.

1946   Sails *Endeavour* from Seattle along the Inside Passage to Cape Spencer for *National Geographic*; his article "Endeavour Sails the Inside Passage" appears in the June 1947 issue; Buzz Holmstrom, Burg's companion on the Colorado River voyage, commits suicide on the Grande Ronde River in northeastern Oregon.

1947–57   Continues lecturing throughout the United States and filming for
          EBF overseas; voyages aboard the SS *North Star* from Sitka to Barrow,
          a three-month, eleven-thousand-mile journey for his *National Geo-
          graphic* article "*North Star* Cruises America's Wild West" (appeared in
          the July 1952 issue); covers Alaska's 1898 Gold Rush for *National
          Geographic*, with his article "Along the Yukon Trail" (appeared in the
          September 1953 issue); serves as fishery inspector/patrol officer for
          US Fish and Wildlife along the Inside Passage for three years; accepts
          contract to do film fieldwork for the Alaska Department of Fish
          and Game, the start of a two-decade career as editor, filmmaker,
          and writer for the department's Information and Education divi-
          sion; continues to gather and record stories from the "Class of '98"
          (the original Gold Rushers) at the Pioneer's Home in Sitka; after a
          lengthy illness, Burg's mother dies in October 1952, in Portland.

1958   Marries Carolyn Warren in Juneau, his adopted home, on June 2; sells
          Dorjun to his friend Andrew Yunker for one dollar; becomes the
          first Information and Education director for the Alaska Depart-
          ment of Fish and Game.

1959   Alaska becomes the forty-ninth state.

1961–65   Construction begins on the Burgs' home on Douglas Island over-
          looking the Gastineau Channel; continues to make films for the
          ADFG, traveling throughout Alaska.

1966   Presents the promotional film *Juneau, Alaska's Capital City* in Juneau.

1968   At age sixty-six, returns to the Athabaska and Mackenzie Rivers for
          another voyage.

1969   Returns to the Mackenzie delta to complete his voyage on the Bell
          and Porcupine Rivers.

1972   Begins "Campfire Reflections," a popular column for *Alaska Fish and
          Game*, the department's magazine.

1974   Retires as Information and Education officer at the ADFG; continues
          to write articles for the department as well as "Sourdough Sam," a
          column for the *Juneau Empire* newspaper.

1976   Undergoes triple-bypass heart surgery at the University Hospital in
          Seattle.

1977   Makes the first of numerous voyages down the Yukon River from
          Whitehorse to Carmacks, Alaska, with family and friends.

1978   At age seventy-six, diagnosed with prostate cancer; begins radiation
          treatment, which continues off and on for the next eight years; in
          July, returns to run the Snake River in Hells Canyon and the Yukon
          River with his former shipmate, Roy Pepper, his family, and mutual
          friends.

1980   Bone scans reveal his cancer has spread; Burg and Carolyn travel
          along the upper Yukon River by automobile to retrace earlier voy-
          ages; meets author, river guide, and river historian Cort Conley.

1982   Endeavour Breakfast Club starts; sells *Endeavour* to Fritz Funk.

1983   Western River Guides present Burg an award for "early and signifi-
          cant voyages on American rivers"; Burg retraces early river voyages
          on the Columbia and Snake by automobile; begins negotiations
          with the Oregon Historical Society for his letters, diaries, photo-
          graphs, and memorabilia.

1984   His "A Voyageur's Lament" appears in *Alaska Fish and Game* maga-
          zine; Alaska Sportsmen's Council honors Burg as "Conservationist
          of the Year." Nancy Long begins videotaping Burg for a documen-
          tary; *The Journey of Amos Burg* appears on Alaskan Public Television
          on December 3, 1992.

1986   June 11, Amos Burg dies in Juneau; a memorial service is held in
          Portland.

Appendix 2. Amos Burg's Boats

Charlie
In the early 1990s, in an effort to commemorate Amos Burg's 1925 Snake River
voyage, Breck O'Neill, owner of Mad River Boat Trips in Jackson Hole, Wyoming, persuaded the Utah Historical Society to release *Charlie* for public display.
O'Neill had opened a space for a river runners' museum next to the gift shop
in his river business in Jackson Hole. The boat, faded and peeling, was placed on
display in a glass case. As part of the agreement with the Utah Historical Society,
he had *Charlie* appraised for insurance purposes by the Maritime Museum in
San Francisco. The curator listed the craft as priceless in terms of historical value.
In May 2012 *Charlie* was returned to Utah Historical Society in Salt Lake City,
Utah. The fate of the historical boat remains unknown.

Dorjun
On Memorial Day 1948, *Dorjun* broke away from her moorings near Gault
Harbor, when the Columbia River breached a levy and flooded Vanport City,
outside of Portland. Heavily damaged, the boat lay in the mudflat for two years
until Burg and dentist Andrew Yunker hauled it to Yunker's home in Oak Grove,
near Portland. Over the years Yunker attempted cosmetic repairs on the aging
craft. In 1958, Burg sold *Dorjun* to Yunker for one dollar. Thirty years later, in
October 1988, Yunker sold the boat to Bruce Garman, his son-in-law, again for
one dollar. Garman hauled the boat to his home in South Colby, Washington.
Garman and his wife, Virginia, brought *Dorjun* to Louchard's Boat Shop in Port
Townsend, Washington, for restoration in 1992. Shipwrights Ed Louchard and
Steve Chapin, along with a devoted restoration crew, set to work. Eight months

later, on September 13, 1992, the restored *Dorjun* made its maiden voyage at the annual Wooden Boat Festival in Port Townsend. The Wooden Boat Foundation continues to use *Dorjun* in its educational programs.

Endeavour

After purchasing *Endeavour* from Burg in 1982, Fritz Funk spent the next five years restoring the vessel, a major undertaking. For the next two decades he sailed the waters of the Inside Passage. In July 2005 he donated *Endeavour* to the Michigan Lighthouse Conservancy in Fenton, Michigan. The boat has been stabilized and shrink-wrapped to prevent further damage. Restoration is in the preliminary planning phase while donations are being sought.

Song o' the Winds

Throughout his river-running career, Burg found, bought, borrowed, wrecked, and repaired a number of canoes. He began his voyages with a derelict craft he found in the Columbia Slough but soon converted to Old Town canoes. In the late 1920s he switched to Chestnut canoes. At least two of these were damaged, one beyond repair. (He left one on the bottom of the Snake River, below Hoback Junction near Jackson Hole; the other he gave to a Native guide on the lower Yukon River after the boat had been blown off the beach into the river in a storm). In 1968 he purchased a nineteen-foot Chestnut for voyages down the Mackenzie and Yukon Rivers. In his later years he paddled the Chestnut on short outings on the Gastineau Channel, near his home in Juneau, with his wife, Carolyn. The last reincarnation of *Song o' the Winds* is stored in the Oregon Historical Society's warehouse in Gresham, Oregon.

Appendix 3. A Brief History of Western Dams

Mica Dam

The Mica Dam, eighty-one miles north of Revelstoke, British Columbia, was completed in 1973. Today Surprise Rapids lies beneath Kinbasket Lake.

Rock Island Dam

Construction of the Rock Island Dam, the first to span the Columbia River, began in 1930 and was completed in 1933. A "gently inclined" fish ladder was included in the design. Development of the dam, near Wenatchee, Washington, continued over the next fifty years as powerhouses and improvements were added. The same year the Rock Island Dam was completed, construction on the Grand Coulee Dam, 143 miles upstream, began.

The Dalles Dam

On March 10, 1957, Celilo Falls, along with the fishing platforms and the village of Celilo, was submerged under the rising waters of Lake Celilo, created by The Dalles Dam.

Bonneville Dam

Completed in 1896, the Cascade Locks and Canal allowed steamboats on the Columbia River to bypass Cascade Rapid, a significant obstacle to river travel and commerce at the time. With completion of the Bonneville Dam in 1938, the Cascade Locks and Canal as well as Cascade Rapid were submerged beneath the waters of Lake Bonneville.

Lower Granite, Little Goose, Lower Monumental, and Ice Harbor Dams
Between 1955 and 1972 four dams and locks were constructed on the lower Snake between Lewiston, Idaho, and the confluence with the Columbia River: Lower Granite, Little Goose, Lower Monumental, and Ice Harbor.

Palisades Dam
By 1958, Grand Valley had disappeared beneath the reservoir formed by the Palisades Dam, fifty-five miles southeast of Idaho Falls.

Minidoka Dam
In 1906 mile-wide Minidoka Dam, the first reclamation project on the Snake, began to back up the waters of the Snake River. Within weeks, thirty-four-mile-long Lake Walcott had swallowed nearby forest and farmland. Dam boosters claimed that the useless, uninhabited sagebrush desert surrounding Rupert and Burley, in Idaho, would blossom into an agricultural Garden of Eden. People eagerly awaited its arrival.

Swan Falls Dam
Completed in 1901, the year Burg was born, the Swan Falls Dam was the first hydroelectric dam on the Snake River. Built to generate electricity to light the mines in Silver City, south of Boise, the mines folded before the electricity arrived. The reservoir behind the dam backed up the Snake River for 150 miles.

Brownlee, Oxbow, and Hells Canyon Dams
In 1955 the Federal Power Commission granted a license to the Idaho Power Company to build three dams (called the Hells Canyon Project) on the lower Snake River. The Brownlee Dam was completed in 1958 and backed up fifty-three miles of river. In 1961 the Oxbow Dam, downriver from Brownlee, came on line, followed by the Hells Canyon Dam in 1967. Together the three dams drown five of the seven major rapids Burg had fretted over—Steamboat Creek Rapid, Sawpit Rapid, Buck Rapid, Squaw Creek Rapid, and Kinney Creek Rapid—each comparable in size and ferocity to rapids on the Colorado River in the Grand Canyon. The seasonal runs of Chinook and steelhead salmon were devastated as a result.

High Mountain Sheep and Nez Perce Dams
In the late 1950s power companies applied to place two dams in the vicinity of the confluence of the Salmon and Snake Rivers. The High Mountain Sheep Dam, one mile above the mouth of the Lower Salmon, would have backed up water for fifty-eight miles, virtually flooding Hells Canyon. The Nez Perce Dam, downriver from the mouth of the Lower Salmon, would have flooded the Lower Salmon, wiping out anadromous fish runs to the Salmon and its tributaries. In June 1967 the Supreme Court, with Justice William O. Douglas writing the lead opinion, overturned an appeals court decision. The dams were never built.

Whitehorse Rapids Dam
Notorious Whitehorse Rapids—a formidable obstacle for Gold Rush stampeders, sternwheeler captains, and Amos Burg—disappeared beneath Lake Schwatka in

1958 with the completion of the Whitehorse Rapids Dam. In 1959 the Whitehorse Fishway, one of the longest wooden fish ladders in the world, was completed, allowing the ancient migration of Chinook salmon to continue.

Ramparts Dam

In 1954, Ernest Gruening, the territorial governor of Alaska, began spearhead-
ing a proposal by the US Army Corp of Engineers to build a dam in the Ramparts region of the lower Yukon, three hundred miles downstream from Circle.
The proposed Ramparts Dam would flood more than ten thousand square miles
of the Yukon Flats, creating a body of water roughly the size of Lake Erie. A
coalition of Native Americans, conservation groups, and scientists contested the
project. In 1967 the secretary of the interior, Stuart Udall, formally opposed
construction of the dam and the project was shelved. In 1980, President Jimmy
Carter created the Yukon Flats National Wildlife Sanctuary.

Flaming Gorge and Glen Canyon Dams

After a protracted political battle with environmental organizations in the mid-
1950s, the Bureau of Reclamation agreed to not build two downriver dams
at Echo Park and Split Mountain on the Green River. In exchange, the environmental organizations promised to not challenge dam proposals for Flaming
Gorge (1958–64) on the Green River and Glen Canyon (1956–66) on the Colorado River. Some historians of the West view the controversy as the start of the
environmental movement.

Marble Gorge and Bridge Canyon Dams

Since the early 1950s, the Bureau of Reclamation had seriously contemplated
building two dams, one in Marble Gorge (Mile 32) and another at Bridge Canyon (Mile 235) as part of the Pacific Southwest Water Plan. The Marble Gorge
Dam would have created a reservoir forty miles long, reaching up to and past Lees
Ferry. The Bridge Canyon Dam would have backed up water ninety-three miles,
flooding Lava Falls (Mile 179), one of the more spectacular rapids on the river, and
lower Havasu Creek (Mile 157), a side canyon known for its plant life, quiet pools,
travertine formations, and waterfalls. Substantial opposition from the public, led by
such environmental organizations as the Sierra Club, halted the project in 1968.

Middle Fork and Main Salmon Rivers

To this day there are no dams on the Middle Fork and Main Salmon Rivers.

Hells Canyon Wilderness Act

In 1975, Congress passed the Hells Canyon Wilderness Act. The 31.5-mile reach
of the Snake River from Hells Canyon Dam to Pittsburg Landing was granted
"wild river" designation and the thirty-six-mile reach from Pittsburg Landing to
the Washington border, a "scenic river" designation.

Appendix 4. Sources

Institutions

The Oregon Historical Society in Portland and the Alaska State Library in Juneau
each house extensive Amos Burg collections. Other Burg sources include the

Gary Topping Collection at the Utah State Historical Society in Salt Lake City and the Dock Marston Collection at Huntington Library in Pasadena, California.

Amos Burg Films and Magazine Articles

In the 1920s Burg wrote numerous travel pieces for Portland's *Oregon Journal*. From 1974 to 1984 he wrote popular columns for the *Juneau Empire* ("Sourdough Sam") and *Alaska Fish and Game* ("Campfire Reflections").

National Geographic Articles and Photographs

"Today on the Yukon Trail of 1898," July 1930
"On Mackenzie's Trail to the Polar Sea," August 1931
"A Native Son's Rambles in Oregon," February 1934
"Coconuts and Coral Islands," March 1934 (Amos Burg, photographer)
"Land of the Free in Asia," May 1934 (Amos Burg, photographer)
"Inside Cape Horn," December 1937
"Britain Just before the Storm," August 1940
"Strategic Alaska Looks Ahead," September 1942 (Amos Burg, photographer)
"Cruising Colombia's Ol' Man River," May 1947
"*Endeavour* Sails the Inside Passage," June 1947
"*North Star* Cruises Alaska's Wild West," July 1952
"Along the Yukon Trail," September 1953

Films (1928–1976)

Burg began his film career freelancing for Jesse Sill, a Portland photographer and filmmaker. He went on to work for numerous film companies, including Paramount Pictures, 20th Century Fox, Bray Picture Corp., ERPI Classrooms, Encyclopedia Britannica Films, and the Alaska Department of Fish and Game.

Alaska Wilds (1928, 1935)
Bering Sea Voyage: King Island to Nunivak (1928)
Yukon River (1929)
Camargo Voyage (1931–32)
Giants of the North (1932)
Creosoting Douglas Fir (1935)
Canals of England (1938)
Conquering the Colorado (Green and Colorado Rivers) (1939)
The Cattlemen (1940)
Seeing Is Believing (Middle Fork Salmon River) (1940)
Children of China (1940–41)
Children of Japan (1940–41)
People of Western China (1940–41)
Eskimo Children (1941)
Alaska, Reservoir of Resources (1941–42)
Far Western States (1942–43)
The Middle States (1942–43)
The Northwestern States (1942–43)
The Southwestern States (1942–43)

West Indies (1943–44)
Venezuela and Colombia (1945)
Milk (1946)
British Isles (1947)
Distributing America's Goods (1947)
English Children (1947–49)
Iberian Peninsula (1947–49)
Norwegian Children (1947–49)
Spanish Children (1947–49)
White Whales of the Bering Sea (1954–58)
Quest for Better Fishing (1956–57)
Coho Carnival (1956–60)
Rainbows for the Sportsmen (1956–60)
Return of the Musk Oxen (1956–60)
Sheefish, Eskimo Tarpon (1956–60)
Valley of the Kings (1958)
King of the Sea (1959)
Alaska Big Game Safari (1960)
The Pink Salmon Story (1960–69)
Scandinavia (1962)
The Sea Lion (1962)
British Isles, Second Edition (1963)
Angling under the Midnight Sun (1963–64)
The King Crab Story (1963–64)
Juneau, Alaska's Capital City (1966)
Quest for Grayling (1970–73)
The Bristol Bay Story (1972)
Wealth from the Navajo Forest (1974–76)

Films and Publications about Amos Burg

Canoeing North into the Unknown: A Record of River Travel: 1874–1974. By Bruce W. Hodgins and Gwyneth Hoyle. Toronto: Natural Heritage/Natural History Inc., 1994.

Exploration of Cape Horn Region, 1934. National Geographic Society Research Reports (1890–1954). Washington, D.C.: National Geographic Society, 1975. Pages 31–34.

Explorers Journal. Volume 60 (March 1982): 4–7. By Ashon Agathon. Official journal of the Explorers Club of New York.

Interviewing Saints and Sinners. By David Hazen. Portland, Oregon: Binfords & Mort, 1942. Page 150.

The Journey of Amos Burg. Produced and directed by Nancy Long. Alaska Public Television. 1988.

National Geographic Expedition Atlas. Washington, D.C.: National Geographic Society, 2000. Pages 167–70.

The Snake River of Hells Canyon. By Johnny Carrey, Cort Conley, and Ace Barton. Cambridge, Idaho: Backeddy Books, 1979. Pages 73–77.

Through Hell and High Water. Edited by the Explorers Club. New York. Robert M. McBride & Company, 1941. Pages 109–20.

Appendix 5. Selected Bibliography

Audette, Susan T., and David E. Baker. *The Old Town Canoe Company: Our First Hundred Years.* Gardiner, Maine: Tilbury House, 1998.

Belknap, Buzz. *Grand Canyon River Guide.* Evergreen, Colo.: Westwater Books, 1969.

Benidickson, Jamie. *Idleness, Water, and a Canoe: Reflections on Paddling for Pleasure.* Toronto: University of Toronto Press International, 1997.

Benke, Arthur C., and Colbert E. Cushing. *Rivers of North America.* San Diego: Elsevier Academic Press, 2005.

Bennett, Dennis J. *Nine o'clock in the Morning.* South Plainfield, New Jersey: Bridge Publishing, Inc., 1970.

Bennett, Jeff. *The Complete Whitewater Rafter.* Camden, Maine: Ragged Mountain Press, 1996.

Bridges, E. Lucas. *Uttermost Part of the Earth: A History of Tierra del Fuego and the Fuegians.* London: Hodder and Stoughton, Ltd., 1948.

Carrey, Johnny, and Cort Conley. *The Middle Fork: A Guide.* Cambridge, Idaho: Backeddy Books, 1992.

Carrey, Johnny, Cort Conley, and Ace Barton. *Snake River of Hells Canyon.* Cambridge, Idaho: Backeddy Books, 1979.

Clark, Robert. *River of the West: Stories from the Columbia.* New York: HarperCollins West, 1995.

Cody, Robin. *Voyage of a Summer Sun.* Seattle: Sasquatch Books, 1995.

Conley, Cort. *Idaho Loners: Hermits, Solitaires, and Individualists.* Cambridge, Idaho: Backeddy Books, 1994.

Cooper Jr., John M. *Pivotal Decades: The United States, 1900–1920.* New York: W. W. Norton and Company, 1990.

Dietrich, William. *Northwest Passage: The Great Columbia River.* Seattle: University of Washington Press, 1996.

Dimock, Brad. *Every Rapid Speaks Plainly: The Salmon, Green, and Colorado River Journals of Buzz Holmstrom.* Flagstaff, Arizona: Fretwater Press, 2003.

Eddy, Clyde. *Voyaging down the Thames.* New York: Frederick A. Stokes Company, 1938.

Fleischmann, Julius. *Footsteps in the Sea.* New York: G. P. Putnam's and Sons, 1935.

Fletcher, Roger. *Drift Boats and River Dories: Their History, Design Construction, and Use.* Mechanicsburg, Pennsylvania: Stackpole Books, 2007.

Freeman, Lewis. *Down the Columbia.* New York: Dodd, Mead, and Company, 1921.

———. *Down the Grand Canyon.* New York: Dodd, Mead, and Company, 1924.

———. *Down the Yellowstone.* New York: Dodd, Mead, and Company, 1922.

———. *Many Rivers.* New York: Dodd, Mead, and Company, 1937.

———. "Trailing History down the Big Muddy." *National Geographic,* July 1928. Pp. 73–120.

Gulick, Bill. *Snake River Country.* Photographs by Earl Roberge. Caldwell, Idaho: Claxton Press, 1971.

Halliburton, Richard. *The Glorious Adventure.* New York: Bobbs-Merrill Company, 1927.

———. *Halliburton's Book of Marvels.* New York: Bobbs-Merrill Company, Inc., 1937.

Harden, Blaine. *A River Lost: The Life and Death of the Columbia.* New York: W. W. Norton & Company, 1996.

Huser, Verne. *On the River with Lewis and Clark.* College Station: Texas A&M University Press, 2004.

———. *Wyoming's Snake River: A River Guide's Chronicle of People and Places, Plants and Animals.* Salt Lake City: University of Utah Press, 2001.

Kolb, Ellsworth. *Through the Grand Canyon from Wyoming to Mexico.* New York: Macmillan Company, 1914.

Lansing, Jewel. *Portland: People, Politics, and Power, 1851–2001.* Corvallis: Oregon State University Press, 2003.

Lavender, David. *River Runners of the Grand Canyon.* Tucson, Arizona: Grand Canyon Natural History Association, 1985.

Layman, William D. *River of Memory: The Everlasting Columbia.* Seattle: University of Washington Press, 2006.

Leydet, Francois. *Time and the River Flowing: Grand Canyon.* Edited by David Brower. San Francisco: Sierra Club Books, 1964.

Lockely, Fred. *Oregon Folks.* New York: The Knickerbocker Press, 1927.

Lorraine, M. J. *The Columbia Unveiled.* Los Angeles: The Times-Mirror Press, 1924.

Lyman, William. *The Columbia River: Its History, Its Myths, Its Scenery, Its Commerce.* Fourth edition. Portland, Oregon: Binfords & Mort, 1963.

McKinney, Sam. *Sailing Uphill.* Victoria, British Columbia: Horsdal & Scubert Publishers, 2000.

McPhee, John. *Coming into the Country.* New York: Farrar, Strauss, and Giroux, Inc., 1977.

Meloy, Ellen. *Raven's Exile: A Season on the Green.* New York: Henry Holt and Company, 1994.

Moore, Greg, and Don McClaran. *Idaho Whitewater.* McCall, Idaho: Class VI Whitewater Company, 1989.

Nash, Roderick. *Wilderness and the American Mind.* New Haven, Connecticut: Yale University Press, Boston, 1967.

Nisbet, Jack. *Sources of the River: Tracking David Thompson across Western North America.* Seattle, Washington: Sasquatch Books, 1994.

Nute, Grace Lee. *The Voyageur.* St. Paul, Minnesota: D. Appleton and Company, 1931.

O'Neill, Dan. *A Land Gone Lonesome: An Inland Voyage along the Yukon River.* New York: Counterpoint Press, 2006.

Palmer, Tim. *The Columbia: Sustaining a Modern Resource.* Seattle, Washington: The Mountaineers Books, 1997.

————. *The Snake River: Window to the West*. Washington, D.C.: Island Press, 1991.

Petersen, Keith C., and Mary E. Reed. *Controversy, Conflict, and Compromise: A History of the Lower Snake River Development*. Walla Walla, Washington: US Army Corps of Engineers, 1994.

Podruchny, Carolyn. *Making the Voyageur World: Travelers and Traders in the Northern American Fur Trade*. Lincoln: University of Nebraska Press, 2006.

Poole, Robert M. *Explorers House*. New York: Penguin Press, 2004.

Reisner, Marc. *Cadillac Desert: The American West and Its Disappearing Water*. New York: Viking Penguin Ltd., 1986.

Roberts, Wilma. *Celilo Falls: Remembering Thunder*. The Dalles, Oregon: Wasco County Historical Museum Press, 1997.

Rothman, Hal K. *Devil's Bargains: Tourism in the Twentieth Century American West*. Lawrence: University Press of Kansas, 1998.

Satterfield, Archie. *Exploring the Yukon River*. Mechanicsburg, Pennsylvania: Stackpole Press, 1979.

Schwatka, Frederick. *Along Alaska's Great River*. 1885; reprint, Anchorage: Alaska Northwest Publishing Company, 1983.

Scott, Alastair. *Tracks across Alaska*. London: John Murray Publishers Ltd., 1990.

Sherman, Harold. *Your Key to Happiness*. Greenwich, Connecticut: Fawcett Publishers, Inc. 1935.

Shuler, Loel. *Alaska in the Wake of the North Star*. Blaine, Washington: Hancock House Publishers, 2005.

Solway, Kenneth. *The Story of the Chestnut Canoe*. Halifax, Nova Scotia: Nimbus Publishing, 1997.

Stelmok, Jerry, and Rollin Thurlow. *The Wood and Canvas Canoe: A Complete Guide to Its History, Construction, Restoration, and Maintenance*. Gardiner, Maine: The Harpswell Press, 1987.

Voss, J. C. *The Venturesome Voyages of Captain Voss*. Sidney, British Columbia: Gray's Publishing Ltd., 1976.

Wake-Walker, Edward. *Lost Photographs of the RNLI*. Stroud, Gloucestershire, England: Sutton Publishing, 2004.

Webb, Robert H., Jayne Belnap, and John S. Weisheit. *Cataract Canyon: A Human and Environmental History of the Rivers in Canyonlands*. Salt Lake City: University of Utah Press, 2004.

Webb, Roy. *High, Wide, and Handsome: The River Journals of Norm Nevills*. Salt Lake City: Utah State University Press, 2005.

Welch, Vince, Cort Conley, and Brad Dimock. *The Doing of the Thing: Brief, Brilliant Whitewater Career of Buzz Holmstrom*. Flagstaff, Arizona: Fretwater Press, 1998.

Zimmerly, David W. *Qayaq: Kayaks of Alaska and Siberia*. Fairbanks: University of Alaska Press, 2000.

Zwinger, Ann. *Run, River, Run: A Naturalist's Journey down One of the Great Rivers of the American West*. Tucson: University of Arizona Press, 1975.

INDEX

A

Admiralty Island, 132

Air Cruisers, 186

Alakalufs, 158, 164

Alaska Department of Fish and Game, 260, 262, 271, 277

Alaska Department of Fisheries, 256–59

Alaska Fish and Game, 272, 278, 294

Alaska Highway Department, 273

Alaska Wilds, 97

Alpine Canyon, 53

Arctic Red River, 110, 268

Arroyo, Captain, 144

B

Bailey Creek Rapids, 52

barges, 174, 176

Barton, Otis, 121

Beagle Channel, 156, 159

Beebe, Fred C., 139

Beebe, William, 121–23

Bell, John, 111

Bennett, Elaine, 167–68

Bennett Lake, 73

Bennett Range, 79

Bergenham, Pete, 24, 29

Bering Sea, 244–56

Biederman, Ed "Adolph," 87

Big Bend, 22, 24–25, 30–31

Boat Encampment, 31

Boulder Dam, 177

Boxer, 94

Bracher, Vic, 262–63

brothers, 26

Brown, Don, 278–81, 285, 299

Buck Creek Rapids, 65

Burg, Amos Sr., 18, 211–12

Burg, Annie, 22, 213, 236, 253, 255

Burg, Carolyn. *See* Warren, Carolyn

C

Cabo de Hornos, 148–49, 155

Camargo, 123–29

cameras, 22, 51, 72, 125

Canadian Rockies, 23

Canal Flats, 23

canals, 172–73, 177

Canoe River, 31, 120

canoes, 19, 22–23, 25, 33, 35, 37, 50–51, 54–55, 57, 65, 73, 92, 99

Carmacks, 287

Cascade Locks, 39, 68, 166

Castlegar, 34

Cataract Canyon, 197–99, 201

Celilo Falls, 39, 300

Charley, Alfred, 112–14

Charlie, 196, 198–99, 202–03, 205–08, 210,

219–20, 283, 291–92

China, 226–27, 231

Circle City, 87

Cockburn Channel, 150

Colorado River, 178, 180–213

Columbia Gorge, 37, 293

Columbia River, 18–45, 167, 289

Columbia River, 19

Columbia Slough, 27

Conley, Cort, 288–93, 299–300

Conquering the Colorado, 212–13, 237

Cranbrook, 23

Cuba, 232

D

dams, 166, 177, 294–95

death, 299

Deh Cho, 98–116

Dellenbaugh, Frederick, 180–81

diary, 31–32, 73, 76, 82–84, 86, 89, 101–04, 107, 109–12, 114–15, 134, 153–54, 189, 194, 197, 201, 285

Distributor, 108

Dorjun, 140–41, 143–45, 149, 151–52, 159, 161–63, 165, 169–70, 177, 240–41, 296–97

E

Eddy, Clyde, 180

education, 26–28, 43

Educational Britannica Films (EBF), 239–40, 242, 254

Electrical Research Products, Inc., 171, 177, 225, 228, 231–32, 236

Emerald, The, 44

Endeavour, 225, 228–31, 234, 236, 238–39, 251, 257, 274, 292–93

Eskimos, 247

Explorers Club, 118–19, 121, 132–33, 136, 189, 227

F

films/filming, 72–73, 80, 94, 97, 129, 131, 167, 171, 173, 177, 207, 224–25, 228, 231, 236, 258–59, 261

Finley, William, 166

Fitzgerald, 103

Five Fingers Rapids, 83

Flat Creek, 51

Fleischmann, Julius, 123–29, 140, 167

Fletcher, Jack, 120

Fogleberry, Harry, 19, 47–55, 92, 294

Fort McPherson, 111

Fort Simpson, 267

Fort Smith, 265

Fort Yukon, 87, 115, 271

Fortier, Alfred, 84–85

Francis, Abraham, 111–12

Frazier, Russell "Doc," 187, 218, 223, 234

Freeman, Lewis, 21, 30, 42

G

Gabriel Channel, 147

Glenn's Ferry, 60

Golden, 21, 24–25, 29

Good Hope, 94

Goodlad, Bill, 252–53, 267, 280, 296

Grand Canyon, 181, 194, 204–5, 237

Grand Valley, 55

Great Slave Lake, 105, 266–67

Green River, 178, 180–213

Green River Lakes, 188–89

Grosvenor, Gilbert, 116, 261

Gurtlers, 88–89

H

Hamilton, Basil, 21–24

Hansen, Earl F., 118

Harderlie, Charlie, 55–56

Harvey, Lawrence, 39

Hasselborg, Al, 131–32

Hay River, 105–06, 266

Hells Canyon, 55, 60, 63–64, 66–68, 282, 284, 294

Hill, Fred "Spokane," 46–47, 74–78, 80–87, 93–95, 140, 169, 244, 251

Hoback River, 52

Hollister, Gloria, 123

Holmstrom, Haldane "Buzz," 177–78, 182–86, 188–95, 197–99, 201, 203–13, 218, 236–38, 289

Holy Cross, 89

Homestead, 61–62

Hossman, Slim "Bacon Rind," 52, 54, 294

Hubbard, Gerard F., 169–70

Hudson, Bill, 40–41

Hunt, Wilson Price, 46

I

Idaho Falls, 57

illness, 233, 279, 296–99

Inside Passage, 75, 96, 169–70, 228

Inuvik, 269

J

Jackson Lake, 48–49, 120

Japan, 225–27, 231

Johnson, Willis "Bill," 195–96, 204–5, 210, 219–20, 229–30, 294

Julius F., 187–92, 196, 199–200, 203–7, 210

K

kayaks, 89–91

Kelly, Charles, 219–21

Kerns Rapids, 63

Kettle Falls Rapid, 35

Kicking Horse River, 24–25

Kinbasket Rapids, 30

King Island, 248–50

Kinney Creek Rapid, 64

Kiser, Fred, 47

knee injury, 23

Knowles Summit, 176

Knudsen, K. C., 25, 28–29, 32

Kolb, Emery, 204–5

Kootenay River, 23

L

La Gorce, John Oliver, 123–24, 129–30, 137

Lage, Bill, 56

Lake Athabaska, 98, 102, 264

Lake Columbia, 21, 23, 74

Lake Laberge, 81

Lake Walcott, 58

Lake Windermere, 24

Larsen, A. C., 142

Larsen, L. M., 141

Lawrence, Martin, 157–59

lectures, 115–16, 119, 169

legging, 175

Leonore III, 41

Little Dalles Rapids, 34

Little Salmon, 82, 85

locks, 175–76

London, 170–77

Long, Nancy, 276–77

Lorraine, M. J., 21, 25, 29–30, 36, 42

Lower Arrow Lake, 32–34

Lundstrom, Phil, 190–93, 195

Lyman, William, 19

Lynch Creek, 64

M

Mackenzie River, 98–116, 128, 257–74, 300

MacMurray, 101

Magallanes, 143–46, 148, 150, 164

Magdalena River, 233

Mahar, Jim, 188, 190–91

Main Salmon River, 218–42, 288

Malad River, 59

marriage, 260

Marsh Lake, 79–80

Martin, John, 112

McKenzie River, 44

McLean, Joe, 269–70

McMurray, 264, 268

Menner's Ferry, 50

Meskin Canal, 146

Middle Fork River, 218–42, 289

Mile Long Rapid, 199–200

Miles Canyon, 251

Miller, Hack, 219, 221–22

Milner Dam, 58

Mississippi River, 20

Moore, Harvey, 77

Mullins, John, 61–64, 66, 285, 289

N

Narrows, The, 33

National Geographic, 22–23, 48, 74, 79, 83, 96–97, 99, 109, 115–16, 122, 129–30, 132–34, 154, 156, 165, 169–70, 177, 204, 232, 239, 241–42, 245, 251, 253, 261–62

Natives, 85–86, 114, 128

Nelson ranch, 56

Neuberger, Richard, 212

New York, 235–36, 241

Nonsuch Island, 121, 124

North Star, 244–48, 250

O

Offing Island, 143

Ohio River, 20

Olmsted, Frederick Law, 27

Oregon Agriculture College, 43

Owyhee River, 131

P

Patagonia archipelagos, 136–65

Patterson, Pat, 234, 236

Peel River, 110–11

Pend d'Oreille River, 34

Pepper, Randy, 284, 286, 290

Pepper, Roy, 142–45, 147, 149–53, 162–64, 169–70, 283–84, 286–87, 290, 296–98

Petoch, John, 76

Pond, James "Bim," 116, 118

Porcupine River, 113–14, 270–71

Powell, John Wesley, 180–81, 193, 208

Prospector canoe, 99

prostate cancer, 281, 290

Q

qayaqs, 89–91

R

Raft River, 58

rafts, 99–100, 113, 120, 185–86, 188, 283, 285, 292

Rankin, Oliver P., 224–25, 228, 230

rapids, 29–30, 34–35, 37–39, 52–53, 63–66, 80–81, 83, 199–200, 203, 206, 235, 252, 279

Rebec, George, 100–09, 133

Red Creek, 54

Redgrave Canyon, 29

retirement, 277

Revelstoke, 31–32

Rimer, Alfred, 41–42, 138

Rink Rapids, 83

Rio Grande River, 125

River Thames, 170–77

Rock Island Rapids, 37

Roderick, Hans, 108–10

Royal National Lifeboat Institution, 240–41

Russian Mission, 90–92

S
Sacramento, 127

Salt River, 55–56

Seagull Anchorage, 161–62

Selkirk Mountains, 31

Shumaker, Ralph, 61–62

Sierra, 95–96

Sill, Jesse, 40, 44, 47, 72–73, 96–97, 120, 135

Simpson, 106–07

sisters, 26, 236

Skagway, 76–77

Slave River, 98, 103, 265–66

Snake River, 37, 46–70, 73, 92, 120, 234, 285, 289, 294, 299

Song o' the Winds, 19, 22–23, 25, 28, 30–31, 35–36, 41–42, 46, 48–49, 54–55, 61, 68, 74, 76, 78, 86, 88, 90–92, 100, 102, 109, 111, 120, 169, 171–72, 175–76, 229, 238, 262–64, 267, 270–71, 291, 293

Sparks, Frank, 119–20

speeches, 115–16, 119, 168–69, 227–28

Squaw Creek Rapids, 64

Steamboat Rapids, 66

Surprise Rapids, 29–30

Swain, Frank, 219, 221–23

Swan Falls Dam, 60

Swan Valley, 56

T
Tee-Van, John, 121–22

Thirty-Two Point Rapids, 66

Thomas, Lowell, 212, 227

Thompson, David, 24, 31, 42

Thornthwaite, Corporal, 114

Topping, Gary, 292

Tring Summit, 175

Tug Bay, 151

Twin Falls, 57

U
Umatilla Rapids, 38

umiaks, 248–49

Upper Arrow Lake, 32–33

Ushuaia, 156–57, 163–64

V
vulcanization, 184–85, 190

W
Warren, Carolyn, 255, 259–60, 272–73, 276, 286, 299

Warrenton, 130

West Camargo, 165

West Mahwah, 141–43, 164

Wheeler, Charles, 171, 185, 187, 234, 277–78

Whitehorse Rapids, 80–81, 252, 279

Wilbur, Ray, 131

Williamette River, 18, 26–27, 140

Williams, Ken, 159–63

Wisherd, Andy, 125–26

Wolf Creek, 53

Wollaston Islands, 145, 160

Wood River, 31

Wrigley, 107

writings, 23, 31, 68–69, 83, 92–93, 95–97, 103–04, 109–10, 114–15, 201, 261, 289, 295

Y
Yaghans, 158–60

Yanert, William, 88

Yukon, 75

Yukon Flats, 72

Yukon River, 72–97, 128, 244–56, 279, 285, 299

V ince Welch has spent his life around water, fresh and salt. Before
working as a professional river guide in Grand Canyon and on
numerous other western rivers, he surfed, sailed, and labored as a fisherman, marine domestic, and abalone diver on the West Coast. His
wandering has carried him to Europe, Mexico, Hawaii, New Zealand,
and the South Pacific. Despite the occasional close encounter with
near-drowning, he continues to voyage down the rivers of the west in
his wooden dory, *Music Temple*, with other ancient mariners.

In 1998, Welch co-authored *The Doing of the Thing—The Brief
Brilliant Whitewater Career of Buzz Holmstrom*. He has written for *Boatman's Quarterly Review*, *Oregon Coast*, *Wend*, *Rivers*, *Utne*, and *Mountain
Gazette* where he is a senior correspondent and writes a bi-monthly
blog, *Rivermouth*.

When he is not running rivers or roaming the Oregon coast, he
lives in Portland, Oregon, with his wife, Helen, daughter, Gwen, and
a bunch of chickens.